Learning the Korn Shell

Second Edition

Bill Rosenblatt and Arnold Robbins

O'REILLY®

Beijing · Cambridge · Farnham · Köln · Paris · Sebastopol · Taipei · Tokyo

Learning the Korn Shell, Second Edition
by Bill Rosenblatt and Arnold Robbins

Published by O'Reilly & Associates, Inc., 1005 Gravenstein Highway North, Sebastopol, CA
95472.

O'Reilly & Associates books may be purchased for educational, business, or sales promotional
use. Online editions are also available for most titles (*safari.oreilly.com*). For more information
contact our corporate/institutional sales department: 800-998-9938 or *corporate@oreilly.com*.

Editor: Michael Loukides

Production Editor: Leanne Clarke Soylemez

Cover Designer: Edie Freedman

Printing History:

January 1993:	First Edition.
April 2002:	Second Edition.

ISBN: 0-596-00195-9
[M]

To Margot Lorraine Rosenblatt, born April 16, 2001.

—Bill Rosenblatt

To my wife, Miriam, for your love and support.
To my children, Chana, Rivka, Nachum, and Malka.

—Arnold Robbins

Table of Contents

Preface

The long, tortuous history of the Unix operating system has resulted in systems with all kinds of permutations and combinations of features. This means that whenever you walk up to an unfamiliar Unix system, you need to find out certain things about it in order to use it properly. And even on a given system, you may have a number of choices you can make about what features you want to use.

The most important such decision—if you get to make it—is what *shell* to use. "Shell" is Unix jargon for the program that allows you to communicate with the computer by entering commands and getting responses. The shell is completely separate from the Unix operating system per se; it's just a program that runs on Unix. With other systems such as MS-DOS, Microsoft Windows, Macintosh,* Open-VMS, and VM/CMS, the command interpreter or user interface is an integral part of the operating system.

Nowadays there are dozens of different shells floating around, ranging from the original standard, the Bourne shell, to menu-based and graphical interfaces. The most important shells have been the Bourne shell, the C shell, and the Korn shell—the subject of this book.

Korn Shell Versions

Specifically, this book describes the 1993 version of the Korn shell. The 1993 version is distributed with the three major commercial versions of Unix: Solaris, HP-UX, and AIX, albeit as part of the Common Desktop Environment (CDE), in */usr/dt/bin/dtksh*. The 1988 version is also available on modern Unix systems, usually

---

* At least up until MacOS X. MacOS X has a Unix-like system at its core—Darwin, which is derived from Mach and 4.4–BSD–Lite.

as */usr/bin/ksh*. There are various other versions, variations, and implementations on other operating systems; these, along with the differences between the 1988 and 1993 versions of the Korn shell are described in Appendix A.

The 1993 version is now available in both source code form and as precompiled executables for many common systems. Downloading and building it is described in Appendix C. The latest, downloadable version of *ksh* has a number of features not in earlier versions. We cover all of those features, too. We have made an effort to point out when something may not be in an earlier version, but caveat emptor; if you need a feature and your system's version of the 1993 Korn shell doesn't have it, you may need to download a prebuilt executable or download the source and build your own executable.

To find out which version you have, type the command set -o emacs, then press CTRL-V. You should see a date followed by a version letter (the letter is generally unimportant). If you do, you have one of the official versions, the 1993 version, the 1988 version, or an older one. But if you don't, you have a nonstandard version, such as *pdksh*, the public domain Korn shell discussed in Appendix A.

Summary of Korn Shell Features

The Korn shell is the most advanced of the shells that are "officially" distributed with Unix systems. It's a backward-compatible evolutionary successor to the Bourne shell that includes most of the C shell's major advantages as well as a number of new features of its own.

Features appropriated from the C shell include:

Job control
> The ability to stop jobs with CTRL-Z and move them to the foreground or background with the *fg* and *bg* commands.

Aliases
> The ability to define shorthand names for commands or command lines.

Functions
> The ability to store your own shell code in memory instead of files. Functions increase programmability and efficiency. (Functions have been common in the Bourne shell for many years.)

Command history
> The ability to recall previously entered commands.

The Korn shell's major new features include:

Command-line editing

This feature allows you to use *vi* or Emacs-style editing commands on your command lines.

Integrated programming features

The functionality of several external Unix commands, including *test, expr, getopt,* and *echo,* has been integrated into the shell itself, enabling common programming tasks to be done more cleanly and without creating extra processes.

Control structures

Additional flow-control structures, especially the `select` construct, enable easy menu generation.

Debugging primitives

These features make it possible to write tools that help programmers debug their shell code.

Regular expressions

Well known to users of Unix utilities like *grep* and *awk,* regular expressions (albeit with a different syntax) have been added to the standard set of filename wildcards and to the shell variable facility.

Advanced I/O features

Several new facilities for control of process I/O, including the ability to do two-way communication with concurrent processes (coroutines), and to connect to network services.

New options and variables

These options and variables give you more ways to customize your environment than the standard Unix shells do.

Increased speed

The Korn shell often executes the same shell program considerably faster than the Bourne shell does.

Security features

Features designed to help protect against "Trojan horses" and other types of break-in schemes.

Major new features in the 1993 version include:

POSIX compliance

Compliance with POSIX, an international standard for portable shell programming, makes it possible to write and use portable shell scripts.

Arithmetic for loops
This new control structure lets you program more naturally when looping a fixed number of times.

Floating-point arithmetic
The ability to use floating-point numbers and new built-in arithmetic functions enrich the shell as a programming language.

Structured variable names
New syntax for variable names provides facilities similar to C structures and Ada records for grouping related items together in a variable.

Indirect variable references
This facility eases shell function programming for manipulating global variables.

Associative arrays
A powerful data-management facility that is similar to those in *awk* or *perl*.

Additional text manipulation facilities
There are even more ways to match patterns and substitute variables.

More built-in commands
Additional commands improve efficiency and increase script portability.

Intended Audience

This book is designed to appeal most to casual Unix users who are just above the "raw beginner" level. You should be familiar with the process of logging in, entering commands, and doing simple things with files. Although Chapter 1 reviews concepts such as the tree-like file and directory scheme, you may find that it moves too quickly if you're a complete neophyte. In that case, we recommend the book *Learning the Unix Operating System* by Jerry Peek, Grace Todino, and John Strang, published by O'Reilly & Associates, Inc.

If you're an experienced user, you may wish to skip Chapter 1 altogether. But if your experience is with the C shell, you may find that Chapter 1 reveals a few subtle differences between the Korn and C shells.

No matter what your level of experience, you will undoubtedly learn many things in this book that will make you a more productive Korn shell user—from major features down to details at the "nook-and-cranny" level that you weren't aware of.

If you are interested in shell programming (writing shell scripts and functions that automate everyday tasks or serve as system utilities), you should find this book useful too. However, we have deliberately avoided drawing a strong distinction between interactive shell use (entering commands during a login session) and shell programming. We see shell programming as a natural, inevitable outgrowth of increasing experience as a user.

Accordingly, each chapter depends on those prior to it, and although the first three chapters are oriented toward interactive use only, subsequent chapters describe interactive user-oriented features in addition to programming concepts.

In fact, if this book has an overriding message, it is this: "The Korn shell is an incredibly powerful and grossly undervalued Unix programming environment. You—yes, *you*—can write useful shell programs, even if you just learned how to log on last week and have never programmed before."

Toward that end, we have decided not to spend much time on features of interest exclusively to low-level systems programmers. Concepts like file descriptors, special file types, etc., can only confuse the casual user, and anyway, we figure that those of you who understand such things are smart enough to extrapolate the necessary information from our cursory discussions.

Code Examples

This book is full of examples of shell commands and programs that are designed to be useful in your everyday life as a user, not just to illustrate the feature being explained. From Chapter 4 onwards, we include various programming problems, which we call *tasks*, that illustrate particular shell programming concepts. Some tasks have solutions that are refined in subsequent chapters. The later chapters also include programming exercises, many of which build on the tasks in the chapter.

You should feel free to use any code you see in this book and pass it along to friends and colleagues. We especially encourage you to modify and enhance it yourself. The code is available from this book's web site: *http://www.oreilly.com/catalog/korn2/*.

If you want to try examples but you don't use the Korn shell as your login shell, you must put the following line at the top of each shell script:

```
#! /bin/ksh
```

If your Korn shell isn't installed as the file */bin/ksh*, or if */bin/ksh* is the 1988 version, substitute the full pathname for your version of *ksh93* in the above.

Chapter Summary

If you want to investigate specific topics rather than read the entire book through, here is a chapter-by-chapter summary:

Chapter 1, Korn Shell Basics
Introduces the Korn shell and tells you how to install it as your login shell. It then introduces the basics of interactive shell use, including overviews of the Unix file and directory scheme, standard I/O, and background jobs.

Chapter 2, Command-Line Editing
Discusses the shell's command history mechanism, including the emacs and vi editing modes and the *hist* history command.

Chapter 3, Customizing Your Environment
Covers ways to customize your shell environment without programming, by using the *.profile* and environment files. Aliases, options, and shell variables are the customization techniques discussed.

Chapter 4, Basic Shell Programming
Introduces shell programming. This chapter explains the basics of shell scripts and functions, and discusses several important "nuts-and-bolts" programming features: string manipulation operators, regular expressions, command-line arguments (positional parameters), and command substitution.

Chapter 5, Flow Control
Continues the discussion of shell programming by describing command exit status, conditional expressions, and the shell's flow-control structures: if, for, case, select, while, and until.

Chapter 6, Command-Line Options and Typed Variables
Goes into depth about positional parameters and command-line option processing, then discusses special types and properties of variables, such as integer and floating-point arithmetic, the arithmetic version of the for loop, indexed and associative arrays, and the *typeset* command.

Chapter 7, Input/Output and Command-Line Processing
Gives a detailed description of Korn shell I/O, filling in the information omitted in Chapter 1. All of the shell's I/O redirectors are covered, along with the shell's ability to make TCP/IP socket connections and the line-at-a-time I/O commands *read*, *print*, and *printf*. The chapter then discusses the shell's command-line processing mechanism and the *eval* command.

Chapter 8, Process Handling
Covers process-related issues in detail. It starts with a discussion of job control and then gets into various low-level information about processes, including

process IDs, signals, and traps. The chapter then moves out to a higher level of abstraction to discuss coroutines, two-way pipes, and subshells.

Chapter 9, Debugging Shell Programs

Discusses various debugging techniques, starting with simple ones like trace and verbose modes and "fake signal" traps. Next, this chapter describes discipline functions. Finally, it presents *kshdb*, a Korn shell debugging tool that you can use to debug your own code.

Chapter 10, Korn Shell Administration

Gives information for system administrators, including techniques for implementing system-wide shell customization, customizing the built-in editors, and features related to system security.

Appendix A, Related Shells

Compares the 1993 Korn shell to several similar shells, including the standard SVR4 Bourne shell, the 1988 Korn shell, the IEEE 1003.2 POSIX shell standard, the CDE Desk Top Korn shell (*dtksh*), *tksh* (which blends Tcl/Tk with *ksh*), the public domain Korn shell (*pdksh*), the Free Software Foundation's *bash*, the Z shell (*zsh*), and a number of Bourne-style shells (really Unix-emulation environments) for Microsoft Windows.

Appendix B, Reference Information

Contains lists of shell invocation options, built-in commands, predefined aliases, built-in variables, conditional test operators, *set* command options, *typeset* command options, and emacs and vi editing mode commands. This appendix also covers the full details for using the *getopts* built-in command.

Appendix C, Building ksh from Source Code

Describes how to download the source for *ksh93* and build a working executable. This appendix also covers downloading prebuilt executables for a number of different systems.

Appendix D, AT&T ast Source Code License Agreement

Presents the licensing terms for the *ksh93* source code.

Conventions Used in This Handbook

We leave it as understood that, when you enter a shell command, you press ENTER at the end. ENTER is labeled RETURN on some keyboards.

Characters called CTRL-*X*, where *X* is any letter, are entered by holding down the CTRL (or CTL, or CONTROL) key and pressing that letter. Although we give the letter in uppercase, you can press the letter without the SHIFT key.

Other special characters are newline (which is the same as CTRL-J), BACKSPACE (same as CTRL-H), ESC, TAB, and DEL (sometimes labeled DELETE or RUBOUT).

This book uses the following font conventions:

Italic

> Used when discussing Unix filenames, external and built-in commands, alias names, command options, shell options, and shell functions. *Italic* is also used in the text when discussing dummy parameters that should be replaced with an actual value, to distinguish the *vi* and *emacs* programs from their Korn-shell modes, and to highlight special terms the first time they are defined.

`Constant width`

> Used for variable names and shell keywords, filename suffixes, and in examples to show the contents of files or the output from commands, as well as for command lines when they are within regular text.

`Constant width bold`

> Used in examples to show interaction between the user and the shell; any text the user types in is shown in **`constant width bold`**. For example:

```
$ pwd
/home/billr/ora/kb
$
```

`Constant width italic`

> Used in the text and in example command lines for dummy parameters that should be replaced with an actual value. For example:

```
$ cd directory
```

Reverse video

> Used in Chapter 2 to show the position of the cursor on the command line being edited. For example:

```
grep -l Bob < ~pete/wk/names
```

Indicates a tip, suggestion, or general note.

Indicates a warning or caution.

Standard Unix utility commands are sometimes mentioned with a number in parentheses (usually 1) following the command's name. The number refers to the section of the Unix User's Manual in which you'll find reference documentation (a.k.a. "the man page") on the utility in question. For example, *grep*(1) means the man page for *grep* in Section 1.

When there is an important difference between the 1988 and 1993 versions of the Korn shell, we refer to them as *ksh88* and *ksh93* respectively. Most of this book applies to all versions of the 1993 Korn shell. When we need to distinguish among different versions of the 1993 Korn shell, we add the minor release to the name, such as *ksh93h*, or *ksh93l+*.

About the Second Edition

The first edition of this book covered the 1988 version of the Korn shell. Shortly after it was published, David Korn released the 1993 version, which included compatibility with the POSIX 1003.2 shell standard, as well as many new features.

Although *ksh93* has been slow to spread to the commercial Unix world, source code is now available, so anyone who wants a copy of the latest and greatest version of *ksh93* has but to download the source and compile it. With this in mind, we have made *ksh93* the focus of the second edition, with a summary of the differences available in an appendix. This edition covers the most recent *ksh93* release available at the time of writing, which includes some significant features not found in earlier versions.

The basic structure and flow of the book remains the same, although we have fixed a number of mistakes and typos in the first edition and updated *kshdb*, the Korn Shell Debugger, to work with *ksh93*. Appendix A now includes more information about Korn shell work-alikes, both for Unix and Windows systems.

Also included with this edition is a reference card that covers many of the features of *ksh93* described in this book. This card is copyrighted by Specialized Systems Consultants, Inc. (SSC), and is reprinted by permission. SSC sells a four-color, 26-panel, 3.5-inch by 8.5-inch version of the card that covers both *ksh88* and *ksh93* in considerably more detail. See *http://www.ssc.com* for more information.

We'd Like to Hear From You

Please address comments and questions concerning this book to the publisher:

O'Reilly & Associates, Inc.
1005 Gravenstein Highway North
Sebastopol, CA 95472
(800) 998-9938 (in the United States or Canada)
(707) 829-0515 (international or local)
(707) 829-0104 (fax)

We have a web page for this book, where we list examples, errata, or any additional information. You can access this page at:

> *http://www.oreilly.com/catalog/korn2/*

To comment or ask technical questions about this book, send email to:

> *bookquestions@oreilly.com*

For more information about our books, conferences, Resource Centers, and the O'Reilly Network, see our web site at:

> *http://www.oreilly.com*

Acknowledgments

Writing a book from scratch isn't easy. Updating a book is even harder; the trick is to make it impossible (or at least difficult) for the reader to tell which author wrote what parts. I hope I've succeeded in that. I want to acknowledge Bill Rosenblatt for writing the first edition and giving me an excellent body of material with which to work. This is one of the best O'Reilly books I've ever read, and it was a pleasure to work with it.

I would like to thank (in alphabetical order) Nelson A. Beebe (University of Utah Mathematics department), Dr. David G. Korn (AT&T Research), Chet Ramey (maintainer of *bash*), Bill Rosenblatt (GiantSteps/Media Technology Strategies), and Dr. Eugene H. Spafford (Purdue University Computer Science department) for reviewing the book and providing many helpful comments. Mike Loukides, the book's editor, was very patient with me during several delays in the update. David Chu, of O'Reilly's editorial staff, did a great job making sure that many of the "nuts and bolts" parts of the project got done, for which I'm grateful.

David Korn, now of AT&T Research Laboratories, and author of the Korn shell, answered a number of questions and provided early access to *ksh93l* documentation, which helped considerably, as well as prerelease access to *ksh93n*. Glenn Fowler, also of AT&T Research, helped with compilation issues under GNU/Linux, as well as helping me understand a number of the finer points of *ksh* usage. Steve Alston provided some improvements to the *kshdb* debugger in Chapter 9. George Kraft IV provided helpful information on *dtksh* for Appendix A. Glenn Barry, of Sun Microsystems, provided information on *zsh* for Appendix A.

Thanks to Phil Hughes, president of SSC, for permission to reprint parts of their *ksh* reference card.

Several other staff members at O'Reilly contributed to the book, as well: Leanne Soylemez was the production editor and proofreader; Mary Brady and Jane Ellin provided additional quality control; Brenda Miller wrote the index.

Finally, thanks to my wonderful wife Miriam, for not demanding the attention she was entitled to on way too many nights while I worked on this book. Without her, nothing would be worth doing.

Arnold Robbins
Nof Ayalon
ISRAEL

Acknowledgments from the First Edition

Many people contributed to this book in many ways. I'd like to thank the following people for technical advice and assistance: for system administration help, John van Vlaanderen and Alexis Rosen. For information on alternative shells, John (again), Sean Wilson (of MKS), Ed Ravin, Mel Rappaport, and Chet Ramey. For identifying the need for a shell debugger, expertise in SunOS and system security, and, indeed, a significant portion of my career, Hal Stern. For debugger suggestions, Tan Bronson. For humanitarian aid, Jessica Lustig. And much thanks to David Korn for all kinds of great "horse's mouth" information—and, of course, for the Korn shell itself.

Thanks to our technical reviewers: Jim Baumbach, Jim Falk, David Korn, Ed Miner, Eric Pearce, and Ed Ravin. I especially appreciate the cooperation of Ed and Ed (in that order) during my "Whaddya mean, it doesn't work?!?" phase.

Several people at O'Reilly & Associates contributed to this effort: Gigi Estabrook and Clairemarie Fisher O'Leary proofread multiple drafts of the manuscript, Kismet McDonough and Donna Woonteiler copyedited the manuscript, Len Muellner implemented the book design macro package, Jennifer Niederst designed the cover and the format of the book, and Chris Reilley created the figures. Finally, an ocean of gratitude to Mike Loukides—editor, motivator, facilitator, constructive nitpicker, and constant voice of reason. He and the other folks at O'Reilly & Associates are some of the most innovative, interesting, and motivated people I've ever had the privilege to work with.

Bill Rosenblatt

1

Korn Shell Basics

You've used your computer for simple tasks, such as invoking your favorite application programs, reading your electronic mail, and perhaps examining and printing files. You know that your machine runs the Unix operating system, or maybe you know it under some other name, like Solaris, HP-UX, AIX, or SunOS. (Or you may be using a system such as GNU/Linux or one of the 4.4–BSD-derived systems that is not based on the original Unix source code.) But apart from that, you may not have given too much thought to what goes on inside the machine when you type in a command and hit ENTER.

It is true that several layers of events take place whenever you enter a command, but we're going to consider only the top layer, known as the *shell*. Generally speaking, a shell is any user interface to the Unix operating system, i.e., any program that takes input from the user, translates it into instructions that the operating system can understand, and conveys the operating system's output back to the user.

There are various types of user interface. The Korn shell belongs to the most common category, known as *character-based user interfaces*. These interfaces accept lines of textual commands that the user types; they usually produce text-based output. Other types of interface include the now-common *graphical user interfaces* (GUI), which add the ability to display arbitrary graphics (not just typewriter characters) and to accept input from mice and other pointing devices, touch-screen interfaces (such as those you see on some automatic teller machines), and so on.

What Is a Shell?

The shell's job, then, is to translate the user's command lines into operating system instructions. For example, consider this command line:

```
sort -n phonelist > phonelist.sorted
```

This means, "Sort lines in the file *phonelist* in numerical order, and put the result in the file *phonelist.sorted*." Here's what the shell does with this command:

1. Breaks up the line into the pieces `sort`, `-n`, `phonelist`, `>`, and `phonelist.sorted`. These pieces are called *words*.

2. Determines the purpose of the words: `sort` is a command; `-n` and `phonelist` are arguments; `>` and `phonelist.sorted`, taken together, are I/O instructions.

3. Sets up the I/O according to `> phonelist.sorted` (output to the file *phonelist.sorted*) and some standard, implicit instructions.

4. Finds the command *sort* in a file and runs it with the option *–n* (numerical order) and the argument *phonelist* (input filename).

Of course, each step really involves several substeps, and each substep includes a particular instruction to the underlying operating system.

Remember that the shell itself is not Unix—just the user interface to it. This is illustrated in Figure 1-1. Unix is one of the first operating systems to make the user interface independent of the operating system.

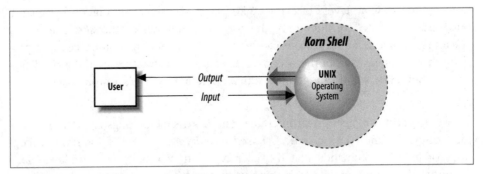

Figure 1-1. The shell is a layer around the Unix operating system

Scope of This Book

In this book, you will learn about the Korn shell, which is the most recent and powerful of the shells distributed with commercial Unix systems. There are two ways to use the Korn shell: as a user interface and as a programming environment.

This chapter and the next cover interactive use. These two chapters should give you enough background to use the shell confidently and productively for most of your everyday tasks.

After you have been using the shell for a while, you will undoubtedly find certain characteristics of your environment (the shell's "look and feel") that you would like to change and tasks that you would like to automate. Chapter 3 shows several ways of doing this.

Chapter 3 also prepares you for shell programming, the bulk of which is covered in Chapter 4 through Chapter 6. You need not have any programming experience to understand these chapters and learn shell programming. Chapter 7 and Chapter 8 give more complete descriptions of the shell's I/O and process handling capabilities, and Chapter 9 discusses various techniques for finding and removing problems in your shell programs.

You'll learn a lot about the Korn shell in this book; you'll also learn about Unix utilities and the way the Unix operating system works in general. It's possible to become a virtuoso shell programmer without any previous programming experience. At the same time, we've carefully avoided going down past a certain level of detail about Unix internals. We maintain that you shouldn't have to be an internals expert to use and program the shell effectively, and we won't dwell on the few shell features that are intended specifically for low-level systems programmers.

History of Unix Shells

The independence of the shell from the Unix operating system per se has led to the development of dozens of shells throughout Unix history, though only a few have achieved widespread use.

The first major shell was the Bourne shell (named after its inventor, Stephen Bourne); it was included in the first widely popular version of Unix, Version 7, starting in 1979. The Bourne shell is known on the system as *sh*. Although Unix has gone through many, many changes, the Bourne shell is still popular and essentially unchanged. Several Unix utilities and administration features depend on it.

The first widely used alternative shell was the C shell, or *csh*. It was written by Bill Joy at the University of California at Berkeley as part of the Berkeley Software Distribution (BSD) version of Unix that came out a couple of years after Version 7. It's included in essentially all recent Unix versions. (A popular variant is the so-called Twenex *csh*, *tcsh*.)

The C shell gets its name from the resemblance of its commands to statements in the C programming language, which makes the shell easier for programmers on

Unix systems to learn. It supports a number of operating system features (e.g., job control; see Chapter 8) that were once unique to BSD Unix but by now have migrated to just about all other modern versions. It also has a few important features (e.g., aliases; see Chapter 3) that make it easier to use in general.

The Korn Shell

The Korn shell, or *ksh*, was invented by David Korn of AT&T Bell Laboratories in the mid-1980s. It is almost entirely upwardly compatible with the Bourne shell,* which means that Bourne shell users can use it right away, and all system utilities that use the Bourne shell can use the Korn shell instead. In fact, some systems have the Korn shell installed as if it were the Bourne shell.

The Korn shell began its public life in 1986 as part of AT&T's "Experimental Toolchest," meaning that its source code was available at very low cost to anyone who was willing to use it without technical support and with the knowledge that it might still have a few bugs. Eventually, AT&T's Unix System Laboratories (USL) decided to give it full support as a Unix utility. As of USL's version of Unix called System V Release 4 (SVR4 for short, 1989), it was distributed with all USL Unix systems, all third-party versions of Unix derived from SVR4, and many other versions.

Late in 1993, David Korn released a newer version, popularly known as *ksh93*. This version is distributed with many commercial Unix systems as part of the Common Desktop Environment (CDE), typically as the "desktop Korn shell," */usr/dt/ bin/dtksh*.

Although Unix itself has changed owners several times since then, David Korn remained at Bell Laboratories until 1996, when AT&T (voluntarily, this time) split itself apart into AT&T Corporation, Lucent Technologies, and NCR. At that time, he moved to AT&T Research Laboratories from Bell Labs (which remained part of Lucent). Although both Lucent and AT&T retained full rights to the Korn shell, all enhancements and changes now come from David Korn at AT&T.

On March 1, 2000, AT&T released the *ksh93* source code under an Open Source–style license. Getting the source code is discussed further in Appendix C, and the license is presented in Appendix D.

This book focuses on the 2001 version of *ksh93*. Occasionally, the book notes a significant difference between the 1993 and 1988 versions. Where necessary, we distinguish them as *ksh93* and *ksh88*, respectively. Appendix A describes the differences between the 1988 and 1993 versions in an orderly fashion, and other shell versions are summarized briefly in that appendix, as well.

---

* With a few extremely minor exceptions. See Chapter 10 for the only important one.

Features of the Korn Shell

Although the Bourne shell is still known as the "standard" shell, the Korn shell is also popular. In addition to its Bourne shell compatibility, it includes the best features of the C shell as well as several advantages of its own. It also runs more efficiently than any previous shell.

The Korn shell's command-line editing modes are the features that tend to attract people to it at first. With command-line editing, it's much easier to go back and fix mistakes than it is with the C shell's history mechanism—and the Bourne shell doesn't let you do this at all.

The other major Korn shell feature that is intended mostly for interactive users is job control. As Chapter 8 explains, job control gives you the ability to stop, start, and pause any number of commands at the same time. This feature was borrowed almost verbatim from the C shell.

The rest of the Korn shell's important advantages are mainly meant for shell customizers and programmers. It has many new options and variables for customization, and its programming features have been significantly expanded to include function definition, more control structures, built-in regular expressions and arithmetic, associative arrays, structured variables, advanced I/O control, and more.

Getting the 1993 Korn Shell

This book covers the 1993 version of the Korn shell. A large amount of what's covered is unique to that shell; a subset of what is unique applies only to the recent versions available directly from AT&T. In order to make best use of the book, you should be using the 1993 Korn shell. Use the following sequence of instructions to determine what shell you currently have and whether the 1993 Korn shell exists on your system, and to make the 1993 Korn shell be your login shell.

1. Determine which shell you are using. The SHELL variable denotes your login shell. Log in to your system and type echo $SHELL at the prompt. You will see a response containing sh, csh, or ksh; these denote the Bourne, C, and Korn shells, respectively. (There's also a good chance that you're using a third-party shell such as *bash* or *tcsh*.) If the response is ksh, go to step 3. Otherwise, continue to step 2.

2. See if some version of *ksh* exists on your system in a standard directory. Type ksh. If that works (prints a $ prompt), you have a version of the Korn shell; proceed to step 3. Otherwise, proceed to step 5.

3. Check the version. Type `echo ${.sh.version}`. If that prints a version, you're all set; skip the rest of these instructions. Otherwise, continue to step 4.

4. You don't have the 1993 version of the Korn shell. To find out what version you do have, type the command `set -o emacs`, then press CTRL-V. This will tell you if you have the 1988 version or the Public Domain Korn shell. In either case, continue to step 5.

5. Type the command `/usr/dt/bin/dtksh`. If this gives you a $ prompt, you have the Desktop Korn Shell, which is based on an early version of *ksh93*. You may use this version; almost everything in this book will work. Go to step 7.

6. You need to download an executable version of *ksh93* or download the source and build an executable from it. These tasks are described in Appendix C. It would be best to enlist the help of your system administrator for this step. Once you have a working *ksh93*, continue to step 7.

7. Install *ksh93* as your login shell. There are two situations; pick the one appropriate to you:

    Single-user system

    On a single-user system, where you are the administrator, you will probably need to add the full path to *ksh93* to the file */etc/shells* as the first step. Then, you should be able to change your login shell by typing `chsh ksh-name`, where *ksh-name* is the full path to the *ksh93* executable. If this works, you'll be prompted for your password. Type in your password, then log out and log back in again to start using the Korn shell.

    If *chsh* doesn't exist or doesn't work, check the man page for *passwd*(1). Look for either the *-e* or *-s* options for updating your password file information. Use whatever is appropriate for your system to change your login shell.

    If none of the above works, you can resort to editing the */etc/passwd* file while logged in as root. If you have the *vipw*(8) command, you should use that to edit your password file. Otherwise, edit the file manually with your favorite text editor.

    Large multi-user system

    This situation is even more complex than the single-user case. It is best to let your system administrator handle changing the shell for you. Most large installations have a "helpdesk" (accessible via email or phone, or both) for entering such requests.

Interactive Shell Use

When you use the shell interactively, you engage in a login session that begins when you log in and ends when you exit or press CTRL-D.* During a login session, you type *command lines* into the shell; these are lines of text ending in ENTER that you type into your terminal or workstation.† By default, the shell prompts you for each command with a dollar sign, though, as you will see in Chapter 3 the prompt can be changed.

Commands, Arguments, and Options

Shell command lines consist of one or more words, which are separated on a command line by spaces or TABs. The first word on the line is the *command.* The rest (if any) are *arguments* (also called *parameters*) to the command, which are names of things on which the command will act.

For example, the command line lpr myfile consists of the command *lpr* (print a file) and the single argument *myfile. lpr* treats *myfile* as the name of a file to print. Arguments are often names of files, but not necessarily: in the command line mail billr, the *mail* program treats *billr* as the name of the user to which a message will be sent.

An *option* is a special type of argument that gives the command specific information on what it is supposed to do. Options usually consist of a dash followed by a letter; we say "usually" because this is a convention rather than a hard-and-fast rule. The command lpr -h myfile contains the option *–h*, which tells *lpr* not to print the "banner page" before it prints the file.

Sometimes options take their own arguments. For example, lpr -P hp3si -h myfile has two options and one argument. The first option is *–P hp3si*, which means "Send the output to the printer called *hp3si.*" The second option and argument are as above.

Built-in Help

Almost all the built-in commands in *ksh* have both minimal and more extensive "online" help. If you give a command the *–?* option, it prints a short usage summary:

---

* You can set up your shell so that it doesn't accept CTRL-D, i.e., it requires you to type exit to end your session. We recommend this, because CTRL-D is too easy to type by accident; see the section on options in Chapter 3.

† Although we assume that there are few people still using real serial terminals, modern windowing systems provide shell access through a terminal *emulator.* Thus, at least when it comes to interactive shell use, the term "terminal" applies equally well to a windowing environment.

```
$ cd -?
Usage: cd [-LP] [directory]
   Or: cd [ options ] old new
```

(You may wish to quote the ?, since, as we will see later, it is special to the shell.)
You may also give the *--man* option to print help in the form of the traditional
Unix man page.* The output uses ANSI standard escape sequences to produce a
visible change on the screen, rendered here using a bold font:

```
$ cd --man
NAME
   cd - change working directory


SYNOPSIS
   cd [ options ] [directory]
   cd [ options ] old new


DESCRIPTION
   cd changes the current working directory of the current shell environment.

   In the first form with one operand, if directory begins with /, or if the
   first component is . or .., the directory will be changed to this directory.
   ...
```

Similarly, the *--html* option produces output in HTML format for later rendering
with a web browser.

Finally, the *--nroff* option let's you produce each command's help in the form of
nroff--man input.† This is convenient for formatting the help for printed output.

For POSIX compliance, a few commands don't accept these options: *echo, false,
jobs, login, newgrp, true,* and *:.* For *test,* you have to type test --man -- to get the
online help.

Files

Although arguments to commands aren't always files, files are the most important
types of "things" on any Unix system. A file can contain any kind of information,
and there are different types of files. Four types are by far the most important:

Regular files

> Also called *text files*; these contain readable characters. For example, this
> book was created from several regular files that contain the text of the book
> plus human-readable DocBook XML formatting instructions.

---

* Starting with *ksh93i*.

† All of the help options send their output to standard error (which is described later in this chapter).
This means you have to use shell facilities that we don't cover until Chapter 7 to catch their output.
For example, cd --man 2>&1 | more runs the online help through the pager program *more*.

Executable files

Also called programs; these are invoked as commands. Some can't be read by humans; others—the shell scripts that we'll examine in this book—are just special text files. The shell itself is a (not human-readable) executable file called *ksh*.

Directories

Like folders that contain other files—possibly other directories (called *subdirectories*).

Symbolic links

A kind of "shortcut" from one place in the system's directory hierarchy to another. We will see later in this chapter how symbolic links can affect interactive use of the Korn shell.

Directories

Let's review the most important concepts about directories. The fact that directories can contain other directories leads to a hierarchical structure, more popularly known as a *tree*, for all files on a Unix system. Figure 1-2 shows part of a typical directory tree; ovals are regular files and rectangles are directories.

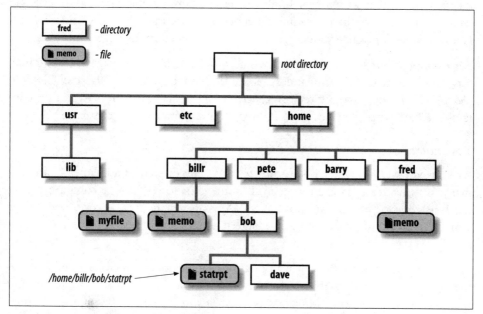

Figure 1-2. A tree of directories and files

The top of the tree is a directory called "root" that has no name on the system.* All files can be named by expressing their location on the system relative to root; such names are built by listing all the directory names (in order from root), separated by slashes (/), followed by the file's name. This way of naming files is called a *full* (or *absolute*) *pathname*.

For example, say there is a file called *memo* in the directory *fred*, which is in the directory *home*, which is in the root directory. This file's full pathname is */home/fred/memo*.

The working directory

Of course, it's annoying to have to use full pathnames whenever you need to specify a file, so there is also the concept of the *working directory* (sometimes called the *current directory*), which is the directory you are "in" at any given time. If you give a pathname with no leading slash, the location of the file is worked out relative to the working directory. Such pathnames are called *relative* pathnames; you'll use them much more often than full pathnames.

When you log in to the system, your working directory is initially set to a special directory called your *home* (or *login*) directory. System administrators often set up the system so that everyone's home directory name is the same as their login name, and all home directories are contained in a common directory under root. It is now common practice to use */home* as the top directory for home directories.

For example, */home/billr* is a typical home directory. If this is your working directory and you give the command `lp memo`, the system looks for the file *memo* in */home/billr*. If you have a directory called *bob* in your home directory, and it contains the file *statrpt*, you can print *statrpt* with the command `lp bob/statrpt`.

Tilde notation

As you can well imagine, home directories occur often in pathnames. Although many systems are organized so that all home directories have a common parent (such as */home*), you should not have to rely on that being the case, nor should you even have to know what the absolute pathname of someone's home directory is.

Therefore, the Korn shell has a way of abbreviating home directories: just precede the name of the user with a tilde (˜). For example, you could refer to the file *memo* in user fred's home directory as ˜*fred/memo*. This is an absolute pathname, so it doesn't matter what your working directory is when you use it. If fred's home

---

* Most introductory Unix tutorials say that root has the name /. We stand by this alternative explanation because it is more logically consistent.

directory has a subdirectory called *bob* and the file is in there instead, you can use *~fred/bob/memo* as its name.

Even more conveniently, a tilde by itself refers to your own home directory. You can refer to a file called *notes* in your home directory as *~/notes* (note the difference between that and *~notes*, which the shell would try to interpret as user notes's home directory). If *notes* is in your *bob* subdirectory, you can call it *~/bob/notes*. This notation is handiest when your working directory is not in your home directory tree, e.g., when it's some "system" directory like */tmp*.

Changing working directories

If you want to change your working directory, use the command *cd*. If you don't remember your working directory, the command *pwd* tells the shell to print it.

cd takes as argument the name of the directory you want to become your working directory. It can be relative to your current directory, it can contain a tilde, or it can be absolute (starting with a slash). If you omit the argument, *cd* changes to your home directory (i.e., it's the same as cd ~).

Table 1-1 gives some sample *cd* commands. Each command assumes that your working directory is */home/billr* just before the command is executed, and that your directory structure looks like Figure 1-2.

Table 1-1. Sample cd commands

Command	New working directory
cd bob	*/home/billr/bob*
cd bob/dave	*/home/billr/bob/dave*
cd ~/bob/dave	*/home/billr/bob/dave*
cd /usr/lib	*/usr/lib*
cd ..	*/home*
cd ../pete	*/home/pete*
cd ~pete	*/home/pete*
cd billr pete	*/home/pete*
cd illr arry	*/home/barry*

The first four are straightforward. The next two use a special directory called .. (two dots, pronounced "dot dot"), which means "parent of this directory." Every directory has one of these; it's a universal way to get to the directory above the current one in the hierarchy—which is called the parent directory.

Each directory also has the special directory . (single dot), which just means "this directory." Thus, cd . effectively does nothing. Both . and .. are actually special hidden files in each directory that point to the directory itself and to its parent directory, respectively. The root directory is its own parent.

The last two examples in the table use a new form of the *cd* command, which is not included in most Bourne shells. The form is cd *old new*. It takes the full pathname of the current working directory and tries to find the string *old* in it. If it finds the string, it substitutes *new* and changes to the resulting directory.

In the first of the two examples, the shell substitutes *pete* for *billr* in the current directory name and makes the result the new current directory. The last example shows that the substitution need not be a complete filename: substituting *arry* for *illr* in */home/billr* yields */home/barry*. (If the *old* string can't be found in the current directory name, the shell prints an error message.)

Another feature of the Korn shell's *cd* command is the form cd -, which changes to whatever directory you were in before the current one. For example, if you start out in */usr/lib*, type cd without an argument to go to your home directory, and then type cd -, you will be back in */usr/lib*.

Symbolic links to directories

Modern Unix systems provide *symbolic links*. Symbolic links (sometimes called *soft links*) provide a kind of "shortcut" to files in a different part of the system's file hierarchy. You can make a symbolic link to either a file or a directory, using either full or relative pathnames. When you access a file or directory via a symbolic link, Unix "follows the link" to the real file or directory.

Symbolic links to directories can generate surprising behavior. To explain why, let's start by assuming that you're using the regular Bourne shell, *sh*.* Now, suppose that we and user fred are working together on a project, and the primary directory for the project is under his home directory, say */home/fred/projects/ important/wonderprog*. That's a fairly long pathname to have to type, even if using the tilde notation (which we can't in the Bourne shell, but that's another story). To make life easier, let's create a symbolic link to the *wonderprog* directory in our home directory:

```
$ sh                Use the Bourne shell
$ cd                Make sure we're in our home directory
$ pwd               Show where we are
/home/billr
Create the symbolic link
$ ln -s /home/fred/projects/important/wonderprog wonderprog
```

---

* If you have a system where the Korn shell is installed as */bin/sh*, this example won't work.

Now, when we type cd `wonderprog`, we end up in */home/fred/projects/important/wonderprog*:

```
$ cd wonderprog
$ pwd
/home/fred/projects/important/wonderprog
```

After working for a while adding important new features* to *wonderprog*, we remember that we need to update the *.profile* file in our home directory. No problem: just *cd* back there and start work on the file, by looking at it first with *more*.

```
$ cd ..                    Go back up one level
$ more .profile            Look at .profile
.profile: No such file or directory
```

What happened? The cd `..` didn't take us back the way we came. Instead, it went up one level in the *physical* filesystem hierarchy:

```
$ pwd
/home/fred/projects/important
```

This is the "gotcha" with symbolic links; the logical view of the filesystem hierarchy presented by a symbolic link to a directory breaks down to the underlying physical reality when you *cd* to the parent directory.

The Korn shell works differently. It understands symbolic links and, by default, always presents you with a logical view of the filesystem. Not only is *cd* built into the shell, but so is *pwd*. Both commands accept the same two options: *–L*, to perform logical operations (the default), and *–P*, to perform the operations on the actual directories. Let's start over in the Korn shell:

```
$ cd wonderprog ; pwd              cd through the symbolic link
/home/billr/wonderprog             Answer is logical location
$ pwd -P                           What is the physical location?
/home/fred/projects/important/wonderprog    Answer is physical location
$ cd .. ; pwd                      Go back up one level
/home/billr                        Traversal was again logical

$ cd -P wonderprog; pwd            Do a physical cd
/home/fred/projects/important/wonderprog    Logical now equals physical
$ cd .. ; pwd                      Go back up up one level
/home/fred/projects/important      Logical still equals physical
```

As shown, the *–P* option to *cd* and *pwd* lets you "get around" the Korn shell's default use of logical positioning. Most of the time, though, logical positioning is exactly what you want.

---

* "Important new features" are those that the marketing department wants, whether or not the customers actually need them.

The shell sets the PWD and OLDPWD variables correspondingly whenever you do a *cd*; the results of typing pwd and print $PWD should always be the same.

As an unrelated note that rounds out the discussion, Unix systems also provide "hard links" (or just plain *links*) to files. Each name for a file is called a link; all hard links refer to the same data on disk, and if the file is changed by one name, that change is seen when looking at it from a different name. Hard links have certain restrictions, which symbolic links overcome. (See *ln*(1) for more information.) However, you cannot make hard links to directories, so symbolic links are all that matter for *cd* and *pwd*.

Filenames and Wildcards

Sometimes you need to run a command on more than one file at a time. The most common example of such a command is *ls*, which lists information about files. In its simplest form, without options or arguments, it lists the names of all files in the working directory except special hidden files, whose names begin with a dot (.).

If you give *ls* filename arguments, it will list those files, which is sort of silly: if your current directory has the files *bob* and *fred* in it, and you type ls bob fred, the system will simply parrot the filenames back at you.

Actually, ls is more often used with options that tell it to list information about the files, like the −*l* (long) option, which tells *ls* to list the file's owner, group, size, time of last modification, and other information, or −*a* (all), which also lists the hidden files described above. But sometimes you want to verify the existence of a certain group of files without having to know all of their names; for example, if you design web pages, you might want to see which files in your current directory have names that end in *.html*.

Filenames are so important in Unix that the shell provides a built-in way to specify the pattern of a set of filenames without having to know all of the names themselves. You can use special characters, called *wildcards*, in filenames to turn them into patterns. We'll show the three basic types of wildcards that all major Unix shells support, and we'll save the Korn shell's set of advanced wildcard operators for Chapter 4. Table 1-2 lists the basic wildcards.

Table 1-2. Basic wildcards

Wildcard	Matches
?	Any single character
*	Any string of characters
[*set*]	Any character in *set*
[!*set*]	Any character *not* in *set*

The ? wildcard matches any single character, so that if your directory contains the files *program.c, program.log,* and *program.o,* then the expression program.? matches *program.c* and *program.o* but not *program.log.*

The asterisk (*) is more powerful and far more widely used; it matches any string of characters. The expression program.* will match all three files in the previous paragraph; web designers can use the expression *.html to match their input files.*

Table 1-3 should give you a better idea of how the asterisk works. Assume that you have the files *bob, darlene, dave, ed, frank,* and *fred* in your working directory.

Notice that * can stand for nothing: both *ed and *e* match *ed.* Also notice that the last example shows what the shell does if it can't match anything: it just leaves the string with the wildcard untouched.

*Table 1-3. Using the * wildcard*

Expression	Yields
fr*	*frank fred*
*ed	*ed fred*
b*	*bob*
e	*darlene dave ed fred*
r	*darlene frank fred*
*	*bob darlene dave ed frank fred*
d*e	*darlene dave*
g*	*g**

Files are kept within directories in an unspecified order; the shell sorts the results of each wildcard expansion. (On some systems, the sorting may be subject to an ordering that is appropriate to the system's location, but that is different from the

---

* MS-DOS, Windows, and OpenVMS users should note that there is nothing special about the dot (.) in Unix filenames (aside from the leading dot, which "hides" the file); it's just another character. For example, ls * lists all files in the current directory; you don't need *.* as you do on other systems.

underlying machine collating order. Unix traditionalists can use export LANG=C to get the behavior they're used to.)

The remaining wildcard is the *set* construct. A set is a list of characters (e.g., abc), an inclusive range (e.g., a-z), or some combination of the two. If you want the dash character to be part of a list, just list it first or last. Table 1-4 (which assumes an ASCII environment) should explain things more clearly.

Table 1-4. Using the set construct wildcards

Expression	Matches
[abc]	*a*, *b*, or *c*
[.,;]	Period, comma, or semicolon
[-_]	Dash and underscore
[a-c]	*a*, *b*, or *c*
[a-z]	All lowercase letters
[!0-9]	All non-digits
[0-9!]	All digits and exclamation point
[a-zA-Z]	All lower- and uppercase letters
[a-zA-Z0-9_-]	All letters, all digits, underscore, and dash

In the original wildcard example, program.[co] and program.[a-z] both match *program.c* and *program.o*, but not *program.log*.

An exclamation point after the left bracket lets you "negate" a set. For example, [!.;] matches any character except period and semicolon; [!a-zA-Z] matches any character that isn't a letter.

The range notation is handy, but you shouldn't make too many assumptions about what characters are included in a range. It's generally safe to use a range for uppercase letters, lowercase letters, digits, or any subranges thereof (e.g., [f-q], [2-6]). Don't use ranges on punctuation characters or mixed-case letters: e.g., [a-z] and [A-z] should not be trusted to include all of the letters and nothing more. The problem is that such ranges are not entirely portable between different types of computers.*

Another problem is that modern systems support different *locales*, which are ways of describing how the local character set works. In most countries, the default locale's character set is different from that of plain ASCII. In Chapter 4, we show

---

* Specifically, ranges depend on the character encoding scheme your computer uses. The vast majority use ASCII, but IBM mainframes use EBCDIC. (Actually, on EBCDIC systems, not even the upper- and lowercase letters make a contiguous range.)

you how to use POSIX bracket expressions to denote letters, digits, punctuation, and other kinds of characters in a portable fashion.

The process of matching expressions containing wildcards to filenames is called *wildcard expansion.* This is just one of several steps the shell takes when reading and processing a command line; another that we have already seen is *tilde expansion,* where tildes are replaced with home directories where applicable. We'll see others in later chapters, and the full details of the process are enumerated in Chapter 7.

However, it's important to be aware that the commands that you run see only the *results* of wildcard expansion. (Indeed, this is true of all expansions.) That is, they just see a list of arguments, and they have no knowledge of how those arguments came into being. For example, if you type `ls fr*` and your files are as described earlier, then the shell expands the command line to `ls fred frank` and invokes the command *ls* with arguments *fred* and *frank.* If you type `ls g*`, then (because there is no match) *ls* will be given the literal string `g*` and will complain with the error message, `g* not found.`* (The actual message is likely to vary from system to system.)

Here is another example that should help you understand why this is important. Suppose you are a C programmer. This just means that you deal with files whose names end in .c (programs, a.k.a. source files), .h (header files for programs), and .o (object code files that aren't human-readable), as well as other files.

Let's say you want to list all source, object, and header files in your working directory. The command `ls *.[cho]` does the trick. The shell expands `*.[cho]` to all files whose names end in a period followed by a c, h, or o and passes the resulting list to *ls* as arguments.

In other words, *ls* will see the filenames just as if they were all typed in individually—but notice that we assumed no knowledge of the actual filenames whatsoever! We let the wildcards do the work.

As you gain experience with the shell, reflect on what life would be like without wildcards. Pretty miserable, we would say.

A final note about wildcards. You can set the variable `FIGNORE` to a shell pattern describing filenames to *ignore* during pattern matching. (The full pattern capabilities of the shell are described later, in Chapter 4.) For example, *emacs* saves backup versions of files by appending a ~ to the original filename. Often, you

---

* This is different from the C shell's wildcard mechanism, which prints an error message and doesn't execute the command at all.

don't need to see these files. To ignore them, you might add the following to your *.profile* file:

```
export FIGNORE='*~'
```

As with wildcard expansion, the test against FIGNORE applies to all components of a pathname, not just the final one.

Input and Output

The software field—really, any scientific field—tends to advance most quickly and impressively on those few occasions when someone (i.e., not a committee) comes up with an idea that is small in concept yet enormous in its implications. The standard input and output scheme of Unix has to be on the short list of such ideas, along with such classic innovations as the LISP language, the relational data model, and object-oriented programming.

The Unix I/O scheme is based on two dazzlingly simple ideas. First, Unix file I/O takes the form of arbitrarily long sequences of characters (bytes). In contrast, file systems of older vintage have more complicated I/O schemes (e.g., "block," "record," "card image," etc.). Second, everything on the system that produces or accepts data is treated as a file; this includes hardware devices like disk drives and terminals. Older systems treated every device differently. Both of these ideas have made systems programmers' lives much more pleasant.

Standard I/O

By convention, each Unix program has a single way of accepting input called *standard input*, a single way of producing output called *standard output*, and a single way of producing error messages called *standard error output*, usually shortened to *standard error*. Of course, a program can have other input and output sources as well, as we will see in Chapter 7.

Standard I/O was the first scheme of its kind that was designed specifically for interactive users, rather than the older batch style of use that usually involved decks of punch-cards. Since the Unix shell provides the user interface, it should come as no surprise that standard I/O was designed to fit in very neatly with the shell.

All shells handle standard I/O in basically the same way. Each program that you invoke has all three standard I/O channels set to your terminal or workstation window, so that standard input is your keyboard, and standard output and error are your screen or window. For example, the *mail* utility prints messages to you on the standard output, and when you use it to send messages to other users, it accepts your input on the standard input. This means that you view messages on your screen and type new ones in on your keyboard.

When necessary, you can redirect input and output to come from or go to a file instead. If you want to send the contents of a preexisting file to someone as mail, you redirect *mail*'s standard input so that it reads from that file instead of your keyboard.

You can also hook up programs into a *pipeline*, in which the standard output of one program feeds directly into the standard input of another; for example, you could feed *mail* output directly to the *lp* program so that messages are printed instead of shown on the screen.

This makes it possible to use Unix utilities as building blocks for bigger programs. Many Unix utility programs are meant to be used in this way: they each perform a specific type of filtering operation on input text. Although this isn't a textbook on Unix utilities, they are essential to productive shell use. The more popular filtering utilities are listed in Table 1-5.

Table 1-5. Popular Unix data filtering utilities

Utility	Purpose
cat	Copy input to output
grep	Search for strings in the input
sort	Sort lines in the input
cut	Extract columns from input
sed	Perform editing operations on input
tr	Translate characters in the input to other characters

You may have used some of these before and noticed that they take names of input files as arguments and produce output on standard output. You may not know, however, that all of them (and most other Unix utilities) accept input from standard input if you omit the argument.*

For example, the most basic utility is *cat*, which simply copies its input to its output. If you type cat with a filename argument, it will print out the contents of that file on your screen. But if you invoke it with no arguments, it will read standard input and copy it to standard output. Try it: *cat* will wait for you to type a line of text; when you type ENTER, *cat* will parrot the text back at you. To stop the

---

* If a particular Unix utility doesn't accept standard input when you leave out the filename argument, try using – as the argument. This is a common, although not universal, convention.

process, hit CTRL-D at the beginning of a line (see below for what this character means). You will see ^D when you type CTRL-D. Here's what this should look like:

```
$ cat
Here is a line of text.
Here is a line of text.
This is another line of text.
This is another line of text.
^D
$
```

I/O Redirection

cat is actually short for "catenate," i.e., link together. It accepts multiple filename arguments and copies them to the standard output. But let's pretend, for the moment, that *cat* and other utilities don't accept filename arguments and accept only standard input. As we said above, the shell lets you redirect standard input so that it comes from a file. The notation `command < filename` does this; it sets things up so that *command* takes standard input from a file instead of from a terminal.

For example, if you have a file called *fred* that contains some text, then cat < fred will print *fred*'s contents out onto your terminal. sort < fred will sort the lines in the *fred* file and print the result on your terminal (remember: we're pretending that utilities don't take filename arguments).

Similarly, `command > filename` causes *command*'s standard output to be redirected to the named file. The classic "canonical" example of this is date > now: the *date* command prints the current date and time on the standard output; the above command saves it in a file called *now*.

Input and output redirectors can be combined. For example, the *cp* command is normally used to copy files; if for some reason it didn't exist or was broken, you could use *cat* in this way:

```
cat < file1 > file2
```

This would be similar to cp file1 file2.

As a mnemonic device, think of < and > as "data funnels." Data goes into the big end and comes out the small end.

When used interactively, the Korn shell lets you use a shell wildcard after an I/O redirection operator. If the pattern matches *exactly* one file, that file is used for I/O redirection. Otherwise, the pattern is left unchanged, and the shell attempts to open a file whose name is exactly what you typed. In addition, it is invalid to attempt a redirection with the null string as the filename (such as might happen when using the value of a variable, and the variable happens to be empty).

Finally, it is tempting to use the same file for both input and output:

```
sort < myfile > myfile        Sort myfile in place? No!
```

This does *not* work! The shell truncates *myfile* when opening it for output, and there won't be any data there for *sort* to process when it runs.

Pipelines

It is also possible to redirect the output of one command into the standard input of another running command instead of a file. The construct that does this is called the pipe, notated as |. A command line that includes two or more commands connected with pipes is called a *pipeline*.

Pipes are very often used with the *more* command, which works just like *cat* except that it prints its output screen by screen, pausing for the user to type SPACE (next screen), ENTER (next line), or other commands. If you're in a directory with a large number of files and you want to see details about them, `ls -l | more` will give you a detailed listing a screen at a time.

Pipelines can get very complex (see, for example, the *lsd* function in Chapter 4 or the pipeline version of the C compiler driver in Chapter 7); they can also be combined with other I/O redirectors. To see a sorted listing of the file *fred* a screen at a time, type `sort < fred | more`. To print it instead of viewing it on your terminal, type `sort < fred | lp`.

Here's a more complicated example. The file */etc/passwd* stores information about users' accounts on a Unix system. Each line in the file contains a user's login name, user ID number, encrypted password, home directory, login shell, and other info. The first field of each line is the login name; fields are separated by colons (:). A sample line might look like this:

```
billr:5Ae40BGR/tePk:284:93:Bill Rosenblatt:/home/billr:/bin/ksh
```

To get a sorted listing of all users on the system, type:

```
cut -d: -f1 < /etc/passwd | sort
```

(Actually, you can omit the <, since *cut* accepts input filename arguments.) The *cut* command extracts the first field (*-f1*), where fields are separated by colons (*-d:*), from the input. The entire pipeline prints a list that looks like this:

```
al
billr
bob
chris
dave
```

```
ed
frank
...
```

If you want to send the list directly to the printer (instead of your screen), you can extend the pipeline like this:

```
cut -d: -f1 < /etc/passwd | sort | lp
```

Now you should see how I/O redirection and pipelines support the Unix building block philosophy. The notation is extremely terse and powerful. Just as important, the pipe concept eliminates the need for messy temporary files to store output of commands before it is fed into other commands.

For example, to do the same sort of thing as the above command line on other operating systems (assuming that equivalent utilities were available), you would need three commands. On Compaq's OpenVMS system, they might look like this:

```
$ cut [etc]passwd /d=":" /f=1 /out=temp1
$ sort temp1 /out=temp2
$ print temp2
```

After sufficient practice, you will find yourself routinely typing in powerful command pipelines that do in one line what in other operating systems would require several commands (and temporary files) to accomplish.

Background Jobs

Pipes are actually a special case of a more general feature: doing more than one thing at a time. any other commercial operating systems don't have this capability, because of the rigid limits that they tend to impose upon users. Unix, on the other hand, was developed in a research lab and meant for internal use, so it does relatively little to impose limits on the resources available to users on a computer—as usual, leaning towards uncluttered simplicity rather than overcomplexity.

"Doing more than one thing at a time" means running more than one program at the same time. You do this when you invoke a pipeline; you can also do it by logging on to a Unix system as many times simultaneously as you wish. (If you try that on an IBM VM/CMS system, for example, you get an obnoxious "already logged in" message.)

The shell also lets you run more than one command at a time during a single login session. Normally, when you type a command and hit ENTER, the shell lets the command have control of your terminal until it is done; you can't run further commands until the first one finishes. But if you want to run a command that does not require user input and you want to do other things while the command is running, put an ampersand (&) after the command.

This is called running the command in the background, and a command that runs in this way is called a *background job*; for contrast, a job run the normal way is called a *foreground job*. When you start a background job, you get your shell prompt back immediately, enabling you to enter other commands.

The most obvious use for background jobs is programs that can take a long time to run, such as *sort* or *gunzip* on large files. For example, assume you just got an enormous compressed file loaded into your directory from magnetic tape. Today, the *gzip* utility is the de-facto file compression utility. *gzip* often achieves 50% to 90% compression of its input files. The compressed files have names of the form *filename.gz*, where *filename* is the name of the original uncompressed file. Let's say the file is *gcc–3.0.1.tar.gz*, which is a compressed archive file that contains well over 36 MB of source code files.

Type `gunzip gcc-3.0.1.tar.gz &`, and the system starts a job in the background that uncompresses the data "in place" and ends up with the file *gcc–3.0.1.tar*. Right after you type the command, you see a line like this:

```
[1]     4692
```

followed by your shell prompt, meaning that you can enter other commands. Those numbers give you ways of referring to your background job; Chapter 8 explains them in detail.

You can check on background jobs with the command *jobs*. For each background job, *jobs* prints a line similar to the above but with an indication of the job's status:

```
[1]  +  Running            gunzip gcc-3.0.1.tar.gz
```

When the job finishes, you see a message like this right before your shell prompt:

```
[1]  +  Done               gunzip gcc-3.0.1.tar.gz
```

The message changes if your background job terminated with an error; again, see Chapter 8 for details.

Background I/O

Jobs you put in the background should not do I/O to your terminal. Just think about it for a moment and you'll understand why.

By definition, a background job doesn't have control over your terminal. Among other things, this means that only the foreground process (or, if none, the shell itself) is "listening" for input from your keyboard. If a background job needs keyboard input, it will often just sit there doing nothing until you do something about it (as described in Chapter 8).

If a background job produces screen output, the output will just appear on your screen. If you are running a job in the foreground that also produces output, the output from the two jobs will be randomly (and often annoyingly) interspersed.

If you want to run a job in the background that expects standard input or produces standard output, the obvious solution is to redirect it so that it comes from or goes to a file. The only exception is that some programs produce small, one-line messages (warnings, "done" messages, etc.); you may not mind if these are interspersed with whatever other output you are seeing at a given time.

For example, the *diff* utility examines two files, whose names are given as arguments, and prints a summary of their differences on the standard output. If the files are exactly the same, *diff* is silent. Usually, you invoke *diff* expecting to see a few lines that are different.

diff, like *sort* and *gzip*, can take a long time to run if the input files are very large. Suppose you have two large files called *warandpeace.html* and *warand-peace.html.old*. The command `diff warandpeace.html.old warandpeace.html` reveals that the author decided to change the name "Ivan" to "Aleksandr" throughout the entire file—i.e., hundreds of differences, resulting in large amounts of output.

If you type `diff warandpeace.html.old warandpeace.html &`, then the system will spew lots and lots of output at you, which it will be very difficult to stop—even with the techniques explained in Chapter 7. However, if you type:

```
diff warandpeace.html.old warandpeace.html > wpdiff &
```

the differences will be saved in the file *wpdiff* for you to examine later.

Background Jobs and Priorities

Background jobs can save you a lot of thumb-twiddling time (or can help you diet by eliminating excuses to run to the candy machine). But remember that there is no free lunch; background jobs take resources that become unavailable to you or other users on your system. Just because you're running several jobs at once doesn't mean that they will run faster than they would if run sequentially—in fact, it's usually worse.

Every job on the system is assigned a *priority*, a number that tells the operating system how much priority to give the job when it doles out resources (the higher the number, the lower the priority). Foreground commands that you enter from the shell usually have the same, standard priority. But background jobs, by default, have lower priority.* You'll find out in Chapter 3 how you can override this priority assignment so that background jobs run at the same priority as foreground jobs.

If you're on a large multiuser system, running lots of background jobs may eat up more than your fair share of the shared resources, and you should consider whether having your job run as fast as possible is really more important than being a good citizen.

On the other hand, if you have a dedicated workstation with a fast processor and loads of memory and disk, then you probably have cycles to spare and shouldn't worry about it as much. The typical usage pattern on such systems largely obviates the need for background processes anyway: you can just start a job and then open another window and keep working.

nice

Speaking of good citizenship, there is also a shell command that lets you lower the priority of any job: the aptly-named *nice*. If you type the following, the command will run at a lower priority:

```
nice command
```

You can control just how much lower by giving *nice* a numerical argument; consult the man page for details.†

Special Characters and Quoting

The characters <, >, |, and & are four examples of *special characters* that have particular meanings to the shell. The wildcards we saw earlier in this chapter (*, ?, and [...]) are also special characters.

Table 1-6 gives indications of the meanings of all special characters within shell command lines only. Other characters have special meanings in specific situations, such as the regular expressions and string-handling operators we'll see in Chapter 3 and Chapter 4.

---

* This feature was borrowed from the C shell; it is not present in most Bourne shells.

† If you are a system administrator logged in as root, you can also use *nice* to raise a job's priority.

Table 1-6. Special characters

Character	Meaning	See chapter
~	Home directory	1
`	Command substitution (archaic)	4
#	Comment	4
$	Variable expression	3
&	Background job	1
*	String wildcard	1
(	Start subshell	8
)	End subshell	8
\	Quote next character	1
|	Pipe	1
[	Start character-set wildcard	1
]	End character-set wildcard	1
{	Start code block	7
}	End code block	7
;	Shell command separator	3
'	Strong quote	1
"	Weak quote	1
<	Input redirect	1
>	Output redirect	1
/	Pathname directory separator	1
?	Single-character wildcard	1
%	Job name/number identifier	8

Quoting

Sometimes you will want to use special characters literally, i.e., without their special meanings. This is called *quoting*. If you surround a string of characters with single quotes, you strip all characters within the quotes of any special meaning they might have.

The most obvious situation where you might need to quote a string is with the *print* command, which just takes its arguments and prints them to the standard output. What is the point of this? As you will see in later chapters, the shell does quite a bit of processing on command lines—most of which involves some of the special characters listed in Table 1-6. *print* is a way of making the result of that processing available on the standard output.

But what if we wanted to print the string, 2 * 3 > 5 is a valid inequality? Suppose you typed this:

```
print 2 * 3 > 5 is a valid inequality.
```

You would get your shell prompt back, as if nothing happened! But then there would be a new file, with the name *5*, containing "2", the names of all files in your current directory, and then the string 3 is a valid inequality. Make sure you understand why.*

However, if you type:

```
print '2 * 3 > 5 is a valid inequality.'
```

the result is the string, taken literally. You needn't quote the entire line, just the portion containing special characters (or characters you think *might* be special, if you just want to be sure):

```
print '2 * 3 > 5' is a valid inequality.
```

This has exactly the same result.

Notice that Table 1-6 lists double quotes (") as weak quotes. A string in double quotes is subjected to *some* of the steps the shell takes to process command lines, but not all. (In other words, it treats only some special characters as special.) You'll see in later chapters why double quotes are sometimes preferable; Chapter 7 contains the most comprehensive explanation of the shell's rules for quoting and other aspects of command-line processing. For now, though, you should stick to single quotes.

Backslash-Escaping

Another way to change the meaning of a character is to precede it with a backslash (\). This is called *backslash-escaping* the character. In most cases, when you backslash-escape a character, you quote it. For example:

```
print 2 \* 3 \> 5 is a valid inequality.
```

produces the same results as if you surrounded the string with single quotes. To use a literal backslash, just surround it with quotes ('\') or, even better, backslash-escape it (\\).

Here is a more practical example of quoting special characters. A few Unix commands take arguments that often include wildcard characters, which need to be

---

* This should also teach you something about the flexibility of placing I/O redirectors anywhere on the command line—even in places where they don't seem to make sense.

escaped so the shell doesn't process them first. The most common such command is *find*, which searches for files throughout entire directory trees.

To use *find*, you supply the root of the tree you want to search and arguments that describe the characteristics of the file(s) you want to find. For example, the command `find . -name` *string* `-print` searches the directory tree whose root is your current directory for files whose names match the string, and prints their names. (Other arguments allow you to search by the file's size, owner, permissions, date of last access, etc.)

You can use wildcards in the string, but you must quote them, so that the *find* command itself can match them against names of files in each directory it searches. The command `find . -name '*.c'` will match all files whose names end in `.c` anywhere in your current directory, subdirectories, sub-subdirectories, etc.

Quoting Quotation Marks

You can also use a backslash to include double quotes within a string. For example:

```
print \"2 \* 3 \> 5\" is a valid inequality.
```

produces the following output:

```
"2 * 3 > 5" is a valid inequality.
```

Within a double-quoted string, only the double quotes need to be escaped:

```
$ print "\"2 * 3 > 5\" is a valid inequality."
"2 * 3 > 5" is a valid inequality.
```

However, this won't work with single quotes inside quoted expressions. For example, `print 'Bob\'s hair is brown'` will not give you `Bob's hair is brown`. You can get around this limitation in various ways. First, try eliminating the quotes:

```
print Bob\'s hair is brown
```

If no other characters are special (as is the case here), this works. Otherwise, you can use the following command:

```
print 'Bob'\''s hair is brown'
```

That is, `'\''` (i.e., single quote, backslash, single quote, single quote) acts like a single quote within a quoted string. Why? The first `'` in `'\''` ends the quoted string we started with `'Bob`, the `\'` inserts a literal single quote, and the next `'` starts another quoted string that ends with the word "brown". If you understand this, you will have no trouble resolving the other bewildering issues that arise from the shell's often cryptic syntax.

A somewhat more legible mechanism, specific to *ksh93*, is available for cases where you need to quote single quotes. This is the shell's extended quoting mechanism: `$'...'`. This is known in *ksh* documentation as *ANSI C quoting*, since the rules closely resemble those of ANSI/ISO Standard C. The full details are provided in Chapter 7. Here is how to use ANSI C quoting for the previous example:

```
$ print $'Bob\'s hair is brown'
Bob's hair is brown
```

Continuing Lines

A related issue is how to continue the text of a command beyond a single line on your terminal or workstation window. The answer is conceptually simple: just quote the ENTER key. After all, ENTER is really just another character.

You can do this in two ways: by ending a line with a backslash or by not closing a quote mark (i.e., by including ENTER in a quoted string). If you use the backslash, there must be nothing between it and the end of the line—not even spaces or TABs.

Whether you use a backslash or a single quote, you are telling the shell to ignore the special meaning of the ENTER character. After you press ENTER, the shell understands that you haven't finished your command line (i.e., since you haven't typed a "real" ENTER), so it responds with a secondary prompt, which is > by default, and waits for you to finish the line. You can continue a line as many times as you wish.

For example, if you want the shell to print the first sentence of Thomas Hardy's *The Return of the Native*, you can type this:

```
$ print A Saturday afternoon in November was approaching the \
> time of twilight, and the vast tract of unenclosed wild known \
> as Egdon Heath embrowned itself moment by moment.
```

Or you can do it this way:

```
$ print 'A Saturday afternoon in November was approaching the
> time of twilight, and the vast tract of unenclosed wild known
> as Egdon Heath embrowned itself moment by moment.'
```

There is a difference between the two methods. The first prints the sentence as one long line. The second preserves the embedded newlines. Try both, and you'll see the difference.

Control Keys

Control keys—those that you type by holding down the CONTROL (or CTRL) key and hitting another key—are another type of special character. These normally don't print anything on your screen, but the operating system interprets a few of them as special commands. You already know one of them: ENTER is actually the same as CTRL-M (try it and see). You have probably also used the BACKSPACE or DEL key to erase typos on your command line.

Actually, many control keys have functions that don't really concern you—yet you should know about them for future reference and in case you type them by accident.

Perhaps the most difficult thing about control keys is that they can differ from system to system. The usual arrangement is shown in Table 1-7, which lists the control keys that all major modern versions of Unix support. Note that CTRL-\ and CTRL-| (control-backslash and control-pipe) are the same character notated two different ways; the same is true of DEL and CTRL-?.

You can use the *stty*(1) command to find out what your settings are and change them if you wish; see Chapter 8 for details. On modern Unix systems (including GNU/Linux), use stty -a to see your control-key settings:

```
$ stty -a
speed 38400 baud; rows 24; columns 80; line = 0;
intr = ^C; quit = ^\; erase = ^H; kill = ^U; eof = ^D; eol = <undef>;
eol2 = <undef>; start = ^Q; stop = ^S; susp = ^Z; rprnt = ^R; werase = ^W;
lnext = ^V; flush = ^O; min = 1; time = 0;
...
```

The ^*X* notation stands for CTRL-*X*.

Table 1-7. Control keys

Control key	stty name	Function description
CTRL-C	intr	Stop current command.
CTRL-D	eof	End of input.
CTRL-\ or CTRL-|	quit	Stop current command, if CTRL-C doesn't work.
CTRL-S	stop	Halt output to screen.
CTRL-Q	start	Restart output to screen.
BACKSPACE or CTRL-H	erase	Erase last character. This is the most common setting.
DEL or CTRL-?	erase	Erase last character. This is a common alternative setting. for the erase character
CTRL-U	kill	Erase entire command line.

Table 1-7. Control keys (continued)

Control key	stty name	Function description
CTRL-Z	susp	Suspend current command (see Chapter 8).
CTRL-R	rprnt	Reprint the characters entered so far.

The control key you will probably use most often is CTRL-C, sometimes called the *interrupt* key. This stops—or tries to stop—the command that is currently running. You will want to use this when you enter a command and find that it's taking too long, when you gave it the wrong arguments by mistake, when you change your mind about wanting to run it, and so on.

Sometimes CTRL-C doesn't work; in that case, if you really want to stop a job, try CTRL-\. But don't just type CTRL-\; always try CTRL-C first! Chapter 8 explains why in detail. For now, suffice it to say that CTRL-C gives the running job more of a chance to clean up before exiting, so that files and other resources are not left in funny states.

We've already seen an example of CTRL-D. When you are running a command that accepts standard input from your keyboard, CTRL-D (as the first character on the line) tells the process that your input is finished—as if the process were reading a file and it reached the end of the file. *mail* is a utility in which this happens often. When you are typing in a message, you end by typing CTRL-D. This tells *mail* that your message is complete and ready to be sent. Most utilities that accept standard input understand CTRL-D as the end-of-input character, though many such programs accept commands like q, quit, exit, etc. The shell itself understands CTRL-D as the end-of-input character: as we saw earlier in this chapter, you can normally end a login session by typing CTRL-D at the shell prompt. You are just telling the shell that its command input is finished.

CTRL-S and CTRL-Q are called flow-control characters. They represent an antiquated way of stopping and restarting the flow of output from one device to another (e.g., from the computer to your terminal) that was useful when the speed of such output was low. They are rather obsolete in these days of high-speed local networks and dialup lines. In fact, under the latter conditions, CTRL-S and CTRL-Q are basically a nuisance. The only thing you really need to know about them is that if your screen output becomes "stuck," then you may have hit CTRL-S by accident. Type CTRL-Q to restart the output; any keys you may have hit in between will then take effect.

The final group of control characters gives you rudimentary ways to edit your command line. BACKSPACE or CTRL-H acts as a backspace key (in fact, some systems use the DEL or CTRL-? keys as "erase" instead of BACKSPACE); CTRL-U

erases the entire line and lets you start over. Again, most of these are outmoded.*
Instead of using these, go to the next chapter and read about the Korn shell's editing modes, which are among its most exciting features.

---

* Why are so many outmoded control keys still in use? They have nothing to do with the shell per se;
  instead, they are recognized by the *tty driver*, an old and hoary part of the operating system's lower
  depths that controls input and output to/from your terminal. It is, in fact, the tty driver that understands CTRL-D and signals end-of-input to programs reading from the terminal, not the programs
  themselves.

2

Command-Line Editing

It's always possible to make mistakes when you type at a computer keyboard, but perhaps even more so when you are using a Unix shell. Unix shell syntax is powerful, yet terse, full of odd characters, and not particularly mnemonic, making it possible to construct command lines that are as cryptic as they are complex. The Bourne and C shells exacerbate this situation by giving you extremely limited ways of editing your command lines.

In particular, there is no way to recall a previous command line so that you can fix a mistake. For example, in Chapter 7 we'll see complex command lines like:

```
eval cat \$srcname \| ccom \| optimize \| as \> \$objname
```

If you are an experienced Bourne shell user, undoubtedly you know the frustration of having to retype lines like this. You can use the backspace key to edit, but once you hit ENTER, it's gone forever!

The C shell provides a small improvement via its *history* mechanism, which provides a few very awkward ways of editing previous commands. But there are more than a few people who have wondered, "Why can't I edit my Unix command lines in the same way I can edit text with an editor?"

This is exactly what the Korn shell allows you to do. It has editing modes that allow you to edit command lines with editing commands similar to those of the two most popular Unix editors, *vi* and Emacs.* It also provides a much-extended analogue to the C shell history mechanism called *hist* (for "history") that, among

---

* For some unknown reason, the documentation on emacs-mode has been removed from the *ksh*(1) manual pages on some Unix systems. This does not mean, however, that the mode doesn't exist or doesn't work properly.

other things, allows you to use your favorite editor directly for editing your command lines.

In this chapter, we discuss features common to all of the Korn shell's command-history facilities; then we deal with each such facility in detail. If you use *vi* or Emacs, you may wish to read only the section on the emulation mode for the one you use.* If you use neither *vi* or Emacs but are interested in learning one of the editing modes anyway, we suggest emacs-mode, because it is more of a natural extension of the minimal editing capability you get with the bare shell.

We should mention up front that both emacs- and vi-modes introduce the potential for clashes with control keys set up by the Unix terminal interface. Recall the control keys shown in Chapter 1 in Table 1-7 and the sample *stty* command output. The control keys shown there override their functions in the editing modes.

During the rest of this chapter, we warn you when an editing command clashes with the default setting of a terminal-interface control key. But if you (or your system administrator) choose to customize your terminal interface, as we show in Chapter 8, you're on your own as far as the editing modes are concerned.

Enabling Command-Line Editing

There are two ways of entering either editing mode. First, you can set your editing mode by using the environment variable VISUAL. The Korn shell checks to see if this variable ends with vi or macs.† An excellent way to set VISUAL is to put a line like the following in your *.profile* or environment file:

```
VISUAL=$(whence emacs)
```

or

```
VISUAL=$(whence vi)
```

As you will find out in Chapter 3 and Chapter 4, the *whence* built-in command takes the name of another command as its argument and writes the command's full pathname on the standard output; the form $(*command*) returns the standard output generated by *command* as a string value. Thus, the line above finds out the full pathname of your favorite editor and stores it in the environment variable VISUAL. The advantage of this code is that it is portable to other systems, which may have the executables for editors stored in different directories.

---

* You will get the most out of these sections if you are already familiar with the editor(s) in question. Good sources for more complete information on the editors are *Learning the vi Editor* by Linda Lamb and Arnold Robbins and *Learning GNU Emacs* by Debra Cameron, Bill Rosenblatt, and Eric Raymond. Both are published by O'Reilly & Associates.

† GNU Emacs is sometimes installed as *gmacs* or *gnumacs*.

The second way of selecting an editing mode is to set the option explicitly with the *set –o* command:

```
set -o emacs
```

or

```
set -o vi
```

vi users may wish to add:

```
set -o viraw
```

along with `set -o vi`. This enables TAB completion in recent versions of *ksh93*. The additional overhead, particularly on single-user systems, is nominal and, in any case, is no worse than that of emacs-mode. (Starting with *ksh93n*, the *viraw* option is automatically enabled when you use vi-mode.)

You will find that the vi and emacs editing modes are good at emulating the basic commands of these editors, but not advanced features; their main purpose is to let you transfer "finger habits" from your favorite editor to the shell. *hist* is a powerful facility; it is mainly meant to supplant C shell history and as an "escape hatch" for users of editors other than *vi* or Emacs. Therefore the section on *hist* is recommended mostly to C shell users and those who don't use either standard editor.

Before diving into the details, it's worth mentioning two other points that apply to both editing modes:

- *ksh* indicates that a line is wider than your screen by marking the last column of the visible line with a special character: < indicates that there is more text on the left side of what you currently see, > indicates there is more text to the right of what you see, and * indicates there is text on both sides of what is currently visible.

  ```
  $ print this is a very long line that just runs on and >
  ```

- Customization of the *ksh93* editing modes is possible but requires knowledge of advanced features we haven't covered yet. See Chapter 10 for the details.*

The History File

All of the Korn shell's command history facilities depend on a file that stores commands as you type them in. This file is normally *.sh_history* in your home directory, but you can call it whatever you like by setting the environment variable

---

* The public domain Korn shell, *bash*, and zsh have editing modes that are customizable, but in a different way from *ksh93*. See Appendix A.

HISTFILE (see Chapter 3). When you run one of the Korn shell's editing modes, you are actually running a mini-editor on your history file.

If you run more than one login session at a time (e.g., more than one *xterm* on an X Windows workstation), you may find it advantageous to maintain a separate history file for each login session. Put the following line in your *.profile*:

```
HISTFILE=~/.hist.$(tty | sed 's;.*/;;')
```

This creates a history file whose name ends with the last component of your terminal's device name. For example, your window's terminal device name might be */dev/pts/42*. The *sed* command strips everything through the last slash, leaving just the *42*. The history file then becomes *~/.hist.42*. You can remove the history file at logout, as explained in Chapter 4. Or you can leave the files around, and your history will be there the next time you start a window on that same terminal device. (Preserving history between sessions is the point of the history file, after all.)

An attractive alternative is to use a single history file for *all* your windows. Each running instance of the Korn shell is smart enough to share its file with other running instances; from a second window, you can recall and edit the commands run in the first window.

Another environment variable, HISTSIZE, can be used to determine the maximum number of commands accessible from the history file. The default is 128 (i.e., the 128 most recent commands), which should be more than adequate.

Emacs Editing Mode

If you are an Emacs user, you will find it most useful to think of emacs editing mode as a simplified Emacs with a single, one-line window. All of the basic commands are available for cursor motion, cut and paste, and search.

Basic Commands

Emacs-mode uses control keys for the most basic editing functions. If you aren't familiar with Emacs, you can think of these as extensions of the rudimentary "erase" character (usually backspace or DEL) that Unix provides through its interface to users' terminals. In fact, emacs-mode figures out what your erase character is and uses that as its delete-backward key. For the sake of consistency, we'll assume your erase character is DEL from now on; if it is CTRL-H or something else, you will need to make a mental substitution. The most basic control-key commands are shown in Table 2-1.

Table 2-1. Basic emacs-mode commands

Command	Description
CTRL-B	Move backward one character (without deleting)
CTRL-F	Move forward one character
DEL	Delete one character backward
CTRL-D	Delete one character forward
CTRL-Y	Retrieve ("yank") last item deleted

 Remember that typing CTRL-D when your command line is empty may log you off!

The basic finger habits of emacs-mode are easy to learn, but they do require that you assimilate a couple of concepts that are peculiar to the Emacs editor.

The first of these is the use of CTRL-B and CTRL-F for backward and forward cursor motion. These keys have the advantage of being obvious mnemonics, but many people would rather use the arrow keys that are on just about every keyboard nowadays.

Unfortunately, emacs-mode doesn't use the arrow keys,* because the codes that they transmit to the computer aren't completely standardized; emacs-mode was designed to work on the widest variety of terminals possible without the heavy-duty customization that the full Emacs needs. Just about the only hardware requirements of emacs-mode are that the SPACE character overwrite the character on top of which it is typed, and that BACKSPACE moves to the left without overwriting the current character.

In emacs-mode, the *point* (sometimes also called *dot*) is an imaginary place just to the left of the character the cursor is on. In the command descriptions in Table 2-1, some say "forward" while others say "backward." Think of forward as "to the right of point" and backward as "to the left of point."

---

* In fact, as described in Appendix B, starting with *ksh93h*, if your terminal uses ANSI-standard escape sequences for the arrow keys, you can use them.

For example, let's say you type in a line and, instead of typing ENTER, you type CTRL-B and hold it down so that it repeats. The cursor will move to the left until it is over the first character on the line, like this:

```
$ fgrep -1 Bob < ~pete/wk/names
```

Now the cursor is on the f, and point is at the beginning of the line, just before the f. If you type DEL, nothing will happen because there are no characters to the left of point. However, if you press CTRL-D (the "delete character forward" command) you will delete the first letter:

```
$ grep -1 Bob < ~pete/wk/names
```

Point is still at the beginning of the line. If this were the desired command, you could hit ENTER now and run it; you don't need to move the cursor back to the end of the line. However, if you wanted to, you could type CTRL-F repeatedly to get there:

```
$ grep -1 Bob < ~pete/wk/names
```

At this point, typing CTRL-D wouldn't do anything, but hitting DEL would erase the final s. If you type DEL and decide you want the s back again, just press CTRL-Y to yank it back. If you think this example is silly, you're right in this particular case, but bear in mind that CTRL-Y undoes the last delete command of any kind, including the delete-word and delete-line commands that we will see shortly.*

If you make multiple deletes in sequence, CTRL-Y brings back everything that you've deleted. Its memory goes back to the last keystroke that wasn't a delete; the deletes don't have to be of the same type. For example, if you type DEL SPACE DEL SPACE CTRL-D CTRL-K, typing CTRL-Y retrieves the result of the last three operations but not the first delete.

Word Commands

The basic commands are really all you need to get around a command line, but a set of more advanced commands lets you do it with fewer keystrokes. These commands operate on *words* rather than on single characters; emacs-mode defines a word to be a sequence of one or more alphanumeric characters or underscores. (For the rest of this discussion, it will help to think of the underscore as a letter, even though it really isn't.)

The word commands are shown in Table 2-2. Whereas the basic commands are all single characters, the word commands consist of two keystrokes, ESC followed by

---

* Emacs users should note that this usage of CTRL-Y is different from the full editor, which doesn't save character deletes.

a letter. You will notice that the command ESC *X*, where *X* is any letter, often does for a word what CTRL-*X* does for a single character. The multiplicity of choices for delete-word-backward arises from the fact that your erase character could be either CTRL-H or DEL.

Table 2-2. Emacs-mode word commands

Command	Description
ESC b	Move one word backward
ESC f	Move one word forward
ESC DEL, ESC h, ESC CTRL-H	Delete one word backward
ESC d	Delete one word forward

To return to our example: if we type ESC b, point moves back a word. Since / is not an alphanumeric character, emacs-mode stops there:

```
$ grep -l Bob < ~pete/wk/names
```

The cursor is on the n in *names*, and point is between the / and the n. Now let's say we want to change the –*l* option's argument of this command from *Bob* to *Dave*. We need to move back on the command line, so we type ESC b two more times. This gets us here:

```
$ grep -l Bob < ~pete/wk/names
```

If we type ESC b again, we end up at the beginning of *Bob*:

```
$ grep -l Bob < ~pete/wk/names
```

Why? Remember that a word is defined as a sequence of alphanumeric characters only; therefore < is not a word, and the next word in the backward direction is *Bob*. We are now in the right position to delete *Bob*, so we type ESC d and get:

```
$ grep -l < ~pete/wk/names
```

Now we can type in the desired argument:

```
$ grep -l Dave< ~pete/wk/names
```

The CTRL-Y "undelete" command will retrieve an entire word, instead of a character, if a word was the last thing deleted.

Line Commands

There are still more efficient ways of moving around a command line in emacs-mode. A few commands deal with the entire line; they are shown in Table 2-3.

Table 2-3. Emacs-mode line commands

Command	Description
CTRL-A	Move to beginning of line
CTRL-E	Move to end of line
CTRL-K	Delete ("kill") forward to end of line
CTRL-C	Capitalize character after point

CTRL-C is often the "interrupt" key that Unix provides through its interface to your terminal. If this is the case, CTRL-C in emacs-mode will erase the entire line, as if CTRL-A and CTRL-K were pressed. On systems where the interrupt key is set to something else (often DEL), CTRL-C capitalizes the current character.

Using CTRL-A, CTRL-E, and CTRL-K should be straightforward. Remember that CTRL-Y will always undelete the last thing deleted, whether that was from a single delete command or several delete commands in a row. If you use CTRL-K, that could be quite a few characters.

Moving Around in the History File

Now we know how to get around the command line efficiently and make changes. But that doesn't address the original issue of recalling previous commands by accessing the history file. Emacs-mode has several commands for doing this, summarized in Table 2-4.

Table 2-4. Emacs-mode commands for moving through the history file

Command	Description
CTRL-P	Move to previous line
CTRL-N	Move to next line
CTRL-R	Search backward
ESC <	Move to first line of history file
ESC >	Move to last line of history file

CTRL-P is by far the one you will use most often—it's the "I made a mistake; let me go back and fix it" key. You can use it as many times as you wish to scroll back through the history file. If you want to get back to the last command you entered, you can hold down CTRL-N until the Korn shell beeps at you, or just type ESC >. As an example, you hit ENTER to run the command above, but you get an error message telling you that your option letter was incorrect. You want to change it without retyping the whole thing. First, you would type CTRL-P to recall the bad command. You get it back with point at the end:

```
$ grep -l Dave < ~pete/wk/names▋
```

After CTRL-A, ESC f, two CTRL-Fs, and CTRL-D, you have:

```
$ grep -▋Dave < ~pete/wk/names
```

You decide to try –*s* instead of –*l*, so you type s and hit ENTER. You get the same error message, so you give up and look it up in the manual. You find out that the command you want is *fgrep*—not *grep*—after all. You sigh heavily and go back and find the *fgrep* command you typed in an hour ago. To do this, you type CTRL-R; whatever was on the line disappears and is replaced by ^R. Then type fgrep, and you see this:

```
$ ^Rfgrep
```

Hit ENTER, and the shell searches backwards through the history file for a line containing "fgrep". If it doesn't find one, it beeps. But if it finds one, it displays it, and your "current line" will be that line (i.e., you will be somewhere in the middle of the history file, not at the end as usual):

```
$ fgrep -l Bob < ~pete/wk/names▋
```

Typing CTRL-R without an argument (i.e., just CTRL-R followed by ENTER) causes the shell to repeat your last backward search. If you try the *fgrep* command by hitting ENTER again, two things happen. First, of course, the command runs. Second, the executed command line is entered into the history file at the end, and your "current line" will be at the end as well. You will no longer be in the middle of the history file.

CTRL-P and CTRL-R are clearly the most important emacs-mode commands that deal with the history file, and you might use CTRL-N occasionally. The others are less useful, and we suspect that they were included mainly for compatibility with the full Emacs editor.

Emacs users should also note that the full editor's "deluxe" search capabilities, such as incremental and regular expression search, are not available in the Korn shell's emacs-mode—with one minor exception: if you use CTRL-R and precede your search string with a ^ (caret character), it matches only commands that have the search string at the beginning of the line.

Filename and Variable Completion and Expansion

One of the most powerful (and typically underused) features of emacs-mode is its *filename completion* facility, inspired by similar features in the full Emacs editor, the C shell, and (originally) the old DEC TOPS-20 operating system.

The premise behind filename completion is that when you need to type a filename, you should not have to type more than is necessary to identify the file unambiguously. This is an excellent feature; there is an analogous one in vi-mode. We recommend that you get it under your fingers, since it will save you quite a bit of typing.

There are three commands in emacs-mode that relate to filename completion. The most important is TAB. (Emacs users will find this familiar; it is the same as minibuffer completion with the TAB key.) When you type in a word of text followed by TAB, the Korn shell attempts to complete the name of a file in the current directory. Then one of four things can happen:

1. If there is no file whose name begins with the word, the shell beeps and nothing further happens.

2. If there is exactly one way to complete the filename, and the file is a regular file, the shell types the rest of the filename and follows it with a space so you can type in more command arguments.

3. If there is exactly one way to complete the filename, and the file is a directory, the shell completes the filename and follows it with a slash.

4. If there is more than one way to complete the filename, the shell completes out to the longest common prefix among the available choices.

For example, assume you have a directory with the files *program.c* and *problem.c*. You want to compile the first of these by typing cc program.c. You type cc pr followed by TAB. This is an ambiguous prefix, since the prefix "pro" is common to both filenames, so the shell only completes out to cc pro. You need to type more letters to disambiguate, so you type g and hit TAB again. Then the shell completes out to "cc program.c ", leaving the extra space for you to type in other filenames or options.

A related command is ESC *, which expands the prefix to all possible choices. ESC * acts like the standard * shell wildcard character except that it expands the choices for you to see and does not execute the command. In the previous example, if you type ESC * instead of TAB, the shell will expand to "cc problem.c program.c ". If you type ESC = instead of ESC *, you will see a numbered list of expansions printed to standard error.

Starting with *ksh93m*, the ESC = command accepts a numeric prefix. When a prefix is provided, the shell treats it as the number of one of the commands shown by a previous ESC = listing and completes the filename. (An example is provided later in this chapter where the vi-mode version of this command is described.)

When TAB, ESC *, and ESC = are used on the first word of the command line, they expand aliases, functions, and commands. This very useful feature is known as *command completion*.

For backwards compatibility with *ksh88* and versions of *ksh93* prior to *ksh93h*, you may instead type ESC ESC for filename and command completion.

Starting with *ksh93l*, the editing modes understand *ksh* quoting rules; expansions are ignored inside quotes. However, if you have typed a leading quote but no closing quote yet, the completion commands do work. In addition, all three expansions work on variable names as well. (Variables are discussed in Chapter 4.) When *ksh* sees either a $ or "$ and part of a variable name, you may use any of the three expansions to see which variable names match what you've typed.

Miscellaneous Commands

Several miscellaneous commands complete emacs editing mode; they are shown in Table 2-5.

Table 2-5. Emacs-mode miscellaneous commands

Command	Description
CTRL-J	Same as ENTER.
CTRL-L	Redisplay the line.
CTRL-M	Same as ENTER.
CTRL-O	Same as ENTER, then display next line in history file.
CTRL-T	Transpose the characters on either side of point. This is like GNU Emacs.[a]
CTRL-U	Repeat the following command four times.
CTRL-V	Print the version of the Korn shell.
CTRL-W	Delete ("wipe") all characters between point and "mark." "Mark" is discussed later in this section.
CTRL-X CTRL-E	Invoke an editor—usually the *emacs* program—on the current command.
CTRL-X CTRL-X	Exchange point and mark.
CTRL-[	Same as ESC (most keyboards).
CTRL-] *x*	Search forward on current line for *x*, where *x* is any character.
CTRL-@	Set mark at point.
ESC c	Change word after point to all capital letters.
ESC l	Change word after point to all lowercase letters.

Table 2-5. Emacs-mode miscellaneous commands (continued)

Command	Description
ESC p	Save all characters between point and mark as if they were deleted.
ESC .	Insert last word in previous command line after point.
ESC _	Same as previous entry.
ESC CTRL-] x	Search backward for x, where x is any character.
ESC SPACE	Set mark at point.
ESC #	Prepend # (comment character) to the line and send it to the history file; useful for saving a command to be executed later without having to retype it. If the line already starts with a #, remove the leading # and any other comment characters that follow newlines in a multi-line command.

[a] This is a difference from *ksh88*, which transposes two characters to the right of point and moves point forward by one. CTRL-T behaves slightly differently if you put set –o gmacs (instead of emacs) in your *.profile*. In this case, it transposes the two characters to the left of point, leaving point unmoved. This is the only difference between emacs and gmacs modes; the latter conforms to the once-popular James Gosling version of the Emacs editor (a.k.a. Unipress Emacs, now no longer available).

Several of these commands may clash with terminal interface control keys on your system. CTRL-U is the default key for "kill line" on most versions of Unix. Modern Unix systems use CTRL-V and CTRL-W as default settings for the "quote next character" and "word erase" terminal interface functions, respectively. CTRL-V is particularly confusing, since it is meant to override other terminal interface control keys but has no effect on emacs-mode commands. However, emacs-mode works by directly interpreting every character you type, so the *stty* settings are largely ignored.

A few miscellaneous commands are worth discussing, even though they may not be among the most useful emacs-mode commands.

CTRL-O is useful for repeating a sequence of commands you have already entered. Just go back to the first command in the sequence and press CTRL-O instead of ENTER. This executes the command and brings up the next command in the history file. Press CTRL-O again to enter this command and bring up the next one. Repeat this until you see the last command in the sequence; then just hit ENTER.

CTRL-U, if it doesn't perform the line-delete function of your system's terminal interface, repeats the next command four times. If you type CTRL-U twice, the repeat factor becomes 16; for 3 CTRL-Us it's 64; and so on. CTRL-U is possibly most useful when navigating through your history file. If you want to recall a command that you entered a while ago, you could type CTRL-U CTRL-P to go back through the history file four lines at a time; you could think of this as a "fast rewind" through your command history.

Another possible use of CTRL-U is when you want to go from one end of a long pathname to the other. Unlike vi-mode, emacs-mode does not have a concept of "word" that is flexible enough to distinguish between pathnames and filename components. The emacs-mode word motion commands (ESC b and ESC f) move through a pathname only one component at a time, because emacs-mode treats the slash as a word separator. You can use CTRL-U to help get around this limitation. If you have a line that looks like this:

```
$ ls -1 /a/very/long/pathname/filename▊
```

and you need to go back and change "very" to "really", you can type CTRL-U ESC b and your cursor will end up here:

```
$ ls -1 /a/▊ery/long/pathname/filename
```

Then you can make the change. First, get rid of "very" by typing CTRL-U CTRL-D:

```
$ ls -1 /a/▊long/pathname/filename
```

Then insert the new text:

```
$ ls -1 /a/really▊long/pathname/filename
```

Judicious use of CTRL-U can save you a few keystrokes, but considering the small amount of information you manipulate when you edit command lines, it's probably not an incredibly vital feature. Often, holding down a key to repeat it is just as effective as CTRL-U. Because you'll probably have to use the *stty* command to redefine the terminal driver's line erase key before you can use CTRL-U, it's probably better to do without it.

The mark mentioned in the explanation of CTRL-W should be familiar to Emacs users, but its function in emacs-mode is a subset of that in the full editor. Emacs-mode keeps track of the place at which the last delete operation was performed (whether it was a character, word, line, or whatever); this place is called the *mark*. If nothing has been deleted on the current line, the mark defaults to the beginning of the line. You can also set the mark to where your cursor is by typing ESC SPACE (or, alternatively, CTRL-@). CTRL-X CTRL-X (CTRL-X hit twice) causes the Korn shell to swap point and mark, i.e., to move your cursor to where the mark is and reset mark to where your cursor was before you typed CTRL-X CTRL-X.

The mark concept is not extremely useful because of the small amount of "distance" to travel in command lines. But if you ever have to make a series of changes in the same place in a line, CTRL-X CTRL-X will take you back there. In the previous example, if you wanted to change "really" to "monumentally", one way would be to type CTRL-X CTRL-X to return to the beginning of "really":

```
$ ls -l /a/▊eally/long/pathname/filename
```

Then you could type ESC d to delete "really" and make the change. Of course, you could do this faster by typing ESC DEL instead of CTRL-X CTRL-X and ESC d.

Of the case-changing commands, ESC l (letter ell) is useful when you hit the CAPS LOCK key by accident and don't notice it immediately. Since all-caps words aren't used too often in the Unix world, you may not use ESC c very often.

If it seems like there are too many synonyms for ENTER, bear in mind that CTRL-M is actually the same (ASCII) character as ENTER, and that CTRL-J is actually the same as newline, which Unix usually accepts in lieu of ENTER anyway.

ESC . and ESC _ are useful if you want to run several commands on a given file. The usual Unix convention is that a filename is the last argument to a command. Therefore you can save typing by just entering each command followed by SPACE and then typing ESC . or ESC _. For example, say you want to examine a file using *more*, so you type:

```
$ more myfilewithaverylongname
```

Then you decide you want to print it, using the print command *lp*. You can avoid typing the very long name by typing lp followed by a space and then ESC . or ESC _; the Korn shell inserts *myfilewithaverylongname* for you.

If you're a real Emacs expert and the built-in mode just isn't working for you, use CTRL-X CTRL-E to invoke the *emacs* editor program on your command line. When you exit the editor, if you actually made changes to the file, the shell executes the final command line.

Macro Expansion with Aliases

As you become accustomed to using emacs-mode, you may find that there are sequences of commands that you execute over and over again. Typing these commands repeatedly is difficult and time-wasting. It is better to define a *macro* for them. A macro is a short name that, when entered, expands into the full sequence of commands.

The Korn shell provides a macro facility, using the alias mechanism (described in the next chapter), that lets you set up a sequence of commands and then invoke that sequence with a single emacs-mode command. It works as follows: if you define an alias named _x, where x is a letter, then when you type ESC x, emacs-mode expands the alias, and reads it as input. The alias value may contain regular text, emacs-mode commands, or both.

For example, suppose that you want a command to capitalize the first letter of the current word. You could define an alias as follows:

```
alias _C='^[b^C'          Value is ESC b CTRL-C
```

Now, whenever you type ESC C, the shell moves to the beginning of the current word (ESC b), and then capitalizes the current letter (CTRL-C).

```
$ print here is a word          Type ESC C
$ print here is a Word
```

Vi Editing Mode

Like emacs-mode, vi-mode essentially creates a one-line editing window into the history file. Vi-mode is popular because *vi* is the most standard Unix editor. But the function for which *vi* was designed, writing C programs, has different editing requirements from those of command interpreters. As a result, although it is possible to do complex things in *vi* with relatively few keystrokes, the relatively simple things you need to do in the Korn shell sometimes take too many keystrokes.

Like *vi*, vi-mode has two modes of its own: *input* and *control* mode. The former is for typing commands (as in normal Korn shell use); the latter is for moving around the command line and the history file. When you are in input mode, you can type commands and hit ENTER to run them. In addition, you have minimal editing capabilities via control characters, which are summarized in Table 2-6.

Table 2-6. Editing commands in vi input mode

Command	Description
DEL	Delete previous character
CTRL-W	Erase previous word (i.e., erase until whitespace)
CTRL-V	"Quote" the next character
ESC	Enter control mode (see below)

At least some of these editig commands—depending on which version of Unix you have—are the same as those provided by modern Unix systems in the terminal interface. Vi-mode uses your "erase" character as the "delete previous character" key; usually it is set to DEL or CTRL-H (BACKSPACE). CTRL-V causes the next character you type to appear in the command line as is; i.e., if it is an editing command (or an otherwise special character like CTRL-D), it is stripped of its special meaning.

Under normal circumstances, you just stay in input mode. But if you want to go back and make changes to your command line, or if you want to recall previous commands, you need to go into control mode. To do this, hit ESC.

Simple Control Mode Commands

A full range of *vi* editing commands are available to you in control mode. The simplest of these move you around the command line* and are summarized in Table 2-7. Vi-mode contains two "word" concepts. The simplest is any sequence of non-whitespace characters; we'll call this a *nonblank word*. The other is any sequence of only alphanumeric characters (letters and digits) or any sequence of only non-alphanumeric characters; we'll just call this a *word*.†

Table 2-7. Basic vi control mode commands

Command	Description
h	Move left one character.
l	Move right one character.
space	Move right one character.
w	Move right one word.
b	Move left one word.
W	Move to beginning of next nonblank word.
B	Move to beginning of preceding nonblank word.
e	Move to end of current word.
E	Move to end of current nonblank word.
0	Move to beginning of line.
^	Move to first nonblank character in line.
$	Move to end of line.

All of these commands except the last three can be preceded by a number that acts as a *repeat count*. The last two will be familiar to users of Unix utilities (such as *grep*) that use regular expressions, as well as to *vi* users.

Time for a few examples. Let's say you type in this line and, before you hit ENTER, decide you want to change it:

```
$ fgrep -l Bob < ~pete/wk/names
```

As shown, your cursor is beyond the last character of the line. First, type ESC to enter control mode; your cursor moves back one space so that it is on the s. Then

---

* As with emacs mode, since *ksh93h*, you may use ANSI-standard arrow key sequences for moving back and forth on the command line, and up and down within the history list.

† Neither of these definitions is the same as the definition of a word in emacs-mode.

if you type h, your cursor moves back to the e. If you type 3h from the e, you end up at the n.

Now we look at the difference between the two "word" concepts. Go back to the end of the line by typing $. If you type b, the word in question is "names", and the cursor ends up on the n:

```
$ fgrep -l Bob < ~pete/wk/names
```

If you type b again, the next word is the slash (it's a "sequence" of non-alphanumeric characters), so the cursor ends up over it:

```
$ fgrep -l Bob < ~pete/wk/names
```

However, if you typed B instead of b, the nonblank word would be the entire pathname, and the cursor ends up at the beginning of it—that is, over the tilde:

```
$ fgrep -l Bob < ~pete/wk/names
```

You would have had to type b four times—or just 4b—to get the same effect, since there are four "words" in the part of the pathname to the left of */names*: *wk*, slash, *pete*, and the leading tilde.

At this point, w and W do the opposite: typing w gets you over the p, since the tilde is a "word," while typing W brings you to the end of the line. But whereas w and W take you to the beginning of the next word, e and E take you to the end of the current word. Thus, if you type w with the cursor on the tilde, you get to:

```
$ fgrep -l Bob < ~pete/wk/names
```

Then typing e gets you to:

```
$ fgrep -l Bob < ~pete/wk/names
```

And typing an additional w gets you to:

```
$ fgrep -l Bob < ~pete/wk/names
```

On the other hand, E gets you to the end of the current nonblank word—in this case, the end of the line. (While at first glance the commands may appear nonmnemonic, there is generally some order to the choice of command letters. Each command letter is usually the first letter of the English word for the operation. Lowercase letters work on words, while the uppercase versions work on nonblank words. Getting the hang of this is undoubtedly tougher if English isn't your native language, but that also applies to the emacs-mode commands.)

Entering and Changing Text

Now that you know how to enter control mode and move around on the command line, you need to know how to get back into input mode so you can make changes and type in additional commands. A number of commands take you from control mode into input mode; they are listed in Table 2-8. All of them enter input mode a bit differently.

Table 2-8. Commands for entering vi input mode

Command	Description
i	Text inserted before current character (insert)
a	Text inserted after current character (append)
I	Text inserted at beginning of line
A	Text inserted at end of line
r	Replace one character (doesn't enter input mode)
R	Text overwrites existing text (replace)

Most likely, you will use either i or a consistently, and you may use R occasionally. I and A are abbreviations for 0i and $a respectively. To illustrate the difference between i, a, and R, say we start out with our example line:

```
$ fgrep -l Bob < ~pete/wk/names
```

If you type i followed by end, you get:

```
$ fgrep -l Bob < ~pete/wkend/names
```

That is, the cursor always appears to be over the / before *names*. But if you type a instead of i, you will notice the cursor move one space to the right. Then if you type nick, you get:

```
$ fgrep -l Bob < ~pete/wk/nicknames
```

That is, the cursor is always just after the last character you typed, until you type ESC to end your input. Finally, if you go back to the n in *names*, type R instead, and then type task, you will see:

```
$ fgrep -l Bob < ~pete/wk/tasks
```

In other words, you will be *replacing* (hence R) instead of inserting text.

Why capital R instead of lowercase r? The latter is a slightly different command, which replaces only one character and does not enter input mode. With r, the next single character overwrites the character under the cursor. So if we start with the original command line and type r followed by a semicolon, we get:

```
$ fgrep -1 Bob < ~pete/wk names
```

If you precede r with a number *N*, it allows you to replace the next *N* existing characters on the line—but still not enter input mode. Vi-mode replaces the *N* characters on the line with *N* copies of the character you type after the r. Lower-case r is effective for fixing erroneous option letters, I/O redirection characters, punctuation, etc.

Deletion Commands

Now that you know how to enter commands and move around the line, you need to know how to delete. The basic deletion command in vi-mode is d followed by one other letter. This letter determines what the unit and direction of deletion is, and it corresponds to a motion command, as listed previously in Table 2-7. Table 2-9 shows some commonly used examples.

Table 2-9. Some vi-mode deletion commands

Command	Description
dh	Delete one character backwards.
dl	Delete one character forwards.
db	Delete one word backwards.
dw	Delete one word forwards.
dB	Delete one nonblank word backwards.
dW	Delete one nonblank word forwards.
d$	Delete to end of line.
d0	Delete to beginning of line.

These commands have a few variations and abbreviations. If you use a c instead of d, you enter input mode after it does the deletion. You can supply a numeric repeat count either before or after the d (or c). Table 2-10 lists the available abbreviations.

Most people tend to use D to delete to end of line, dd to delete an entire line, and x (as "backspace") to delete single characters. If you aren't a hardcore *vi* user, you may find it difficult to get some of the more esoteric deletion commands under your fingers.

Table 2-10. Abbreviations for vi-mode delete commands

Command	Description
D	Equivalent to d$ (delete to end of line)
dd	Equivalent to 0d$ (delete entire line)
c	Equivalent to c$ (delete to end of line, enter input mode)
cc	Equivalent to 0c$ (delete entire line, enter input mode)
s	Equivalent to xi (delete current character, enter input mode)
S	Equivalent to cc (delete entire line, enter input mode)
x	Equivalent to dl (delete character forwards)
X	Equivalent to dh (delete character backwards)

Every good editor provides "undelete" commands as well as delete commands, and vi-mode is no exception. Vi-mode maintains a *delete buffer* that stores all of the modifications to text on the current line only (note that this is different from the full *vi* editor). The command u undoes the last text modification command only, while U undoes all such commands on the current line. So if you make one change and want to undo it, type u; if you make lots of changes and find that the original is closer to what you want, you can undo everything by typing U. A related command is . (dot), which redoes the last text modification command.

There is also a way to save text in the delete buffer without having deleted it in the first place: just type in a delete command but use y ("yank") instead of d. This does not modify anything, but it allows you to retrieve the yanked text as many times as you like later on. The command to retrieve yanked text is p, which inserts ("puts") the text on the current line to the right of the cursor. The uppercase version, P, puts text to the left of the cursor. The various cut and paste commands are summarized in Table 2-11.

Table 2-11. Vi-mode cut and paste commands

Command	Description
y	Yank (save) text, don't actually change the line.
p	Put the last yanked or deleted text into the line after the cursor.
P	Put the last yanked or deleted text into the line before the cursor.
u	Undo most recent change.
U	Undo all changes to the line.
. (dot)	Redo last change at current cursor position.

The d and p commands are quite useful together for rearranging the order of options or arguments on a command line. As an example, most Unix C compilers accept a –*l* option that indicates the name of a library to use when linking a compiled program. The *–L* option specifies a directory in which the compiler should look for libraries, besides looking in the standard places for system libraries.

```
cc -o myprog myprog.c -Lmylibdir -lmylib
```

This command looks for the library file *libmylib.a* in the directory *mylibdir* when compiling and linking *myprog.c*. So far so good. The catch is that typically the *–L* option must appear on the command line *before* the *–l* option. Let's suppose you accidentally typed them the other way around, and therefore that the compilation failed. You can use the d and p commands to rearrange things. Start by recalling the line:

```
$ cc -o myprog myprog.c -lmylib -Lmylibdir
```

Next, move to the last option with 5w. Then back up to the preceding space with h. Your command line now looks like this:

```
$ cc -o myprog myprog.c -lmylib -Lmylibdir
```

Type D to delete the rest of the line:

```
$ cc -o myprog myprog.c -lmylib
```

Now move back to the preceding c character with Bhh:

```
$ cc -o myprog myprog.c -lmylib
```

Finally, use p to insert the moved option:

```
$ cc -o myprog myprog.c -Lmylibdir -lmylib
```

Then hit ENTER and you're done. This looks like a lot of typing. But, as we will soon see, there are additional commands that let you search for characters on the command line, making it much easier to move around. And if you're an experienced *vi* user, you'll be right at home.

Moving Around in the History File

The next group of vi control mode commands we cover allows you to move around in and search your history file. This is the all-important functionality that lets you go back and fix an erroneous command without retyping the entire line. These commands are summarized in Table 2-12.

Table 2-12. Vi control mode commands for searching the history file

Command	Description
k or –	Move backward one line.
j or +	Move forward one line.
G	Move to line given by repeat count, or to very first history line if no repeat count.
?*string*	Search backward for *string*.
/*string*	Search forward for *string*.
n	Repeat search in same direction as previous.
N	Repeat search in opposite direction of previous.

The first three can be preceded by repeat counts (e.g., 3k or 3– moves back three lines in the history file).

If you aren't familiar with *vi* and its cultural history, you may be wondering at the wisdom of choosing such seemingly poor mnemonics as h, j, k, and l for backward character, forward line, backward line, and forward character, respectively. Well, there actually is a rationale for the choices—other than that they are all together on the standard keyboard.

Bill Joy originally developed *vi* to run on Lear-Siegler ADM-3a terminals, which were the first popular models with addressable cursors (meaning that a program could send a command to an ADM-3a to make it move the cursor to a specified location on the screen). The ADM-3a's h, j, k, and l keys had little arrows on them, so Joy decided to use those keys for appropriate commands in *vi*.

Another (partial) rationale for the command choices is that CTRL-H is the traditional backspace key, and CTRL-J denotes linefeed. The primary rationale for these choices, however, is that with these keys, it's never necessary to move your hands off the "home row" of the keyboard.

Perhaps + and – are better mnemonics than j and k, but the latter have the advantage of being more easily accessible to touch typists. In either case, these commands are the most basic ones for moving around the history file. To see how they work, let's take the same examples we used when discussing emacs-mode earlier.

You enter the example command (ENTER works in both input and control modes, as does newline or CTRL-J):

```
$ fgrep -l Bob < ~pete/wk/names
```

But you get an error message saying that your option letter was wrong. You want to change it to −*s* without having to retype the entire command. Assuming you are in control mode (you may have to type ESC to put yourself in control mode), you type k or − to get the command back. Your cursor will be at the beginning of the line:

```
$ █grep -1 Bob < ~pete/wk/names
```

Type w to get to the −, then 1 or space to get to the 1. Now you can replace it by typing rs; press ENTER to run the command.

Now let's say you get another error message, and you finally decide to look at the manual page for the *fgrep* command. You remember having done this a while ago today, so rather than typing in the entire *man*(1) command, you search for the last one you used. To do this, type ESC to enter control mode (if you are already in control mode, this has no effect), then type / followed by man or ma. To be on the safe side, you can also type ^ma; the ^ means match only lines that begin with ma.*

But typing /^ma doesn't give you what you want; instead, the shell gives you:

```
$ █ake myprogram
```

To search for "man" again, you can type n, which does another backward search using the last search string. Typing / again without an argument and hitting ENTER accomplishes the same thing.

The G command retrieves the command whose number is the same as the numeric prefix argument you supply. G depends on the command numbering scheme described in the section "Prompting variables," in Chapter 3. Without a prefix argument, it goes to command number 1. This may be useful to former C shell users who still want to use command numbers.

Character-Finding Commands

There are some additional motion commands in vi-mode. These commands allow you to move to the position of a particular character in the line. They are summarized in Table 2-13, in which *x* denotes any character.

All of these commands can be preceded by a repeat count.

---

* Fans of *vi* and search utilities like *grep* should note that caret (^) for beginning-of-line is the only context operator vi-mode provides for search strings.

Table 2-13. Vi-mode character-finding commands

Command	Description
f*x*	Move right to next occurrence of *x* (find).
F*x*	Move left to previous occurrence of *x* (find backwards).
t*x*	Move right to next occurrence of *x*, then back one position (go *to* the character).
T*x*	Move left to previous occurrence of *x*, then forward one position (go backwards to the character).
;	Redo last character-finding command.
,	Redo last character-finding command in opposite direction.
%	Move to matching (,), {, }, [, or].

Starting with the previous example: let's say you want to change *Bob* to *Rob*. Make sure that you're at the end of the line (or, in any case, to the right of the B in *Bob*); then, if you type FB, your cursor moves to the B:

```
$ fgrep -1 Bob < ~pete/wk/names
```

At this point, you could type rR to replace the B with R. But let's say you wanted to change *Bob* to *Blob*. You would need to move one space to the right of the B. Of course, you could just type 1. But, given that you're somewhere to the right of *Bob*, the fastest way to move to the o would be to type TB instead of FB followed by 1.

As an example of how the repeat count can be used with character-finding commands, let's say you want to change the filename from *names* to *namfile*. In this case, assuming your cursor is still on the B, you need to get to the third e to the right, so you can type 3te, followed by 1 to put the cursor back on the e in *names*.

The character-finding commands also have associated delete commands. Read the command definitions in the previous table and mentally substitute "delete" for "move." You'll get what happens when you precede the given character-finding command with a d. The deletion includes the character given as argument. For example, assume that your cursor is under the n in *names*:

```
$ fgrep -1 Bob < ~pete/wk/names
```

If you want to change *names* to *aides*, one possibility is to type dfm. This means "delete right to next occurrence of m," i.e., delete "nam." Then you can type i (to enter input mode) and then "aid" to complete the change.

A better way, though, is to use cfm. This means "change everything from under the cursor up to and including the next occurrence of m." This deletes "nam" and enters input mode for you.

The % command is very useful for finding the matching "pair" character when used with parentheses, square brackets, and curly braces. All of these occur frequently in matched pairs on shell command lines.

One final command rounds out the vi control mode commands for getting around on the current line: you can use the pipe character (|) for moving to a specific column, whose number is given by a numeric prefix argument. Column counts start at 1; count only your input, not the space taken up by the prompt string. The default repeat count is 1, of course, which means that typing | by itself is equivalent to 0 (see Table 2-7).

Filename and Variable Completion and Expansion

Vi-mode provides one additional feature that we think you will use quite often: filename completion. This feature is not part of the real *vi* editor, and it was undoubtedly inspired by similar features in Emacs and, originally, in the TOPS-20 operating system for DEC mainframes.

The rationale behind filename completion is simple: you should have to type only as much of a filename as is necessary to distinguish it from other filenames in the same directory. Backslash (\) is the command that tells the Korn shell to do filename completion in vi-mode. If you type in a word, type ESC to enter control mode, and then type \, one of four things happens; they are the same as for TAB (or ESC ESC) in emacs-mode:

1. If there is no file whose name begins with the word, the shell beeps and nothing further happens.

2. If there is exactly one way to complete the filename, and the file is a regular file, the shell types the rest of the filename, followed by a space in case you want to type in more command arguments.

3. If there is exactly one way to complete the filename, and the file is a directory, the shell completes the filename, followed by a slash.

4. If there is more than one way to complete the filename, the shell completes out to the longest common prefix among the available choices.

As in emacs-mode, starting with *ksh93h*, you may use TAB instead of ESC \. However, this only works if you use *set −o viraw* in addition to *set −o vi*. (The *viraw* option is a bit more CPU-intensive—although probably not noticeably—and is required on some older Unix systems for vi-mode to work at all.) Fortunately, beginning with *ksh93n*, the *viraw* option is automatically enabled when you use vi-mode.

A related command is *, which is the same as ESC * in emacs-mode as described earlier in this chapter.* It behaves similarly to ESC \, but if there is more than one completion possibility (number four in the list above), it lists all of them and allows you to type further. Thus, it resembles the * shell wildcard character.

Finally, the command = does the same kind of filename expansion as the * shell wildcard, but in a different way. Instead of expanding the filenames onto the command line, it prints them in a numbered list with one filename on each line. Then it gives you your shell prompt back and retypes whatever was on your command line before you typed =. For example, if the files in your directory include *program.c* and *problem.c*, and you type pro followed by ESC and then =, you will see this:

```
$ cc pro              ESC = typed at this point
1) problem.c
2) program.c
$ cc pro
```

Beginning with *ksh93m*, prefixing the = command with a count indicates selection of a particular option. Returning to the previous example: after listing both *problem.c* and *program.c*, the command line looks like this:

```
$ cc pro
```

If you want *program.c*, it's enough to type 2 =, and the shell picks expansion number 2. The command line changes to:

```
$ cc program.c
```

As in emacs-mode, you can also do command completion from vi-mode. The *, \, and = commands, when used on the first word of the command line, expand aliases, functions, and commands. Also as in emacs-mode, starting with *ksh93l*, these expansions work when you've opened a quoted string but haven't closed it yet, and for variable expansions with $ and "$.

Miscellaneous Commands

Several miscellaneous commands round out vi-mode; some of them are quite esoteric. They are listed in Table 2-14.

---

* If you count the ESC needed to get out of input mode, the vi-mode command is identical to emacs-mode.

Table 2-14. Miscellaneous vi-mode commands

Command	Description
~	Invert ("twiddle") case of current character(s).
_	Append last word of previous command; enter input mode. A repeat count appends the given *n*th word, starting from the beginning of the command.
v	Run the *hist* command on the current line (actually, run the command `hist -e ${VISUAL:-${EDITOR:-vi}}`); usually this means run the full *vi* on the current line.
CTRL-L	Start a new line and redraw the current line on it; good for when your screen becomes garbled.
CTRL-V	Print the version of the Korn shell.
#	Prepend # (comment character) to the line and send it to the history file;[a] useful for saving a command to be executed later without having to retype it. If the line already starts with a #, remove the leading # and any other comment characters that follow newlines in a multiline command.
@ *x*	Insert expansion of alias *_x* as command mode input (see text).

[a] The line is also "executed" by the shell. However, # is the shell's comment character, so the shell ignores it.

The first of these can be preceded by a repeat count. A repeat count of *n* preceding the ~ changes the case of the next *n* characters.* The cursor advances accordingly.

A repeat count preceding _ causes the *n*th word in the previous command to be inserted in the current line; without the count, the last word is used. Omitting the repeat count is useful because a filename is usually the last thing on a Unix command line, and because users often run several commands in a row on the same file. With this feature, you can type all of the commands (except the first) followed by ESC _, and the shell inserts the filename.

Macro Expansion with Aliases

Just as described earlier for emacs-mode, you may use the shell's alias facility (described in the next chapter) to create *macros*, i.e., single-letter abbreviations for longer sequences of commands. If you create an alias named *_x*, where *x* is a letter, then when you type @ *x*, vi-mode expands the alias and reads it as command-mode input.

---

* This, in our opinion, is a design flaw in the *vi* editor that the Korn shell authors might have corrected. Letting the user append a motion command to ~ and having it behave analogously to d or y would have been much more useful; that way, a word could be case-twiddled with only two keystrokes.

As before, suppose that you want a command to capitalize the first letter of the current word. You could define an alias as follows:

```
alias _C='B~'
```

Now, if you type ESC @ C, the cursor moves to the beginning of the current word (B), and then capitalizes the current letter (~).

```
$ print here is a word        Type ESC @ C
$ print here is a Word
```

The hist Command

hist is a shell built-in command* that provides a superset of the C shell history mechanism. You can use it to examine the most recent commands you entered, to edit one or more commands with your favorite "real" editor, and to run old commands with changes without having to type the entire command in again. We'll look at each of these uses.

The *–l* option for *hist* lists previous commands. It takes arguments that refer to commands in the history file. Arguments can be numbers or alphanumeric strings; numbers refer to the commands in the history file, while strings refer to the most recent command beginning with the string. *hist* treats arguments in a rather complex way:

* If you give two arguments, they serve as the first and last commands to be shown.

* If you specify one number argument, only the command with that number is shown.

* With a single string argument, *hist* searches for the most recent command starting with that string and shows you everything from that command to the most recent command.

* If you specify no arguments, you will see the last 16 commands you entered. Thus, `hist -l` by itself is equivalent to the C shell *history* command, and indeed the Korn shell defines a built-in alias *history* as:

  ```
  alias history='hist -l'
  ```

  As you will find out in Chapter 3, this means that you can type `history` and the Korn shell will run the command `hist -l`.

---

* In *ksh88*, this command is called *fc*, for "fix command." *ksh93* provides a built-in alias for *fc* to *hist*, for those who are used to using the *fc* command. Recent versions also have *fc* as a built-in command that behaves identically to *hist*; this is because POSIX requires that this command be built-in.

A few examples should make these options clearer. Let's say you logged in and entered these commands:

```
ls -l
more myfile
vi myfile
wc -l myfile
pr myfile | lp -h
```

If you type hist -l (or history) with no arguments, you will see the above list with command numbers, as in:

```
1       ls -l
2       more myfile
3       vi myfile
4       wc -l myfile
5       pr myfile | lp -h
```

The option *-n* suppresses the line numbers. If you want to see only commands 2 through 4, type hist -l 2 4. If you want to see only the *vi* command, type hist -l 3. To see everything from the *vi* command up to the present, type hist -l v. Finally, if you want to see commands between *more* and *wc*, you can type hist -l m w, hist -l m 4, hist -l 2 4, etc.

Negative history numbers indicate values relative to the current command number. For example, hist -l -3 shows the 3rd previous command. A less confusing way to to do this is with the *-N* option: hist -l -N 3 does the same thing. This also has the advantage of conforming to the POSIX conventions for options and arguments.

The *-l* option to *hist* is not particularly useful, except as a quick way of remembering what commands you typed recently. Use the *history* alias if you are an experienced C shell user.

The other important option to *hist* is *-e* for "edit." This is useful as an "escape hatch" from vi- and emacs-modes if you aren't used to either of those editors. You can specify the pathname of your favorite editor and edit commands from your history file; then when you have made the changes, the shell actually executes the new lines.

Let's say your favorite editor is a little home-brew gem called *zed*. You could edit your commands by typing:

```
$ hist -e /usr/local/bin/zed
```

This seems like a lot of work just to fix a typo in your previous command; fortunately, there is a better way. You can set the environment variable HISTEDIT to the pathname of the editor you want *hist* to use. If you put a line in your *.profile* or environment file saying:

```
HISTEDIT=/usr/local/bin/zed
```

you get *zed* when you invoke *hist*. HISTEDIT defaults to the old line editor *ed*, so that the overall default is also *ed*.*

hist is usually used to fix a recent command. Therefore, it handles arguments a bit differently than it does for the hist -l variation above:

- With no arguments, *hist* loads the editor with the most recent command.

- With a numeric argument, *hist* loads the editor with the command with that number.

- With a string argument, *hist* loads the most recent command starting with that string.

- With two arguments to *hist*, the arguments specify the beginning and end of a range of commands, as above.

Remember that *hist* actually runs the command(s) after you edit them. Therefore, the last-named choice can be dangerous. The Korn shell attempts to execute all commands in the range you specify when you exit your editor. If you have typed in any multiline constructs (like those we will cover in Chapter 5), the results could be even more dangerous. Although these might seem like valid ways of generating "instant shell programs," a far better strategy would be to direct the output of hist -nl with the same arguments to a file; then edit that file and execute the commands when you're satisfied with them:

```
$ hist -nl cp > lastcommands    List all commands that start with cp into lastcommands
$ vi lastcommands               Edit lastcommands
$ . lastcommands                Run the commands in it
```

In this case, the shell will not try to execute the file when you leave the editor!

There is one final use for *hist*. If you specify the option *–s* (i.e., type hist -s), the Korn shell will skip the editing part and just run the command(s) specified by the argument(s). Why is this useful? For one thing, just typing hist -s causes the previous command to repeat, just like the C shell !! command. The Korn shell provides the built-in alias *r* for this, so that if you type *r* and hit ENTER, you will repeat the last command.

---

* The default is actually a bit complicated in *ksh93*. hist -e runs ${HISTEDIT:-$FCEDIT} to edit the command line. This preserves compatibility with *ksh88*, where the variable for the *fc* command was, not surprisingly, FCEDIT. If neither variable is set, you get */bin/ed*. (The ${HISTEDIT:-$FCEDIT} construct is explained in Chapter 4. The upshot is to use the editor specified by the HISTEDIT variable if it's set; otherwise use the value of the FCEDIT variable.)

This form of *hist* allows yet another type of argument, of the form old=new, meaning "change occurrences of *old* in the specified previous command to *new* and then run it." (Unfortunately, you can't get the Korn shell to make this kind of substitution more than once; it only changes the first occurrence of *old* to *new*.) For example, suppose that you are using *troff* and its preprocessors to work on a document.* If you accidentally ran the *tbl* preprocessor with this command:

```
tbl ch2.tr | troff -ms -Tps > ch2.ps
```

but you needed to run *eqn*, you can redo it by typing hist -s tbl=eqn. (You could also use the alias, r tbl=eqn.) This command would then run:

```
eqn ch2.tr | troff -ms -Tps > ch2.ps
```

The Korn shell prints the modified command before running it.

Finger Habits

To paraphrase the old adage, old finger habits die hard. In fact, that is the primary reason for the choices of *vi* and Emacs for the Korn shell's editing modes. If you are an experienced user of one of these editors, by all means use the corresponding Korn shell editing mode. If you are a *vi* wizard, you probably know how to navigate between any two points on a line in three keystrokes or less.

But if you're not, you should seriously consider adopting emacs-mode finger habits. Because it is based on control keys, just like the minimal editing support you may have already used with the Bourne or C shell, you will find emacs-mode easier to assimilate. Although the full Emacs is an extremely powerful editor, its command structure lends itself very well to small subsetting: there are several "mini-emacs" style editors floating around for Unix, MS-DOS, and other systems.

The same cannot be said for *vi*, because its command structure is really meant for use in a full-screen editor. *vi* is quite powerful too, in its way, but its power becomes evident only when it is used for purposes similar to that for which it was designed: editing source code in C and LISP. Doing complicated things in *vi* takes relatively few keystrokes. But doing simple things takes more keystrokes in vi-mode than it does in emacs-mode. Unfortunately, the ability to do simple things with a minimal number of keystrokes is most desired in a command interpreter, especially nowadays when users are spending more time within applications and less time working with the shell.

Both Korn shell editing modes have quite a few commands; you will undoubtedly develop finger habits that include just a few of them. If you use emacs-mode and

---

* If so, you're one of a rare breed!

you aren't familiar with the full Emacs, here is a subset that is easy to learn yet enables you to do just about anything:

- For cursor motion around a command line, stick to CTRL-A and CTRL-E for beginning and end of line, and CTRL-F and CTRL-B for moving around.

- Delete using DEL (or whatever your "erase" key is) and CTRL-D; as with CTRL-F and CTRL-B, hold down to repeat if necessary. Use CTRL-C to erase the entire line.

- Use CTRL-P to retrieve the last command when you make a mistake.

- Use CTRL-R to search for a command you need to run again.

- Definitely use TAB for filename, command, and variable completion.

After a few hours spent learning these finger habits, you will wonder how you ever got along without command-line editing.

3

Customizing Your Environment

A common synonym for a Unix shell, or for the interface any computer program presents, is an environment. An *environment* is typically a collection of concepts that expresses the things a computer does in terms designed to be understandable and coherent, and a look and feel that is comfortable.

For example, your desk at work is an environment. Concepts involved in desk work usually include memos, phone calls, letters, forms, etc. The tools on or in your desk that you use to deal with these things include paper, staples, envelopes, pens, a telephone, a calculator, etc. Every one of these has a set of characteristics that express how you use it; such characteristics range from location on your desk or in a drawer (for simple tools) to more sophisticated things like which numbers the memory buttons on your phone are set to. Taken together, these characteristics make up your desk's look and feel.

You customize the look and feel of your desk environment by putting pens where you can most easily reach them, programming your phone buttons, etc. In general, the more customization you have done, the more tailored to your personal needs—and therefore the more productive—your environment is.

Similarly, Unix shells present you with such concepts as files, directories, and standard input and output, while Unix itself gives you tools to work with these, such as file manipulation commands, text editors, and print queues. Your Unix environment's look and feel is determined by your keyboard and display, of course, but also by how you set up your directories, where you put each kind of file, and what names you give to files, directories, and commands. There are also more sophisticated ways of customizing your shell environment.

The most basic means of customization that the Korn shell provides are these:

Aliases

 Synonyms for commands or command strings that you can define for convenience.

Options

 Controls for various aspects of your environment, which you can turn on and off.

Variables

 Placeholders for information that tell the shell and other programs how to behave under various circumstances.

There are also more complex ways to customize your environment, mainly the ability to program the shell, which we will see in later chapters. In this chapter, we cover the techniques listed above.

While most of the customizations obtainable with the above techniques are straightforward and apply to everyday Unix use, others are rather arcane and require in-depth technical knowledge to understand. Most of this chapter concentrates on the former. Because we want to explain things from the perspective of tasks you may want to perform, rather than that of the specific features of the Korn shell, a few little details may fall through the cracks (such as miscellaneous options to certain commands). We suggest you look in Appendix B for this type of information.

The .profile File

If you want to customize your environment, it is most important to know about a file called *.profile* in your home (login) directory. This is a file of shell commands, also called a shell script, that the Korn shell reads and runs whenever you log in to your system.

If you use a large machine in an office or department, the odds are good that your system administrator has already set up a *.profile* file for you that contains a few standard things. This is one of the "hidden" files mentioned in Chapter 1; other common hidden files include *.xinitrc* (for the X Window System), *.emacs* (for the GNU Emacs editor), and *.mailrc* (for the Unix *mail* program).

Your *.profile*, together with the environment file that we discuss towards the end of this chapter, will be the source of practically all of the customizations we discuss here as well as in subsequent chapters. Therefore, it is very important for you to become comfortable with a text editor like *vi* or Emacs so that you can try whatever customization techniques strike your fancy.

Bear in mind, however, that if you add commands to your *.profile*, they will not take effect until you log out and log back in again, or type the command `login`.*
Of course, you need not immediately add customization commands to your *.profile*—you can always just test them by typing them in yourself. (Be sure you test your changes though: it is possible to set things up in your *.profile* such that you can't log back in! Test your changes before logging out, by logging in again, perhaps from a new window or virtual console.)

If you already have a *.profile*, it's likely to contain lines similar to some of these:

```
PATH=/sbin:/usr/sbin:/usr/bin:/etc:/usr/ucb:/local/bin:
stty stop ^S intr ^C erase ^?
EDITOR=/usr/local/bin/emacs
SHELL=/bin/ksh
export EDITOR
```

These commands set up a basic environment for you, so you probably shouldn't change them until you learn about what they do—which you will by the end of this chapter. When you edit your *.profile*, just put your additional lines in afterwards.

The /etc/profile File

Every user has a personal *.profile* file in the home directory. While your system administrator may have provided you with an initial *.profile* file when your account was first set up, you are free to customize it as you see fit.

There is an additional, system-wide, customization file known as */etc/profile*. If this file exists, the Korn shell reads and executes it as the very first thing it does, even before reading your personal *.profile* file. This is where your system administrator places commands that should be executed by *every* user upon login, and where he or she places system-wide defaults, such as adding extra directories to the PATH variable (which, as you will see later in this chapter, tells the shell where to look for programs to run).

It pays to be aware of this file, since it may have settings in it that you might wish to override in your own *.profile* file. (At least, once you understand what it's doing!) If the file exists, it will be readable and will contain shell commands in it, just like your *.profile*. It may be worthwhile to peruse the version on your system; you may learn something that way.

---

* This has the same effect as logging out and logging in again, although it actually replaces your login session with a new one without explicitly terminating the old session.

Aliases

Perhaps the easiest and most popular type of customization is the *alias*, which is a synonym for a command or command string. This is one of several Korn shell features that were appropriated from the C shell.* You define an alias by entering (or adding to your *.profile*) a line with the following form:

```
alias new=original
```

(Notice that there are no spaces on either side of the equal sign (=); this is required syntax.) The *alias* command defines *new* to be an alias for *original*; whenever you type new, the Korn shell substitutes original internally. (You cannot use any of the shell's special characters, such as *, $, =, and so on, in alias names.)

There are a few basic ways to use an alias. The first, and simplest, is as a more mnemonic name for an existing command. Many commonly used Unix commands have names that are poor mnemonics and therefore are excellent candidates for aliasing; the classic example is:

```
alias search=grep
```

grep, the Unix file-searching utility, derives its name from the command "g/re/p" in the original *ed* text editor, which does essentially the same thing as *grep*. (The regular expression matching code was carved out of *ed* to make a separate program.)† This acronym may mean something to a computer scientist but probably not to the office administrator who has to find Fred in a list of phone numbers. If you have to find Fred, and you have the word *search* defined as an alias for *grep*, you can type:

```
search Fred phonelist
```

Another popular alias eschews *exit* in favor of a more widely used command for ending a login session:

```
alias logout=exit
```

If you are a C shell user, you may be used to having a *.logout* file of commands that the shell executes just before you log out. The Korn shell doesn't have this feature as such, but you can mimic it quite easily using an alias:

```
alias logout='. ~/.ksh_logout; exit'
```

---

* C shell users should note that the Korn shell's alias feature does not support arguments in alias expansions, as C shell aliases do.

† Thanks to Dennis Ritchie and Brian Kernighan of Bell Labs for verifying this for me. ADR.

This executes the commands in the file *.ksh_logout* in your home directory and then logs you out. The semicolon acts as a statement separator, allowing you to have more than one command on the same line.

Notice the quotes around the full value of the alias; these are necessary if the string being aliased consists of more than one word.*

You might want the file *.ksh_logout* to "clean up" your history files, as we discussed in the last chapter. Recall that we created history files with names like *.hist.42*, which guarantees a unique name for every serial line or window. To remove these files when the shells exit, just put this line in your *.ksh_logout* file:

```
rm ~/.hist.*
```

Some people who aren't particularly good typists like to use aliases for typographical errors they make often. For example:

```
alias emcas=emacs
alias mali=mail
alias gerp=grep
```

This can be handy, but we feel you're probably better off suffering with the error message and getting the correct spelling under your fingers. Another common way to use an alias is as a shorthand for a longer command string. For example, you may have a directory to which you need to go often. It's buried deeply in your directory hierarchy, so you want to set up an alias that will allow you to *cd* there without typing (or even remembering) the entire pathname:

```
alias cdcm='cd ~/work/projects/devtools/windows/confman'
```

As before, the quotes around the full *cd* command are needed, because the string being aliased has more than one word.

As another example, a useful option to the *ls* command is *-F:* it puts a slash (/) after directory files and an asterisk (*) after executable files. (Depending on your system, it may append other characters after other kinds of files as well.) Since typing a dash followed by a capital letter is inconvenient, many people like to define an alias like this:

```
alias lf='ls -F'
```

A few things about aliases are important to remember. First, the Korn shell makes a textual substitution of the alias for that which it is aliasing; it may help to imagine *ksh* passing your command through a text editor or word processor and issuing a "change" or "substitute" command before interpreting and executing it.

---

* This contrasts with C shell aliases, in which the quotes aren't required.

This, in turn, means that any special characters (such as wildcards like * and ?) that result when the alias is expanded are interpreted properly by the shell. This leads to an important corollary: wildcards and other special characters cannot be used in the names of aliases, i.e., on the left side of the equal sign. For example, to make it easier to print all of the files in your directory, you could define the alias:

```
alias printall='pr * | lp'
```

Second, keep in mind that aliases are recursive, which means that it is possible to alias an alias. A legitimate objection to the previous example is that the alias, while mnemonic, is too long and doesn't save enough typing. If we want to keep this alias but add a shorter abbreviation, we could define:

```
alias pa=printall
```

Recursive aliasing makes it possible to set up an "infinite loop" of definitions, wherein an alias ends up (perhaps after several lookups) being defined as itself. For example, the command:

```
alias ls='ls -l'
```

sets up a possible infinite loop. Luckily, the shell has a mechanism to guard against such dangers. The above command works as expected (typing ls produces a long list with permissions, sizes, owners, etc.). Even more pathological situations work, such as these:

```
alias listfile=ls
alias ls=listfile
```

If you type *listfile*, *ls* runs.

Aliases can only be used for the beginning of a command string—albeit with certain exceptions. In the *cd* example above, you might want to define an alias for the directory name alone, not for the entire command. But if you define:

```
alias cm=work/projects/devtools/windows/confman
```

and then type cd cm, the Korn shell will probably print a message like ksh: cd: cm: [No such file or directory].

An obscure, rather ugly feature of the Korn shell's alias facility—one not present in the analogous C shell feature—provides a way around this problem. If the value of an alias (the right side of the equal sign) ends in a space or a tab, then the Korn shell tries to do alias substitution on the next word on the command line. To make the value of an alias end in a space, you need to surround it with quotes.

This feature exists so that it is possible to have aliases for commands that themselves run other commands, such as *nohup* and *nice*. For example, *nohup* is aliased to 'nohup '. That way, when you type:

```
nohup my_favorite_alias somefile
```

the shell will expand *my_favorite_alias* just as it would when typed without the preceding *nohup* command. (The *nohup* command is described in Chapter 8.)

Here is how you would use this capability to allow aliases for directory names, at least for use with the *cd* command:

```
alias cd='cd '
```

This causes the Korn shell to search for an alias for the directory name argument to *cd*, which in the previous example would enable it to expand the alias *cm* correctly.

The Korn shell provides an efficiency feature called "tracked aliases." We delay discussion of these until the section "PATH and tracked aliases." Also, a number of aliases are predefined by the shell; they are listed in Appendix B.

Finally, there are a few useful adjuncts to the basic *alias* command. If you type alias *name* without an equal sign (=) and value, the shell prints the alias's value or *name*: alias not found if it is undefined. If you type alias without any arguments, you get a list of all the aliases you have defined as well as several that are built-in. If you type alias -p, the shell prints all your aliases, with each one preceded by the alias keyword. This is useful for saving all your aliases in a way that allows them to be re-read by the shell at a later time. The command unalias *name* removes any alias definition for its argument. If you type unalias -a, the shell removes all aliases.

Aliases are very handy for creating a comfortable environment, but they are really just kid stuff compared to more advanced customization techniques like scripts and functions, which we will see in the next chapter. These give you everything aliases do plus much more, so if you become proficient at them, you may find that you don't need aliases anymore. However, aliases are ideal for novices who find Unix to be a rather forbidding place, full of terseness and devoid of good mnemonics.

Options

While aliases let you create convenient names for commands, they don't really let you change the shell's behavior. *Options* are one way of doing this. A shell option is a setting that is either "on" or "off." While several options relate to arcane shell features that are of interest only to programmers, those that we cover here are of interest to all users.

The basic commands that relate to options are set -o *optionnames* and set +o *optionnames*, where *optionnames* is a list of option names separated by whitespace. The use of plus (+) and minus (–) signs is counterintuitive: the – turns the named option on, while the + turns it off. The reason for this incongruity is that the dash (–) is the conventional Unix way of specifying options to a command, while the use of + is an afterthought.

Most options also have one-letter abbreviations that can be used in lieu of the set -o command; for example, set -o noglob can be abbreviated set -f. These abbreviations are carry-overs from the Bourne shell. Like several other "extra" Korn shell features, they exist to ensure upward compatibility; otherwise, their use is not encouraged.

Table 3-1 lists the options that are useful to general Unix users. All of them are off by default except as noted.

Table 3-1. Basic shell options

Option	Description
bgnice	Run background jobs at lower priority (on by default).
emacs	Enter emacs editing mode.
ignoreeof	Don't allow use of CTRL-D to log off; require the exit command.
markdirs	When expanding filename wildcards, append a slash (/) to directories.
noclobber	Don't allow output redirection (>) to clobber an existing file.
noglob	Don't expand filename wildcards like * and ? (wildcard expansion is sometimes called *globbing*).
nounset	Indicate an error when trying to use a variable that is undefined.
trackall	Turn on alias tracking. (The shell actually ignores the setting of this option; alias tracking is always turned on. This is discussed in the section "PATH and tracked aliases," later in this chapter.)
vi	Enter vi editing mode.

There are several other options (22 in all; Appendix B lists them). To check the status of an option, just type set -o. The Korn shell prints a list of all options along with their settings. There is no command for testing single options, but here is a simple shell function to do it:

```
function testopt {
    if [[ -o $1 ]] ; then
        print Option $1 is on.
```

```
    else
        print Option $1 is off.
    fi
}
```

Shell functions are covered in the next chapter. For now, though, if you want to use the *testopt* function, just type it into your *.profile* or environment file (see the section "The Environment File," later in this chapter), type either `login` or `. .profile`. (Yes, the period, or "dot," is actually a command; see the section "Shell Scripts and Functions" in Chapter 4.) Then you can type `testopt` *optionname* to check the status of an option.

Shell Variables

There are several characteristics of your environment that you may want to customize but that cannot be expressed as an on/off choice. Characteristics of this type are specified in shell variables. Shell variables can specify everything from your prompt string to how often the shell checks for new mail.

Like an alias, a shell variable is a name that has a value associated with it. The Korn shell keeps track of several built-in shell variables; shell programmers can add their own. By convention, built-in variables have names in all capital letters. The syntax for defining variables is somewhat similar to the syntax for aliases:

> *varname=value*

There must be no space on either side of the equal sign, and if the value is more than one word, it must be surrounded by quotes. To use the value of a variable in a command, precede its name by a dollar sign ($).

You can delete a variable with the command `unset` *varname*. Normally, this isn't useful, since all variables that don't exist are assumed to be null, i.e., equal to the empty string `""`. But if you use the option *nounset* (see Table 3-1), which causes the shell to indicate an error when it encounters an undefined variable, you may be interested in *unset*.

The easiest way to check a variable's value is to use the *print* built-in command.* All *print* does is print its arguments, but not until the shell has evaluated them. This includes—among other things that will be discussed later—taking the values

---

* The Korn shell supports the old command *echo*, which does much the same thing, for backward compatibility reasons. However, we strongly recommend *print* because its options are the same on all Unix systems, whereas *echo*'s options differ among different Unix versions. This is not likely to change; the POSIX standard says that *echo*'s options are implementation-defined.

of variables and expanding filename wildcards. So, if the variable *fred* has the value bob, typing the following causes the shell to simply print bob:

```
print "$fred"
```

If the variable is undefined, the shell prints a blank line. A more verbose way to do this is:

```
print "The value of \$varname is \"$varname\"."
```

The first dollar sign and the inner double quotes are backslash-escaped (i.e., preceded with \ so the shell doesn't try to interpret them; see Chapter 1) so that they appear literally in the output, which for the above example would be:

```
The value of $fred is "bob".
```

Variables and Quoting

Notice that we used double quotes around variables (and strings containing them) in these *print* examples. In Chapter 1 we said that some special characters inside double quotes are still interpreted (while none are interpreted inside single quotes).

Perhaps the most important special character that "survives" double quotes is the dollar sign—meaning that variables are evaluated. It's possible to do without the double quotes in some cases; for example, we could have written the above *print* command this way:

```
print The value of \$varname is \"$varname\".
```

But double quotes are more generally correct.

Here's why. Suppose we did this:

```
fred='Four spaces between these    words.'
```

Then if we entered the command print $fred, the result would be:

```
Four spaces between these words.
```

What happened to the extra spaces? Without the double quotes, the shell splits the string into words after substituting the variable's value, as it normally does when it processes command lines. The double quotes circumvent this part of the process (by making the shell think that the whole quoted string is a single word).

Therefore the command print "$fred" prints this:

```
Four spaces between these    words.
```

This becomes especially important when we start dealing with variables that contain user or file input later on. In particular, it's increasingly common to find directories made available on Unix systems via the network from Apple Macintosh and Microsoft Windows systems, where spaces and other unusual characters are common in filenames.

Double quotes also allow other special characters to work, as we'll see in Chapter 4, Chapter 6, and Chapter 7. But for now, we'll revise the "When in doubt, use single quotes" rule in Chapter 1 by adding, "...unless a string contains a variable, in which case you should use double quotes."

Built-in Variables

As with options, some built-in shell variables are meaningful to general Unix users, while others are arcana for professional programmers. We'll look at the more generally useful ones here, and we'll save some of the more obscure ones for later chapters. Again, Appendix B contains a complete list.

Editing mode variables

Several shell variables relate to the command-line editing modes that we saw in the previous chapter. These are listed in Table 3-2.

The first two of these are sometimes used by text editors and other screen-oriented programs, which rely on the variables being set correctly. Although the Korn shell and most windowing systems should know how to set them correctly, you should look at the values of COLUMNS and LINES if you are having display trouble with a screen-oriented program.

Table 3-2. Editing mode variables

Variable	Meaning
COLUMNS	Width, in character columns, of your terminal. The standard value is 80 (sometimes 132), though if you are using a windowing system like X, you could give a terminal window any size you wish.
LINES	Length of your terminal in text lines. The standard value for terminals is 24, but for IBM PC–compatible monitors it's 25; once again, if you are using a windowing system, you can usually resize to any amount.
HISTFILE	Name of history file on which the editing modes operate.
EDITOR	Pathname of your favorite text editor; the suffix (macs[a] or vi) determines which editing mode to use.
VISUAL	Similar to EDITOR; if set, used in preference to EDITOR to choose editing mode.
HISTEDIT	Pathname of editor to use with the *hist* command.

[a] This suffix also works if your editor is a different version of Emacs whose name doesn't end in emacs.

Mail variables

Since the *mail* program is not running all the time, there is no way for it to inform you when you get new mail; therefore the shell does this instead.* The shell can't actually check for incoming mail, but it can look at your mail file periodically and determine whether the file has been modified since the last check. The variables listed in Table 3-3 let you control how this works.

Table 3-3. Mail variables

Variable	Meaning
MAIL	Name of file to check for incoming mail (i.e., your mail file)
MAILCHECK	How often, in seconds, to check for new mail (default 600 seconds, or 10 minutes)
MAILPATH	List of filenames, separated by colons (:), to check for incoming mail
_ (underscore)	When used inside $MAILPATH, name of mail file that changed; see text for other uses

Under the simplest scenario, you use the standard Unix mail program, and your mail file is */var/mail/yourname* or something similar. In this case, you would just set the variable MAIL to this filename if you want your mail checked:

```
MAIL=/var/mail/yourname
```

If your system administrator hasn't already done it for you, put a line like this in your *.profile.*

However, some people use nonstandard mailers that use multiple mail files; MAIL-PATH was designed to accommodate this. The Korn shell uses the value of MAIL as the name of the file to check, unless MAILPATH is set, in which case the shell checks each file in the MAILPATH list for new mail. You can use this mechanism to have the shell print a different message for each mail file: for each mail filename in MAILPATH, append a question mark followed by the message you want printed.

For example, let's say you have a mail system that automatically sorts your mail into files according to the username of the sender. You have mail files called */var/ mail/you/fritchie, /var/mail/you/droberts, /var/mail/you/jphelps*, etc. You define your MAILPATH as follows:

```
MAILPATH=/var/mail/you/fritchie:/var/mail/you/droberts:\
/var/mail/you/jphelps
```

---

* The commonly available *biff* command does a better job of this; while the Korn shell only prints "you have mail" messages right before it prints command prompts, *biff* can tell you who the mail is from.

If you get mail from Jennifer Phelps, the file */var/mail/you/jphelps* changes. The Korn shell notices the change within 10 minutes and prints the message:

```
you have mail in /var/mail/you/jphelps.
```

If you are in the middle of running a command, the shell waits until the command finishes (or is suspended) to print the message. To customize this further, you could define MAILPATH to be:

```
MAILPATH=\
/var/mail/you/fritchie?You have mail from Fiona.:\
/var/mail/you/droberts?Mail from Dave has arrived.:\
/var/mail/you/jphelps?There is new mail from Jennifer.
```

The backslashes at the end of each line allow you to continue your command on the next line. But be careful: you can't indent subsequent lines. Now, if you get mail from Jennifer, the shell prints:

```
There is new mail from Jennifer.
```

Within the message parts of MAILPATH, you may use the special variable _ (underscore) for the name of the file that is triggering the message:

```
MAILPATH='/var/mail/you/fritchie?You have mail from Fiona in $_.'
MAILPATH+=':/var/mail/you/droberts?Mail from Dave has arrived, check $_.'
MAILPATH+=':/var/mail/you/jphelps?There is new mail from Jennifer, look at $_.'
```

The meaning of $_ actually varies depending on where and how it's used:

Inside the value of MAILPATH
> As just described, use $_ for the name of the file that triggers a message in the value of MAILPATH.

The last argument of the last interactive command
> When used on a command line entered interactively, $_ represents the last word on the previous command line:

```
$ print hi            Run a command
hi
$ print $_            Verify setting of $_
hi
$ print hello         New last argument
hello
$ print $_
hello
$ print "hi there"    Usage is word based
hi there
$ print $_
hi there
```

This usage of $_ is similar to the !$ feature of the C shell's history mechanism.

Inside a script

When accessed from inside a shell script, $_ is the full pathname used to find and invoke the script:

```
$ cat /tmp/junk        Show test program
print _ is $_
$ PATH=/tmp:$PATH       Add directory to PATH
$ junk                  Run the program
_ is /tmp/junk
```

Prompting variables

If you have seen enough experienced Unix users at work, you may already have realized that the shell's prompt is not engraved in stone. It seems as though one of the favorite pastimes of professional Unix programmers is thinking of cute or innovative prompt strings. We'll give you some of the information you need to do your own here; the rest comes in the next chapter.

Actually, the Korn shell uses four prompt strings. They are stored in the variables PS1, PS2, PS3, and PS4. The first of these is called the primary prompt string; it is your usual shell prompt, and its default value is "$ " (a dollar sign followed by a space). Many people like to set their primary prompt string to something containing their login name. Here is one way to do this:

```
PS1="($LOGNAME)-> "
```

LOGNAME is another built-in shell variable, which is set to your login name when you log in.* So, PS1 becomes a left parenthesis, followed by your login name, followed by ")-> ". If your login name is fred, your prompt string will be "(fred)-> ".If you are a C shell user and, like many such people, are used to having a command number in your prompt string, the Korn shell can do this similarly to the C shell: if there is an exclamation point in the prompt string, it substitutes the command number. Thus, if you define your prompt string to be the following, your prompts will look like (fred 1)->, (fred 2)->, and so on:

```
PS1="($LOGNAME !)->"
```

Perhaps the most useful way to set up your prompt string is so that it always contains your current directory. Then you needn't type pwd to remember where you are. Putting your directory in the prompt is more complicated than the above examples, because your current directory changes during your login session,

---

* Some very old systems use USER instead. Thankfully, such systems are becoming more and more rare with time.

unlike your login name and the name of your machine. But we can accommodate this by taking advantage of the different kinds of quotes. Here's how:

```
PS1='($PWD)-> '
```

The difference is the single quotes, instead of double quotes, surrounding the string on the right side of the assignment. The trick is that this string is evaluated twice: once when the assignment to PS1 is done (in your *.profile* or environment file) and then again after every command you enter. Here's what each of these evaluations does:

1. The first evaluation observes the single quotes and returns what is inside them without further processing. As a result, PS1 contains the string ($PWD)-> .

2. After every command, the shell evaluates ($PWD)->. PWD is a built-in variable that is always equal to the current directory, so the result is a primary prompt that always contains the current directory.*

We'll discuss the subtleties of quoting and delayed evaluation in more depth in Chapter 7.

PS2 is called the secondary prompt string; its default value is "> " (a greater-than sign followed by a single space). It is used when you type an incomplete line and hit ENTER, as an indication that you must finish your command. For example, assume that you start a quoted string but don't close the quote. Then if you hit ENTER, the shell prints > and waits for you to finish the string:

```
$ x="This is a long line,          PS1 for the command
> which is terminated down here"    PS2 for the continuation
$                                   PS1 for the next command
```

PS3 and PS4 relate to shell programming and debugging, respectively; they are explained in Chapter 5 and Chapter 9.

Using history command numbers

The current history command number is available in the HISTCMD environment variable. You can see the current history number in your prompt by placing a ! (or $HISTCMD) somewhere in the value of the PS1 variable:

```
$ PS1="command !> "
command 42> ls -FC *.xml
appa.xml  appd.xml  ch01.xml  ch04.xml  ch07.xml  ch10.xml
appb.xml  appf.xml  ch02.xml  ch05.xml  ch08.xml  colo1.xml
appc.xml  ch00.xml  ch03.xml  ch06.xml  ch09.xml  copy.xml
command 43>
```

---

* The shell also does command and arithmetic substitution on the value of PS1, but we haven't covered those features yet. See Chapter 6.

To get a literal ! into the value of your prompt, place !! into PS1.

Terminal types

Today, the most common use of the shell is from inside a terminal emulator window displayed on the high resolution screen of a workstation or PC. However, the terminal emulator program still does emulate the facilities provided by the actual serial CRT terminals of yesteryear. As such, the shell variable TERM is vitally important for any program that uses your entire window, like a text editor. Such programs include traditional screen editors (such as *vi* and Emacs), pager programs like *more*, and countless third-party applications.

Because users are spending more and more time within programs and less and less using the shell itself, it is extremely important that your TERM is set correctly. It's really your system administrator's job to help you do this (or to do it for you), but in case you need to do it yourself, here are a few guidelines.

The value of TERM must be a short character string with lowercase letters that appears as a filename in the *terminfo* database.* This database is a two-tiered directory of files under the root directory */usr/share/terminfo*.† This directory contains subdirectories with single-character names; these in turn contain files of terminal information for all terminals whose names begin with that character. Each file describes how to tell the terminal in question to do certain common things like position the cursor on the screen, go into reverse video, scroll, insert text, and so on. The descriptions are in binary form (i.e., not readable by humans).

Names of terminal description files are the same as that of the terminal being described; sometimes an abbreviation is used. For example, the DEC VT100 has a description in the file */usr/share/terminfo/v/vt100*; the GNU/Linux character-based console has a description in the file */usr/share/terminfo/l/linux*. An *xterm* terminal window under the X Window System has a description in */usr/share/terminfo/x/xterm*.

Sometimes your Unix software will not set up TERM correctly; this often happens for X terminals and PC-based Unix systems. Therefore, you should check the value of TERM by typing print $TERM before going any further. If you find that your Unix system isn't setting the right value for you (especially likely if your terminal is of a different make than your computer), you need to find the appropriate value of TERM yourself.

---

* Versions of Unix not derived from System V use *termcap*, an older-style database of terminal capabilities that uses the single text file */etc/termcap* for all terminal descriptions. Modern systems often have both the */etc/termcap* file and the *terminfo* database available. Current BSD systems use a single-file indexed database, */usr/share/misc/termcap.db*.

† This is the typical location on modern systems. Older systems have it in */usr/lib/terminfo*.

The best way to find the TERM value—if you can't find a local guru to do it for you—is to guess the *terminfo* name and search for a file of that name under */usr/share/terminfo* by using *ls*. For example, if your terminal is a Blivitz BL-35A, you could try:

```
$ cd /usr/share/terminfo
$ ls b/bl*
```

If you are successful, you will see something like this:

```
bl35a          blivitz35a
```

In this case, the two names are likely to be synonyms for (links to) the same terminal description, so you could use either one as a value of TERM. In other words, you could put *either* of these two lines in your *.profile*:

```
TERM=bl35a
TERM=blivitz35a
```

If you aren't successful, *ls* won't print anything, and you will have to make another guess and try again. If you find that *terminfo* contains nothing that resembles your terminal, all is not lost. Consult your terminal's manual to see if the terminal can emulate a more popular model; nowadays the odds of this are excellent.

Conversely, *terminfo* may have several entries that relate to your terminal, for submodels, special modes, etc. If you have a choice of which entry to use as your value of TERM, we suggest you test each one out with your text editor or any other screen-oriented programs you use and see which one works best.

The process is much simpler if you are using a windowing system, in which your "terminals" are logical portions of the screen rather than physical devices. In this case, operating system–dependent software was written to control your terminal window(s), so the odds are very good that if it knows how to handle window resizing and complex cursor motion, it is capable of dealing with simple things like TERM. The X Window System, for example, automatically sets "xterm" as its value for TERM in an *xterm* terminal window.

Command search path

Another important variable is PATH, which helps the shell find the commands you enter.

As you probably know, every command you use is actually a file that contains code for your machine to run.* These files are called *executable files* or just *executables* for short. They are stored in various directories. Some directories, like

---

* Unless it's a built-in command (like *cd* and *print*), in which case the code is simply part of the executable file for the entire shell.

/bin or */usr/bin,* are standard on all Unix systems; some depend on the particular version of Unix you are using; some are unique to your machine; if you are a programmer, some may even be your own. In any case, there is no reason why you should have to know where a command's executable file is in order to run it.

That is where PATH comes in. Its value is a list of directories that the shell searches every time you enter a command name that does not contain a slash; the directory names are separated by colons (:), just like the files in MAILPATH. For example, if you type print $PATH, you will see something like this:

```
/sbin:/usr/sbin:/usr/bin:/etc:/usr/X11R6/bin:/local/bin
```

Why should you care about your path? There are three main reasons. First, there are security aspects to its value, which we touch on shortly. Second, once you have read the later chapters of this book and you try writing your own shell programs, you will want to test them and eventually set aside a directory for them. Third, your system may be set up so that certain "restricted" commands' executable files are kept in directories that are not listed in PATH. For example, there may be a directory */usr/games* in which there are executables that are verboten during regular working hours.

Therefore you may want to add directories to the default PATH you get when you login. Let's say you have created a *bin* directory under your login directory for your own shell scripts and programs. To add this directory to your PATH so that it is there every time you log in, put this line in your *.profile*:

```
PATH="$PATH:$HOME/bin"
```

This sets PATH to whatever it was before, followed immediately by a colon and $HOME/bin (your personal *bin* directory). This is a rather typical usage. (Using $HOME lets your system administrator move your home directory around, without your having to fix your *.profile* file.)

There is an important additional detail to understand about how PATH works. This has to do with empty (or "null") elements in the PATH. A null element can occur in one of three ways: placing a lone colon at the front of PATH, placing a lone colon at the end of PATH, or placing two adjacent colons in the middle of PATH. The shell treats a null element in PATH as a synonym for ".", the current directory, and searches in whatever directory you happen to be in at that point in the path search.

```
PATH=:$HOME/bin:/usr/bin:/usr/local/bin      Search current directory first
PATH=$HOME/bin:/usr/bin:/usr/local/bin:      Search current directory last
PATH=$HOME/bin::/usr/bin:/usr/local/bin      Search current directory second
```

Finally, if you need to know which directory a command comes from, you need not look at directories in your PATH until you find it. The shell built-in command *whence* prints the full pathname of the command you give it as argument, or just the command's name if it's a built-in command itself (like *cd*), an alias, or a function (as we'll see in Chapter 4).

PATH security considerations

How you set up your PATH variable can have important implications for security.

First, having the current directory in your path is a real security hole, especially for system administrators, and the root account should *never* have a null element (or explicit dot) in its search path. Why? Consider someone who creates a shell script named, for example, *ls*, makes it executable, and places it in a directory that root might *cd* to, such as */tmp*:

```
rm -f /tmp/ls          Hide the evidence
/bin/ls "$@"           Run real ls
nasty stuff here       Silently run other stuff as root
```

If root has the current directory first in PATH, then cd /tmp; ls does whatever the miscreant wants, and root is none the wiser. (This is known in the security world as a "trojan horse.") While less serious for regular users, there are many experts who would still advise against having the current directory in PATH.

Secondly, the safest way to add your personal bin to PATH is at the end. When you enter a command, the shell searches directories in the order they appear in PATH until it finds an executable file. Therefore, if you have a shell script or program whose name is the same as an existing command, the shell will use the existing command—unless you type in the command's full pathname to disambiguate. For example, if you have created your own version of the *more* command in $HOME/bin and your PATH has $HOME/bin at the end, to get your version you will need to type $HOME/bin/more (or just ~/bin/more).

The more reckless way of resetting your path is to tell the shell to look in your directory first by putting it before the other directories in your PATH:

```
PATH="$HOME/bin:$PATH"
```

This is less safe because you are trusting that your own version of the *more* command works properly. But it is also risky since it might allow for trojan horses (similar to the *ls* example we just saw). If your *bin* directory is writable by others on your system, they can install a program that does something nasty.

Proper use of PATH is just one of many aspects of system security. See Chapter 10 for more details. In short, we recommend leaving the current directory out of your PATH (both implicitly and explicitly), adding your personal *bin* directory at the end of PATH, and making sure that *only* you can create, remove, or change files in your personal *bin* directory.

PATH and tracked aliases

It is worth noting that a search through the directories in your PATH can take time. You won't exactly die if you hold your breath for the length of time it takes for most computers to search your PATH, but the large number of disk I/O operations involved in some PATH searches can take longer than the command you invoked takes to run!

The Korn shell provides a way to circumvent PATH searches, called a tracked alias. First, notice that if you specify a command by giving its full pathname, the shell won't even use your PATH—instead, it just goes directly to the executable file.

Tracked aliases do this for you automatically. The first time you invoke a command, the shell looks for the executable in the normal way (through PATH). Then it creates an alias for the full pathname, so that the next time you invoke the command, the shell uses the full pathname and does not bother with PATH at all. If you ever change your PATH, the shell marks tracked aliases as "undefined," so that it searches for the full pathnames again when you invoke the corresponding commands.

In fact, you can add tracked aliases for the sole purpose of avoiding PATH lookup of commands that you use particularly often. Just put a "trivial alias" of the form alias -t *command* in your *.profile* or environment file; the shell substitutes the full pathname itself.

For example, the first time you invoke *emacs*, the shell does a PATH search. Upon finding the location of *emacs* (say */usr/local/bin/emacs*), the shell creates a tracked alias:

```
    alias -t emacs=/usr/local/bin/emacs     Automatic tracked alias
```

The next time you run *emacs*, the shell expands the *emacs* alias into the full path */usr/local/bin/emacs*, and executes the program directly, not bothering with a PATH search.

You can also define individual tracked aliases yourself, with the option *−t* to the *alias* command, and you can list all such tracked aliases by typing alias -t by itself. (For compatibility with the System V Bourne shell, *ksh* predefines the alias hash='alias -t --'; the *hash* command in that shell displays the internal table of found commands. The Korn shell's tracked alias mechanism is more flexible.)

Although the shell's documentation and *trackall* option indicate that you can turn alias tracking on and off, the shell's actual behavior is different: alias tracking is always on. *alias −t* lists all of the automatically-created tracked aliases. However, *alias −p* does not print tracked aliases. This is because, conceptually, tracked aliases are just a performance enhancement; they are really unrelated to the aliases that you define for customization.

Directory search path

CDPATH is a variable whose value, like that of PATH, is a list of directories separated by colons. Its purpose is to augment the functionality of the *cd* built-in command.

By default, CDPATH isn't set (meaning that it is null), and when you type cd *dirname*, the shell looks in the current directory for a subdirectory called *dirname*. Similar to PATH, this search is disabled when *dirname* starts with a slash. If you set CDPATH, you give the shell a list of places to look for *dirname*; the list may or may not include the current directory.

Here is an example. Consider the alias for the long *cd* command from earlier in this chapter:

```
alias cdcm="cd work/projects/devtools/windows/confman"
```

Now suppose there were a few directories under this directory to which you need to go often; they are called *src*, *bin*, and *doc*. You define your CDPATH like this:

```
CDPATH=:~/work/projects/devtools/windows/confman
```

In other words, you define your CDPATH to be the empty string (meaning the current directory, wherever you happen to be) followed by ~/work/projects/devtools/windows/confman.

With this setup, if you type cd doc, then the shell looks in the current directory for a (sub)directory called *doc*. Assuming that it doesn't find one, it looks in the directory *~/work/projects/devtools/windows/confman*. The shell finds the *doc* directory there, so you go directly to it.

This works for any relative pathname. For example, if you have a directory *src/whizprog* in your home directory, and your CDPATH is :$HOME (the current directory and your home directory), typing cd src/whizprog takes you to *$HOME/src/whizprog* from anywhere on the system.

This feature gives you yet another way to save typing when you need to *cd* often to directories that are buried deep in your file hierarchy. You may find yourself going to a specific group of directories often as you work on a particular project, and then changing to another set of directories when you switch to another project. This implies that the CDPATH feature is only useful if you update it whenever your work habits change; if you don't, you may occasionally find yourself where you don't want to be.

Miscellaneous variables

We have covered the shell variables that are important from the standpoint of customization. There are also several that serve as status indicators and for various other miscellaneous purposes. Their meanings are relatively straightforward; the more basic ones are summarized in Table 3-4.

The first two variables are set by the *login* program, before the shell starts. The shell sets the value of the next two whenever you change directories. The final variable's value changes dynamically, as time elapses. Although you can also set the values of any of these, just like any other variables, it is difficult to imagine any situation where you would want to.

Table 3-4. Status variables

Variable	Meaning
HOME	Name of your home (login) directory. This is the default argument for the *cd* command.
SHELL	Pathname of the shell that programs should use to run commands.
PWD	Current directory.
OLDPWD	Previous directory before the last *cd* command.
SECONDS	Number of seconds since the shell was invoked.

Customization and Subprocesses

Some of the variables discussed above are used by commands you may run—as opposed to the shell itself—so that they can determine certain aspects of your environment. The majority, however, are not even known outside the shell.

This dichotomy begs an important question: which shell "things" are known outside the shell, and which are only internal? This question is at the heart of many misunderstandings about the shell and shell programming. Before we answer, we'll ask it again in a more precise way: which shell "things" are known to subprocesses? Remember that whenever you enter a command, you are telling the shell to run that command in a subprocess; furthermore, some complex programs may start their own subprocesses.

The answer is actually fairly simple. Subprocesses inherit only environment variables. They are available automatically, without the subprocess having to take any explicit action. All the other "things"—shell options, aliases, and functions—must be made explicitly available. The *environment file* is how you do this. Furthermore, only interactive shells process the environment file. The next two sections describe environment variables and the environment file, respectively.

Environment Variables

By default, only one kind of thing is known to all kinds of subprocesses: a special class of shell variables called *environment variables*. Some of the built-in variables we have seen are actually environment variables: HISTFILE, HOME, LOGNAME, PATH, PWD, OLDPWD, SHELL, and TERM.

It should be clear why these and other variables need to be known by subprocesses. We have already seen the most obvious example: text editors like *vi* and Emacs need to know what kind of terminal you are using; TERM is their way of determining this. As another example, most Unix mail programs allow you to edit a message with your favorite text editor. How does *mail* know which editor to use? The value of EDITOR (or sometimes VISUAL).

Any variable can become an environment variable, and new variables can be created that are environment variables. Environment variables are created with the command:

```
export varnames
```

(*varnames* can be a list of variable names separated by whitespace.) If the names in *varnames* already exist, then those variables become environment variables. If they don't, the shell creates new variables that are environment variables.

With *ksh*, you may assign a value and export the variable in one step:

```
export TMPDIR=/var/tmp
```

You can also define variables to be in the environment of a particular subprocess (command) only, by preceding the command with the variable assignment, like this:

```
varname=value command
```

You can put as many assignments before the command as you want.* For example, assume you're using the Emacs editor. You are having problems getting it to work with your terminal, so you're experimenting with different values of TERM. You can do this most easily by entering commands that look like:

```
TERM=trythisone emacs filename
```

emacs has trythisone defined as its value of TERM, yet the environment variable in your shell keeps whatever value (if any) it had before. This syntax is not very widely used, so we won't see it very often throughout the remainder of this book.

---

* There is an obscure option, *keyword*, that (if turned on) lets you put this type of environment variable definition *anywhere* on the command line, not just at the beginning.

Nevertheless, environment variables are important. Most *.profile* files include definitions of environment variables; the sample *.profile* earlier in this chapter contained two such definitions:

```
EDITOR=/usr/local/bin/emacs
SHELL=/bin/ksh
export EDITOR SHELL
```

For some reason, the Korn shell doesn't make EDITOR an environment variable by
default. This means, among other things, that *mail* will not know which editor to
use when you want to edit a message.* Therefore you would have to export it
yourself by using the *export* command in your *.profile*.

The second line in the previous code is meant for systems that do not have the
Korn shell installed as the default shell, i.e., as */bin/sh*. Some programs run shells
as subprocesses within themselves (e.g., many mail programs and the Emacs editor's shell mode); by convention, they use the SHELL variable to determine which
shell to use.

You can find out which variables are environment variables and what their values
are by typing *export* without arguments.

The Environment File

Although environment variables are always known to subprocesses, the shell must
be explicitly told which other variables, options, aliases, etc., are to be communi-
cated to subprocesses. The way to do this is to put all such definitions in a special
file called the *environment file* instead of your *.profile*.

You can call the environment file anything you like, as long as you set the environment variable ENV to the file's name. The usual way to do this is as follows:

1.   Decide which definitions in your *.profile* you want to propagate to subpro-
     cesses. Remove them from *.profile* and put them in a file you designate as
     your environment file.

2.   Put a line in your *.profile* that tells the shell where your environment file is:

     ```
     ENV=envfilename
     export ENV
     ```

     It is important that the value of ENV be exported, so that shell subprocesses are
     able to find it.

---

* Actually, it will default to the line editor *ed*. You don't want that, now, do you?

3. For the changes to take effect immediately, logout and then log back in again.* (You can't just use `.  ~/.profile`; the shell does not rerun the $ENV file when the value of ENV changes.)

The idea of the environment file comes from the C shell's *.cshrc* file; thus, many Korn shell users who came from the C shell world call their environment files *.kshrc*. (The `rc` suffix for initialization files is practically universal throughout the Unix world. It stands for "run commands" and entered the Unix lexicon by way of MIT's Compatible Time Sharing System (CTSS)).

As a general rule, you should put as few definitions as possible in *.profile* and as many as possible in your environment file. Because definitions add to rather than take away from an environment, there is little chance that they will cause something in a subprocess not to work properly. (An exception might be name clashes if you go overboard with aliases.)

The only things that really need to be in *.profile* are commands that aren't definitions but actually run or produce output when you log in. Option and alias definitions should go into the environment file. In fact, there are many Korn shell users who have tiny *.profile* files, e.g.:

```
stty stop ^S intr ^C erase ^?
date
from
export ENV=~/.kshrc
```

(The *from* command, in some versions of Unix, checks if you have any mail and prints a list of message headers if you do.) Although this is a small *.profile*, this user's environment file could be huge.

There is an important difference between *ksh88* and *ksh93*. In *ksh88*, the environment file is always executed. In *ksh93*, only *interactive* shells (those not reading from a script, but rather from a terminal) execute the environment file. Thus, it is best that the environment file contain only commands that are useful for interactive use, such as alias and option settings.

Another difference between the two shell versions is that *ksh88* only does variable substitution on the value of ENV, while *ksh93* does variable, command, and arithmetic substitution on its value. (Command substitution is described in Chapter 4. Arithmetic substitution is described in Chapter 6.)

---

* This assumes that the Korn shell is defined as your login shell. If it isn't, you should have your system administrator install it as your login shell.

Customization Hints

You should feel free to try any of the techniques presented in this chapter. The best strategy is to test something out by typing it into the shell during your login session; if you decide you want to make it a permanent part of your environment, add it to your *.profile*.

A nice, painless way to add to your *.profile* without going into a text editor makes use of the *print* command and one of the Korn shell's editing modes. If you type a customization command in and later decide to add it to your *.profile*, you can recall it via CTRL-P or CTRL-R (in emacs-mode) or j, -, or / (vi-mode). Let's say the line is:

```
PS1="($LOGNAME !)->"
```

After you recall it, edit it so that it is preceded by a *print* command, surrounded by *single* quotes, and followed by an I/O redirector that (as you will see in Chapter 7) appends the output to ˜/.profile:

```
print 'PS1="($LOGNAME !)->"' >> ~/.profile
```

Remember that the single quotes are important because they prevent the shell from trying to interpret things like dollar signs, double quotes, and exclamation points.

You should also feel free to snoop around other peoples' *.profile* files for customization ideas. A quick way to examine everyone's *.profile* is as follows: let's assume that all login directories are under */home*. Then you can type:

```
cat /home/*/.profile > ~/other_profiles
```

and examine other people's *.profile* files with a text editor at your leisure (assuming you have read permission on them). If other users have environment files, the file you just created will show what they are, and you can examine them as well.

Finally, be sure that no one else but you has write permission on your *.profile* and environment files.

4

*Basic Shell
Programming*

If you have become familiar with the customization techniques we presented in the previous chapter, you have probably run into various modifications to your environment that you want to make but can't—yet. Shell programming makes these possible.

The Korn shell has some of the most advanced programming capabilities of any command interpreter of its type. Although its syntax is nowhere near as elegant or consistent as that of most conventional programming languages, its power and flexibility are comparable. In fact, the Korn shell can be used as a complete environment for writing software prototypes.

Some aspects of Korn shell programming are really extensions of the customization techniques we have already seen, while others resemble traditional programming language features. We have structured this chapter so that if you aren't a programmer, you can read this chapter and do quite a bit more than you could with the information in the previous chapter. Experience with a conventional programming language like Pascal or C is helpful (though not strictly necessary) for subsequent chapters. Throughout the rest of the book, we will encounter occasional programming problems, called *tasks*, whose solutions make use of the concepts we cover.

Shell Scripts and Functions

A *script*, or file that contains shell commands, is a shell program. Your *.profile* and environment files, discussed in Chapter 3, are shell scripts.

You can create a script using the text editor of your choice. Once you have created one, there are a number of ways to run it. One, which we have already covered, is to type . *scriptname* (i.e., the command is a dot). This causes the commands in the script to be read and run as if you typed them in.

Two more ways are to type ksh *script* or ksh < *script*. These explicitly invoke the Korn shell on the script, requiring that you (and your users) be aware that they are scripts.

The final way to run a script is simply to type its name and hit ENTER, just as if you were invoking a built-in command. This, of course, is the most convenient way. This method makes the script look just like any other Unix command, and in fact several "regular" commands are implemented as shell scripts (i.e., not as programs originally written in C or some other language), including *spell, man* on some systems, and various commands for system administrators. The resulting lack of distinction between "user command files" and "built-in commands" is one factor in Unix's extensibility and, hence, its favored status among programmers.

You can run a script by typing its name only if . (the current directory) is part of your command search path, i.e., is included in your PATH variable (as discussed in Chapter 3). If . isn't on your path, you must type ./*scriptname*, which is really the same thing as typing the script's relative pathname (see Chapter 1).

Before you can invoke the shell script by name, you must also give it "execute" permission. If you are familiar with the Unix filesystem, you know that files have three types of permissions (read, write, and execute) and that those permissions apply to three categories of user (the file's owner, a group of users, and everyone else). Normally, when you create a file with a text editor, the file is set up with read and write permission for you and read-only permission for everyone else.*

Therefore you must give your script execute permission explicitly, by using the *chmod*(1) command. The simplest way to do this is like so:

    chmod +x *scriptname*

Your text editor preserves this permission if you make subsequent changes to your script. If you don't add execute permission to the script, and you try to invoke it, the shell prints the message:

    ksh: *scriptname*: cannot execute [Permission denied]

But there is a more important difference between the two ways of running shell scripts. While the "dot" method causes the commands in the script to be run as if they were part of your login session, the "just the name" method causes the shell to do a series of things. First, it runs another copy of the shell as a subprocess.

---

* This actually depends on the setting of your *umask*, an advanced feature described in Chapter 10.

The shell subprocess then takes commands from the script, runs them, and terminates, handing control back to the parent shell.

Figure 4-1 shows how the shell executes scripts. Assume you have a simple shell script called *fred* that contains the commands *bob* and *dave*. In Figure 4-1.a, typing `. fred` causes the two commands to run in the same shell, just as if you had typed them in by hand. Figure 4-1.b shows what happens when you type just `fred`: the commands run in the shell subprocess while the parent shell waits for the subprocess to finish.

You may find it interesting to compare this with the situation in Figure 4-1.c, which shows what happens when you type `fred &`. As you will recall from Chapter 1, the `&` makes the command run in the *background*, which is really just another term for "subprocess." It turns out that the only significant difference between Figure 4-1.c and Figure 4-1.b is that you have control of your terminal or workstation while the command runs—you need not wait until it finishes before you can enter further commands.

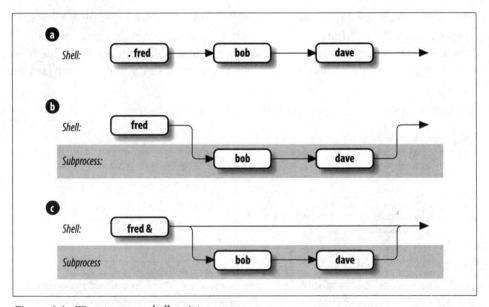

Figure 4-1. Ways to run a shell script

There are many ramifications to using shell subprocesses. An important one is that the *export*ed environment variables that we saw in the last chapter (e.g., TERM, LOG-NAME, PWD) are known in shell subprocesses, whereas other shell variables (such as any that you define in your *.profile* without an *export* statement) are not.

Other issues involving shell subprocesses are too complex to go into now; see Chapter 7 and Chapter 8 for more details about subprocess I/O and process characteristics, respectively. For now, just bear in mind that a script normally runs in a shell subprocess.

Functions

The Korn shell's *function* feature is an expanded version of a similar facility in the System V Bourne shell and a few other shells. A function is sort of a script-within-a-script; you use it to define some shell code by name and store it in the shell's memory, to be invoked and run later.

Functions improve the shell's programmability significantly, for two main reasons. First, when you invoke a function, it is already in the shell's memory (except for automatically loaded functions; see the section "Automatically loading functions," later in this chapter); therefore a function runs faster. Modern computers have plenty of memory, so there is no need to worry about the amount of space a typical function takes up. For this reason, most people define as many functions as possible rather than keep lots of scripts around.

The other advantage of functions is that they are ideal for organizing long shell scripts into modular "chunks" of code that are easier to develop and maintain. If you aren't a programmer, ask one what life would be like without functions (also called *procedures* or *subroutines* in other languages) and you'll probably get an earful.

To define a function, you can use either one of two forms:

```
function functname {       Korn shell semantics
    shell commands
}
```

or:

```
functname () {             POSIX semantics
    shell commands
}
```

The first form provides access to the full power and programmability of the Korn shell. The second is compatible with the syntax for shell functions introduced in the System V Release 2 Bourne shell. This form obeys the semantics of the POSIX standard, which are less powerful than full Korn shell-style functions. (We discuss the differences in detail shortly.) We always use the first form in this book. You can delete a function definition with the command unset -f *functname*.

When you define a function, you tell the shell to store its name and definition (i.e., the shell commands it contains) in memory. If you want to run the function later, just type in its name followed by any arguments, as if it were a shell script.

You can find out what functions are defined in your login session by typing functions.* (Note the s at the end of the command name.) The shell will print not just the names but also the definitions of all functions, in alphabetical order by function name. Since this may result in long output, you might want to pipe the output through *more* or redirect it to a file for examination with a text editor.

Apart from the advantages, there are two important differences between functions and scripts. First, functions do not run in separate processes, as scripts do when you invoke them by name; the "semantics" of running a function are more like those of your *.profile* when you log in or any script when invoked with the "dot" command. Second, if a function has the same name as a script or executable program, the function takes precedence.

This is a good time to show the order of precedence for the various sources of commands. When you type a command to the shell, it looks in the following places until it finds a match:

1. Keywords, such as function and several others (e.g., if and for) that we will see in Chapter 5

2. Aliases (although you can't define an alias whose name is a shell keyword, you can define an alias that expands to a keyword, e.g., alias aslongas=while; see Chapter 7 for more details)

3. Special built-ins, such as *break* and *continue* (the full list is . (dot), :, *alias, break, continue, eval, exec, exit, export, login, newgrp, readonly, return, set, shift, trap, typeset, unalias,* and *unset*)

4. Functions

5. Non-special built-ins, such as *cd* and *whence*

6. Scripts and executable programs, for which the shell searches in the directories listed in the PATH environment variable

We'll examine this process in more detail in the section on command-line processing in Chapter 7.

If you need to know the exact source of a command, there is an option to the *whence* built-in command that we saw in Chapter 3. *whence* by itself will print the pathname of a command if the command is a script or executable program, but it

---

* This is actually an alias for typeset -f; see Chapter 6.

will only parrot the command's name back if it is anything else. But if you type whence -v *commandname*, you get more complete information, such as:

```
$ whence -v cd
cd is a shell builtin
$ whence -v function
function is a keyword
$ whence -v man
man is a tracked alias for /usr/bin/man
$ whence -v ll
ll is an alias for 'ls -l'
```

For compatibility with the System V Bourne shell, the Korn shell predefines the alias type='whence -v'. This definitely makes the transition to the Korn shell easier for long-time Bourne shell users; *type* is similar to *whence*. The *whence* command actually has several options, described in Table 4-1.

Table 4-1. Options for the whence command

Option	Meaning
-a	Print all interpretations of given name.
-f	Skip functions in search for name.
-p	Search $PATH, even if name is a built-in or function.
-v	Print more verbose description of name.

Throughout the remainder of this book we refer mainly to scripts, but unless we note otherwise, you should assume that whatever we say applies equally to functions.

Automatically loading functions

At first glance, it would seem that the best place to put your own function definitions is in your *.profile* or environment file. This is great for interactive use, since your login shell reads ˜*/.profile*, and other interactive shells read the environment file. However, any shell scripts that you write don't read either file. Furthermore, as your collection of functions grows, so too do your initialization files, making them hard to work with.

ksh93 works around both of these issues by integrating the search for functions with the search for commands. Here's how it works:

1. Create a directory to hold your function definitions. This can be your private *bin* directory, or you may wish to have a separate directory, such as ˜*/funcs*. For the sake of discussion, assume the latter.

2. In your *.profile* file, add this directory to *both* the variables PATH and FPATH:

    ```
    PATH=$PATH:~/funcs
    FPATH=~/funcs
    export PATH FPATH
    ```

3. In *~/funcs*, place the definition of each of your functions into a separate file.
    Each function's file should have the same name as the function:

    ```
    $ mkdir ~/funcs
    $ cd ~/funcs
    $ cat > whoson
    # whoson --- create a sorted list of logged-on users
    function whoson {
        who | awk '{ print $1 }' | sort -u
    }
    ^D
    ```

Now, the first time you type whoson, the shell looks for a command named *whoson*
using the search order described earlier. It will not be found as a special-built-in,
as a function, or as a regular built-in. The shell then starts a search along $PATH.
When it finally finds *~/funcs/whoson*, the shell notices that *~/funcs* is also in
$FPATH. ("Aha!" says the shell.) When this is the case, the shell expects to find the
definition of the function named *whoson* inside the file. It reads and executes the
entire contents of the file and only then runs the function *whoson*, with any supplied arguments. (If the file found in both $PATH and $FPATH doesn't actually define
the function, you'll get a "not found" error message.)

The next time you type whoson, the function is already defined, so the shell finds it
immediately, without the need for the path search.

Note that directories listed in FPATH but not in PATH won't be searched for functions, and that as of *ksh93l*, the current directory must be listed in FPATH via an
explicit dot; a leading or trailing colon doesn't cause the current directory to be
searched.

As a final wrinkle, starting with *ksh93m*, each directory named in PATH may contain a file named *.paths*. This file may contain comments and blank lines, and specialized variable assignments. The first allowed assignment is to FPATH, where the
value should name an existing directory. If that directory contains a file whose
name matches the function being searched for, that file is read and executed as if
via the . (dot) command, and then the function is executed.

In addition, one other environment variable may be assigned to. The intended use
of this is to specify a relative or absolute path for a library directory containing the
shared libraries for executables in the current bin directory. On many Unix systems, this variable is LD_LIBRARY_PATH, but some systems have a different variable—check your local documentation. The given value is prepended to the

existing value of the variable when the command is executed. (This mechanism may open security holes. System administrators should use it with caution!)

For example, the AT&T Advanced Software Tools group that distributes *ksh93* also has many other tools, often installed in a separate *ast/bin* directory. This feature allows the *ast* programs to find their shared libraries, without the user having to manually adjust `LD_LIBRARY_PATH` in the *.profile* file.* For example, if a command is found in */usr/local/ast/bin*, and the *.paths* file in that directory contains the assignment `LD_LIBRARY_PATH=../lib`, the shell prepends `/usr/local/ast/lib:` to the value of `LD_LIBRARY_PATH` before running the command.

Readers familiar with *ksh88* will notice that this part of the shell's behavior has changed significantly. Since *ksh88* always read the environment file, whether or not the shell was interactive, it was simplest to just put function definitions there. However, this could still yield a large, unwieldy file. To get around this, you could create files in one or more directories listed in `$FPATH`. Then, in the environment file, you would mark the functions as being *autoloaded*:

```
autoload whoson
...
```

Marking a function with *autoload*[†] tells the shell that this name is a function, and to find the definition by searching `$FPATH`. The advantage to this is that the function is not loaded into the shell's memory if it's not needed. The disadvantage is that you have to explicitly list all your functions in your environment file.

ksh93's integration of `PATH` and `FPATH` searching thus simplifies the way you add shell functions to your personal shell function "library."

POSIX functions

As mentioned earlier, functions defined using the POSIX syntax obey POSIX semantics and not Korn shell semantics:

```
functname () {
    shell commands
}
```

The best way to understand this is to think of a POSIX function as being like a dot script. Actions within the body of the function affect *all* the state of the current script. In contrast, Korn shell functions have much less shared state with the parent shell, although they are not identical to totally separate scripts.

---

* *ksh93* point releases *h* through *l+* used a similar but more restricted mechanism, via a file named *.fpath*, and they hard-wired the setting of the library path variable. As this feature was not widespread, it was generalized into a single file starting with point release *m*.

† *autoload* is actually an alias for *typeset –fu*.

The technical details follow; they include information that we haven't covered yet. So come back and reread this section after you've learned about the *typeset* command in Chapter 6 and about traps in Chapter 8.

- POSIX functions share variables with the parent script. Korn shell functions can have their own local variables.

- POSIX functions share traps with the parent script. Korn shell functions can have their own local traps.

- POSIX functions cannot be recursive (call themselves).* Korn shell functions can.

- When a POSIX function is run, $0 is *not* changed to the name of the function.

If you use the dot command with the name of a Korn shell function, that function will obey POSIX semantics, affecting all the state (variables and traps) of the parent shell:

```
$ function demo {                          Define a Korn shell function
>    typeset myvar=3                        Set a local variable myvar
>    print "demo: myvar is $myvar"
> }
$ myvar=4                                   Set the global myvar
$ demo ; print "global: myvar is $myvar"    Run the function
demo: myvar is 3
global: myvar is 4
$ . demo                                    Run with POSIX semantics
demo: myvar is 3
$ print "global: myvar is $myvar"           See the results
global: myvar is 3
```

Shell Variables

A major piece of the Korn shell's programming functionality relates to shell variables. We've already seen the basics of variables. To recap briefly: they are named places to store data, usually in the form of character strings, and their values can be obtained by preceding their names with dollar signs ($). Certain variables, called *environment variables*, are conventionally named in all capital letters, and their values are made known (with the *export* statement) to subprocesses.

This section presents the basics for shell variables. Discussion of certain advanced features is delayed until later in the chapter, after covering regular expressions.

If you are a programmer, you already know that just about every major programming language uses variables in some way; in fact, an important way of characterizing differences between languages is comparing their facilities for variables.

---

* This is a restriction imposed by the Korn shell, not by the POSIX standard.

The chief difference between the Korn shell's variable schema and those of conventional languages is that the Korn shell's schema places heavy emphasis on character strings. (Thus it has more in common with a special-purpose language like SNOBOL than a general-purpose one like Pascal.) This is also true of the Bourne shell and the C shell, but the Korn shell goes beyond them by having additional mechanisms for handling integers and double-precision floating point numbers explicitly, as well as simple arrays.

Positional Parameters

As we have already seen, you can define values for variables with statements of the form *varname=value*, e.g.:

```
$ fred=bob
$ print "$fred"
bob
```

Some environment variables are predefined by the shell when you log in. There are other built-in variables that are vital to shell programming. We look at a few of them now and save the others for later.

The most important special, built-in variables are called *positional parameters*. These hold the command-line arguments to scripts when they are invoked. Positional parameters have names 1, 2, 3, etc., meaning that their values are denoted by $1, $2, $3, etc. There is also a positional parameter 0, whose value is the name of the script (i.e., the command typed in to invoke it).

Two special variables contain all of the positional parameters (except positional parameter 0): * and @. The difference between them is subtle but important, and it's apparent only when they are within double quotes.

"$*" is a single string that consists of all of the positional parameters, separated by the first character in the variable IFS (internal field separator), which is a space, TAB, and newline by default. On the other hand, "$@" is equal to "$1" "$2" ... "$N", where N is the number of positional parameters. That is, it's equal to N separate double-quoted strings, which are separated by spaces. We'll explore the ramifications of this difference in a little while.

The variable # holds the number of positional parameters (as a character string). All of these variables are "read-only," meaning that you can't assign new values to them within scripts. (They can be changed, just not via assignment. See the section "Changing the positional parameters," later in this chapter.)

For example, assume that you have the following simple shell script:

```
print "fred: $*"
print "$0: $1 and $2"
print "$# arguments"
```

Assume further that the script is called *fred*. Then if you type `fred bob dave`, you will see the following output:

```
fred: bob dave
fred: bob and dave
2 arguments
```

In this case, $3, $4, etc., are all unset, which means that the shell substitutes the empty (or null) string for them (unless the option *nounset* is turned on).

Positional parameters in functions

Shell functions use positional parameters and special variables like * and # in exactly the same way that shell scripts do. If you wanted to define *fred* as a function, you could put the following in your *.profile* or environment file:

```
function fred {
    print "fred: $*"
    print "$0: $1 and $2"
    print "$# arguments"
}
```

You get the same result if you type `fred bob dave`.

Typically, several shell functions are defined within a single shell script. Therefore each function needs to handle its own arguments, which in turn means that each function needs to keep track of positional parameters separately. Sure enough, each function has its own copies of these variables (even though functions don't run in their own subprocess, as scripts do); we say that such variables are *local* to the function.

Other variables defined within functions are not local; they are *global*, meaning that their values are known throughout the entire shell script.* For example, assume that you have a shell script called *ascript* that contains this:

```
function afunc {
    print in function $0: $1 $2
    var1="in function"
}
var1="outside of function"
print var1: $var1
print $0: $1 $2
```

---

* However, see the section on *typeset* in Chapter 6 for a way of making variables local to functions.

```
afunc funcarg1 funcarg2
print var1: $var1
print $0: $1 $2
```

If you invoke this script by typing `ascript arg1 arg2`, you will see this output:

```
var1: outside of function
ascript: arg1 arg2
in function afunc: funcarg1 funcarg2
var1: in function
ascript: arg1 arg2
```

In other words, the function *afunc* changes the value of the variable `var1` from "outside of function" to "in function," and that change is known outside the function, while $0, $1, and $2 have different values in the function and the main script. Figure 4-2 shows this graphically.

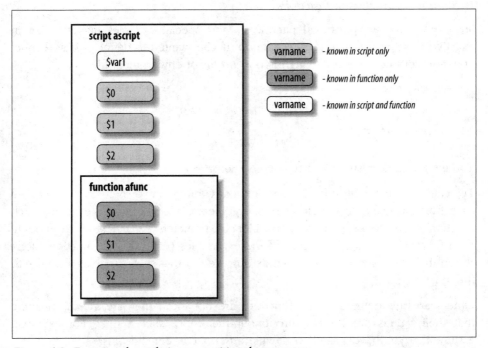

Figure 4-2. Functions have their own positional parameters

It is possible to make other variables local to functions by using the *typeset* command, which we'll see in Chapter 6. Now that we have this background, let's take a closer look at `"$@"` and `"$*"`. These variables are two of the shell's greatest idiosyncrasies, so we'll discuss some of the most common sources of confusion.

• Why are the elements of `"$*"` separated by the first character of IFS instead of just spaces? To give you output flexibility. As a simple example, let's say you

want to print a list of positional parameters separated by commas. This script
would do it:

```
IFS=,
print "$*"
```

Changing IFS in a script is fairly risky, but it's probably OK as long as nothing
else in the script depends on it. If this script were called *arglist*, the command
arglist bob dave ed would produce the output bob,dave,ed. Chapter 10 contains another example of changing IFS.

• Why does "$@" act like *N* separate double-quoted strings? To allow you to use
them again as separate values. For example, say you want to call a function
within your script with the same list of positional parameters, like this:

```
function countargs {
    print "$# args."
}
```

Assume your script is called with the same arguments as *arglist* above. Then if
it contains the command countargs "$*", the function prints 1 args. But if the
command is countargs "$@", the function prints 3 args.

Being able to retrieve the arguments as they came in is also important in case
you need to preserve any embedded white space. If your script was invoked
with the arguments "hi", "howdy", and "hello there", here are the different
results you might get:

```
$ countargs $*
4 args
$ countargs "$*"
1 args
$ countargs $@
4 args
$ countargs "$@"
3 args
```

Because "$@" always exactly preserves arguments, we use it in just about all
the example programs in this book.

Changing the positional parameters

Occasionally, it's useful to change the positional parameters. We've already mentioned that you cannot set them directly, using an assignment such as 1="first".
However, the built-in command *set* can be used for this purpose.

The *set* command is perhaps the single most complicated and overloaded command in the shell. It takes a large number of options, which are discussed in
Chapter 9. What we care about for the moment is that additional non-option arguments to *set* replace the positional parameters. Suppose our script was invoked
with the three arguments "bob", "fred", and "dave". Then countargs "$@" tells us

that we have three arguments. Upon using *set* to change the positional parameters, $# is updated too.

```
$ set one two three "four not five"    Change the positional parameters
$ countargs "$@"                       Verify the change
4 args
```

The *set* command also works inside a shell function. The shell function's positional parameters are changed, but not those of the calling script:

```
$ function testme {
>       countargs "$@"                 Show the original number of parameters
>       set a b c                      Now change them
>       countargs "$@"                 Print the new count
> }
$ testme 1 2 3 4 5 6                   Run the function
6 args                                 Original count
3 args                                 New count
$ countargs "$@"                       No change to invoking shell's parameters
4 args
```

More on Variable Syntax

Before we show the many things you can do with shell variables, we have to make a confession: the syntax of $*varname* for taking the value of a variable is not quite accurate. Actually, it's the simple form of the more general syntax, which is ${*varname*}.

Why two syntaxes? For one thing, the more general syntax is necessary if your code refers to more than nine positional parameters: you must use ${10} for the tenth instead of $10. (This ensures compatibility with the Bourne shell, where $10 means ${1}0.) Aside from that, consider the Chapter 3 example of setting your primary prompt variable (PS1) to your login name:

```
PS1="($LOGNAME)-> "
```

This happens to work because the right parenthesis immediately following LOGNAME isn't a valid character for a variable name, so the shell doesn't mistake it for part of the variable name. Now suppose that, for some reason, you want your prompt to be your login name followed by an underscore. If you type:

```
PS1="$LOGNAME_ "
```

then the shell tries to use "LOGNAME_" as the name of the variable, i.e., to take the value of $LOGNAME_. Since there is no such variable, the value defaults to *null* (the empty string, ""), and PS1 is set just to a single space.

For this reason, the full syntax for taking the value of a variable is ${*varname*}. So if we used:

```
PS1="${LOGNAME}_ "
```

we would get the desired *yourname_*. It is safe to omit the curly braces ({ }) if the variable name is followed by a character that isn't a letter, digit, or underscore.

Appending to a Variable

As mentioned, Korn shell variables tend to be string-oriented. One operation that's very common is to append a new value onto an existing variable. (For example, collecting a set of options into a single string.) Since time immemorial, this was done by taking advantage of variable substitution inside double quotes:

```
myopts="$myopts $newopt"
```

The values of myopts and newopt are concatenated together into a single string, and the result is then assigned back to myopts. Starting with *ksh93j*, the Korn shell provides a more efficient and intuitive mechanism for doing this:

```
myopts+=" $newopt"
```

This accomplishes the same thing, but it is more efficient, and it also makes it clear that the new value is being added onto the string. (In C, the += operator adds the value on the right to the variable on the left; x += 42 is the same as x = x + 42.)

Compound Variables

ksh93 introduces a new feature, called *compound variables*. They are similar in nature to a Pascal or Ada record or a C struct, and they allow you to group related items together under the same name. Here are some examples:

```
now="May 20 2001 19:44:57"        Assign current date to variable now
now.hour=19                       Set the hour
now.minute=44                     Set the minute
...
```

Note the use of the period in the variable's name. Here, now is called the *parent* variable, and it must exist (i.e., have a value) before you can assign a value to an individual component (such as hour or minute). To access a compound variable, you must enclose the variable's name in curly braces. If you don't, the period ends the shell's scan for the variable's name:

```
$ print ${now.hour}
19
$ print $now.hour
May 20 2001 19:44:57.hour
```

Compound Variable Assignment

Assigning to individual elements of a compound variable is tedious. In particular the requirement that the parent variable exist previously leads to an awkward programming style:

```
person="John Q. Public"
person.firstname=John
person.initial=Q.
person.lastname=Public
```

Fortunately, you can use a *compound assignment* to do it all in one fell swoop:

```
person=(firstname=John initial=Q. lastname=Public)
```

You can retrieve the value of either the entire variable, or a component, using *print*.

```
$ print $person                              Simple print
( lastname=Public initial=Q. firstname=John )
$ print -r "$person"                         Print in full glory
(
        lastname=Public
        initial=Q.
        firstname=John
)
$ print ${person.initial}                    Print just the middle initial
Q.
```

The second *print* command preserves the whitespace that the Korn shell provides when returning the value of a compound variable. The *−r* option to *print* is discussed in Chapter 7.

 The order of the components is different from what was used in the initial assignment. This order depends upon how the Korn shell manages compound variables internally and cannot be controlled by the programmer.

A second assignment syntax exists, similar to the first:

```
person=(typeset firstname=John initial=Q. lastname=Public ;
        typeset -i age=42)
```

By using the *typeset* command, you can specify that a variable is a number instead of a string. Here, `person.age` is an integer variable. The rest remain strings. The *typeset* command and its options are presented in Chapter 6. (You can also use *readonly* to declare that a component variable cannot be changed.)

Just as you may use += to append to a regular variable, you can add components to a compound variable as well:

```
person+= (typeset spouse=Jane)
```

A space is allowed after the = but not before. This is true for compound assignments with both = and +=.

The Korn shell has additional syntaxes for compound assignment that apply only to array variables; they are also discussed in Chapter 6.

Finally, we'll mention that the Korn shell has a special compound variable named .sh. The various components almost all relate to features we haven't covered yet, except ${.sh.version}, which tells you the version of the Korn shell that you have:

```
$ print ${.sh.version}
Version M 1993-12-28 m
```

We will see another component of .sh later in this chapter, and the other components are covered as we introduce the features they relate to.

Indirect Variable References (namerefs)

Most of the time, as we've seen so far, you manipulate variables directly, by name (x=1, for example). The Korn shell allows you to manipulate variables *indirectly*, using something called a *nameref*. You create a nameref using *typeset –n*, or the more convenient predefined alias, *nameref*. Here is a simple example:

```
$ name="bill"                      Set initial value
$ nameref firstname=name           Set up the nameref
$ print $firstname                 Actually references variable name
bill
$ firstname="arnold"               Now change the indirect reference
$ print $name                      Shazzam! Original variable is changed
arnold
```

To find out the name of the real variable being referenced by the nameref, use ${!*variable*}:

```
$ print ${!firstname}
name
```

At first glance, this doesn't seem to be very useful. The power of namerefs comes into play when you pass a variable's *name* to a function, and you want that function to be able to update the value of that variable. The following example illustrates how it works:

```
$ date                                Current day and time
Wed May 23 17:49:44 IDT 2001
$ function getday {                   Define a function
>     typeset -n day=$1               Set up the nameref
>     day=$(date | awk '{ print $1 }')   Actually change it
> }
$ today=now                           Set initial value
$ getday today                        Run the function
$ print $today                        Display new value
Wed
```

The default output of *date*(1) looks like this:

```
$ date
Wed Nov 14 11:52:38 IST 2001
```

The *getday* function uses *awk* to print the first field, which is the day of the week. The result of this operation, which is done inside command substitution (described later in this chapter), is assigned to the local variable day. But day is a nameref; the assignment actually updates the global variable today. Without the nameref facility, you have to resort to advanced tricks like using *eval* (see Chapter 7) to make something like this happen.

To remove a nameref, use unset -n, which removes the nameref itself, instead of unsetting the variable the nameref is a reference to. Finally, note that variables that are namerefs may not have periods in their names (i.e., be components of a compound variable). They may, though, be references to a compound variable.

String Operators

The curly-brace syntax allows for the shell's *string operators*. String operators allow you to manipulate values of variables in various useful ways without having to write full-blown programs or resort to external Unix utilities. You can do a lot with string-handling operators even if you haven't yet mastered the programming features we'll see in later chapters.

In particular, string operators let you do the following:

*   Ensure that variables exist (i.e., are defined and have non-null values)

*   Set default values for variables

*   Catch errors that result from variables not being set

*   Remove portions of variables' values that match patterns

Syntax of String Operators

The basic idea behind the syntax of string operators is that special characters that denote operations are inserted between the variable's name and the right curly brace. Any argument that the operator may need is inserted to the operator's right.

The first group of string-handling operators tests for the existence of variables and allows substitutions of default values under certain conditions. These are listed in Table 4-2.

Table 4-2. Substitution operators

Operator	Substitution
${varname:-word}	If *varname* exists and isn't null, return its value; otherwise return *word*.
Purpose:	Returning a default value if the variable is undefined.
Example:	${count:-0} evaluates to 0 if count is undefined.
${varname:=word}	If *varname* exists and isn't null, return its value; otherwise set it to *word* and then return its value.[a]
Purpose:	Setting a variable to a default value if it is undefined.
Example:	${count:=0} sets count to 0 if it is undefined.
${varname:?message}	If *varname* exists and isn't null, return its value; otherwise print varname: *message*, and abort the current command or script. Omitting *message* produces the default message parameter null or not set. Note, however, that interactive shells do not abort.
Purpose:	Catching errors that result from variables being undefined.
Example:	${count:?"undefined!"} prints count: undefined! and exits if count is undefined.
${varname:+word}	If *varname* exists and isn't null, return *word*; otherwise return null.
Purpose:	Testing for the existence of a variable.
Example:	${count:+1} returns 1 (which could mean "true") if count is defined.

[a] Pascal, Modula, and Ada programmers may find it helpful to recognize the similarity of this to the assignment operators in those languages.

The colon (:) in each of these operators is actually optional. If the colon is omitted, then change "exists and isn't null" to "exists" in each definition, i.e., the operator tests for existence only.

The first two of these operators are ideal for setting defaults for command-line arguments in case the user omits them. We'll actually use all four in Task 4-1, which is our first programming task.

Task 4-1

You have a large album collection, and you want to write some software to keep track of it. Assume that you have a file of data on how many albums you have by each artist. Lines in the file look like this:

```
14      Bach, J.S.
1       Balachander, S.
21      Beatles
6       Blakey, Art
```

Write a program that prints the *N* highest lines, i.e., the *N* artists by whom you have the most albums. The default for *N* should be 10. The program should take one argument for the name of the input file and an optional second argument for how many lines to print.

By far the best approach to this type of script is to use built-in Unix utilities, combining them with I/O redirectors and pipes. This is the classic "building-block" philosophy of Unix that is another reason for its great popularity with program-mers. The building-block technique lets us write a first version of the script that is only one line long:

```
sort -nr "$1" | head -${2:-10}
```

Here is how this works: the *sort*(1) program sorts the data in the file whose name is given as the first argument ($1). (The double quotes allow for spaces or other unusual characters in file names, and also prevent wildcard expansion.) The −*n* option tells *sort* to interpret the first word on each line as a number (instead of as a character string); the −*r* tells it to reverse the comparisons, so as to sort in descending order.

The output of *sort* is piped into the *head*(1) utility, which, when given the argu-ment −*N*, prints the first *N* lines of its input on the standard output. The expression -${2:-10} evaluates to a dash (–) followed by the second argument, if it is given, or to 10 if it's not; notice that the variable in this expression is 2, which is the sec-ond positional parameter.

Assume the script we want to write is called *highest*. Then if the user types high-est myfile, the line that actually runs is:

```
sort -nr myfile | head -10
```

Or if the user types highest myfile 22, the line that runs is:

```
sort -nr myfile | head -22
```

Make sure you understand how the :- string operator provides a default value.

This is a perfectly good, runnable script—but it has a few problems. First, its one line is a bit cryptic. While this isn't much of a problem for such a tiny script, it's not wise to write long, elaborate scripts in this manner. A few minor changes makes the code more readable.

First, we can add comments to the code; anything between # and the end of a line is a comment. At minimum, the script should start with a few comment lines that indicate what the script does and the arguments it accepts. Next, we can improve the variable names by assigning the values of the positional parameters to regular variables with mnemonic names. Last, we can add blank lines to space things out; blank lines, like comments, are ignored. Here is a more readable version:

```
#       highest filename [howmany]
#
#       Print howmany highest-numbered lines in file filename.
#       The input file is assumed to have lines that start with
#       numbers.  Default for howmany is 10.

filename=$1

howmany=${2:-10}
sort -nr "$filename" | head -$howmany
```

The square brackets around howmany in the comments adhere to the convention in Unix documentation that square brackets denote optional arguments.

The changes we just made improve the code's readability but not how it runs. What if the user invoked the script without any arguments? Remember that positional parameters default to null if they aren't defined. If there are no arguments, then $1 and $2 are both null. The variable howmany ($2) is set up to default to 10, but there is no default for filename ($1). The result would be that this command runs:

```
sort -nr | head -10
```

As it happens, if *sort* is called without a filename argument, it expects input to come from standard input, e.g., a pipe (|) or a user's keyboard. Since it doesn't have the pipe, it will expect the keyboard. This means that the script will appear to hang! Although you could always type CTRL-D or CTRL-C to get out of the script, a naive user might not know this.

Therefore we need to make sure that the user supplies at least one argument. There are a few ways of doing this; one of them involves another string operator. We'll replace the line:

```
filename=$1
```

with:

```
filename=${1:?"filename missing."}
```

This causes two things to happen if a user invokes the script without any arguments: first, the shell prints the somewhat unfortunate message to the standard
error output:

```
highest: line 1: : filename missing.
```

Second, the script exits without running the remaining code.

With a somewhat "kludgy" modification, we can get a slightly better error message. Consider this code:

```
filename=$1
filename=${filename:?"missing."}
```

This results in the message:

```
highest: line 2: filename: filename missing.
```

(Make sure you understand why.) Of course, there are ways of printing whatever
message is desired; we'll find out how in Chapter 5.

Before we move on, we'll look more closely at the two remaining operators in
Table 4-2 and see how we can incorporate them into our task solution. The :=
operator does roughly the same thing as :-, except that it has the side effect of
setting the value of the variable to the given word if the variable doesn't exist.

Therefore we would like to use := in our script in place of :-, but we can't; we'd
be trying to set the value of a positional parameter, which is not allowed. But if
we replaced:

```
howmany=${2:-10}
```

with just:

```
howmany=$2
```

and moved the substitution down to the actual command line (as we did at the
start), then we could use the := operator:

```
sort -nr "$filename" | head -${howmany:=10}
```

Using := has the added benefit of setting the value of howmany to 10 in case we
need it afterwards in later versions of the script.

The final substitution operator is `:+`. Here is how we can use it in our example: let's say we want to give the user the option of adding a header line to the script's output. If he types the option *–h*, the output will be preceded by the line:

```
ALBUMS ARTIST
```

Assume further that this option ends up in the variable `header`, i.e., `$header` is `-h` if the option is set or null if not. (Later we see how to do this without disturbing the other positional parameters.)

The expression:

```
${header:+"ALBUMS ARTIST\n"}
```

yields null if the variable `header` is null or `ALBUMS ARTIST\n` if it is non-null. This means that we can put the line:

```
print -n ${header:+"ALBUMS ARTIST\n"}
```

right before the command line that does the actual work. The *–n* option to *print* causes it *not* to print a newline after printing its arguments. Therefore this *print* statement prints nothing—not even a blank line—if `header` is null; otherwise it prints the header line and a newline (\n).

Patterns and Regular Expressions

We'll continue refining our solution to Task 4-1 later in this chapter. The next type of string operator is used to match portions of a variable's string value against *patterns*. Patterns, as we saw in Chapter 1, are strings that can contain wildcard characters (`*`, `?`, and `[ ]` for character sets and ranges).

Wildcards have been standard features of all Unix shells going back (at least) to the Version 6 Thompson shell.* But the Korn shell is the first shell to add to their capabilities. It adds a set of operators, called *regular expression* (or *regexp* for short) operators, that give it much of the string-matching power of advanced Unix utilities like *awk*(1), *egrep*(1) (extended *grep*(1)), and the Emacs editor, albeit with a different syntax. These capabilities go beyond those that you may be used to in other Unix utilities like *grep*, *sed*(1), and *vi*(1).

Advanced Unix users will find the Korn shell's regular expression capabilities useful for script writing, although they border on overkill. (Part of the problem is the inevitable syntactic clash with the shell's myriad other special characters.) Therefore we won't go into great detail about regular expressions here. For more comprehensive information, the "very last word" on practical regular expressions in

---

* The Version 6 shell was written by Ken Thompson. Stephen Bourne wrote the Bourne shell for Version 7.

Unix is *Mastering Regular Expressions,* by Jeffrey E. F. Friedl. A more gentle introduction may found in the second edition of *sed & awk,* by Dale Dougherty and Arnold Robbins. Both are published by O'Reilly & Associates. If you are already comfortable with *awk* or *egrep,* you may want to skip the following introductory section and go to the section "Korn shell versus awk/egrep regular expressions," later in this chapter, where we explain the shell's regular expression mechanism by comparing it with the syntax used in those two utilities. Otherwise, read on.

Regular expression basics

Think of regular expressions as strings that match patterns more powerfully than the standard shell wildcard schema. Regular expressions began as an idea in theoretical computer science, but they have found their way into many nooks and crannies of everyday, practical computing. The syntax used to represent them may vary, but the concepts are very much the same.

A shell regular expression can contain regular characters, standard wildcard characters, and additional operators that are more powerful than wildcards. Each such operator has the form *x(exp)*, where *x* is the particular operator and *exp* is any regular expression (often simply a regular string). The operator determines how many occurrences of *exp* a string that matches the pattern can contain. Table 4-3 describes the shell's regular expression operators and their meanings.

Table 4-3. Regular expression operators

Operator	Meaning
*(exp)	0 or more occurrences of *exp*
+(exp)	1 or more occurrences of *exp*
?(exp)	0 or 1 occurrences of *exp*
@(exp1|exp2|...)	Exactly one of *exp1* or *exp2* or ...
!(exp)	Anything that doesn't match *exp*[a]

[a] Actually, !(exp) is not a regular expression operator by the standard technical definition, although it is a handy extension.

As shown for the @(*exp1*|*exp2*|...) pattern, an *exp* within any of the Korn shell operators can be a series of *exp1*|*exp2*|... alternatives.

A little-known alternative notation is to separate each *exp* with the ampersand character, &. In this case, *all* the alternative expressions must match. Think of the | as meaning "or," while the & means "and." (You can, in fact, use both of them in the same pattern list. The & has higher precedence, with the meaning "match this and that, OR match the next thing.") Table 4-4 provides some example uses of the shell's regular expression operators.

Table 4-4. Regular expression operator examples

Expression	Matches
x	*x*
* (*x*)	Null string, *x*, *xx*, *xxx*, ...
+ (*x*)	*x*, *xx*, *xxx*, ...
? (*x*)	Null string, *x*
! (*x*)	Any string except *x*
@ (*x*)	*x* (see below)

Regular expressions are extremely useful when dealing with arbitrary text, as you already know if you have used *grep* or the regular-expression capabilities of any Unix editor. They aren't nearly as useful for matching filenames and other simple types of information with which shell users typically work. Furthermore, most things you can do with the shell's regular expression operators can also be done (though possibly with more keystrokes and less efficiency) by piping the output of a shell command through *grep* or *egrep*.

Nevertheless, here are a few examples of how shell regular expressions can solve filename-listing problems. Some of these will come in handy in later chapters as pieces of solutions to larger tasks.

1. The Emacs editor supports customization files whose names end in *.el* (for Emacs LISP) or *.elc* (for Emacs LISP Compiled). List all Emacs customization files in the current directory.

2. In a directory of C source code, list all files that are not necessary. Assume that "necessary" files end in .c or .h or are named *Makefile* or *README*.

3. Filenames in the OpenVMS operating system end in a semicolon followed by a version number, e.g., *fred.bob;23*. List all OpenVMS-style filenames in the current directory.

Here are the solutions:

1. In the first of these, we are looking for files that end in *.el* with an optional *c*. The expression that matches this is `*.el?(c)`.

2. The second example depends on the four standard subexpressions `*.c`, `*.h`, `Makefile`, and `README`. The entire expression is `!(*.c|*.h|Makefile|README)`, which matches anything that does not match any of the four possibilities.

3. The solution to the third example starts with `*\;`, the shell wildcard `*` followed by a backslash-escaped semicolon. Then, we could use the regular expression `+([0-9])`, which matches one or more characters in the range `[0-9]`, i.e., one or more digits. This is almost correct (and probably close enough), but it

doesn't take into account that the first digit cannot be 0. Therefore the correct expression is `*\;[1-9]*([0-9])`, which matches anything that ends with a semicolon, a digit from 1 to 9, and zero or more digits from 0 to 9.

POSIX character class additions

The POSIX standard formalizes the meaning of regular expression characters and operators. The standard defines two classes of regular expressions: Basic Regular Expressions (BREs), which are the kind used by *grep* and *sed*, and Extended Regular Expressions, which are the kind used by *egrep* and *awk*.

In order to accommodate non-English environments, the POSIX standard enhanced the ability of character set ranges (e.g., [a-z]) to match characters not in the English alphabet. For example, the French è is an alphabetic character, but the typical character class [a-z] would not match it. Additionally, the standard provides for sequences of characters that should be treated as a single unit when matching and collating (sorting) string data. (For example, there are locales where the two characters ch are treated as a unit and must be matched and sorted that way.)

POSIX also changed what had been common terminology. What we saw earlier in Chapter 1 as a "range expression" is often called a "character class" in the Unix literature. It is now called a "bracket expression" in the POSIX standard. Within bracket expressions, besides literal characters such as a, ;, and so on, you can also have additional components:

Character classes

A POSIX character class consists of keywords bracketed by [: and :]. The keywords describe different classes of characters such as alphabetic characters, control characters, and so on (see Table 4-5).

Collating symbols

A collating symbol is a multicharacter sequence that should be treated as a unit. It consists of the characters bracketed by [. and .].

Equivalence classes

An equivalence class lists a set of characters that should be considered equivalent, such as e and è. It consists of a named element from the locale, bracketed by [= and =].

All three of these constructs must appear inside the square brackets of a bracket expression. For example [[:alpha:]!] matches any single alphabetic character or the exclamation point; [[.ch.]] matches the collating element ch but does not match just the letter c or the letter h. In a French locale, [[=e=]] might match any of e, è, or é. Classes and matching characters are shown in Table 4-5.

Table 4-5. POSIX character classes

Class	Matching characters
`[:alnum:]`	Alphanumeric characters
`[:alpha:]`	Alphabetic characters
`[:blank:]`	Space and tab characters
`[:cntrl:]`	Control characters
`[:digit:]`	Numeric characters
`[:graph:]`	Printable and visible (non-space) characters
`[:lower:]`	Lowercase characters
`[:print:]`	Printable characters (includes whitespace)
`[:punct:]`	Punctuation characters
`[:space:]`	Whitespace characters
`[:upper:]`	Uppercase characters
`[:xdigit:]`	Hexadecimal digits

The Korn shell supports all of these features within its pattern matching facilities. The POSIX character class names are the most useful, because they work in different locales.

The following section compares Korn shell regular expressions to analogous features in *awk* and *egrep*. If you aren't familiar with these, skip to the section "Pattern-Matching Operators."

Korn shell versus awk/egrep regular expressions

Table 4-6 is an expansion of Table 4-3: the middle column shows the equivalents in *awk/egrep* of the shell's regular expression operators.

Table 4-6. Shell versus egrep/awk regular expression operators

Korn shell	egrep/awk	Meaning
`*(exp)`	exp*	0 or more occurrences of *exp*
`+(exp)`	exp+	1 or more occurrences of *exp*
`?(exp)`	exp?	0 or 1 occurrences of *exp*
`@(exp1|exp2|...)`	exp1|exp2|...	*exp1* or *exp2* or ...
`!(exp)`	(none)	Anything that doesn't match *exp*
`\N`	\N (grep)	Match same text as matched by previous parenthesized subexpression number *N*

These equivalents are close but not quite exact. Because the shell would interpret an expression like `dave|fred|bob` as a pipeline of commands, you must use `@(dave|fred|bob)` for alternates by themselves.

The *grep* command has a feature called *backreferences* (or *backrefs*, for short). This facility provides a shorthand for repeating parts of a regular expression as part of a larger whole. It works as follows:

```
grep '\(abc\).*\1' file1 file2
```

This matches *abc*, followed by any number of characters, followed again by *abc*. Up to nine parenthesized sub-expressions may be referenced this way. The Korn shell provides an analogous capability. If you use one or more regular expression patterns within a full pattern, you can refer to previous ones using the \N notation as for *grep*.

For example:

- @(dave|fred|bob) matches dave, fred, or bob.

- @(*dave*&*fred*) matches davefred, and freddave. (Notice the need for the * characters.)

- @(fred)*\1 matches freddavefred, fredbobfred, and so on.

- *(dave|fred|bob) means, "0 or more occurrences of dave, fred, or bob". This expression matches strings like the null string, dave, davedave, fred, bobfred, bobbobdavefredbobfred, etc.

- +(dave|fred|bob) matches any of the above except the null string.

- ?(dave|fred|bob) matches the null string, dave, fred, or bob.

- !(dave|fred|bob) matches anything except dave, fred, or bob.

It is worth reemphasizing that shell regular expressions can still contain standard shell wildcards. Thus, the shell wildcard ? (match any single character) is equivalent to . in *egrep* or *awk*, and the shell's character set operator [...] is the same as in those utilities.* For example, the expression +([[:digit:]]) matches a number, i.e., one or more digits. The shell wildcard character * is equivalent to the shell regular expression *(?). You can even nest the regular expressions: +([[:digit:]]|!([[:upper:]])) matches one or more digits or non-uppercase letters.

Two *egrep* and *awk* regexp operators do not have equivalents in the Korn shell:

- The beginning- and end-of-line operators ^ and $.

- The beginning- and end-of-word operators \< and \>.

These are hardly necessary, since the Korn shell doesn't normally operate on text files and does parse strings into words itself. (Essentially, the ^ and $ are implied

---

* And, for that matter, the same as in *grep*, *sed*, *ed*, *vi*, etc. One notable difference is that the shell uses
  ! inside [...] for negation, while the various utilities all use ^.

as always being there. Surround a pattern with * characters to disable this.) Read on for even more features in the very latest version of *ksh*.

Pattern matching with regular expressions

Starting with *ksh93l*, the shell provides a number of additional regular expression capabilities. We discuss them here separately, because your version of *ksh93* quite likely doesn't have them, unless you download a *ksh93* binary or build *ksh93* from source. The facilities break down as follows.

New pattern matching operators
Several new pattern matching facilities are available. They are described briefly in Table 4-7. More discussion follows after the table.

Subpatterns with options
Special parenthesized subpatterns may contain options that control matching within the subpattern or the rest of the expression.

New [:word:] character class
The character class `[:word:]` within a bracket expression matches any character that is "word constituent." This is basically any alphanumeric character or the underscore (_).

Escape sequences recognized within subpatterns
A number of escape sequences are recognized and treated specially within parenthesized expressions.

Table 4-7. New pattern matching operators in ksh93l and later

Operator	Meaning
{*N*}(*exp*)	Exactly *N* occurrences of *exp*
{*N,M*}(*exp*)	Between *N* and *M* occurrences of *exp*
*-(*exp*)	0 or more occurrences of *exp*, shortest match
+-(*exp*)	1 or more occurrences of *exp*, shortest match
?-(*exp*)	0 or 1 occurrences of *exp*, shortest match
@-(*exp1* | *exp2* | ...)	Exactly one of *exp1* or *exp2* or ..., shortest match
{*N*}-(*exp*)	Exactly *N* occurrences of *exp*, shortest match
{*N,M*}-(*exp*)	Between *N* and *M* occurrences of *exp*, shortest match

The first two operators in this table match facilities in *egrep*(1), called *interval expressions*. They let you specify that you want to match exactly *N* items, no more and no less, or that you want to match between *N* and *M* items.

The rest of the operators perform shortest or "non-greedy" matching. Normally, regular expressions match the *longest* possible text. A non-greedy match is one of the shortest possible text that matches. Non-greedy matching was first popularized by the *perl* language. These operators work with the pattern matching and substitution operators described in the next section; we delay examples of greedy vs. non-greedy matching until there. Filename wildcarding effectively always does greedy matching.

Within operations such as @(...), you can provide a special subpattern that enables or disables options for case independent and greedy matching. This subpattern has one of the following forms:

~(+*options*:*pattern list*)   *Enable options*
~(-*options*:*pattern list*)   *Disable options*

The *options* are one or both of i for case-independent matching and g for greedy matching. If the :*pattern list* is omitted, the options apply to the rest of the enclosing pattern. If provided, they apply to just that pattern list. Omitting the *options* is possible, as well, but doing so doesn't really provide you with any new value.

The bracket expression [[:word:]] is a shorthand for [[:alnum:]_]. It is a notational convenience, but one that can increase program legiblity.

Within parenthesized expressions, *ksh* recognizes all the standard ANSI C escape sequences, and they have their usual meaning. (See the the section "Extended quoting," in Chapter 7.) Additionally, the escape sequences listed in Table 4-8 are recognized and can be used for pattern matching.

Table 4-8. Regular expression escape sequences

Escape sequence	Meaning
\d	Same as [[:digit:]]
\D	Same as [![:digit:]]
\s	Same as [[:space:]]
\S	Same as [![:space:]]
\w	Same as [[:word:]]
\W	Same as [![:word:]]

Whew! This is all fairly heady stuff. If you feel a bit overwhelmed by it, don't worry. As you learn more about regular expressions and shell programming and begin to do more and more complex text processing tasks, you'll come to appreciate the fact that you can do all this *within the shell itself,* instead of having to resort to external programs such as *sed, awk,* or *perl.*

Pattern-Matching Operators

Table 4-9 lists the Korn shell's pattern-matching operators.

Table 4-9. Pattern-matching operators

Operator	Meaning
${*variable*#*pattern*}	If the pattern matches the beginning of the variable's value, delete the shortest part that matches and return the rest.
${*variable*##*pattern*}	If the pattern matches the beginning of the variable's value, delete the longest part that matches and return the rest.
${{*variable*%*pattern*}	If the pattern matches the end of the variable's value, delete the shortest part that matches and return the rest.
${*variable*%%*pattern*}	If the pattern matches the end of the variable's value, delete the longest part that matches and return the rest.

These can be hard to remember, so here's a handy mnemonic device: # matches the front because number signs *precede* numbers; % matches the rear because percent signs *follow* numbers. Another mnemonic comes from the typical placement (in the U.S.A., anyway) of the # and % keys on the keyboard. Relative to each other, the # is on the left, and the % is on the right.

The classic use for pattern-matching operators is in stripping components from pathnames, such as directory prefixes and filename suffixes. With that in mind, here is an example that shows how all of the operators work. Assume that the variable path has the value /home/billr/mem/long.file.name; then:

```
Expression        Result
${path##/*/}                    long.file.name
${path#/*/}            billr/mem/long.file.name
$path            /home/billr/mem/long.file.name
${path%.*}       /home/billr/mem/long.file
${path%%.*}      /home/billr/mem/long
```

The two patterns used here are /*/, which matches anything between two slashes, and .*, which matches a dot followed by anything.

Starting with *ksh93l*, these operators automatically set the .sh.match array variable. This is discussed in the section "The .sh.match Variable," later in this chapter.

We will incorporate one of these operators into our next programming task, Task 4-2.

Task 4-2

You are writing a C compiler, and you want to use the Korn shell for your front-end.*

Think of a C compiler as a pipeline of data processing components. C source code is input to the beginning of the pipeline, and object code comes out of the end; there are several steps in between. The shell script's task, among many other things, is to control the flow of data through the components and designate output files.

You need to write the part of the script that takes the name of the input C source file and creates from it the name of the output object code file. That is, you must take a filename ending in .c and create a filename that is similar except that it ends in .o.

The task at hand is to strip the .c off the filename and append .o. A single shell statement does it:

```
objname=${filename%.c}.o
```

This tells the shell to look at the end of `filename` for .c. If there is a match, return `$filename` with the match deleted. So if `filename` had the value `fred.c`, the expression `${filename%.c}` would return `fred`. The .o is appended to make the desired `fred.o`, which is stored in the variable `objname`.

If `filename` had an inappropriate value (without .c) such as `fred.a`, the above expression would evaluate to `fred.a.o`: since there was no match, nothing is deleted from the value of `filename`, and .o is appended anyway. And, if `filename` contained more than one dot—e.g., if it were the *y.tab.c* that is so infamous among compiler writers—the expression would still produce the desired *y.tab.o*. Notice that this would not be true if we used `%%` in the expression instead of `%`. The former operator uses the longest match instead of the shortest, so it would match `.tab.o` and evaluate to `y.o` rather than `y.tab.o`. So the single `%` is correct in this case.

A longest-match deletion would be preferable, however, for Task 4-3.

---

* Don't laugh—once upon a time, many Unix compilers had shell scripts as front-ends.

Task 4-3

You are implementing a filter that prepares a text file for printer output. You want to put the file's name—without any directory prefix—on the "banner" page. Assume that, in your script, you have the pathname of the file to be printed stored in the variable pathname.

Clearly the objective is to remove the directory prefix from the pathname. The following line does it:

```
bannername=${pathname##*/}
```

This solution is similar to the first line in the examples shown before. If pathname were just a filename, the pattern */ (anything followed by a slash) would not match, and the value of the expression would be $pathname untouched. If pathname were something like fred/bob, the prefix fred/ would match the pattern and be deleted, leaving just bob as the expression's value. The same thing would happen if pathname were something like /dave/pete/fred/bob: since the ## deletes the longest match, it deletes the entire /dave/pete/fred/.

If we used #*/ instead of ##*/, the expression would have the incorrect value dave/pete/fred/bob, because the shortest instance of "anything followed by a slash" at the beginning of the string is just a slash (/).

The construct ${variable##*/} is actually quite similar to to the Unix utility *basename*(1). In typical use, *basename* takes a pathname as argument and returns the filename only; it is meant to be used with the shell's command substitution mechanism (see below). *basename* is less efficient than ${variable##/*} because it may run in its own separate process rather than within the shell.* Another utility, *dirname*(1), does essentially the opposite of *basename*: it returns the directory prefix only. It is equivalent to the Korn shell expression ${variable%/*} and is less efficient for the same reason.

Pattern Substitution Operators

Besides the pattern-matching operators that delete bits and pieces from the values of shell variables, you can do substitutions on those values, much as in a text editor. (In fact, using these facilities, you could almost *write* a line-mode text editor as a shell script!) These operators are listed in Table 4-10.

---

* *basename* may be built-in in some versions of *ksh93*. Thus it's not guaranteed to run in a separate process.

Table 4-10. Pattern substitution operators

Operator	Meaning
`${variable:start}` `${variable:start:length}`	These represent substring operations. The result is the value of *variable* starting at position *start* and going for *length* characters. The first character is at position 0, and if no *length* is provided, the rest of the string is used.
	When used with `$*` or `$@` or an array indexed by `*` or `@` (see Chapter 6), *start* is a starting index and *length* is the count of elements. In other words, the result is a slice out of the positional parameters or array. Both *start* and *length* may be arithmetic expressions.
	Beginning with *ksh93m*, a negative *start* is taken as relative to the end of the string. For example, if a string has 10 characters, numbered 0 to 9, a start value of −2 means 7 (9 − 2 = 7). Similarly, if *variable* is an indexed array, a negative *start* yields an index by working backwards from the highest subscript in the array.
`${variable/pattern/replace}`	If *variable* contains a match for *pattern*, the first match is replaced with the text of *replace*.
`${variable//pattern/replace}`	This is the same as the previous operation, except that *every* match of the pattern is replaced.
`${variable/pattern}`	If *variable* contains a match for *pattern*, delete the first match of *pattern*.
`${variable/#pattern/replace}`	If *variable* contains a match for *pattern*, the first match is replaced with the text of *replace*. The match is constrained to occur at the beginning of *variable*'s value. If it doesn't match there, no substitution occurs.
`${variable/%pattern/replace}`	If *variable* contains a match for *pattern*, the first match is replaced with the text of *replace*. The match is constrained to occur at the end of *variable*'s value. If it doesn't match there, no substitution occurs.

The `${variable/pattern}` syntax is different from the `#`, `##`, `%`, and `%%` operators we saw earlier. Those operators are constrained to match at the beginning or end of the variable's value, whereas the syntax shown here is not. For example:

```
$ path=/home/fred/work/file
$ print ${path/work/play}              Change work into play
/home/fred/play/file
```

Let's return to our compiler front-end example and look at how we might use these operators. When turning a C source filename into an object filename, we could do the substitution this way:

```
objname=${filename/%.c/.o}              Change .c to .o, but only at end
```

If we had a list of C filenames and wanted to change all of them into object file-names, we could use the so-called *global* substitution operator:

```
$ allfiles="fred.c dave.c pete.c"
$ allobs=${allfiles//.c/.o}
$ print $allobs
fred.o dave.o pete.o
```

The patterns may be any Korn shell pattern expression, as discussed earlier, and the replacement text may include the \N notation to get the text that matched a subpattern.

Finally, these operations may be applied to the positional parameters and to arrays, in which case they are done on all the parameters or array elements at once. (Arrays are described in Chapter 6.)

```
$ print "$@"
hi how are you over there
$ print ${@/h/H}                        Change h to H in all parameters
Hi How are you over tHere
```

Greedy versus non-greedy matching

As promised, here is a brief demonstration of the differences between greedy and non-greedy matching regular expressions:

```
$ x='12345abc6789'
$ print ${x//+([[:digit:]])/X}          Substitution with longest match
XabcX
$ print ${x//+-([[:digit:]])/X}         Substitution with shortest match
XXXXXabcXXXX
$ print ${x##+([[:digit:]])}            Remove longest match
abc6789
$ print ${x#+([[:digit:]])}             Remove shortest match
2345abc6789
```

The first *print* replaces the longest match of "one or more digits" with a single x, everywhere throughout the string. Since this is a longest match, both groups of digits are replaced. In the second case, the shortest match for "one or more digits" is just a single digit, and thus each digit is replaced with an x.

Similarly, the third and fourth cases demonstrate removing text from the front of the value, using longest and shortest matching. In the third case, the longest match removes all the digits; in the fourth case, the shortest match removes just a single digit.

Variable Name Operators

A number of operators relate to shell variable names, as seen in Table 4-11.

Table 4-11. Name-related operators

Operator	Meaning
${!variable}	Return the name of the real variable referenced by the nameref *variable*.
${!base*}	List of all variables whose names begin with *base*.
${!base@}	

Namerefs were discussed in the section "Indirect Variable References (namerefs)," earlier in this chapter. See there for an example of ${!*name*}.

The last two operators in Table 4-11 might be useful for debugging and/or tracing the use of variables in a large script. Just to see how they work:

```
$ print ${!HIST*}
HISTFILE HISTCMD HISTSIZE
$ print ${!HIST@}
HISTFILE HISTCMD HISTSIZE
```

Several other operators related to array variables are described in Chapter 6.

Length Operators

There are three remaining operators on variables. One is ${#*varname*}, which returns the number of characters in the string.* (In Chapter 6 we see how to treat this and similar values as actual numbers so they can be used in arithmetic expressions.) For example, if filename has the value fred.c, then ${#filename} would have the value 6. The other two operators (${#*array*[*]} and ${#*array*[@]}) have to do with array variables, which are also discussed in Chapter 6.

The .sh.match Variable

The .sh.match variable was introduced in *ksh93l*. It is an indexed array (see Chapter 6), whose values are set every time you do a pattern matching operation on a variable, such as ${filename%%*/}, with any of the #, % operators (for the shortest match), or ##, %% (for the longest match), or / and // (for substitutions). .sh.match[0] contains the text that matched the entire pattern. .sh.match[1] contains the text that matched the first parenthesized subexpression, .sh.match[2] the text that matched the second, and so on. The values of .sh.match become invalid (meaning, don't try to use them) if the variable on which the pattern matching was done changes.

---

* This may be more than the number of bytes for multibyte character sets.

Again, this is a feature meant for more advanced programming and text processing, analogous to similar features in other languages such as *perl*. If you're just starting out, don't worry about it.

Command Substitution

From the discussion so far, we've seen two ways of getting values into variables: by assignment statements and by the user supplying them as command-line arguments (positional parameters). There is another way: *command substitution*, which allows you to use the standard output of a command as if it were the value of a variable. You will soon see how powerful this feature is.

The syntax of command substitution is:

```
$(Unix command)
```

The command inside the parenthesis is run, and anything the command writes to standard output (and to standard error) is returned as the value of the expression. These constructs can be nested, i.e., the Unix command can contain command substitutions.

Here are some simple examples:

- The value of $(pwd) is the current directory (same as the environment variable $PWD).

- The value of $(ls) is the names of all files in the current directory, separated by newlines.

- To find out detailed information about a command if you don't know where its file resides, type ls -l $(whence -p *command*). The *−p* option forces *whence* to do a pathname lookup and not consider keywords, built-ins, etc.

- To get the contents of a file into a variable, you can use *varname*=$(< *filename*). $(cat *filename*) will do the same thing, but the shell catches the former as a built-in shorthand and runs it more efficiently.

- If you want to edit (with Emacs) every chapter of your book on the Korn shell that has the phrase "command substitution," assuming that your chapter files all begin with *ch*, you could type:

  ```
  emacs $(grep -l 'command substitution' ch*.xml)
  ```

  The *−l* option to *grep* prints only the names of files that contain matches.

Command substitution, like variable expansion, is done within double quotes. (Double quotes inside the command substitution are not affected by any enclosing double quotes.) Therefore, our rule in Chapter 1 and Chapter 3 about using single quotes for strings unless they contain variables will now be extended: "When in doubt, use single quotes, unless the string contains variables, or command substitutions, in which case use double quotes."

(For backwards compatibility, the Korn shell supports the original Bourne shell (and C shell) command substituion notation using backquotes: `...`. However, it is considerably harder to use than $(...), since quoting and nested command substitutions require careful escaping. We don't use the backquotes in any of the programs in this book.)

You will undoubtedly think of many ways to use command substitution as you gain experience with the Korn shell. One that is a bit more complex than those mentioned previously relates to a customization task that we saw in Chapter 3: personalizing your prompt string.

Recall that you can personalize your prompt string by assigning a value to the variable PS1. If you are on a network of computers, and you use different machines from time to time, you may find it handy to have the name of the machine you're on in your prompt string. Most modern versions of Unix have the command *hostname*(1), which prints the network name of the machine you are on to standard output. (If you do not have this command, you may have a similar one like *uname.*) This command enables you to get the machine name into your prompt string by putting a line like this in your *.profile* or environment file:

```
PS1="$(hostname) $ "
```

(Here, the second dollar sign does not need to be preceded by a backslash. If the character after the $ isn't special to the shell, the $ is included literally in the string.) For example, if your machine had the name coltrane, then this statement would set your prompt string to "coltrane $ ".

Command substitution helps us with the solution to the next programming task, Task 4-4, which relates to the album database in Task 4-1.

Task 4-4

The file used in Task 4-1 is actually a report derived from a bigger table of data about albums. This table consists of several columns, or *fields*, to which a user refers by names like "artist," "title," "year," etc. The columns are separated by vertical bars (|, the same as the Unix pipe character). To deal with individual columns in the table, field names need to be converted to field numbers.

Suppose there is a shell function called *getfield* that takes the field name as argument and writes the corresponding field number on the standard output. Use this routine to help extract a column from the data table.

The *cut*(1) utility is a natural for this task. *cut* is a data filter: it extracts columns from tabular data.* If you supply the numbers of columns you want to extract from the input, *cut* prints only those columns on the standard output. Columns can be character positions or—relevant in this example—fields that are separated by TAB characters or other delimiters.

Assume that the data table in our task is a file called *albums* and that it looks like this:

```
Coltrane, John|Giant Steps|Atlantic|1960|Ja
Coltrane, John|Coltrane Jazz|Atlantic|1960|Ja
Coltrane, John|My Favorite Things|Atlantic|1961|Ja
Coltrane, John|Coltrane Plays the Blues|Atlantic|1961|Ja
...
```

Here is how we would use *cut* to extract the fourth (year) column:

```
cut -f4 -d\| albums
```

The *–d* argument is used to specify the character used as field delimiter (TAB is the default). The vertical bar must be backslash-escaped so that the shell doesn't try to interpret it as a pipe.

From this line of code and the *getfield* routine, we can easily derive the solution to the task. Assume that the first argument to *getfield* is the name of the field the user wants to extract. Then the solution is:

```
fieldname=$1
cut -f$(getfield $fieldname) -d\| albums
```

If we ran this script with the argument **year**, the output would be:

```
1960
1960
1961
1961
...
```

Task 4-5 is another small task that makes use of *cut*.

Task 4-5

Assume that you are logged into a large server or mainframe that supports many simultaneous users. Send a mail message to everyone who is currently logged in.

---

* Some very old BSD-derived systems don't have *cut*, but you can use *awk* instead. Whenever you see a command of the form cut -f*N* -d*C* *filename*, use this instead: awk -F*C* '{ print $*N* }' *filename*.

The command *who*(1) tells you who is logged in (as well as which terminal they're on and when they logged in). Its output looks like this:

```
billr      console      May 22 07:57
fred       tty02        May 22 08:31
bob        tty04        May 22 08:12
```

The fields are separated by spaces, not TABs. Since we need the first field, we can get away with using a space as the field separator in the *cut* command. (Otherwise we'd have to use the option to *cut* that uses character columns instead of fields.) To provide a space character as an argument on a command line, you can surround it by quotes:

```
who | cut -d' ' -f1
```

With the above *who* output, this command's output would look like this:

```
billr
fred
bob
```

This leads directly to a solution to the task. Just type:

```
mail $(who | cut -d' ' -f1)
```

The command `mail billr fred bob` will run and then you can type your message.

Task 4-6 is another task that shows how useful command pipelines can be in command substitution.

Task 4-6

The *ls* command gives you pattern-matching capability with wildcards, but it doesn't allow you to select files by *modification date*. Devise a mechanism that lets you do this.

This task was inspired by the feature of the OpenVMS operating system that lets you specify files by date with *BEFORE* and *SINCE* parameters.

Here is a function that allows you to list all files that were last modified on the date you give as argument. Once again, we choose a function for speed reasons. No pun is intended by the function's name:

```
function lsd {
    date=$1
    ls -l | grep -i "^.\{41\}$date" | cut -c55-
}
```

This function depends on the column layout of the `ls -l` command. In particular, it depends on dates starting in column 42 and filenames starting in column 55. If this isn't the case in your version of Unix, you will need to adjust the column numbers.*

We use the *grep* search utility to match the date given as argument (in the form *Mon DD*, e.g., Jan 15 or Oct 6, the latter having two spaces) to the output of ls -l. (The regular expression argument to *grep* is quoted with double quotes, in order to perform the variable substitution.) This gives us a long listing of only those files whose dates match the argument. The *−i* option to *grep* allows you to use all lowercase letters in the month name, while the rather fancy argument means, "Match any line that contains 41 characters followed by the function argument." For example, typing lsd 'jan 15' causes *grep* to search for lines that match any 41 characters followed by jan 15 (or Jan 15).

The output of *grep* is piped through our ubiquitous friend *cut* to retrieve just the filenames. The argument to *cut* tells it to extract characters in column 55 through the end of the line.

With command substitution, you can use this function with *any* command that accepts filename arguments. For example, if you want to print all files in your current directory that were last modified today, and today is January 15, you could type:

```
lp $(lsd 'jan 15')
```

The output of *lsd* is on multiple lines (one for each filename), but because the variable IFS (see earlier in this chapter) contains newline by default, the shell uses newline to separate words in *lsd*'s output, just as it normally does with space and TAB.

Advanced Examples: pushd and popd

We conclude this chapter with a couple of functions that you may find handy in your everyday Unix use. They solve the problem presented by Task 4-7.

Task 4-7

In the C shell, the commands *pushd* and *popd* implement a *stack* of directories that enable you to move to another directory temporarily and have the shell remember where you were. The *dirs* command prints the stack. The Korn shell does not provide these commands. Implement them as shell functions.

---

* For example, ls -l on GNU/Linux has dates starting in column 43 and filenames starting in column 57.

We start by implementing a significant subset of their capabilities and finish the implementation in Chapter 6. (For ease of development and explanation, our implementation ignores some things that a more bullet-proof version should handle. For example, spaces in filenames will cause things to break.)

If you don't know what a stack is, think of a spring-loaded dish receptacle in a cafeteria. When you place dishes on the receptacle, the spring compresses so that the top stays at roughly the same level. The dish most recently placed on the stack is the first to be taken when someone wants food; thus, the stack is known as a "last-in, first-out" or *LIFO* structure. (Victims of a recession or company takeovers will also recognize this mechanism in the context of corporate layoff policies.) Putting something onto a stack is known in computer science parlance as *pushing*, and taking something off the top is called *popping*.

A stack is very handy for remembering directories, as we will see; it can "hold your place" up to an arbitrary number of times. The cd - form of the *cd* command does this, but only to one level. For example: if you are in *firstdir* and then you change to *seconddir*, you can type cd - to go back. But if you start out in *firstdir*, then change to *seconddir*, and then go to *thirddir*, you can use cd - only to go back to *seconddir*. If you type cd - again, you will be back in *thirddir*, because it is the previous directory.*

If you want the "nested" remember-and-change functionality that will take you back to *firstdir*, you need a stack of directories along with the *dirs*, *pushd* and *popd* commands. Here is how these work:†

- *pushd dir* does a *cd* to *dir* and then pushes *dir* onto the stack.

- *popd* does a *cd* to the top directory, then pops it off the stack.

For example, consider the series of events in Table 4-12. Assume that you have just logged in and that you are in your home directory (*/home/you*).

We will implement a stack as an environment variable containing a list of directories separated by spaces.

---

* Think of cd - as a synonym for cd $OLDPWD; see the previous chapter.

† We've done it here differently from the C shell. The C shell *pushd* pushes the initial directory onto the stack first, followed by the command's argument. The C shell *popd* removes the top directory off the stack, revealing a new top. Then it *cd*s to the new top directory. We feel that this behavior is less intuitive than our design here.

Table 4-12. pushd/popd example

Command	Stack contents (top on left)	Result directory
`pushd fred`	*/home/you/fred*	*/home/you/fred*
`pushd /etc`	*/etc /home/you/fred*	*/etc*
`cd /usr/tmp`	*/etc /home/you/fred*	*/usr/tmp*
`popd`	*/home/you/fred*	*/etc*
`popd`	(empty)	*/home/you/fred*

Your directory stack should be initialized to your home directory when you log in. To do so, put this in your *.profile*:

```
DIRSTACK="$PWD"
export DIRSTACK
```

Do *not* put this in your environment file if you have one. The *export* statement guarantees that DIRSTACK is known to all subprocesses; you want to initialize it only once. If you put this code in an environment file, it will get reinitialized in every interactive shell subprocess, which you probably don't want.

Next, we need to implement *dirs*, *pushd*, and *popd* as functions. Here are our initial versions:

```
function dirs {          # print directory stack (easy)
    print $DIRSTACK
}

function pushd {         # push current directory onto stack
    dirname=$1
    cd ${dirname:?"missing directory name."}
    DIRSTACK="$PWD $DIRSTACK"
    print "$DIRSTACK"
}

function popd {          # cd to top, pop it off stack
    top=${DIRSTACK%% *}
    DIRSTACK=${DIRSTACK#* }
    cd $top
    print "$PWD"
}
```

Notice that there isn't much code! Let's go through the functions and see how they work. *dirs* is easy; it just prints the stack. The fun starts with *pushd*. The first line merely saves the first argument in the variable *dirname* for readability reasons.

The second line's main purpose is to change to the new directory. We use the :? operator to handle the error when the argument is missing: if the argument is given, the expression ${dirname:?"missing directory name."} evaluates to

`$dirname`, but if it is not given, the shell prints the message `ksh: pushd: line 2: dirname: missing directory name.` and exits from the function.

The third line of the function pushes the new directory onto the stack. The expression within double quotes consists of the full pathname for the current directory, followed by a single space, followed by the contents of the directory stack (`$DIRSTACK`). The double quotes ensure that all of this is packaged into a single string for assignment back to `DIRSTACK`.

The last line merely prints the contents of the stack, with the implication that the leftmost directory is both the current directory and at the top of the stack. (This is why we chose spaces to separate directories, rather than the more customary colons as in `PATH` and `MAILPATH`.)

The *popd* function makes yet another use of the shell's pattern-matching operators. The first line uses the `%%` operator, which deletes the longest match of " *" (a space followed by anything). This removes all but the top of the stack. The result is saved in the variable `top`, again for readability reasons.

The second line is similar, but going in the other direction. It uses the `#` operator, which tries to delete the shortest match of the pattern "* " (anything followed by a space) from the value of `DIRSTACK`. The result is that the top directory (and the space following it) is deleted from the stack.

The third line actually changes directory to the previous top of the stack. (Note that *popd* doesn't care where you are when you run it; if your current directory is the one on the top of the stack, you won't go anywhere.) The final line just prints a confirmation message.

This code is deficient in the following ways: first, it has no provision for errors. For example:

- What if the user tries to push a directory that doesn't exist or is invalid?
- What if the user tries *popd* and the stack is empty?

Test your understanding of the code by figuring out how it would respond to these error conditions. The second deficiency is that the code implements only some of the functionality of the C shell's *pushd* and *popd* commands—albeit the most useful parts. In the next chapter, we will see how to overcome both of these deficiencies.

The third problem with the code is that it will not work if, for some reason, a directory name contains a space. The code will treat the space as a separator character. We'll accept this deficiency for now. However, when you read about arrays in Chapter 6, think about how you might use them to rewrite this code and eliminate the problem.

In this chapter:
• if/else
• for
• case
• select
• while and until

5

Flow Control

If you are a programmer, you may have read the last chapter—with its claim at the outset that the Korn shell has an advanced set of programming capabilities—and wondered where many features from conventional languages are. Perhaps the most glaringly obvious "hole" in our coverage thus far concerns *flow control* constructs like if, for, while, and so on.

Flow control gives a programmer the power to specify that only certain portions of a program run, or that certain portions run repeatedly, according to conditions such as the values of variables, whether or not commands execute properly, and others. We call this the ability to control the flow of a program's execution.

Almost every shell script or function shown thus far has had no flow control—they have just been lists of commands to be run! Yet the Korn shell, like the C and Bourne shells, has all the flow control abilities you would expect and more; we examine them in this chapter. We'll use them to enhance the solutions to some of the programming tasks we saw in the last chapter and to solve tasks that we introduce here.

Although we have attempted to explain flow control so that nonprogrammers can understand it, we also sympathize with programmers who dread having to slog through yet another *tabula rasa* explanation. For this reason, some of our discussions relate the Korn shell's flow-control mechanisms to those that programmers should know already. Therefore you will be in a better position to understand this chapter if you already have a basic knowledge of flow control concepts.

The Korn shell supports the following flow control constructs:

`if/else`
> Execute a list of statements if a certain condition is/is not true.

`for`
> Execute a list of statements a fixed number of times.

`while`
> Execute a list of statements repeatedly *while* a certain condition holds true.

`until`
> Execute a list of statements repeatedly *until* a certain condition holds true.

`case`
> Execute one of several lists of statements depending on the value of a variable.

In addition, the Korn shell provides a new type of flow-control construct:

`select`
> Allow the user to select one of a list of possibilities from a menu.

We will cover each of these, but be warned: the syntax is unusual.

if/else

The simplest type of flow control construct is the *conditional*, embodied in the Korn shell's `if` statement. You use a conditional when you want to choose whether or not to do something, or to choose among a small number of things to do, according to the truth or falsehood of *conditions*. Conditions test values of shell variables, characteristics of files, whether or not commands run successfully, and other factors. The shell has a large set of built-in tests that are relevant to the task of shell programming.

The `if` construct has the following syntax:

```
if condition
then
    statements
[elif condition
    then statements ...]
[else
    statements]
fi
```

The simplest form (without the `elif` and `else` parts, a.k.a. *clauses*) executes the *statements* only if the *condition* is true. If you add an `else` clause, you get the ability to execute one set of statements if a condition is true or another set of statements if the condition is false. You can use as many `elif` (a contraction of "else if") clauses as you wish; they introduce more conditions and thus more choices for which set of statements to execute. If you use one or more `elifs`, you can think of the `else` clause as the "if all *else* fails" part.

Exit Status and Return

Perhaps the only aspect of this syntax that differs from that of conventional languages like C and Pascal is that the "condition" is really a list of statements rather than the more usual Boolean (true or false) expression. How is the truth or falsehood of the condition determined? It has to do with a general Unix concept that we haven't covered yet: the *exit status* of commands.

Every Unix command, whether it comes from source code in C, some other language, or a shell script/function, returns an integer code to its calling process—the shell in this case—when it finishes. This is called the exit status. 0 is *usually* the "OK" exit status, while anything else (1 to 255) *usually* denotes an error.* The way *ksh* handles exit statuses for built-in commands is described in more detail later in this section.

`if` checks the exit status of the *last* statement in the list following the `if` keyword.† (The list is usually just a single statement.) If the status is 0, the condition evaluates to true; if it is anything else, the condition is considered false. The same is true for each condition attached to an `elif` statement (if any).

This enables us to write code of the form:

```
if command ran successfully
then
    normal processing
else
    error processing
fi
```

More specifically, we can now improve on the *pushd* function that we saw in the last chapter:

```
function pushd {          # push current directory onto stack
    dirname=$1
    cd ${dirname:?"missing directory name."}
    DIRSTACK="$dirname $DIRSTACK"
    print "$DIRSTACK"
}
```

---

* Because this is a "convention" and not a "law," there are exceptions. For example, *diff*(1) (find differences between two files) returns 0 for "no differences," 1 for "differences found," or 2 for an error such as an invalid filename argument.

† LISP programmers will find this idea familiar.

This function requires a valid directory as its argument. Let's look at how it handles error conditions: if no argument is given, the second line of code prints an error message and exits. This is fine.

However, the function reacts deceptively when an argument is given that isn't a valid directory. In case you didn't figure it out when reading the last chapter, here is what happens: the *cd* fails, leaving you in the same directory you were in. This is also appropriate. But then the third line of code pushes the bad directory onto the stack anyway, and the last line prints a message that leads you to believe that the push was successful.

We need to prevent the bad directory from being pushed and to print an error message. Here is how we can do this:

```
function pushd {                        # push current directory onto stack
    dirname=$1
    if cd ${dirname:?"missing directory name."}    # if cd was successful
    then
        DIRSTACK="$dirname $DIRSTACK"
        print $DIRSTACK
    else
        print still in $PWD.
    fi
}
```

The call to *cd* is now inside an `if` construct. If *cd* is successful, it returns 0; the next two lines of code are run, finishing the *pushd* operation. But if the *cd* fails, it returns with exit status 1, and *pushd* prints a message saying that you haven't gone anywhere.

You can usually rely on built-in commands and standard Unix utilities to return appropriate exit statuses, but what about your own shell scripts and functions? For example, we'd like *pushd* to return an appropriate status so that it too can be used in an `if` statement:

```
if pushd some-directory
then
    what we need to do
else
    handle problem case
fi
```

The problem is that the exit status is reset by every command, so it "disappears" if you don't save it immediately. In this function, the built-in *cd*'s exit status disappears when the *print* statement runs (and sets its own exit status).

Therefore, we need to save the status that *cd* sets and use it as the entire function's exit status. Two shell features we haven't seen yet provide the way. First is the special shell variable ?, whose value ($?) is the exit status of the last command that ran. For example:

```
cd baddir
print $?
```

causes the shell to print 1, while:

```
cd gooddir
print $?
```

causes the shell to print 0.

Return

The second feature we need is the statement *return N*, which causes the surrounding script or function to exit with exit status *N*. *N* is actually optional; it defaults to the exit value of the last command that was run. Scripts that finish without a *return* statement (i.e., every one we have seen so far) return whatever the last statement returned. If you use *return* within a function, it just exits the function. (In contrast, the statement *exit N* exits the entire script, no matter how deeply you are nested in functions.)

Getting back to our example: we save the exit status in both branches of the if, so that we can use it when we're done:

```
function pushd {                    # push current directory onto stack
    dirname=$1
    if cd ${dirname:?"missing directory name."}   # if cd was successful
    then
        es=$?
        DIRSTACK="$dirname $DIRSTACK"
        print $DIRSTACK
    else
        es=$?
        print still in $PWD.
    fi
    return $es
}
```

The assignment es=$? saves the exit status of *cd* in the variable es; the last line returns it as the function's exit status.

Exit statuses aren't very useful for anything other than their intended purpose. In particular, you may be tempted to use them as "return values" of functions, as you would with functions in C or Pascal. That won't work; you should use variables or command substitution instead to simulate this effect.

Advanced example: overriding a built-in command

Using the exit status and the *return* command, and taking advantage of the shell's command search order, we can write a *cd* function that overrides the built-in command.

Suppose we want our *cd* function to print the old and new directories automatically. Here is a version to put in your *.profile* or environment file:

```
function cd {
        command cd "$@"
        es=$?
        print "$OLDPWD -> $PWD"
        return $es
}
```

This function relies on the search order for commands listed in the last chapter. *cd* is a non-special built-in command, which means that it's found *after* functions. Thus, we can name our function *cd*, and the shell will find it first.

But how do we get to the "real" *cd* command? We need it to do the actual changing of directories. The answer is the built-in command named, oddly enough, *command*. Its job is to do exactly what we need: skip any functions named by the first argument, instead finding the built-in or external command and running it with the supplied arguments. In the Korn shell, using *command* followed by one of the special built-in commands keeps errors in that command from aborting the script. (This happens to be mandated by POSIX.)

The *command* built-in is *not* special. If you define a function named *command*, there's no way to get to the real one anymore (except by removing the function, of course).

Anyway, back to the example. The first line uses *command* to run *cd*. It then saves the exit status in es, as we did earlier, so that it can be returned to the calling program or interactive shell. Finally, it prints the desired message and then returns the saved exit status. We'll see a more substantial "wrapper" for *cd* in Chapter 7.

Pipeline exit status

The exit status for a single command is just a simple number, whose value, as we've seen, is available in the special variable $?. But what about a pipeline? After all, you can hook an arbitrary number of commands together with pipes. Is the exit status of a pipeline that of the first command, the last command, or some command in between? By default, it is the exit status of the *last* command in the pipeline. (This is required by POSIX.)

The advantage to this behavior is that it's well-defined. If a pipeline fails, you know that it was the last command that failed. But if some intermediate process in the pipeline failed, you don't know about it. The *set –o pipefail* option allows you to change this behavior.* When you enable this option, the exit status of the pipeline is changed to that of the last command to fail. If no command fails, the exit status is 0. This still doesn't tell you which command in a pipeline failed, but at least you can tell that something went wrong somewhere and attempt to take corrective action.

Interpreting exit status values

For *ksh93*, the exit status values for built-in commands and several exceptional cases have been regularized as follows:

Value	Meaning
1–125	Command exited with failure
2	Invalid usage, with usage message (built-in commands)
126	Command found, but file is not executable
127	Command not found
128–255	External command exited with failure
≥ 256	Command died with a signal; subtract 256 to get signal number

Signals are a more advanced feature; they are described in Chapter 8.

Combinations of Exit Statuses

One of the more obscure parts of Korn shell syntax allows you to combine exit statuses logically, so that you can test more than one thing at a time.

The syntax `statement1 && statement2` means, "execute *statement1*, and if its exit status is 0, execute *statement2*." The syntax `statement1 || statement2` is the converse: it means, "execute *statement1*, and if its exit status is *not* 0, execute *statement2*."

At first, these look like "if/then" and "if not/then" constructs, respectively. But they are really intended for use within conditions of `if` constructs—as C programmers will readily understand.

---

* This option is available starting with *ksh93g*.

It's much more useful to think of these constructs as "and" and "or," respectively. Consider this:

```
if statement1 && statement2
then
    ...
fi
```

In this case, *statement1* is executed. If it returns a 0 status, then presumably it ran without error. Then *statement2* runs. The then clause is executed if *statement2* returns a 0 status. Conversely, if *statement1* fails (returns a nonzero exit status), *statement2* doesn't even run; the "last statement" in the condition was *statement1*, which failed—so the then clause doesn't run. Taken all together, it's fair to conclude that the then clause runs if *statement1* and *statement2* both succeeded.

Similarly, consider this:

```
if statement1 || statement2
then
    ...
fi
```

If *statement1* succeeds, *statement2* does *not* run. This makes *statement1* the last statement, which means that the then clause runs. On the other hand, if *statement1* fails, *statement2* runs, and whether the then clause runs or not depends on the success of *statement2*. The upshot is that the then clause runs if *statement1* or *statement2* succeeds.

As a simple example, assume that we need to write a script that checks a file for the presence of two words and just prints a message saying whether *either* word is in the file or not. We can use *grep* for this: it returns exit status 0 if it found the given string in its input, nonzero if not:

```
filename=$1
word1=$2
word2=$3
if grep $word1 $filename > /dev/null || grep $word2 $filename > /dev/null
then
    print "$word1 or $word2 is in $filename."
fi
```

To ensure that all we get is the exit status, we've redirected the output of both *grep* invocations to the special file */dev/null*, which is colloquially known as the "bit bucket." Any output directed to */dev/null* effectively disappears. Without this redirection, the output would include the matching lines that contain the words, as well as our message. (Some versions of *grep* support a –*s* option for "silent," meaning no output. POSIX *grep* uses –*q*, meaning "quiet," for this. The most portable solution is to redirect output to */dev/null*, as we've done here.)

The then clause of this code runs if either *grep* statement succeeds. Now assume that we want the script to say whether or not the input file contains *both* words. Here's how to do it:

```
filename=$1
word1=$2
word2=$3
if grep $word1 $filename > /dev/null && grep $word2 $filename > /dev/null
then
    print "$word1 and $word2 are both in $filename."
fi
```

A minor note: when used with commands, && and || have equal precedence. However, when used inside [[...]] (discussed shortly), && has higher precedence than ||.

We'll see more examples of these logical operators later in this chapter and in the code for the *kshdb* debugger in Chapter 9.

Reversing the Sense of a Test

Sometimes, the most natural way to phrase a condition is in the negative. ("If Dave isn't there, then ...") Suppose we need to know that neither of two words is in a source file. In most scripts, when such is the case, you will see code like this:

```
if grep $word1 $filename > /dev/null || grep $word2 $filename > /dev/null
then
    :    # do nothing
else
    print "$word1 and $word2 are both absent from $filename."
fi
```

The : command does nothing. The meaning, then, is "if word1 or word2 are present in filename, do nothing; otherwise, print a message." The Korn shell lets you do this more elegantly using the ! keyword (introduced in POSIX):

```
filename=$1
word1=$2
word2=$3
if ! grep $word1 $filename > /dev/null &&
   ! grep $word2 $filename > /dev/null
then
    print "$word1 and $word2 are both absent from $filename."
fi
```

Condition Tests

Exit statuses are the only things an `if` construct can test. But that doesn't mean you can check only whether or not commands ran properly. The shell provides a way of testing a variety of conditions with the `[[...]]` construct.*

You can use the construct to check many different attributes of a file (whether it exists, what type of file it is, what its permissions and ownership are, etc.), compare two files to see which is newer, do comparisons and pattern matching on strings, and more.

`[[ condition ]]` is actually a statement just like any other, except that the only thing it does is return an exit status that tells whether *condition* is true. Thus it fits within the `if` construct's syntax of `if` *statements*.

String comparisons

The double square brackets (`[[...]]`) surround expressions that include various types of *operators*. We start with the string comparison operators, which are listed in Table 5-1. (Notice that there are no operators for "greater than or equal" or "less than or equal.") In the table, *str* refers to an expression with a string value, and *pat* refers to a pattern that can contain wildcards (just like the patterns in the string-handling operators we saw in the last chapter). Note that these operators compare the lexicographic values of strings, so "10" < "2".

Table 5-1. String comparison operators

Operator	True if...
`str`	*str* is non-null.
`str == pat`	*str* matches *pat*.
`str = pat`	*str* matches *pat* (obsolete).
`str != pat`	*str* does not match *pat*.
`str1 < str2`	*str1* is less than *str2*.
`str1 > str2`	*str1* is greater than *str2*.
`-n str`	*str* is not null (has length greater than 0).
`-z str`	*str* is null (has length 0).

---

* The Korn shell also accepts the `[...]` and *test* commands. (There are built-in commands in all versions of *ksh*; they behave like the original external versions.) The `[[...]]` construct has many more options and is better integrated into the Korn shell language: specifically, word splitting and wildcard expansion aren't done within `[[` and `]]`, making quoting less necessary. In addition, you can always tell operators from operands, since the operators cannot be the result of expansion.

We can use one of these operators to improve our *popd* function, which reacts badly if you try to pop and the stack is empty. Recall that the code for *popd* is:

```
function popd {          # cd to top, pop it off stack
    top=${DIRSTACK%% *}
    DIRSTACK=${DIRSTACK#* }
    cd $top
    print "$PWD"
}
```

If the stack is empty, $DIRSTACK is the null string, as is the expression ${DIRSTACK%% *}. This means that you will change to your home directory; instead, we want *popd* to print an error message and do nothing.

To accomplish this, we need to test for an empty stack, i.e., whether $DIRSTACK is null or not. Here is one way to do it:

```
function popd {                    # pop directory off the stack, cd there
    if [[ -n $DIRSTACK ]]; then
        top=${DIRSTACK%% *}
        DIRSTACK=${DIRSTACK#* }
        cd $top
        print "$PWD"
    else
        print "stack empty, still in $PWD."
        return 1
    fi
}
```

Notice that instead of putting then on a separate line, we put it on the same line as the if after a semicolon, which is the shell's standard statement separator character. (There's a subtlety here. The shell only recognizes keywords such as if and then when they are at the beginning of a statement. This is so you can type, for example, print if then else is neat without getting syntax errors. Newlines and semicolons separate statements. Thus, the then on the same line as the if is correctly recognized after a semicolon, whereas without the semicolon, it would not be.)

We could have used operators other than *−n*. For example, we could have used *−z* and switched the code in the then and else clauses. We also could have used:

```
if [[ $DIRSTACK == "" ]]; then
    ...
```

While we're cleaning up code we wrote in the last chapter, let's fix up the error handling in the *highest* script (Task 4-1). The code for that script is:

```
filename=${1:?"filename missing."}
howmany=${2:-10}
sort -nr $filename | head -$howmany
```

[[...]] Versus the Test and [...] Commands

We wrote our test `[[ $DIRSTACK == "" ]]`. This is *not* the correct usage for the older `[...]` or *test* syntax.

In this syntax, which the Korn shell still supports, and which is all you have in the Bourne shell, if `$DIRSTACK` evaluates to the null string, the shell will complain about a missing argument. This leads to the requirement of enclosing both strings in double quotes (`[ "$DIRSTACK" = "" ]`), which is the most readable way to do it, or to the common hack of adding an extra character in front of the strings, like so: `[ x$DIRSTACK = x ]`. The latter works, since if `$DIRSTACK` is null, the `[...]` command only sees the two x characters, but it's not very obvious what's going on, especially to the novice.

Also note that the the Korn shell's preferred operator is ==, while *test* requires a single = character.

Recall that if you omit the first argument (the filename), the shell prints the message `highest: 1: filename missing`. We can make this better by substituting a more standard "usage" message:

```
if [[ -z $1 ]]; then
    print 'usage: highest filename [N]'
else
    filename=$1
    howmany=${2:-10}
    sort -nr $filename | head -$howmany
fi
```

It is considered better programming style to enclose all of the code in the *if-then-else*, but such code can get confusing if you are writing a long script in which you need to check for errors and bail out at several points along the way. Therefore, a more usual style for shell programming is this:

```
if [[ -z $1 ]]; then
    print 'usage: highest filename [-N]'
    exit 1
fi
filename=$1
howmany=${2:-10}
sort -nr $filename | head -$howmany
```

The *exit* statement informs any calling program that needs to know whether it ran successfully or not. (You can also use *return*, but we feel that *return* should be reserved for use in functions.)

As an example of the == and != operators, we can add to our solution for Task 4-2, the shell script front-end to a C compiler. Recall that we are given a filename ending in .c (the source code file), and we need to construct a filename that is the same but ends in .o (the object code file). The modifications we will make have to do with other types of files that can be passed to a C compiler.

About C compilers

Before we get to the shell code, it is necessary to understand a few things about C compilers. We already know that they translate C source code into object code. Actually, they are part of *compilation systems* that also perform several other tasks. The term "compiler" is often used instead of "compilation system," so we'll use it in both senses.

We're interested here in two tasks that compilers perform other than compiling C code: they can translate *assembly language* code into object code, and they can *link* object code files together to form an *executable* program.

Assembly language works at a level that is close to the bare computer; each assembly statement is directly translatable into a statement of object code—as opposed to C or other higher-level languages, in which a single source statement could translate to dozens of object code instructions. Translating a file of assembly language code into object code is called, not surprisingly, *assembling* the code.

Although many people consider assembly language to be quaintly old-fashioned—like a typewriter in this age of WYSIWYG word processing and desktop publishing—some programmers still need to use it when dealing with precise details of computer hardware. It's not uncommon for a program to consist of several files' worth of code in a higher-level language (such as C or C++) and a few low-level routines in assembly language.

The other task we'll worry about is called *linking*. Most real-world programs, unlike those assigned for a first-year programming class, consist of several files of source code, possibly written by several different programmers. These files are compiled into object code; then the object code must be combined to form the final, runnable program, known as an *executable*. The task of combining is often called "linking": each object code component usually contains references to other components, and these references must be resolved or "linked" together.

C compilation systems are capable of assembling files of assembly language into object code and linking object code files into executables. In particular, a compiler calls a separate *assembler* to deal with assembly code and a *linker* (also known as a "loader," "linking loader," or "link editor") to deal with object code files. These separate tools are known in the Unix world as *as* and *ld*, respectively. The C compiler itself is invoked with the command *cc*.

We can express all of these steps in terms of the suffixes of files passed as arguments to the C compiler. Basically, the compiler does the following:

1. If the argument ends in .c it's a C source file; compile into a .o object code file.

2. If the argument ends in .s, it's assembly language; assemble into a .o file.

3. If the argument ends in .o, do nothing; save for the linking step later.

4. If the argument ends in some other suffix, print an error message and exit.*

5. Link all .o object code files into an executable file called *a.out*. This file is usually renamed to something more descriptive.

Step 3 allows object code files that have already been compiled (or assembled) to be reused to build other executables. For example, an object code file that implements an interface to a CD-ROM drive could be useful in any program that reads from CD-ROMs.

Figure 5-1 should make the compilation process clearer; it shows how the compiler processes the C source files *a.c* and *b.c*, the assembly language file *c.s*, and the already-compiled object code file *d.o*. In other words, it shows how the compiler handles the command cc a.c b.c c.s d.o.

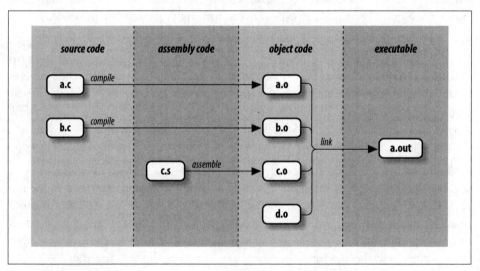

Figure 5-1. Files produced by a C compiler

Here is how we would begin to implement this behavior in a shell script. Assume that the variable filename holds the argument in question, and that *ccom* is the

---

* For the purposes of this example. We know this isn't strictly true in real life.

name of the program that actually compiles a C source file into object code. Assume further that *ccom* and *as* (assembler) take arguments for the names of the source and object files:

```
if [[ $filename == *.c ]]; then
    objname=${filename%.c}.o
    ccom "$filename" "$objname"
elif [[ $filename == *.s ]]; then
    objname=${filename%.s}.o
    as "$filename" "$objname"
elif [[ $filename != *.o ]]; then
    print "error: $filename is not a source or object file."
    exit 1
fi
further processing ...
```

Recall from the previous chapter that the expression ${filename%.c}.o deletes .c from filename and appends .o; ${filename%.s}.o does the analogous thing for files ending in .s.

The "further processing" is the link step, which we will see when we complete this example later in the chapter.

File attribute checking

The other kind of operator that can be used in conditional expressions checks a file for certain properties. There are 24 such operators. We cover those of most general interest here; the rest refer to arcana like sticky bits, sockets, and file descriptors, and thus are of interest only to systems programmers. Refer to Appendix B for the complete list. Table 5-2 lists those that interest us now.

Table 5-2. File attribute operators

Operator	True if ...
-e *file*	*file* exists
-d *file*	*file* is a directory
-f *file*	*file* is a regular file (i.e., not a directory or other special type of file)
-L *file*	*file* is a symbolic link
-r *file*	You have read permission on *file*
-s *file*	*file* exists and is not empty
-w *file*	You have write permission on *file*
-x *file*	You have execute permission on *file* or directory search permission if it is a directory
-O *file*	You own *file* (the effective UID matches that of *file*)
-G *file*	Your effective group ID is the same as that of *file*
file1 -nt *file2*	*file1* is newer than *file2*[a]

Table 5-2. File attribute operators (continued)

Operator	True if ...
file1 -ot *file2*	*file1* is older than *file2*
file1 -ef *file2*	*file1* and *file2* are the same file

a Specifically, the –nt and –ot operators compare *modification times* of two files.

Before we get to an example, you should know that conditional expressions inside [[and]] can also be combined using the logical operators && and ||, just as we saw with plain shell commands in the section "Combinations of Exit Statuses," earlier in this chapter. It's also possible to combine shell commands with conditional expressions using logical operators, like this:

```
if command && [[ condition ]]; then
    ...
```

Chapter 7 contains an example of this combination.

You can also negate the truth value of a conditional expression by preceding it with an exclamation point (!), so that ! *expr* evaluates to true only if *expr* is false. Furthermore, you can make complex logical expressions of conditional operators by grouping them with parentheses. (It turns out that this is true outside of the [[...]] construct as well. As we will see in Chapter 8, the construct (*statement list*) runs the statement list in a subshell, whose exit status is that of the last statement in the list.)

Here is how we would use two of the file operators to embellish (yet again) our *pushd* function. Instead of having *cd* determine whether the argument given is a valid directory—i.e., by returning with a bad exit status if it's not—we can do the checking ourselves. Here is the code:

```
function pushd {                    # push current directory onto stack
    dirname=$1
    if [[ -d $dirname && -x $dirname ]]; then
        cd "$dirname"
        DIRSTACK="$dirname DIRSTACK"
        print "$DIRSTACK"
    else
        print "still in $PWD."
        return 1
    fi
}
```

The conditional expression evaluates to true only if the argument $1 is a directory (*–d*) *and* the user has permission to change to it (*–x*).* Notice that this conditional also handles the case where the argument is missing: $dirname is null, and since the null string isn't a valid directory name, the conditional will fail.

Task 5-1 presents a more comprehensive example of the use of file operators.

Task 5-1

Write a script that prints essentially the same information as ls -1 but in a more user-friendly way.

Although this task requires relatively long-winded code, it is a straightforward application of many of the file operators:

```
if [[ ! -e $1 ]]; then
    print "file $1 does not exist."
    return 1
fi
if [[ -d $1 ]]; then
    print -n "$1 is a directory that you may "
    if [[ ! -x $1 ]]; then
        print -n "not "
    fi
    print "search."
elif [[ -f $1 ]]; then
    print "$1 is a regular file."
else
    print "$1 is a special type of file."
fi
if [[ -O $1 ]]; then
    print 'you own the file.'
else
    print 'you do not own the file.'
fi
if [[ -r $1 ]]; then
    print 'you have read permission on the file.'
fi
if [[ -w $1 ]]; then
    print 'you have write permission on the file.'
fi
if [[ -x $1 && ! -d $1 ]]; then
    print 'you have execute permission on the file.'
fi
```

---

* Remember that the same permission flag that determines execute permission on a regular file determines search permission on a directory. This is why the *–x* operator checks both things depending on file type.

We'll call this script *fileinfo*. Here's how it works:

- The first conditional tests if the file given as argument does *not* exist (the exclamation point is the "not" operator; the spaces around it are required). If the file does not exist, the script prints an error message and exits with error status.

- The second conditional tests if the file is a directory. If so, the first *print* prints part of a message; remember that the *−n* option tells *print* not to print a newline at the end. The inner conditional checks if you do *not* have search permission on the directory. If you don't have search permission, the word "not" is added to the partial message. Then, the message is completed with "search." and a newline.

- The elif clause checks if the file is a regular file; if so, it prints a message.

- The else clause accounts for the various special file types on recent Unix systems, such as sockets, devices, FIFO files, etc. We assume that the casual user isn't interested in their details.

- The next conditional tests to see if you own the file (i.e., if its owner ID is the same as your effective User ID). If so, it prints a message saying you own it. (Real and effective User and Group IDs are explained in Chapter 10.)

- The next two conditionals test for your read and write permission on the file.

- The last conditional checks if you can execute the file. It checks to see if you have execute permission and that the file is *not* a directory. (If the file were a directory, execute permission would really mean directory search permission.)

As an example of *fileinfo*'s output, assume that you do an ls -l of your current directory and it contains these lines:

```
-rwxr-xr-x   1 billr    other       594 May 28 09:49 bob
-rw-r-r-     1 billr    other     42715 Apr 21 23:39 custom.tbl
drwxr-xr-x   2 billr    other        64 Jan 12 13:42 exp
-r-r-r-      1 root     other       557 Mar 28 12:41 lpst
```

custom.tbl and *lpst* are regular text files, *exp* is a directory, and *bob* is a shell script. Typing fileinfo bob produces this output:

```
bob is a regular file.
you own the file.
you have read permission on the file.
you have write permission on the file.
you have execute permission on the file.
```

Typing `fileinfo custom.tbl` results in this:

```
custom.tbl is a regular file.
you own the file.
you have read permission on the file.
you have write permission on the file.
```

Typing `fileinfo exp` results in this:

```
exp is a directory that you may search.
you own the file.
you have read permission on the file.
you have write permission on the file.
```

Finally, typing `fileinfo lpst` produces this:

```
lpst is a regular file.
you do not own the file.
you have read permission on the file.
```

Arithmetic conditionals

The shell also provides a set of *arithmetic* tests. These are different from *character string* comparisons like < and >, which compare *lexicographic* values of strings, not numeric values. For example, "6" is greater than "57" lexicographically, just as "p" is greater than "ox," but of course the opposite is true when they're compared as numbers.

The arithmetic comparison operators are summarized in Table 5-3. Fortran programmers will find their syntax slightly familiar.

Table 5-3. Arithmetic test operators

Test	Comparison	Test	Comparison
-lt	Less than	-gt	Greater than
-le	Less than or equal	-ge	Greater than or equal
-eq	Equal	-ne	Not equal

You'll find these to be of the most use in the context of the numeric variables we'll see in the next chapter. They're necessary if you want to combine numeric tests with other types of tests within the same conditional expression.

However, the shell has a separate syntax for conditional expressions that involve only numbers. (This syntax is covered in Chapter 6.) It's considerably more efficient, as well as more general, so you should use it in preference to the arithmetic test operators listed above.

In fact, some of the *ksh93* documentation considers these numeric conditionals to be obsolete. Therefore, if you need to combine `[[...]]` and numeric tests, do it using the shell's !, &&, and || operators outside the [[...]], instead of inside them. Again, we'll cover the shell's numeric conditionals in the next chapter.

for

The most obvious enhancement we could make to the previous script is the ability to report on multiple files instead of just one. Tests like *−e* and *−d* only take single arguments, so we need a way of calling the code once for each file given on the command line.

The way to do this—indeed, the way to do many things with the Korn shell—is with a looping construct. The simplest and most widely applicable of the shell's looping constructs is the for loop. We'll use for to enhance *fileinfo* soon.

The for loop allows you to repeat a section of code a fixed number of times. During each time through the code (known as an *iteration*), a special variable called a *loop variable* is set to a different value; this way each iteration can do something slightly different.

The for loop is somewhat, but not entirely, similar to its counterparts in conventional languages like C and Pascal. The chief difference is that the shell's for loop doesn't let you specify a number of times to iterate or a range of values over which to iterate; instead, it only lets you give a fixed list of values. In other words, with the normal for loop, you can't do anything like this Pascal-type code, which executes *statements* 10 times:

```
for x := 1 to 10 do
begin
    statements ...
end
```

(You need the arithmetic for loop, which we'll see in Chapter 6, to do that.)

However, the for loop is ideal for working with arguments on the command line and with sets of files (e.g., all files in a given directory). We'll look at an example of each of these. But first, here is the syntax for the for construct:

```
for name [in list]
do
    statements that can use $name ...
done
```

The *list* is a list of names. (If in *list* is omitted, the list defaults to "$@", i.e., the quoted list of command-line arguments, but we always supply the in *list* for the sake of clarity.) In our solutions to the following task, we show two simple ways to specify lists.

In *ksh93* there is an interesting interaction between the for loop and nameref variables (see Chapter 4). If the control variable is a nameref, then each element in the list of names can be a different shell variable, and the shell assigns the nameref to each variable in turn. For example:

```
$ first="I am first"                              Initialize test variables
$ second="I am in the middle"
$ third="I am last"
$ nameref refvar=first                            Create nameref
$ for refvar in first second third ; do           Loop over variables
>    print "refvar -> ${!refvar}, value: $refvar"  Print referenced var, value
> done
refvar -> first, value: I am first
refvar -> second, value: I am in the middle
refvar -> third, value: I am last
$ print ${!refvar}, $refvar                       Show final state
third, I am last
```

The for loop is instrumental for solving Task 5-2.

Task 5-2

You work in an environment with several computers in a local network. Write a shell script that tells you who is logged in to each machine on the network.

The command *finger*(1) can be used (among other things) to find the names of users logged into a remote system; the command finger @*systemname* does this. Its output depends on the version of Unix, but it looks something like this:

```
[motet.early.com]
Trying 127.146.63.17...
-User-    -Full name-        -What- Idle TTY -Console Location-
hildy     Hildegard von Bingen ksh   2d5h p1  jem.cal (Telnet)
mikes     Michael Schultheiss  csh   1:21 r4  ncd2.cal (X display 0)
orlando   Orlando di Lasso     csh     28 r7  maccala (Telnet)
marin     Marin Marais         mush  1:02 pb  mussell.cal (Telnet)
johnd     John Dowland         tcsh    17 p0  nugget.west.nobis. (X Window)
```

In this output, *motet.early.com* is the full network name of the remote machine.

Assume the systems in your network are called *fred, bob, dave,* and *pete.* Then the following code would do the trick:

```
for sys in fred bob dave pete
do
    finger @$sys
    print
done
```

This works no matter which system you are currently logged into. It prints output for each machine similar to the above, with blank lines in between.

A slightly better solution would be to store the names of the systems in an environment variable. This way, if systems are added to your network and you need a list of their names in more than one script, you need change them in only one place. If a variable's value is several words separated by spaces (or TABS), for will treat it as a list of words.

Here is the improved solution. First, put lines in your *.profile* or environment file that define the variable SYSNAMES and make it an environment variable:

```
SYSNAMES="fred bob dave pete"
export SYSNAMES
```

Then, the script can look like this:

```
for sys in $SYSNAMES
do
    finger @$sys
    print
done
```

The foregoing illustrates a simple use of for, but it's much more common to use for to iterate through a list of command-line arguments. To show this, we can enhance the *fileinfo* script above to accept multiple arguments. First, we write a bit of "wrapper" code that does the iteration:

```
for filename in "$@" ; do
    finfo $filename
    print
done
```

Next, we make the original script into a function called *finfo*:*

```
function finfo {
    if [[ ! -e $1 ]]; then
        print "file $1 does not exist."
        return 1
    fi
    ...
}
```

The complete script consists of the for loop code and the above function. Because the function must be defined before it can be used, the function definition must go first, or else it should be in a directory listed in both PATH and FPATH.

The *fileinfo* script works as follows: in the for statement, "$@" is a list of all positional parameters. For each argument, the body of the loop is run with filename set to that argument. In other words, the function *fileinfo* is called once for each

---

* A function can have the same name as a script; however, this isn't good programming practice.

value of `$filename` as its first argument (`$1`). The call to *print* after the call to *file-info* merely prints a blank line between sets of information about each file.

Given a directory with the same files as the previous example, typing `fileinfo *` would produce the following output:

```
bob is a regular file.
you own the file.
you have read permission on the file.
you have write permission on the file.
you have execute permission on the file.

custom.tbl is a regular file.
you own the file.
you have read permission on the file.
you have write permission on the file.

exp is a directory that you may search.
you own the file.
you have read permission on the file.
you have write permission on the file.

lpst is a regular file.
you do not own the file.
you have read permission on the file.
```

Task 5-3 is a programming task that exploits the other major use of `for`.

Task 5-3

Your Unix system has the ability to transfer files from an MS-DOS system, but it leaves the MS-DOS filenames intact. Write a script that translates the filenames in a given directory from MS-DOS format to a more Unix-friendly format.

Filenames in the old Microsoft MS-DOS system have the format *FILENAME.EXT*. *FILENAME* can be up to eight characters long; *EXT* is an extension that can be up to three characters. Letters are all uppercase. We want to do the following:

1. Translate letters from uppercase to lowercase.

2. If the extension is null, remove the dot.

The first tool we will need for this job is the Unix *tr*(1) utility, which translates characters on a one-to-one basis.* Given the arguments *charset1* and *charset2*, it translates characters in the standard input that are members of *charset1* into corresponding characters in *charset2*. The two sets are ranges of characters enclosed in

---

* As we will see in Chapter 6, it is possible to do the case translation within the shell, without using an external program. We'll ignore that fact for now, though.

square brackets ([...] in standard regular-expression form in the manner of *grep*, *awk*, *ed*, etc.). More to the point, tr [A-Z] [a-z] takes its standard input, converts uppercase letters to lowercase, and writes the converted text to the standard output.*

That takes care of the first step in the translation process. We can use a Korn shell string operator to handle the second. Here is the code for a script we'll call *dosmv*:

```
for filename in ${1:+$1/}* ; do
    newfilename=$(print $filename | tr '[A-Z]' '[a-z]')
    newfilename=${newfilename%.}
    print "$filename -> $newfilename"
    mv $filename $newfilename
done
```

The * in the for construct is *not* the same as $*. It's a wildcard, i.e., all files in a directory.

This script accepts a directory name as argument, the default being the current directory. The expression ${1:+$1/} evaluates to the argument ($1) with a slash appended if the argument is supplied, or the null string if it isn't supplied. So the entire expression ${1:+$1/}* evaluates to all files in the given directory, or all files in the current directory if no argument is given.

Therefore, filename takes on the value of each filename in the list. filename gets translated into newfilename in two steps. (We could have done it in one, but readability would have suffered.) The first step uses *tr* in a pipeline within a command substitution construct. Our old friend *print* makes the value of filename the standard input to *tr*. *tr*'s output becomes the value of the command substitution expression, which is assigned to newfilename. Thus, if $filename were DOS-FILE.TXT, newfilename would become dosfile.txt.

The second step uses one of the shell's pattern-matching operators, the one that deletes the shortest match it finds at the end of the string. The pattern here is ., which means a dot at the end of the string.† This means that the expression ${newfilename%.} will delete a dot from $newfilename only if it's at the end of the string; otherwise the expression will leave $newfilename intact. For example, if $newfilename is dosfile.txt, it will be untouched, but if it's dosfile., the expression will change it to dosfile without the final dot. In either case, the new value is assigned back to newfilename.

---

* Modern POSIX-compliant systems support *locales*, which are ways of using non-ASCII character sets in a portable fashion. On such a system, the correct invocation of *tr* is tr '[:upper:]' '[:lower:]'. Most long-time Unix users tend to forget this, though.

† Unix regular expression mavens should remember that this is shell wildcard syntax, in which dots are not operators and therefore do not need to be backslash-escaped.

The last statement in the for loop body does the file renaming with the standard Unix *mv*(1) command. Before that, a *print* command simply informs the user of what's happening.

There is one little problem with this solution: if there are any files in the given directory that *aren't* MS-DOS files (in particular, if there are files whose names don't contain uppercase letters or don't contain a dot), then the conversion will do nothing to those filenames and *mv* will be called with two identical arguments. *mv* will complain with the message: `mv: ` `filename` ` and ` `filename` ` are identical`. The solution is very simple: test to see if the filenames are identical:

```
for filename in ${1:+$1/}* ; do
    newfilename=$(print $filename | tr '[A-Z]' '[a-z]')
    newfilename=${newfilename%.}
    # subtlety: quote value of $newfilename to do string comparison,
    # not regular expression match
    if [[ $filename != "$newfilename" ]]; then
        print "$filename -> $newfilename"
        mv $filename $newfilename
    fi
done
```

If you are familiar with an operating system other than MS-DOS and Unix, you may want to test your script-writing prowess at this point by writing a script that translates filenames from that system's format into Unix format. Use the above script as a guideline.

In particular, if you know the OpenVMS operating system from Compaq (nee DEC), here's a programming challenge:

1. Write a script called *vmsmv* that is similar to *dosmv* but works on OpenVMS filenames instead of MS-DOS filenames. Remember that OpenVMS filenames end with semicolons and version numbers.

2. Modify your script so that if there are several versions of the same file, it renames only the latest version (with the highest version number).

3. Modify it further so that your script erases old versions of files.

The first of these is a relatively straightforward modification of *dosmv*. Number 2 is difficult; here's a strategy hint:

*   Develop a regular expression that matches OpenVMS filenames (you need this for Number 1 anyway).

*   Get a list of base names (sans version numbers) of files in the given directory by piping *ls* through *grep* (with the above regular expression), *cut*, and *sort* *−u*. Use *cut* with a semicolon as "field separator"; make sure that you quote the semicolon so that the shell doesn't treat it as a statement separator. *sort −u*

removes duplicates after sorting. Use command substitution to save the result-ing list in a variable.

• Use a for loop on the list of base names. For each name, get the highest ver-sion number of the file (just the number, not the whole name). Do this with another pipeline: pipe *ls* through *cut*, *sort –n*, and *tail –1*. *sort –n* sorts in numerical (not lexicographical) order; *tail –N* outputs the last *N* lines of its input. Again, use command substitution to capture the output of this pipeline in a variable.

• Append the highest version number to the base name; this is the file to rename in Unix format.

Once you have completed Number 2, you can do Number 3 by adding a single line of code to your script; see if you can figure out how.

Finally, *ksh93* provides the arithmetic for loop, which is much closer in syntax and style to the C for loop. We present it in the next chapter, after discussing the shell's general arithmetic capabilities.

case

The next flow control construct to cover is case. While the case statement in Pas-cal and the similar switch statement in C can be used to test simple values like integers and characters, the Korn shell's case construct lets you test strings against patterns that can contain wildcard characters. Like its conventional language coun-terparts, case lets you express a series of if-then-else type statements in a concise way.

The syntax of case is as follows:

```
case expression in
    pattern1 )
        statements ;;
    pattern2 )
        statements ;;
    ...
esac
```

Any of the *patterns* can actually be several patterns separated by "OR bar" charac-ters (|, which is the same as the pipe symbol, but in this context means "or"). If *expression* matches one of the patterns, its corresponding statements are executed. If there are several patterns separated by OR bars, the expression can match any of them in order for the associated statements to be run. The patterns are checked in order until a match is found; if none is found, nothing happens.

This rather ungainly syntax should become clearer with an example. An obvious choice is to revisit our solution to Task 4-2, the front-end for the C compiler.

Earlier in this chapter, we wrote some code that processed input files according to their suffixes (.c, .s, or .o for C, assembly, or object code, respectively).

We can improve upon this solution in two ways. First, we can use for to allow multiple files to be processed at one time; second, we can use case to streamline the code:

```
for filename in "$@"; do
    case $filename in
        *.c )
            objname=${filename%.c}.o
            ccom "$filename" "$objname" ;;
        *.s )
            objname=${filename%.s}.o
            as "$filename" "$objname" ;;
        *.o ) ;;
        *   )
            print "error: $filename is not a source or object file."
            exit 1 ;;
    esac
done
```

The case construct in this code handles four cases. The first two are similar to the if and first elif cases in the code earlier in this chapter; they call the compiler or the assembler if the filename ends in .c or .s, respectively.

After that, the code is a bit different. Recall that if the filename ends in .o nothing is to be done (on the assumption that the relevant files will be linked later). We handle this with the case *.o), which has no statements. There is nothing wrong with a "case" for which the script does nothing.

If the filename does not end in .o, there is an error. This is dealt with in the final case, which is *. This is a catchall for whatever didn't match the other cases. (In fact, a * case is analogous to a default case in C and an otherwise case in some Pascal-derived languages.)

The surrounding for loop processes all command-line arguments properly. This leads to a further enhancement: now that we know how to process all arguments, we should be able to write the code that passes all of the object files to the linker (the program *ld*) at the end. We can do this by building up a string of object file names, separated by spaces, and hand that off to the linker when we've processed all of the input files. We initialize the string to null and append an object file name each time one is created, i.e., during each iteration of the for loop. The code for this is simple, requiring only minor additions:

```
objfiles=""
for filename in "$@"; do
    case $filename in
        *.c )
```

```
                objname=${filename%.c}.o
                ccom "$filename" "$objname" ;;
        *.s )
                objname=${filename%.s}.o
                as "$filename" "$objname" ;;
        *.o )
                objname=$filename ;;
        *   )
                print "error: $filename is not a source or object file."
                exit 1 ;;
    esac
    objfiles+=" $objname"
done
ld $objfiles
```

The first line in this version of the script initializes the variable objfiles to null.* We added a line of code in the *.o case to set objname equal to $filename, because we already know it's an object file. Thus, the value of objname is set in every case—except for the error case, in which the routine prints a message and bails out.

The last line of code in the for loop body appends a space and the latest $objname to objfiles. Calling this script with the same arguments as in Figure 5-1 would result in $objfiles being equal to " a.o b.o c.o d.o" when the for loop finishes (the leading space doesn't matter). This list of object filenames is given to *ld* as a single argument, but the shell divides it up into multiple file names properly.

Task 5-4 is a new task whose initial solution uses case.

Task 5-4

You are a system administrator,† and you need to set up the system so that users' TERM environment variables correctly reflect what type of terminal they are on. Write some code that does this.

The code for the solution to this task should go into the file */etc/profile*, which is the master startup file that is run for each user *before* his or her *.profile*.

For the time being, we assume that you have a traditional mainframe-style setup, in which terminals are hard-wired to the computer. This means that you can determine which (physical) terminal is being used by the line (or *tty*) it is on. This is typically a name like */dev/ttyNN*, where *NN* is the line number. You can find your tty with the command *tty*(1), which prints it on the standard output.

---

* This isn't strictly necessary, because all variables are assumed to be null if not explicitly initialized (unless the *nounset* option is turned on). It just makes the code easier to read.

† Our condolences.

Let's assume that your system has ten lines plus a system console line (*/dev/con-sole*), with the following terminals:

- Lines tty01, tty03, and tty04 are Givalt GL35a's (*terminfo* name "gl35a").

- Line tty07 is a Tsoris T-2000 ("t2000").

- Line tty08 and the console are Shande 531s ("s531").

- The rest are Vey VT99s ("vt99").

Here is the code that does the job:

```
case $(tty) in
    /dev/tty0[134]              ) TERM=gl35a ;;
    /dev/tty07                 ) TERM=t2000 ;;
    /dev/tty08 | /dev/console ) TERM=s531  ;;
    *                          ) TERM=vt99  ;;
esac
```

The value that case checks is the result of command substitution. Otherwise, the only thing new about this code is the OR bar after */dev/tty08*. This means that */dev/tty08* and */dev/console* are alternate patterns for the case that sets TERM to "s531".

Note that it is *not* possible to put alternate patterns on separate lines unless you use backslash continuation characters at the end of all but the last line. In other words, the line:

```
/dev/tty08 | /dev/console ) TERM=s531  ;;
```

could be changed to the slightly more readable:

```
/dev/tty08 | \
    /dev/console   ) TERM=s531  ;;
```

The backslash must be at the end of the line. If you omit it, or if there are charac-ters (even spaces) following it, the shell complains with a syntax error message.

This problem is actually better solved using a file that contains a table of lines and terminal types. We'll see how to do it that way in Chapter 7.

When a case appeared inside the $(...) command-substitution construct, *ksh88* had a problem: the) that demarcates each pattern from the code to execute termi-nated the $(...). To get around this, it was necessary to supply a leading (in front of the pattern:

```
result=$(case $input in
         ( dave ) print Dave! ;;        Open paren required in ksh88
         ( bob  ) print Bob! ;;
         esac)
```

ksh93 still accepts this syntax, but it no longer requires it.

Merging Cases

Sometimes, when writing a case-style construct, there are instances where one case is a subset of what should be done for another. The C language handles this by letting one case in a switch "fall through" into the code for another. A little-known fact is that the Korn shell (but not the Bourne shell) has a similar facility.

For example, let's suppose that our C compiler generates only assembly code, and that it's up to our front-end script to turn the assembly code into object code. In this case, we want to fall through from the *.c case into the *.s case. This is done using ;& to terminate the body of the case that does the falling through:

```
objfiles=""
for filename in "$@"; do
    case $filename in
        *.c )
            asmname=${filename%.c}.s
            ccom "$filename" "$asmname"
            filename=$asmname ;&      # fall through!
        *.s )
            objname=${filename%.s}.o
            as "$filename" "$objname" ;;
        *.o )
            objname=$filename ;;
        *   )
            print "error: $filename is not a source or object file."
            exit 1 ;;
    esac
    objfiles+=" $objname"
done
ld $objfiles
```

Before falling through, the *c case has to reset the value of filename so that the *.s case works correctly. It is usually a very good idea to add a comment indicating that the "fall through" is on purpose, although it is more obvious in shell than in C. We'll return to this example once more in Chapter 6 when we discuss how to handle dash options on the command line.

select

Almost all of the flow-control constructs we have seen so far are also available in the Bourne shell, and the C shell has equivalents with different syntax. Our next construct, select, is unique to the Korn shell; moreover, it has no analogue in conventional programming languages.

select allows you to generate simple menus easily. It has concise syntax, but it does quite a lot of work. The syntax is:

```
select name [in list]
do
    statements that can use $name ...
done
```

This is the same syntax as the regular for loop except for the keyword select. And like for, you can omit in list, and it will default to "$@", i.e., the list of quoted command-line arguments.

Here is what select does:

- Generates a menu of each item in *list*, formatted with numbers for each choice

- Prompts the user for a number (with the value of PS3)

- Stores the selected choice in the variable *name* and the selected number in the built-in variable REPLY

- Executes the statements in the body

- Repeats the process forever (but see below for how to exit)

Once again, an example should help make this process clearer. Assume you need to write the code for Task 5-4, but your life is not as simple. You don't have terminals hardwired to your computer; instead, your users communicate through a terminal server, or they log in remotely, via *telnet* or *ssh*. This means, among other things, that the tty number does *not* determine the type of terminal.

Therefore, you have no choice but to prompt the user for his or her terminal type at login time. To do this, you can put the following code in */etc/profile* (assume you have the same choice of terminal types):

```
PS3='terminal? '
select term in gl35a t2000 s531 vt99; do
    if [[ -n $term ]]; then
        TERM=$term
        print TERM is $TERM
        export TERM
        break
    else
        print 'invalid.'
    fi
done
```

When you run this code, you see this menu:

```
1) gl35a
2) t2000
3) s531
4) vt99
terminal?
```

The built-in shell variable PS3 contains the prompt string that select uses; its default value is the not particularly useful "#? ". So the first line of the above code sets it to a more relevant value.*

The select statement constructs the menu from the list of choices. If the user enters a valid number (from 1 to 4), the variable term is set to the corresponding value; otherwise it is null. (If the user just presses ENTER, the shell prints the menu again.)

The code in the loop body checks if term is non-null. If so, it assigns $term to the environment variable TERM, exports TERM, and prints a confirmation message; then the *break* statement exits the select loop. If term is null, the code prints an error message and repeats the prompt (but not the menu).

The *break* statement is the usual way of exiting a select loop. Actually (like its analogue in C), it can be used to exit any surrounding control structure we've seen so far (except case, where the double-semicolons act like *break*) as well as the while and until we will see soon. We haven't introduced *break* until now because some people consider it to be bad coding style to use it to exit a loop. However, it is necessary for exiting select when the user makes a valid choice. (A user can also type CTRL-D—for end-of-input—to get out of a select loop. This gives the user a uniform way of exiting, but it doesn't help the shell programmer much.)

Let's refine our solution by making the menu more user-friendly, so that the user doesn't have to know the *terminfo* name of his or her terminal. We do this by using quoted character strings as menu items and then using case to determine the terminfo name:

```
print 'Select your terminal type:'
PS3='terminal? '
select term in \
    'Givalt GL35a' \
    'Tsoris T-2000' \
    'Shande 531' \
    'Vey VT99'
do
    case $REPLY in
        1 ) TERM=gl35a ;;
        2 ) TERM=t2000 ;;
        3 ) TERM=s531 ;;
        4 ) TERM=vt99 ;;
        * ) print 'invalid.' ;;
    esac
    if [[ -n $term ]]; then
        print TERM is $TERM
        export TERM
```

---

* As for PS1, *ksh* does parameter, command, and arithmetic substitution on the value before printing it.

```
        break
    fi
done
```

This code looks a bit more like a menu routine in a conventional program, though select still provides the shortcut of converting the menu choices into numbers. We list each of the menu choices on its own line for reasons of readability, but once again we need continuation characters to keep the shell from complaining about syntax.

Here is what the user sees when this code is run:

```
Select your terminal type:
1) Givalt GL35a
2) Tsoris T-2000
3) Shande 531
4) Vey VT99
terminal?
```

This is a bit more informative than the previous code's output.

When the body of the select loop is entered, $term equals one of the four strings (or is null if the user made an invalid choice), while the built-in variable REPLY contains the number the user selected. We need a case statement to assign the correct value to TERM; we use the value of REPLY as the case selector.

Once the case statement is finished, the if checks to see if a valid choice was made, as in the previous solution. If the choice was valid, TERM has already been assigned, so the code just prints a confirmation message, exports TERM, and exits the select loop. If it wasn't valid, the select loop repeats the prompt and goes through the process again.

Within a select loop, if REPLY is set to the null string, the shell reprints the menu. This happens, as mentioned, when the user hits ENTER. But you may also explicitly set REPLY to the null string to force the shell to reprint the menu.

The variable TMOUT (time out) can affect the select statement. Before the select loop, set it to some number of seconds *N*, and if nothing is entered within that amount of time, the select will exit. As will be explained later, TMOUT also affects the *read* command and the shell's interactive prompting mechanism.

while and until

The remaining two flow control constructs the Korn shell provides are while and until. These are similar; both allow a section of code to be run repetitively while (or until) a certain condition holds true. They also resemble analogous constructs in Pascal (while/do and repeat/until) and C (while and do/while).

while and until are actually most useful when combined with features we will see in the next chapter, such as arithmetic, input/output of variables, and command-line processing. Yet we can show a useful example even with the machinery we have covered so far.

The syntax for while is:

```
while condition
do
    statements ...
done
```

For until, just substitute until for while in the above example. As with if, the *condition* is really a list of *statements* that are run; the exit status of the last one is used as the value of the condition. You can use a conditional with [[and]] here, just as you can with if.

The *only* difference between while and until is the way the condition is handled. In while, the loop executes as long as the condition is true; in until, it runs as long as the condition is false. So far, so familiar. However, the until condition is checked at the *top* of the loop, *not* at the bottom as it is in analogous constructs in C and Pascal.

The result is that you can convert any until into a while simply by negating the condition. The only place where until might be better is something like this:

```
until command; do
    statements ...
done
```

The meaning of this is essentially, "Do *statements* until *command* runs correctly." This is occasionally useful, such as when waiting for the occurrence of a particular event. However, we use while throughout the rest of this book.

Task 5-5 is a good candidate for while.

Task 5-5

Implement a simplified version of the shell's built-in *whence* command.

By "simplified," we mean that we will implement only the part that checks all the directories in your PATH for the command you give as argument (we won't implement checking for aliases, built-in commands, etc.).

We can do this by picking off the directories in PATH one by one, using one of the shell's pattern-matching operators, and seeing if there is a file with the given name in the directory that you have permission to execute. Here is the code:

```
path=$PATH:
dir=${path%%:*}
while [[ -n $path ]]; do
    if [[ $dir == "" ]] ; then
        dir="."
    fi
    if [[ -x $dir/$1 && ! -d $dir/$1 ]]; then
        print "$dir/$1"
        exit 0
    fi
    path=${path#*:}
    dir=${path%%:*}
done
exit 1
```

The first line of this code saves $PATH in path, our own temporary copy. We append a colon to the end so that every directory in $path ends in a colon (in $PATH, colons are used only *between* directories); subsequent code depends on this being the case.

The next line picks the first directory off $path by using the operator that deletes the longest match of the pattern given. In this case, we delete the longest match of the pattern :*, i.e., a colon followed by anything. This gives us the first directory in $path, which we store in the variable dir.

The condition in the while loop checks if $path is non-null. If it is not null, it first checks that $dir is not null. This could happen for two adjacent colons, which represent the current directory. In this case, dir is explicitly set to dot. Next, the script constructs the full pathname $dir/$1 and sees if there is a file by that name for which you have execute permission (and that is not a directory). If so, it prints the full pathname and exits the routine with a 0 ("OK") exit status.

If a file is not found, this code is run:

```
path=${path#*:}
dir=${path%%:*}
```

The first of these uses another shell string operator: this one deletes the shortest match of the pattern given from the front of the string. By now, this type of operator should be familiar. This line deletes the front directory from $path and assigns the result back to path. The second line is the same as before the while: it finds the (new) front directory in $path and assigns it to dir. This sets up the loop for another iteration.

Thus, the code loops through all of the directories in PATH. It exits when it finds a matching executable file or when it has "eaten up" the entire PATH. If no matching executable file is found, it prints nothing and exits with an error status.

We can enhance this script a bit by taking advantage of the Unix utility *file*(1). *file* examines files given as arguments and determines what type they are, based on the file's *magic number* and various heuristics (educated guesses). A magic number is a field in the header of an executable file that the linker sets to identify what type of executable it is.

If *filename* is an executable program (compiled from C or some other language), typing `file filename` produces output similar to this:

```
filename: ELF 32-bit LSB executable 80386 Version 1
```

However, if *filename* is not an executable program, it will examine the first few lines and try to guess what kind of information the file contains. If the file contains text (as opposed to binary data), *file* will look for indications that it is English, shell commands, C, Fortran, *troff*(1) input, and various other things. *file* is wrong sometimes, but it is usually correct.

Assume that *fred* is an executable file in the directory */usr/bin*, and that *bob* is a shell script in */usr/local/bin*. Typing `file /usr/bin/fred` produces this output:

```
/usr/bin/fred: ELF 32-bit LSB executable 80386 Version 1
```

Typing `file /usr/local/bin/bob` has this result:

```
/usr/local/bin/bob: commands text
```

We can just substitute *file* for *print* to print a more informative message in our script:

```
path=$PATH:
while [[ -n $path ]]; do
    dir=${path%%:*}
    if [[ $dir == "" ]] ; then
        dir="."
    fi
    if [[ -x $dir/$1 && ! -d $dir/$1 ]]; then
        file $dir/$1
        exit 0
    fi
    path=${path#*:}
done
exit 1
```

Notice that by moving the statement `dir=${path%%:*}` to the top of the loop body, it needs to be done only once.

Finally, just to show how little difference there is between while, and until, we note that the line:

```
until [[ ! -n $path ]]; do
```

can be used in place of:

```
while [[ -n $path ]]; do
```

with identical results.

We'll see additional examples of while in the next chapter.

break and continue

Earlier in this chapter, we saw the *break* statement used with the select construct for breaking out of a loop. *break* can be used with any looping construct: for, select, while and until.

The *continue* statement is related; its job is to skip any remaining statements in the body of the loop and start the next iteration.

Both the *break* and *continue* statements take an optional numeric argument (which can be a numeric expression). This indicates how many enclosing loops should be broken out of or continued. For example:

```
while condition1; do              Outer loop
    ...
    while condition2; do          Inner loop
        ...
        break 2                   Breaks out of outer loop
    done
done
...                               Execution continues here after break
```

Programmers will note that the *break* and *continue* statements, particularly with the ability to break or continue multiple loop levels, compensate in a very clean fashion for the lack of a goto keyword in the shell language.

6

In this chapter:
- *Command-Line Options*
- *Numeric Variables and Arithmetic*
- *Arithmetic for*
- *Arrays*
- *typeset*

Command-Line Options and Typed Variables

You should have a healthy grasp of shell programming techniques now that you have gone through the previous chapters. What you have learned up to this point enables you to write many nontrivial, useful shell scripts and functions.

Still, you may have noticed some remaining gaps in the knowledge you need to write shell code that behaves like the Unix commands you are used to. In particular, if you are an experienced Unix user, it might have occurred to you that none of the example scripts shown so far have the ability to handle *options* (preceded by a dash (–)) on the command line. And if you program in a conventional language like C or Pascal, you will have noticed that the only type of data that we have seen in shell variables is character strings; we haven't seen how to do arithmetic, for example.

These capabilities are certainly crucial to the shell's ability to function as a useful Unix programming language. In this chapter, we show how the Korn shell supports these and related features.

Command-Line Options

We have already seen many examples of the *positional parameters* (variables called 1, 2, 3, etc.) that the shell uses to store the command-line arguments to a shell script or function when it runs. We have also seen related variables like * and @ (for the string(s) of all arguments) and # (for the number of arguments).

Indeed, these variables hold all the information on the user's command line. But consider what happens when options are involved. Typical Unix commands have the form *command* [*–options*] *args*, meaning that there can be zero or more options. If a shell script processes the command fred bob pete, then $1 is "bob" and $2 is "pete". But if the command is `fred -o bob pete`, then $1 is *−o*, $2 is "bob", and $3 is "pete".

You might think you could write code like this to handle it:

```
if [[ $1 == -o ]]; then
    code that processes the -o option
    1=$2
    2=$3
fi
normal processing of $1 and $2...
```

But this code has several problems. First, assignments like 1=$2 are illegal because positional parameters are read-only. Even if they were legal, another problem is that this kind of code imposes limitations on how many arguments the script can handle—which is very unwise. Furthermore, if this command had several possible options, the code to handle all of them would get very messy very quickly.

shift

Luckily, the shell provides a way around this problem. The command *shift* performs the function of:

```
1=$2
2=$3
...
```

for every argument, regardless of how many there are. If you supply a numeric argument* to *shift*, it shifts the arguments that many times over; for example, `shift 3` has this effect:

```
1=$4
2=$5
...
```

This leads immediately to some code that handles a single option (call it *−o*) and arbitrarily many arguments:

```
if [[ $1 == -o ]]; then
    process the -o option
    shift
fi
normal processing of arguments ...
```

After the `if` construct, $1, $2, etc., are set to the correct arguments, and $# is automatically adjusted, as well.

---

* The argument can actually be a numeric expression; the shell automatically evaluates it.

We can use *shift* together with the programming features we have seen so far to implement simple option schemes. However, we will need additional help when things get more complex. The *getopts* built-in command, which we introduce later, provides this help.

shift by itself gives us enough power to implement the *-N* option to the *highest* script we saw in Task 4-1. Recall that this script takes an input file that lists artists and the number of albums you have by them. It sorts the list and prints out the *N* highest numbers, in descending order. The code that does the actual data processing is:

```
filename=$1
howmany=${2:-10}
sort -nr $filename | head -$howmany
```

Our original syntax for calling this script was `highest filename [N]`, where *N* defaults to 10 if omitted. Let's change this to a more conventional Unix syntax, in which options are given before arguments: `highest [-N] filename`. Here is how we would write the script with this syntax:

```
if [[ $1 == -+([0-9]) ]]; then
    howmany=$1
    shift
elif [[ $1 == -* ]]; then
    print 'usage: highest [-N] filename'
    exit 1
else
    howmany="-10"
fi
filename=$1
sort -nr $filename | head $howmany
```

In this code, the option is considered to be supplied if $1 matches the pattern `-+([0-9])`. This uses one of the Korn shell's regular expression operators, which we saw in Chapter 4. Notice that we didn't surround the pattern with quotes (even double quotes); if we did, the shell would interpret it literally, not as a pattern. This pattern means "A dash followed by one or more digits." If $1 matches, then we assign it to the variable `howmany`.

If $1 doesn't match, we test to see if it's an option at all, i.e., if it matches the pattern `-*`. If it does, then it's invalid; we print an error message and exit with error status. If we reach the final (`else`) case, we provide the default value for `howmany` and assume that $1 is a filename and treat it as such in the ensuing code. The rest of the script processes the data as before.

We can extend what we have learned so far to a general technique for handling multiple options. For the sake of concreteness, assume that our script is called *bob* and we want to handle the options *-a*, *-b*, and *-c*:

```
while [[ $1 == -* ]]; do
    case $1 in
        -a ) process option -a ;;
        -b ) process option -b ;;
        -c ) process option -c ;;
        *  ) print 'usage: bob [-a] [-b] [-c] args ...'
             exit 1 ;;
    esac
    shift
done
normal processing of arguments ...
```

This code checks $1 repeatedly as long as it starts with a dash (-). Then the case construct runs the appropriate code depending on which option $1 is. If the option is invalid (i.e., if it starts with a dash but isn't *-a*, *-b*, or *-c*), the script prints a usage message and returns with an error exit status. After each option is processed, the arguments are shifted over. The result is that the positional parameters are set to the actual arguments when the while loop finishes.

Notice that by generalizing this code, you can handle options of arbitrary length, not just one letter (e.g., -fred instead of -a).

Options with Arguments

We need to add one more ingredient to make option processing really useful. Recall that many commands have options that take their *own* arguments. For example, the *cut* command, on which we relied heavily in Chapter 4, accepts the option *-d* with an argument that determines the field delimiter (if it is not the default TAB). To handle this type of option, we just use another *shift* when we are processing the option.

Assume that, in our *bob* script, the option *-b* requires its own argument. Here is the modified code that processes it:

```
while [[ $1 == -* ]]; do
    case $1 in
        -a ) process option -a ;;
        -b ) process option -b
             $2 is the option's argument
             shift ;;
        -c ) process option -c ;;
        *  ) print 'usage: bob [-a] [-b barg] [-c] args ...'
             exit 1 ;;
    esac
    shift
done
normal processing of arguments ...
```

getopts

So far, we have a complete, though still constrained, way of handling command-line options. The above code does not allow a user to combine arguments with a single dash, e.g., -abc instead of -a -b -c. It also doesn't allow the user to specify arguments to options without a space in between, e.g., -barg in addition to -b arg.*

The shell provides a built-in way to deal with multiple complex options without these constraints. The built-in command *getopts*† can be used as the condition of the while in an option-processing loop. Given a specification of which options are valid and which require their own arguments, it sets up the body of the loop to process each option in turn.

getopts takes at least two arguments. The first is a string that can contain letters and colons. Each letter is a valid option; if a letter is followed by a colon, the option requires an argument. If the letter is followed by a #, the option requires a numeric argument. The : or # may be followed by [*description*], i.e., a descriptive string enclosed in square brackets that is used when generating usage error messages. If you append a space with more descriptive text to the list of option characters, that text is also printed in error messages.

getopts picks options off the command line and assigns each one (without the leading dash) to a variable whose name is *getopts*'s second argument. As long as there are options left to process, *getopts* returns exit status 0; when the options are exhausted, it returns exit status 1, causing the while loop to exit.

By default, *getopts* loops through "$@", the quoted list of command line arguments. However, you may supply additional arguments to *getopts*, in which case it uses those arguments, instead.

getopts does a few other things that make option processing easier; we'll encounter them as we examine how to use *getopts* in the preceding example:

```
while getopts ":ab:c" opt; do
    case $opt in
        a  ) process option -a ;;
        b  ) process option -b
             $OPTARG is the option's argument ;;
        c  ) process option -c ;;
        \? ) print 'usage: bob [-a] [-b barg] [-c] args ...'
```

---

* Although most Unix commands allow this, it is actually contrary to the Command Syntax Standard Rules originally set forth in *intro*(1) of the Unix System V *User's Manual.* These rules have now been codified by POSIX.

† *getopts* replaces the external command *getopt*(1), used in Bourne shell programming; *getopts* is better integrated into the shell's syntax and runs more efficiently. C programmers will recognize *getopts* as very similar to the standard library routine *getopt*(3).

```
                exit 1 ;;
        esac
   done
   shift $(($OPTIND - 1))
```
normal processing of arguments ...

The call to *getopts* in the while condition sets up the loop to accept the options *–a*, *–b*, and *–c*, and specifies that *–b* takes an argument. (We will explain the ":" that starts the option string in a moment.) Each time the loop body is executed, it has the latest option available, without a dash (-), in the variable opt.

If the user types an invalid option, *getopts* normally prints an error message (of the form cmd: -o: unknown option) and sets opt to ?. *getopts* finishes processing all its options, and if an error was encountered, the shell exits. However—now here's an obscure kludge—if you begin the option letter string with a colon, *getopts* won't print the message, and shell will not exit. This allows you to handle error messages on your own.

You may either supply the leading colon and provide your own error message in a case that handles ? and exits manually, as above, or you may provide descriptive text within the call to *getopts*, and let the shell handle printing the error message. In the latter case, the shell will also automatically exit upon encountering an invalid option.

We have modified the code in the case construct to reflect what *getopts* does. But notice that there are no more *shift* statements inside the while loop: *getopts* does not rely on *shift*s to keep track of where it is. It is unnecessary to shift arguments over until *getopts* is finished, i.e., until the while loop exits.

If an option has an argument, *getopts* stores it in the variable OPTARG, which can be used in the code that processes the option.

The one *shift* statement left is after the while loop. *getopts* stores in the variable OPTIND the number of the next argument to be processed; in this case, that's the number of the first (non-option) command-line argument. For example, if the command line were bob -ab pete, then $OPTIND would be "2". If it were bob -a -b pete, then $OPTIND would be "3". OPTIND is reinitialized to 1 whenever you run a function, which allows you to use *getopts* within a function body.

The expression $(($OPTIND - 1)) is an arithmetic expression (as we'll see later in this chapter) equal to $OPTIND minus 1. This value is used as the argument to *shift*. The result is that the correct number of arguments is shifted out of the way, leaving the "real" arguments as $1, $2, etc.

Before we continue, now is a good time to summarize everything that *getopts* does (including some points not mentioned yet):

1. If given the −*a* option and an argument, *getopts* uses that argument as the program name in any error messages, instead of the default, which is the name of the script. This is most useful if you are using *getopts* within a function, where $0 is the name of the function. In that case, it's less confusing if the error message uses the script name instead of the function name.

2. Its first (non-option) argument is a string containing all valid option letters. If an option requires an argument, a colon follows its letter in the string. An initial colon causes *getopts* not to print an error message when the user gives an invalid option.

3. Its second argument is the name of a variable that holds each option letter (without any leading dash) as it is processed. Upon encountering an error, this variable will contain a literal ? character.

4. Following an option letter with a # instead of a colon indicates that the option takes a numeric argument.

5. When an option takes an argument (the option letter is followed by either a color or a # symbol), appending a question mark indicates that the option's argument is optional (i.e., not required).

6. If additional arguments are given on the *getopts* command line after the option string and variable name, they are used instead of "$@".

7. If an option takes an argument, the argument is stored in the variable OPTARG.

8. The variable OPTIND contains a number equal to the next command-line argument to be processed. After *getopts* is done, it equals the number of the first "real" argument.

9. If the first character in the option string is + (or the second character after a leading colon), then options may start with + as well. In this case, the option variable will have a value that starts with +.

getopts can do much, much more than described here. See Appendix B, which provides the full story.

The advantages of *getopts* are that it minimizes extra code necessary to process options and fully supports the standard command option syntax as specified by POSIX.

As a more concrete example, let's return to our C compiler front-end (Task 4-2). So far, we have given our script the ability to process C source files (ending in .c), assembly code files (.s), and object code files (.o). Here is the latest version of the script:

```
objfiles=""
for filename in "$@"; do
    case $filename in
        *.c )
            objname=${filename%.c}.o
            ccom "$filename" "$objname" ;;
        *.s )
            objname=${filename%.s}.o
            as "$filename" "$objname" ;;
        *.o )
            objname=$filename ;;
        *   )
            print "error: $filename is not a source or object file."
            exit 1 ;;
    esac
    objfiles+=" $objname"
done
ld $objfiles
```

Now we can give the script the ability to handle options. To know what options we'll need, we have to discuss further what compilers do.

More about C compilers

C compilers on typical modern Unix systems tend to have a bewildering array of options. To make life simple, we'll limit ourselves to the most widely-used ones.

Here's what we'll implement. All compilers provide the ability to eliminate the final linking step, i.e., the call to the linker *ld*. This is useful for compiling C code into object code files that will be linked later, and for taking advantage of the compiler's error checking separately before trying to link. The *−c* option (compile only) suppresses the link step, producing only the compiled object code files.

C compilers are also capable of including lots of extra information in an object code file that can be used by a debugger (though it is ignored by the linker and the running program). If you don't know what a debugger is, see Chapter 9. The debugger needs lots of information about the original C code to be able to do its job; the option *−g* directs the compiler to include this information in its object-code output.

If you aren't already familiar with Unix C compilers, you may have thought it strange when you saw in the last chapter that the linker puts its output (the executable program) in a file called *a.out*. This convention is a historical relic that no one ever bothered to change. Although it's certainly possible to change the executable's name with the *mv* command, the C compiler provides the option *−o file-name*, which uses *filename* instead of *a.out*.

Another option we will support here has to do with *libraries*. A library is a collection of object code, *some* of which is to be included in the executable at link time.

(This is in contrast to a precompiled object code file, *all* of which is linked in.) Each library includes a large amount of object code that supports a certain type of interface or activity; typical Unix systems have libraries for things like networking, math functions, and graphics.

Libraries are extremely useful as building blocks that help programmers write complex programs without having to "reinvent the wheel" every time. The C compiler option *–l name* tells the linker to include whatever code is necessary from the library *name** in the executable it builds. One particular library called *c* (the file *libc.a*) is always included. This is known as the C runtime library; it contains code for C's standard input and output capability, among other things. (While Unix compilers normally take library specifications *after* the list of object files, our front-end treats them just like any other option, meaning that they must be listed before the object files.)

Finally, it is possible for a good C compiler to do certain things that make its output object code smaller and more efficient. Collectively, these things are called *optimization*. You can think of an *optimizer* as an extra step in the compilation process that looks back at the object-code output and changes it for the better. The option *–O* invokes the optimizer.

Table 6-1 summarizes the options we will build into our C compiler front-end.

Table 6-1. Popular C compiler options

Option	Meaning
-c	Produce object code only; do not invoke the linker
-g	Include debugging information in object code files
-l *lib*	Include the library *lib* when linking
-o *exefile*	Produce the executable file *exefile* instead of the default *a.out*
-O	Invoke the optimizer

You should also bear in mind this information about the options:

- The options *–o* and *–l lib* are merely passed on to the linker (*ld*), which processes them on its own.

- The *–l lib* option can be used multiple times to link in multiple libraries.

- On most systems, *ld* requires that library options come after object files on the command line. (This also violates the conventions we've been working so hard to adhere to.) In addition, the order of libraries on the command line matters. If a routine in *libA.a* references another routine from *libB.a*, then

---

* This is actually a file called *lib*name.*a* in a standard library directory such as */lib* or */usr/lib*.

libA.a must appear first on the command line (-1A -1B). This implies that the C library (*libc.a*) has to be loaded last, since routines in other libraries almost always depend upon the standard routines in the C library.

* The *–g* option is passed to the *ccom* command (the program that does the actual C compilation).

* We will assume that the optimizer is a separate program called *optimize* that accepts an object file as argument and optimizes it "in place," i.e., without producing a separate output file.

For our front-end, we've chosen to let the shell handle printing the usage message. Here is the code for the script *occ* that includes option processing:

```
# initialize option-related variables
do_link=true
debug=""
link_libs=""
clib="-lc"
exefile=""
opt=false

# process command-line options
while getopts "cgl:[lib]o:[outfile]O files ..." option; do
    case $option in
        c )     do_link=false ;;
        g )     debug="-g" ;;
        l )     link_libs+=" -l $OPTARG" ;;
        o )     exefile="-o $OPTARG" ;;
        O )     opt=true ;;
    esac
done
shift $(($OPTIND - 1))

# process the input files
objfiles=""
for filename in "$@"; do
    case $filename in
        *.c )
            objname=${filename%.c}.o
            ccom $debug "$filename" "$objname"
            if [[ $opt == true ]]; then
                optimize "$objname"
            fi ;;
        *.s )
            objname=${filename%.s}.o
            as "$filename" "$objname" ;;
            if [[ $opt == true ]]; then
                optimize "$objname"
            fi ;;
        *.o )
            objname=$filename ;;
        *    )
```

```
              print "error: $filename is not a source or object file."
              exit 1 ;;
     esac
     objfiles+=" $objname"
 done

 if [[ $do_link == true ]]; then
     ld $exefile $objfiles $link_libs $clib
 fi
```

Let's examine the option-processing part of this code. The first several lines initialize variables that we use later to store the status of each of the options. We use "true" and "false" for truth values for readability; they are just strings and otherwise have no special meaning. The initializations reflect these assumptions:

- We will want to link.

- We will not want the compiler to generate space-consuming debugger information.

- The only object-code library we will need is *c*, the standard C runtime library that is automatically linked in.

- The executable file that the linker creates will be the linker's default file, *a.out*.

- We will not want to invoke the optimizer.

The while, getopts, and case constructs process the options in the same way as the previous example. Here is what the code that handles each option does:

- If the *–c* option is given, the do_link flag is set to "false," which causes the if condition at the end of the script to be false, meaning that the linker will not run.

- If *–g* is given, the debug variable is set to "-g". This is passed on the command line to the compiler.

- Each *–l lib* that is given is appended to the variable link_libs, so that when the while loop exits, $link_libs is the entire string of *–l* options. This string is passed to the linker.

- If *–o file* is given, the exefile variable is set to "-o *file*". This string is passed to the linker.

- If *–O* is specified, the opt flag is set to "true." This specification causes the conditional if [[$opt == true]] to be true, which means that the optimizer will run.

The remainder of the code is a modification of the for loop we have already seen; the modifications are direct results of the above option processing and should be self-explanatory.

Numeric Variables and Arithmetic

The expression $((\$OPTIND - 1))$ in the last example gives a clue as to how the shell can do integer arithmetic. As you might guess, the shell interprets words surrounded by $((\ $ and $))$ as arithmetic expressions. Variables in arithmetic expressions do *not* need to be preceded by dollar signs. It is OK to supply the dollar sign, except when assigning a value to a variable.

Arithmetic expressions are evaluated inside double quotes, like variables and command substitutions. We're *finally* in a position to state the definitive rule about quoting strings: When in doubt, enclose a string in single quotes, unless it contains any expression involving a dollar sign, in which case you should use double quotes.

For example, the *date*(1) command on modern versions of Unix accepts arguments that tell it how to format its output. The argument +%j tells it to print the day of the year, i.e., the number of days since December 31st of the previous year.

We can use +%j to print a little holiday anticipation message:

```
print "Only $(( (365-$(date +%j)) / 7 )) weeks until the New Year!"
```

We'll show where this fits in the overall scheme of command-line processing in Chapter 7.

The arithmetic expression feature is built in to the Korn shell's syntax, and it was available in the Bourne shell (most versions) only through the external command *expr*(1). Thus it is yet another example of a desirable feature provided by an external command (i.e., a syntactic kludge) being better integrated into the shell. [[...]] and *getopts* are also examples of this design trend.

While *expr* and *ksh88* were limited to integer arithmetic, *ksh93* supports floating-point arithmetic. As we'll see shortly, you can do just about any calculation in the Korn shell that you could do in C or most other programming languages.

Korn shell arithmetic operators are equivalent to their counterparts in the C language. Precedence and associativity are the same as in C. (More details on the Korn shell's compatibility with the C language may be found in Appendix B; said details are of interest mostly to people already familiar with C.) Table 6-2 shows the arithmetic operators that are supported, in order from highest precedence to lowest. Although some of these are (or contain) special characters, there is no need to backslash-escape them, because they are within the $((...))$ syntax.

Table 6-2. Arithmetic operators

Operator	Meaning	Associativity
++ --	Increment and decrement, prefix and postfix	Left to right
+ - ! ~	Unary plus and minus; logical and bitwise negation	Right to left
**	Exponentiation[a]	Right to left
* / %	Multiplication, division, and remainder	Left to right
+ -	Addition and subtraction	Left to right
<< >>	Bit-shift left and right	Left to right
< <= > >=	Comparisons	Left to right
== !=	Equal and not equal	Left to right
&	Bitwise and	Left to right
^	Bitwise exclusive-or	Left to right
|	Bitwise or	Left to right
&&	Logical and (short circuit)	Left to right
||	Logical or (short circuit)	Left to right
?:	Conditional expression	Right to left
= += -= *= /= %= &= ^= <<= >>=	Assignment operators	Right to left
,	Sequential evaluation	Left to right

[a] *ksh93m* and newer. The ** operator is not in the C language.

Parentheses can be used to group subexpressions. The arithmetic expression syntax (like C) supports relational operators as "truth values" of 1 for true and 0 for false.

For example, $((3 > 2))$ has the value 1; $(((3 > 2) || (4 <= 1)))$ also has the value 1, since at least one of the two subexpressions is true.

If you're familiar with C, C++ or Java, the operators listed in Table 6-2 will be familiar. But if you're not, some of them warrant a little explanation.

The assignment forms of the regular operators are a convenient shorthand for the more conventional way of updating a variable. For example, in Pascal or Fortran you might write x = x + 2 to add 2 to x. The += lets you do that more compactly: $((x += 2))$ adds 2 to x and stores the result back in x. (Compare this to the recent addition of the += operator to *ksh93* for string concatenation.)

Since adding and subtracting 1 are such frequent operations, the ++ and -- operators provide an even more abbreviated way to do them. As you might guess, ++ adds 1, while -- subtracts 1. These are unary operators. Let's take a quick look at how they work.

```
$ i=5
$ print $((i++)) $i
5 6
$ print $((++i)) $i
7 7
```

What's going on here? In both cases, the value of i is increased by one. But the value returned by the operator depends upon its placement relative to the variable being operated upon. A *postfix* operator (one that occurs after the variable) returns the variable's *old* value as the result of the expression and then increments the variable. By contrast, a *prefix* operator, which comes in front of the variable, increments the variable first and then returns the new value. The -- operator works the same as ++, but it decrements the variable by one, instead of incrementing it.

The shell also supports base *N* numbers, where *N* can be up to 64. The notation *B#N* means "*N* base *B*." Of course, if you omit the *B#*, the base defaults to .10. The digits are 0–9, a–z (10–35), A–Z (36–61), @ (62), and _ (63). (When the base is less than or equal to 36, you may use mixed case letters.) For example:

```
$ print the ksh number 43#G is $((43#G))
the ksh number 43#G is 42
```

Interestingly enough, you can use shell variables to contain subexpressions, and the shell substitutes the value of the variable when doing arithmetic. For example:

```
$ almost_the_answer=10+20
$ print $almost_the_answer
10+20
$ print $(( almost_the_answer + 12 ))
42
```

Built-in Arithmetic Functions

The shell provides a number of built-in arithmetic and trigonometric functions for use with $((...)). They are called using C function call syntax. The trigonometric functions expect arguments to be in radians, not in degrees. (There are 2π radians in a circle.) For example, remembering way back to high-school days, recall that 45 degrees is π divided by 4. Let's say we need the cosine of 45 degrees:

```
$ pi=3.1415927        Approximate value for π
$ print the cosine of pi / 4 is $(( cos(pi / 4) ))
the cosine of pi / 4 is 0.707106772982
```

A better approximation of π may be obtained using the atan function:

```
pi=$(( 4. * atan(1.) ))                          A better value for π
```

Table 6-3 lists the built-in arithmetic functions.

Table 6-3. Built-in arithmetic functions

Function	Returns		Function	Returns
abs	Absolute value		hypot[a]	Euclidean distance
acos	Arc cosine		int	Integer part
asin	Arc sine		log	Natural logarithm
atan	Arc tangent		pow[a]	Exponentiation (x^y)
atan2[a]	Arc tangent of two variables		sin	Sine
cos	Cosine		sinh	Hyperbolic sine
cosh	Hyperbolic cosine		sqrt	Square root
exp	Exponential (e^x)		tan	Tangent
fmod[a]	Floating-point remainder		tanh	Hyperbolic tangent

[a] Added in *ksh93e*.

Arithmetic Conditionals

Another construct, closely related to $((...)), is ((...)) (without the leading dollar sign). We use this for evaluating arithmetic condition tests, just as [[...]] is used for string, file attribute, and other types of tests.

((...)) is almost identical to $((...)). However, it was designed for use in if and while constructs. Instead of producing a textual result, it just sets its exit status according to the truth of the expression: 0 if true, 1 otherwise. So, for example, ((3 > 2)) produces exit status 0, as does (((3 > 2) || (4 <= 1))), but (((3 > 2) && (4 <= 1))) has exit status 1 since the second subexpression isn't true.

You can also use numerical values for truth values within this construct. It's like the analogous concept in C: a value of 0 means *false* (i.e., returns exit status 1), and a non-zero value means *true* (returns exit status 0), e.g., ((14)) is true. See the code for the *kshdb* debugger in Chapter 9 for more examples of this.

Arithmetic Variables and Assignment

The ((...)) construct can also be used to define numeric variables and assign values to them. The statement:

```
(( var=expression ))
```

creates the numeric variable *var* (if it doesn't already exist) and assigns to it the result of *expression*.

The double-parentheses syntax is what's recommended. However, if you prefer to use a command for doing arithmetic, the shell provides one: the built-in command *let*. The syntax is:

```
let var=expression
```

It is not necessary (because it's actually redundant) to surround the expression with $((and)) in a *let* statement. When not using quotes, there must not be any space on either side of the equal sign (=). However, it is good practice to surround expressions with quotes, since many characters are treated as special by the shell (e.g., *, #, and parentheses); furthermore, you must quote expressions that include whitespace (spaces or TABs). See Table 6-4 for examples. Once you have quotes, you can use spaces:

```
let "x = 3.1415927" "y = 1.41421"
```

While *ksh88* only allowed you to use integer variables, *ksh93* no longer has this restriction, and variables may be floating point as well. (An *integer* is what was called a "whole number" in school, a number that doesn't have a fractional part, such as 17 or 42. Floating-point numbers, in contrast, can have fractional parts, such as 3.1415927.) The shell looks for a decimal point in order to determine that a value is floating point. Without one, values are treated as integers. This is primarily an issue for division: integer division truncates any fractional part. The % operator requires an integer divisor.

The shell provides two built-in aliases for declaring numeric variables: *integer* for integer variables and *float* for floating point variables. (These are both aliases for the *typeset* command with different options. More details are provided in the section "Type and Attribute Options," later in this chapter.)

Finally, all assignments to both integer and floating-point variables are automatically evaluated as arithmetic expressions. This means that you don't need to use the *let* command:

```
$ integer the_answer
$ the_answer=12+30
$ print $the_answer
42
```

Table 6-4. Sample expression assignments

Assignment let x=	Value $x
x=1+4	5
'x = 1 + 4'	5
'x = 1.234 + 3'	4.234

Table 6-4. Sample expression assignments (continued)

Assignment let x=	Value $x
'x = (2+3) * 5'	25
'x = 2 + 3 * 5'	17
'x = 17 / 3'	5
'x = 17 / 3.0'	5.66666666667
'17 % 3'	2
'1 << 4'	16
'48 >> 3'	6
'17 & 3'	1
'17	3'	19
'17 ^ 3'	18

Task 6-1 is a small task that makes use of arithmetic.

Task 6-1

Write a script called *pages* that, given the name of a text file, tells how many pages of output it contains. Assume that there are 66 lines to a page, but provide an option allowing the user to override that.

We'll make our option *-N*, a la *head*. The syntax for this single option is so simple that we need not bother with *getopts*. Here is the code:

```
if [[ $1 == -+([0-9]) ]]; then
    (( page_lines = ${1#-} ))
    shift
else
    (( page_lines = 66 ))
fi
let file_lines="$(wc -l < $1)"

(( pages = file_lines / page_lines ))
if (( file_lines % page_lines > 0 )); then
    (( pages++ ))
fi

print "$1 has $pages pages of text."
```

Note that we use the arithmetical conditional ((file_lines % page_lines > 0)) rather than the [[...]] form.

At the heart of this code is the Unix utility *wc*(1), which counts the number of lines, words, and characters (bytes) in its input. By default, its output looks something like this:

```
    8      34      161   bob
```

wc's output means that the file *bob* has 8 lines, 34 words, and 161 characters. *wc* recognizes the options *–l*, *–w*, and *–c*, which tell it to print only the number of lines, words, or characters, respectively.

wc normally prints the name of its input file (given as argument). Since we want only the number of lines, we have to do two things. First, we give it input from file redirection instead, as in `wc -l < bob` instead of `wc -l bob`. This produces the number of lines preceded by one or more spaces.

Unfortunately, that space complicates matters: the statement `let file_lines=$(wc -l < $1)` becomes `let file_lines= N` after command substitution; the space after the equal sign is an error. That leads to the second modification, the quotes around the command substitution expression. The statement `let file_lines=" N"` is perfectly legal, and *let* knows how to remove the leading space.

The first `if` clause in the *pages* script checks to see if the first command line argument is an option. If so, it strips the dash (–) off and assigns the result to the variable `page_lines`. *wc* in the command substitution expression returns the number of lines in the file whose name is given as argument.

The next group of lines calculates the number of pages and, if there is a remainder after the division, adds 1. Finally, the appropriate message is printed.

As a bigger example of arithmetic, we now complete our version of the C shell's *pushd* and *popd* functions (Task 4-7). Remember that these functions operate on DIRSTACK, a stack of directories represented as a string with the directory names separated by spaces. The C shell's *pushd* and *popd* take additional types of arguments:

* `pushd +n` takes the *n*th directory in the stack (starting with 0), rotates it to the top, and *cd*s to it.

* `pushd` without arguments doesn't complain; instead, it swaps the two top directories on the stack and *cd*s to the new top.

* `popd +n` takes the *n*th directory in the stack and just deletes it.

The most useful of these features is the ability to get at the *n*th directory in the
stack. Here are the latest versions of both functions:

```
function pushd {                    # push current directory onto stack
    dirname=$1
    if [[ -d $dirname && -x $dirname ]]; then
        cd $dirname
        DIRSTACK="$dirname DIRSTACK"
        print "$DIRSTACK"
    else
        print "still in $PWD."
        return 1
    fi
}

function popd {                     # pop directory off the stack, cd there
    if [[ -n $DIRSTACK ]]; then
        top=${DIRSTACK%% *}
        DIRSTACK=${DIRSTACK#* }
        cd $top
        print "$PWD"
    else
        print "stack empty, still in $PWD."
        return 1
    fi
}
```

To get at the *n*th directory, we use a while loop that transfers the top directory to
a temporary copy of the stack *n* times. We'll put the loop into a function called
getNdirs that looks like this:

```
function getNdirs {
    stackfront=''
    let count=0
    while (( count < $1 )); do
        stackfront="$stackfront ${DIRSTACK%% *}"
        DIRSTACK=${DIRSTACK#* }
        let count++
    done
}
```

The argument passed to *getNdirs* is the *n* in question. The variable stackfront is
the temporary copy that contains the first *n* directories when the loop is done.
stackfront starts as null; count, which counts the number of loop iterations, starts
as 0.

The first line of the loop body appends the top of the stack (${DIRSTACK%% *}) to
stackfront; the second line deletes the top from the stack. The last line increments
the counter for the next iteration. The entire loop executes *n* times, for values of
count from 0 to *n*−1.

When the loop finishes, the last directory in $stackfront is the *n*th directory. The expression ${stackfront##* } extracts this directory. Furthermore, DIRSTACK now contains the "back" of the stack, i.e., the stack *without* the first *n* directories. With this in mind, we can now write the code for the improved versions of *pushd* and *popd*:

```
function pushd {
    if [[ $1 == ++([0-9]) ]]; then
        # case of pushd +n: rotate n-th directory to top
        num=${1#+}
        getNdirs $num

        newtop=${stackfront##* }
        stackfront=${stackfront%$newtop}

        DIRSTACK="$newtop $stackfront $DIRSTACK"
        cd $newtop

    elif [[ -z $1 ]]; then
        # case of pushd without args; swap top two directories
        firstdir=${DIRSTACK%% *}
        DIRSTACK=${DIRSTACK#* }
        seconddir=${DIRSTACK%% *}
        DIRSTACK=${DIRSTACK#* }
        DIRSTACK="$seconddir $firstdir $DIRSTACK"
        cd $seconddir

    else
        # normal case of pushd dirname
        dirname=$1
        if [[ -d $dirname && -x $dirname ]]; then
            cd $dirname
            DIRSTACK="$dirname $DIRSTACK"
            print "$DIRSTACK"
        else
            print still in "$PWD."
            return 1
        fi
    fi
}

function popd {      # pop directory off the stack, cd to new top
    if [[ $1 == ++([0-9]) ]]; then
        # case of popd +n: delete n-th directory from stack
        num=${1#+}
        getNdirs $num
        stackfront=${stackfront% *}
        DIRSTACK="$stackfront $DIRSTACK"

    else
        # normal case of popd without argument
        if [[ -n $DIRSTACK ]]; then
            top=${DIRSTACK%% *}
```

```
            DIRSTACK=${DIRSTACK#* }
            cd $top
            print "$PWD"
        else
            print "stack empty, still in $PWD."
            return 1
        fi
    fi
}
```

These functions have grown rather large; let's look at them in turn. The `if` at the beginning of *pushd* checks if the first argument is an option of the form +*N*. If so, the first block of code is run. The first statement simply strips the plus sign (+) from the argument and assigns the result—as an integer—to the variable num. This, in turn, is passed to the *getNdirs* function.

The next two assignment statements set newtop to the *n*th directory—i.e., the last directory in $stackfront—and delete that directory from stackfront. The final two lines in this part of *pushd* put the stack back together again in the appropriate order and *cd* to the new top directory.

The `elif` clause tests for no argument, in which case *pushd* should swap the top two directories on the stack. The first four lines of this clause assign the top two directories to firstdir and seconddir and delete these from the stack. Then, as above, the code puts the stack back together in the new order and *cd*s to the new top directory.

The `else` clause corresponds to the usual case, where the user supplies a directory name as argument.

popd works similarly. The `if` clause checks for the +*N* option, which in this case means delete the *N*th directory. num receives the integer count; the *getNdirs* function puts the first *N* directories into stackfront. Then the line stackfront=${stackfront% *} deletes the last directory (the *N*th directory) from stackfront. Finally, the stack is put back together with the *N*th directory missing.

The `else` clause covers the usual case, where the user doesn't supply an argument.

Before we leave this subject, here are a few exercises that should test your understanding of this code:

1. Add code to *pushd* that exits with an error message if the user supplies no argument and the stack contains fewer than two directories.

2. Verify that when the user specifies +*N* and *N* exceeds the number of directories in the stack, both *pushd* and *popd* use the last directory as the *N*th directory.

3. Modify the *getNdirs* function so that it checks for the above condition and exits with an appropriate error message if true.

4. Change *getNdirs* so that it uses *cut* (with command substitution), instead of the while loop, to extract the first *N* directories. This uses less code but runs more slowly because of the extra processes generated.

Arithmetic for

The for loop as described in Chapter 5 has been in Unix shells since the Version 7 Bourne Shell. As mentioned, you can't do Pascal or C-style looping for a fixed number of iterations with that for loop. *ksh93* introduced the arithmetic for loop to remedy this situation and to bring the shell closer to a traditional (some would say "real") programming language.

The syntax resembles the shell's arithmetic facilities that we have just seen. It is almost identical to the syntax of the C for loop, except for the extra set of parentheses:

```
for ((init; condition; increment))
do
    statements ...
done
```

Here, *init* represents something to be done once, at the start of the loop. The *condition* is tested, and as long as it's true, the shell executes *statements*. Before going back to the top of the loop to test the *condition* again, the shell executes *increment*.

Any of *init*, *condition*, and *increment* may be omitted. A missing *condition* is treated as *true*; i.e., the loop body always executes. (The so-called "infinite loop" requires you to use some other method to leave the loop.) We'll use the arithmetic for loop for Task 6-2, which is our next, rather simple task.

Task 6-2

Write a simple script that takes a list of numbers on the command line and adds them up, printing the result.

Here's the code; the explanation follows:

```
sum=0
count=$#
for ((i = 1; i <= count; i++))
do
    let "sum += $1"
    shift
done
print $sum
```

The first line initializes the variable sum to 0. sum accumulates the sum of the arguments. The second line is mostly for readability; count indicates how many arguments there are. The third line starts the loop itself. The variable i is the loop
control variable. The *init* clause sets it to 1, the *condition* clause tests it against the
limit count, and the *increment* clause adds 1 to it each time around the loop. One
thing you'll notice right away is that inside the for loop header, there's no need
for the $ in front of a variable name to get that variable's value. This is true for any
arithmetic expression in the Korn shell.

The body of the loop does the addition. It simply lets *let* do the math: the addition
is accomplished by adding $1 to the value in sum. The *shift* command then moves
the next argument down into $1 for use the next time around the loop. Finally,
when the loop is done, the script prints the result.

The arithmetic for loop is particularly handy for working with all the elements in
an indexed array, which we're about to see in the next section.

Arrays

So far we have seen three types of variables: character strings, integers, and floating-point numbers. The fourth type of variable that the Korn shell supports is an
array. As you may know, an array is like a list of things; you can refer to specific
elements in an array with *indices*, so that a[i] refers to the *i*th element of array a.
The Korn shell provides two kinds of arrays: indexed arrays, and associative
arrays.

Indexed Arrays

The Korn shell provides an indexed array facility that, while useful, is much more
limited than analogous features in conventional programming languages. In particular, indexed arrays can be only one-dimensional (i.e., no arrays of arrays), and
they are limited to 4096 elements.* Indices start at 0. This implies that the maximum index value is 4095. Furthermore, they may be any arithmetic expression:
ksh automatically evaluates the expression to yield the actual index.

There are three ways to assign values to elements of an array. The first is the most
intuitive: you can use the standard shell variable assignment syntax with the array
index in brackets ([]). For example:

```
nicknames[2]=bob
nicknames[3]=ed
```

---

* 4096 is a minimum value in *ksh93*. Recent releases allow up to 64K elements.

These assignments put the values bob and ed into the elements of the array nick-names with indices 2 and 3, respectively. As with regular shell variables, values assigned to array elements are treated as character strings unless the assignment is preceded by *let*, or the array was declared to be numeric with one of the *typeset* options *−i, −ui, −E,* or *−F.* (Strictly speaking, the value assigned with *let* is still a string; it's just that with *let*, the shell evaluates the arithmetic expression being assigned to produce that string.)

The second way to assign values to an array is with a variant of the *set* statement, which we saw in Chapter 3. The statement:

```
set -A aname val1 val2 val3 ...
```

creates the array *aname* (if it doesn't already exist) and assigns *val1* to aname[0], *val2* to aname[1], etc. As you would guess, this is more convenient for loading up an array with an initial set of values.

The third (recommended) way is to use the compound assignment form:

```
aname=(val1 val2 val3)
```

Starting with *ksh93j*, you may use the += operator to add values to an array:

```
aname+=(val4 val5 val6)
```

To extract a value from an array, use the syntax ${*aname[i]*}. For example, ${nicknames[2]} has the value "bob". The index *i* can be an arithmetic expression—see above. If you use * or @ in place of the index, the value will be all elements, separated by spaces. Omitting the index ($nicknames) is the same as specifying index 0 (${nicknames[0]}).

Now we come to the somewhat unusual aspect of Korn shell arrays. Assume that the only values assigned to nicknames are the two we saw above. If you type print "${nicknames[*]}", you will see the output:

```
bob ed
```

In other words, nicknames[0] and nicknames[1] don't exist. Furthermore, if you were to type:

```
nicknames[9]=pete
nicknames[31]=ralph
```

and then type print "${nicknames[*]}", the output would look like this:

```
bob ed pete ralph
```

This is why we said "the elements of nicknames with indices 2 and 3" earlier, instead of "the 2nd and 3rd elements of nicknames". Any array elements with unassigned values just don't exist; if you try to access their values, you get null strings.

You can preserve whatever whitespace you put in your array elements by using "${*aname*[@]}" (with the double quotes) instead of ${*aname*[*]}, just as you can with "$@" instead of $* or "$*".

The shell provides an operator that tells you how many elements an array has defined: ${#*aname*[*]}. Thus ${#nicknames[*]} has the value 4. Note that you need the [*] because the name of the array alone is interpreted as the 0th element. This means, for example, that ${#nicknames} equals the length of nicknames[0] (see Chapter 4). Since nicknames[0] doesn't exist, the value of ${#nicknames} is 0, the length of the null string.

If you think of an array as a mapping from integers to values (i.e., put in a number, get out a value), you can see why arrays are "number-dominated" data structures. Because shell programming tasks are much more often oriented towards character strings and text than towards numbers, the shell's indexed array facility isn't as broadly useful as it might first appear.

Nevertheless, we can find useful things to do with indexed arrays. Here is a cleaner solution to Task 5-4, in which a user can select his or her terminal type (TERM environment variable) at login time. Recall that the "user-friendly" version of this code used select and a case statement:

```
print 'Select your terminal type:'
PS3='terminal? '
select term in \
    'Givalt GL35a' \
    'Tsoris T-2000' \
    'Shande 531' \
    'Vey VT99'
do
    case $REPLY in
        1 ) TERM=gl35a ;;
        2 ) TERM=t2000 ;;
        3 ) TERM=s531 ;;
        4 ) TERM=vt99 ;;
        * ) print "invalid." ;;
    esac
    if [[ -n $term ]]; then
        print "TERM is $TERM"
        export TERM
        break
    fi
done
```

We can eliminate the entire case construct by taking advantage of the fact that the select construct stores the user's numeric choice in the variable REPLY. We just need a line of code that stores all of the possibilities for TERM in an array, in an order that corresponds to the items in the select menu. Then we can use $REPLY to index the array. The resulting code is:

```
set -A termnames gl35a t2000 s531 vt99
print 'Select your terminal type:'
PS3='terminal? '
select term in \
    'Givalt GL35a' \
    'Tsoris T-2000' \
    'Shande 531' \
    'Vey VT99'
do
    if [[ -n $term ]]; then
        TERM=${termnames[REPLY-1]}
        print "TERM is $TERM"
        export TERM
        break
    fi
done
```

This code sets up the array termnames so that ${termnames[0]} is "gl35a", ${termnames[1]} is "t2000", etc. The line TERM=${termnames[REPLY-1]} essentially replaces the entire case construct by using REPLY to index the array.

Notice that the shell knows to interpret the text in an array index as an arithmetic expression, as if it were enclosed in ((and)), which in turn means that the variable need not be preceded by a dollar sign ($). We have to subtract 1 from the value of REPLY because array indices start at 0, while select menu item numbers start at 1.

Think about how you might use arrays to maintain the directory stack for *pushd* and *popd*. The arithmetic for loop might come in handy too.

Associative Arrays

As mentioned in the previous section, shell programming tasks are usually string- or text-oriented, instead of number-oriented. *ksh93* introduced *associative arrays* into the shell to improve the shell's programmability. Associative arrays are a mainstay of programming in languages such as *awk, perl,* and *python.*

An associative array is an array indexed by string values. It provides an *association* between the string index and the value of the array at that index, making programming certain kinds of tasks work much more naturally. You tell the shell that an array is associative by using *typeset –A*:

```
typeset -A person
person[firstname]="frank"
person[lastname]="jones"
```

We can rewrite our terminal example from the previous section using associative arrays:

```
typeset -A termnames                        termnames is associative
termnames=([Givalt GL35a]=gl35a             Fill in the values
           [Tsoris T-2000]=t2000
           [Shande 531]=s531
           [Vey VT99]=vt99)
print 'Select your terminal type:'
PS3='terminal? '
select term in "${!termnames[@]}"           Present menu of array indices
do
    if [[ -n $term ]]; then
        TERM=${termnames[$term]}            Use string to index array
        print "TERM is $TERM"
        break
    fi
done
```

Note that the square brackets in the compound assignment act like double quotes; while it's OK to quote the string indices, it's not necessary. Also note the `"${!termnames[@]}"` construct. It's a bit of a mouthful, but it gives us all the array indices as separate quoted strings that preserve any embedded whitespace, just like `"$@"`. (See the next section.)

Starting with *ksh93j*, as for regular arrays, you may use the += operator to add values to an associative array:

```
termnames+= ([Boosha B-27]=boo27 [Cherpah C-42]=chc42)
```

As a side note, if you apply `typeset -A` to a previously existing nonarray variable, that variable's current value will be placed in index 0. The reason is that the shell treats `$x` as equivalent to `${x[0]}`, so that if you do:

```
x=fred
typeset -A x
print $x
```

you will still get `fred`.

Array Name Operators

In Chapter 4 we saw that the shell provides a large number of ways to access and manipulate the values of shell variables. In particular, we saw operators that work with shell variable *names*. Several additional operators apply to arrays. They are described in Table 6-5.

Table 6-5. Array name-related operators

Operator	Meaning
${!array[subscript]}	Return the actual subscript used to index the array. Subscripts can come from arithmetic expressions or from the values of shell variables.
${!array[*]}	List of all subscripts in the *array* associative array.
${!array[@]}	List of all subscripts in the *array* associative array, but expands to separate words when used inside double quotes.

You can think of the ${!...} construct to produce the actual array as being conceptually similar to its use with nameref variables. There, it indicates the actual variable that a nameref refers to. With arrays, it yields the actual subscript used to access a particular element. This is valuable because subscripts can be generated dynamically, e.g., as arithmetic expressions, or via the various string operations available in the shell. Here is a simple example:

```
$ set -A letters a b c d e f g h i j k l m n o p q r s t u v w x y z
$ print ${letters[20+2+1]}
x
$ print ${!letters[20+2+1]}
23
```

To loop over all elements of an indexed array, you could easily use an arithmetic for loop that went from 0 to, for example, ${#letters[*]} (the number of elements in letters). Associative arrays are different: there are no lower or upper bounds on the indices of the array, since they're all strings. The latter two operators in Table 6-5 make it easy to loop through an associative array:

```
typeset -A bob                             Create associative array
...                                         Fill it in
for index in "${!bob[@]}"; do               For all bob's subscripts
    print "bob[$index] is ${bob[$index]}"   Print each element
    ...
done
```

Analogous to the difference between $* and "$@", it is best to use the @ version of the operator, inside double quotes, to preserve the original string values. (We used "${!var[@]}" with select in the last example in the earlier section on associative arrays.)

typeset

The final Korn shell feature that relates to the kinds of values that variables can hold is the *typeset* command. If you are a programmer, you might guess that *typeset* is used to specify the *type* of a variable (integer, string, etc.); you'd be partially right.

typeset is a rather ad hoc collection of things that you can do to variables that restrict the kinds of values they can take. Operations are specified by options to *typeset*; the basic syntax is:

```
typeset option varname[=value]
```

Here, *option* is an option letter preceded with a hyphen or plus sign. Options can be combined and multiple *varname*s can be used. If you leave out *varname*, the shell prints a list of variables for which the given option is turned on.

The available options break down into two basic categories:

1. String formatting operations, such as right- and left-justification, truncation, and letter case control

2. Type and attribute functions that are of primary interest to advanced programmers

Local Variables in Functions

typeset without options has an important meaning: if a *typeset* statement is used inside a function definition, the variables involved all become *local* to that function (in addition to any properties they may take on as a result of *typeset* options). The ability to define variables that are local to "subprogram" units (procedures, functions, subroutines, etc.) is necessary for writing large programs, because it helps keep subprograms independent of the main program and of each other.

 Local variable names are restricted to simple identifiers. When *typeset* is used with a compound variable name (i.e., one that contains periods), that variable is automatically global, even if the *typeset* statement occurs inside the body of a function.

If you just want to declare a variable local to a function, use *typeset* without any options. For example:

```
function afunc {
    typeset diffvar
    samevar=funcvalue
```

```
        diffvar=funcvalue
        print "samevar is $samevar"
        print "diffvar is $diffvar"
}

samevar=globvalue
diffvar=globvalue
print "samevar is $samevar"
print "diffvar is $diffvar"
afunc
print "samevar is $samevar"
print "diffvar is $diffvar"
```

This code prints the following:

```
samevar is globvalue
diffvar is globvalue
samevar is funcvalue
diffvar is funcvalue
samevar is funcvalue
diffvar is globvalue
```

Figure 6-1 shows this graphically.

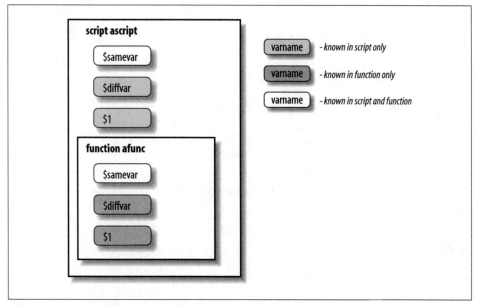

Figure 6-1. Local variables in functions

You will see several additional examples of local variables within functions in Chapter 9.

String Formatting Options

Now let's look at the various options to *typeset*. Table 6-6 lists the string formatting options; the first three take an optional numeric argument.

Table 6-6. Typeset string formatting options

Option	Operation
-L*n*	Left-justify. Remove leading spaces; if *n* is given, fill with spaces or truncate on right to length *n*.
-R*n*	Right-justify. Remove trailing spaces; if *n* is given, fill with spaces or truncate on left to length *n*.
-Z*n*	If used with -R, add leading 0's instead of spaces if needed. If used with -L, strips leading 0's. By itself, acts the same as -RZ.
-l	Convert letters to lowercase.
-u	Convert letters to uppercase.

Here are a few simple examples. Assume that the variable `alpha` is assigned the letters of the alphabet, in alternating case, surrounded by three spaces on each side:

```
alpha="   aBcDeFgHiJkLmNoPqRsTuVwXyZ   "
```

Table 6-7 shows some *typeset* statements and their resulting values (assuming that each of the statements are run "independently").

Table 6-7. Examples of typeset string formatting options

Statement	Value of v
typeset -L v=$alpha	"aBcDeFgHiJkLmNoPqRsTuVwXyZ "
typeset -L10 v=$alpha	"aBcDeFgHiJ"
typeset -R v=$alpha	" aBcDeFgHiJkLmNoPqRsTuVwXyZ"
typeset -R16 v=$alpha	"kLmNoPqRsTuVwXyZ"
typeset -l v=$alpha	" abcdefghijklmnopqrstuvwxyz "
typeset -uR5 v=$alpha	"VWXYZ"
typeset -Z8 v="123.50"	"00123.50"

When you run *typeset* on an existing variable, its effect is *cumulative* with whatever *typesets* may have been used previously. This has the obvious exceptions:

- A typeset -u undoes a typeset -l, and vice versa.
- A typeset -R undoes a typeset -L, and vice versa.

- You may not combine typeset -1 and typeset -u with some of the numeric attributes, such as typeset -E. Note, though, that typeset -ui creates unsigned integers.

- typeset -A and typeset -n (associative array and nameref, respectively) are not cumulative.

You can turn off *typeset* options explicitly by typing typeset +o, where *o* is the option you turned on before. Of course, it is hard to imagine scenarios where you would want to turn multiple *typeset* formatting options on and off over and over again; you usually set a *typeset* option on a given variable only once.

An obvious application for the *−L* and *−R* options is one in which you need fixed-width output. The most ubiquitous source of fixed-width output in the Unix system is reflected in Task 6-3.

Task 6-3

Pretend that *ls* doesn't do multicolumn output; write a shell script that does it.

For the sake of simplicity, we'll assume further that our version of Unix is an ancient one, in which filenames are limited to 14 characters.*

Our solution to this task relies on many of the concepts we have seen earlier in this chapter. It also relies on the fact that set -A (for constructing arrays) can be combined with command substitution in an interesting way: each word (separated by spaces, TABs, or newlines) becomes an element of the array. For example, if the file *bob* contains 50 words, the array fred has 50 elements after the statement:

```
set -A fred $(< bob)
```

Our strategy is to get the names of all files in the given directory into an array variable. We use an arithmetic for loop as we saw earlier in this chapter, to get each filename into a variable whose length has been set to 14. We print that variable in five-column format, with two spaces between each column (for a total of 80 columns), using a counter to keep track of columns. Here is the code:

```
set -A filenames $(ls $1)
typeset -L14 fname
let numcols=5

for ((count = 0; count < ${#filenames[*]} ; count++)); do
    fname=${filenames[count]}
    print -rn "$fname   "
    if (( (count+1) % numcols == 0 )); then
```

---

* We don't know of any modern Unix systems that still have this restriction. But applying it here considerably simplifies the programming problem.

```
        print               # newline
    fi
done

if (( count % numcols != 0 )); then
    print
fi
```

The first line sets up the array `filenames` to contain all the files in the directory given by the first argument (the current directory by default). The *typeset* statement sets up the variable `fname` to have a fixed width of 14 characters. The next line initializes `numcols` to the number of columns per line.

The arithmetic `for` loop iterates once for every element in `filenames`. In the body of the loop, the first line assigns the next array element to the fixed-width variable. The *print* statement prints the latter followed by two spaces; the *−n* option suppresses *print*'s final newline.

Then there is the `if` statement, which determines when to start the next line. It checks the *remainder* of `count` + 1 divided by `$numcols`—remember that dollar signs aren't necessary within a `$((...))` construct—and if the result is 0, it's time to output a newline via a *print* statement without arguments. Notice that even though `$count` increases by 1 with every iteration of the loop, the remainder goes through a cycle of 1, 2, 3, 4, 0, 1, 2, 3, 4, 0, ...

After the loop, an `if` construct outputs a final newline if necessary, i.e., if the `if` within the loop didn't just do it.

We can also use *typeset* options to clean up the code for our *dosmv* script (Task 5-3), which translates filenames in a given directory from MS-DOS to Unix format. The code for the script is:

```
for filename in ${1:+$1/}* ; do
    newfilename=$(print $filename | tr '[A-Z]' '[a-z]')
    newfilename=${newfilename%.}
    # subtlety: quote value of $newfilename to do string comparison,
    # not regular expression match
    if [[ $filename != "$newfilename" ]]; then
        print "$filename -> $newfilename"
        mv $filename $newfilename
    fi
done
```

We can replace the call to *tr* in the `for` loop with one to **typeset** −1 before the loop:

```
typeset -l newfilename
for filename in ${1:+$1/}* ; do
    newfilename=${filename%.}
    # subtlety: quote value of $newfilename to do string comparison,
    # not regular expression match
```

```
        if [[ $filename != "$newfilename" ]]; then
            print "$filename -> $newfilename"
            mv $filename $newfilename
        fi
    done
```

This way, the translation to lowercase letters is done automatically each time a value is assigned to newfilename. Not only is this code cleaner, but it is also more efficient, because the extra processes created by *tr* and command substitution are eliminated.

Type and Attribute Options

The other options to *typeset* are of more use to advanced shell programmers who are "tweaking" large scripts. These options are listed in Table 6-8.

Table 6-8. Typeset type and attribute options

Option	Operation
-A	Create an associative array.
-E*n*	Represent the variable internally as a double-precision floating-point number; improves the efficiency of floating-point arithmetic. If *n* is given, it is the number of significant figures to use in output. Large numbers print in scientific notation: [-]*d.ddd*e±*dd*. Smaller numbers print in regular notation: [-]*ddd.ddd*.
-F*n*	Represent the variable internally as a double-precision floating-point number; improves the efficiency of floating-point arithmetic. If *n* is given, it is the number of decimal places to use in output. All values print in regular notation: [-]*ddd.ddd*.
-H	On non-Unix systems, Unix-style filenames are converted into the format appropriate for the local system.
-i*n*	Represent the variable internally as an integer; improves the efficiency of integer arithmetic. If *n* is given, it is the base used for output. The default base is 10.
-n	Create a nameref variable (see Chapter 4).
-p	When used by itself, prints typeset statements that describe the attributes of each of the shell's variables that have attributes set. With additional options, only prints those variables that have the corresponding attribute set. Intended for dumping the shell's state into a file that can later be sourced by a different shell to recreate the original shell's state.
-r	Make the variable read-only: forbid assignment to it and disallow it from being *unset*. The built-in command *readonly* does the same thing, but *readonly* cannot be used for local variables.
-t	"Tags" the variable. The list of tagged variables is available from *typeset +t*. This option is obsolete.

Table 6-8. Typeset type and attribute options (continued)

Option	Operation
-u*i*n	Represent the variable internally as an *unsigned* integer. This is discussed further in Appendix B. If *n* is given, it is the base used for output. The default base is 10.[a]
-x	This does the same thing as the *export* command, but *export* cannot be used for local variables.
-f	Refer to function names only; see the section "Function Options," later in this chapter.

[a] This feature is only in *ksh93m* and newer.

The *−i* option is the most useful. You can put it in a script when you are done writing and debugging it to make arithmetic run a bit faster, though the speedup will be apparent only if your script does a *lot* of arithmetic. The more readable *integer* is a built-in alias for typeset -i, so that integer x=5 is the same as typeset -i x=5. Similarly, the word *float* is a predefined alias for typeset -E.*

The *−r* option is useful for setting up "constants" in shell scripts; constants are like variables except that you can't change their values once they have been initialized. Constants allow you to give names to values even if you don't want them changed; it is considered good programming practice to use named constants in large programs.

The solution to Task 6-3 contains a good candidate for typeset -r: the variable numcols, which specifies the number of columns in the output. Since numcols is an integer, we could also use the *−i* option, i.e., replace let numcols=5 with typeset -ri numcols=5. If we were to try assigning another value to numcols, the shell would respond with the error message ksh: numcols: is read only.

These options are also useful without arguments, i.e., to see which variables exist that have those options turned on.

Function Options

The *−f* option has various suboptions, all of which relate to functions. These are listed in Table 6-9.

---

* C, C++, and Java programmers may find the choice of the word "float" to be suprising, since internally the shell uses double-precision floating point. We theorize that the name "float" was chosen since its meaning is more obvious to the nonprogrammer than the word "double."

Table 6-9. Typeset function options

Option	Operation
-f	With no arguments, prints all function definitions.
-f *fname*	Prints the definition of function *fname*.
+f	Prints all function names.
-ft	Turns on trace mode for named function(s). (Chapter 9)
+ft	Turns off trace mode for named function(s). (Chapter 9)
-fu	Defines given name(s) as autoloaded function(s). (Chapter 4)

Two of these have built-in aliases that are more mnemonic: *functions* (note the *s*) is an alias for typeset -f and *autoload* is an alias for typeset -fu.

Finally, if you type typeset with no arguments, you will see a list of all variables that have attributes set (in no discernible order), preceded by the appropriate keywords for whatever *typeset* options are turned on. For example, typing *typeset* in an uncustomized shell gives you a listing of most of the shell's built-in variables and their attributes that looks like this:

```
export HISTFILE
integer TMOUT
export FCEDIT
export _AST_FEATURES
export TERM
HISTEDIT
PS2
PS3
integer PPID
export MAIL
export LOGNAME
export EXINIT
integer LINENO
export PATH
integer HISTCMD
export _
export OLDPWD
export PWD
float precision 3 SECONDS
export SHELL
integer RANDOM
export HOME
export VISUAL
export MANPATH
export EDITOR
export ENV
export HISTSIZE
export USER
export LANG
export MORE
```

```
integer OPTIND
integer MAILCHECK
export CDPATH
readonly namespace .sh
```

Here is the output of `typeset -p`:

```
typeset -x HISTFILE
typeset -i TMOUT
typeset -x FCEDIT
typeset -x _AST_FEATURES
typeset -x TERM
typeset -x ASIS_DIR
typeset HISTEDIT
typeset PS2
typeset PS3
typeset -i PPID
typeset -x MAIL
typeset -x LOGNAME
typeset -x EXINIT
typeset -i LINENO
typeset -x PATH
typeset -i HISTCMD
typeset -x _
typeset -x OLDPWD
typeset -x PWD
typeset -F 3 SECONDS
typeset -x SHELL
typeset -i RANDOM
typeset -x HOME
typeset -x VISUAL
typeset -x MANPATH
typeset -x EDITOR
typeset -x ENV
typeset -x HISTSIZE
typeset -x USER
typeset -x LANG
typeset -x MORE
typeset -i OPTIND
typeset -i MAILCHECK
typeset -x CDPATH
typeset -r .sh
```

The following command saves the values and attributes of all the shell's variables for later reuse:

```
{ set ; typeset -p ;} > varlist
```

7

Input/Output and Command-Line Processing

The past few chapters have gone into detail about various shell programming techniques, mostly focused on the flow of data and control through shell programs. In this chapter, we'll switch the focus to two related topics. The first is the shell's mechanisms for doing file-oriented input and output. We present information that expands on what you already know about the shell's basic I/O redirectors.

Second, we zoom in and talk about I/O at the line and word level. This is a fundamentally different topic, since it involves moving information between the domains of files/terminals and shell variables. *print* and command substitution are two ways of doing this that we've seen so far.

Our discussion of line and word I/O then leads into a more detailed explanation of how the shell processes command lines. This information is necessary so that you can understand exactly how the shell deals with *quotation*, and so that you can appreciate the power of an advanced command called *eval*, which we cover at the end of the chapter.

I/O Redirectors

In Chapter 1 you learned about the shell's basic I/O redirectors, <, >, and |. Although these are enough to get you through 95% of your Unix life, you should know that the Korn shell supports a total of 20 I/O redirectors. Table 7-1 lists them, including the three we've already seen. Although some of the rest are useful, others are mainly for systems programmers. We will wait until the next chapter to discuss the last three, which, along with >| and <<<, are not present in most Bourne shell versions.

Table 7-1. I/O redirectors

Redirector	Function
`> file`	Direct standard output to *file*
`< file`	Take standard input from *file*
`cmd1	cmd2`	Pipe; take standard output of *cmd1* as standard input to *cmd2*
`>> file`	Direct standard output to *file*; append to *file* if it already exists
`>| file`	Force standard output to *file* even if *noclobber* is set
`<> file`	Open *file* for both reading and writing on standard input[a]
`<< label`	Here-document; see text
`<<- label`	Here-document variant; see text
`<<< label`	Here-string; see text
`n> file`	Direct output file descriptor *n* to *file*
`n< file`	Set *file* as input file descriptor *n*
`<&n`	Duplicate standard input from file descriptor *n*
`>&n`	Duplicate standard output to file descriptor *n*
`<&n-`	Move file descriptor *n* to standard input
`>&n-`	Move file descriptor *n* to standard output
`<&-`	Close the standard input
`>&-`	Close the standard output
`|&`	Background process with I/O from parent shell
`n<&p`	Move input from coprocess to file descriptor *n*
`n>&p`	Move output to coprocess to file descriptor *n*

[a] Normally, files opened with < are opened read-only.

Notice that some of the redirectors in Table 7-1 contain a digit *n* and that their descriptions contain the term *file descriptor*; we'll cover that in a little while. (In fact, any redirector that starts with < or > may be used with a file descriptor; this is omitted from the table for simplicity.)

The first two new redirectors, >> and >|, are simple variations on the standard output redirector >. The >> appends to the output file (instead of overwriting it) if it already exists; otherwise it acts exactly like >. A common use of >> is for adding a line to an initialization file (such as *.profile* or *.mailrc*) when you don't want to bother with a text editor. For example:

```
$ cat >> .mailrc
> alias fred frederick@longmachinename.longcompanyname.com
> ^D
$
```

As we saw in Chapter 1, *cat* without an argument uses standard input as its input. This allows you to type the input and end it with CTRL-D on its own line. The `alias` line will be appended to the file *.mailrc* if it already exists; if it doesn't, the file is created with that one line.

Recall from Chapter 3 that you can prevent the shell from overwriting a file with `>` *file* by typing `set -o noclobber`. The `>|` operator overrides *noclobber*—it's the "Do it anyway, darn it!" redirector.

Unix systems allow you to open files read-only, write-only, and read-write. The `<` redirector opens the input file read-only; if a program attempts to write on standard input, it will receive an error. Similarly, the `>` redirector opens the output file write-only; attempting to read from standard output generates an error. The `<>` redirector opens a file for both reading and writing, by default on standard input. It is up to the invoked program to notice this and take advantage of the fact, but it is useful in the case where a program may want to update data in a file "in place." This operator is most used for writing networking clients; see the section "Special Filenames," later in this chapter for an example.

Here-Documents

The `<< label` redirector essentially forces the input to a command to be the shell program's text, which is read until there is a line that contains only *label*. The input in between is called a *here-document*. Here-documents aren't very interesting when used from the command prompt. In fact, it's the same as the normal use of standard input except for the label. We could have used a here-document in the previous example of `>>`, like this (EOF, for "end of file," is an often-used label):

```
$ cat >> .mailrc << EOF
> alias fred frederick@longmachinename.longcompanyname.com
> EOF
$
```

Here-documents are meant to be used from within shell scripts; they let you specify "batch" input to programs. A common use of here-documents is with simple text editors like *ed*(1). Task 7-1 uses a here-document in this way.

Task 7-1

The `s` *file* command in *mail*(1) saves the current message in *file*. If the message came over a network (such as the Internet), it has several prepended header lines that give information about network routing. You need this information because you're trying to solve some network routing problems. Write a shell script that extracts just the header lines from the file.

We can use *ed* to delete the body lines, leaving just the header. To do this, we need to know something about the syntax of mail messages, specifically, that there is always a blank line between the header lines and the message text. The *ed*

command /^$/,$d does the trick: it means, "Delete from the first blank line*
through the last line of the file." We also need the *ed* commands w (write the
changed file) and q (quit). Here is the code that solves the task:

```
ed $1 << \EOF
/^$/,$d
w
q
EOF
```

Normally, the shell does parameter (variable) substitution, command substitution,
and arithmetic substitution on text in a here-document, meaning that you can use
shell variables and commands to customize the text. This evaluation is disabled if
any part of the delimiter is quoted, as done in the previous example. (This prevents the shell from treating $d as a variable substitution.)

Often though, you do want the shell to perform its evaluations: perhaps the most
common use of here-documents is for providing templates for form generators or
program text for program generators. Task 7-2 is a simple task for system administrators that shows how this works.

Task 7-2

> Write a script that sends a mail message to a set of users saying that a new
> version of a certain program has been installed in a certain directory.

You can get a list of all users on the system in various ways; perhaps the easiest is
to use *cut* to extract the first field of */etc/passwd*, the file that contains all user
account information. Fields in this file are separated by colons (:).†

Given such a list of users, the following code does the trick:

```
pgmname=$1
for user in $(cut -f1 -d: /etc/passwd); do
    mail $user << EOF
Dear $user,

A new version of $pgmname has been installed in $(whence pgmname).

Regards,
Your friendly neighborhood sysadmin.
EOF
done
```

---

* The line has to be completely empty; no spaces or TABs. That's OK: mail message headers are separated from their bodies by exactly this kind of blank line.

† There are a few possible problems with this; for example, */etc/passwd* usually contains information
   on "accounts" that aren't associated with people, like uucp, lp, and daemon. We'll ignore such problems for the purpose of this example.

The shell substitutes the appropriate values for the name of the program and its directory.

The redirector << has two variations. First, you can prevent the shell from doing parameter, command and arithmetic substitution by surrounding the *label* in single or double quotes. (Actually, it's enough to quote just one character in the *label*.) We saw this in the solution to Task 7-1.

The second variation is <<-, which deletes leading TABs (but not spaces) from the here-document and the label line. This allows you to indent the here-document's text, making the shell script more readable:

```
pgmname=$1
for user in $(cut -f1 -d: /etc/passwd); do
    mail $user <<- EOF
        Dear $user,

        A new version of $pgmname has been installed in $(whence pgmname).

        Regards,

        Your friendly neighborhood sysadmin.
        EOF
done
```

Of course, you need to choose your *label* so that it doesn't appear as an actual input line.

Here-Strings

A common idiom in shell programming is to use *print* to generate some text to be further processed by one or more commands:

```
# start with a mild interrogation
print -r "$name, $rank, $serial_num" | interrogate -i mild
```

This could be rewritten to use a here-document, which is slightly more efficient, although not necessarily any easier to read:

```
# start with a mild interrogation
interrogate -i mild << EOF
$name, $rank, $serial_num
EOF
```

Starting with *ksh93n,** the Korn shell provides a new form of here-document, using three less-than signs:

```
program <<< WORD
```

In this form, the text of *WORD* (followed by a trailing newline) becomes the input to the program. For example:

```
# start with a mild interrogation
interrogate -i mild <<< "$name, $rank, $serial_num"
```

This notation first originated in the Unix version of the *rc* shell, where it is called a "here string." It was later picked up by the Z shell, *zsh* (see Appendix A), from which the Korn shell borrowed it. This notation is simple, easy to use, efficient, and visually distinguishable from regular here-documents.

File Descriptors

The next few redirectors in Table 7-1 depend on the notion of a *file descriptor.* This is a low-level Unix I/O concept that is vital to understand when programming in C or C++. It appears at the shell level when you want to do anything that doesn't involve standard input, standard output and standard error. You can get by with a few basic facts about them; for the whole story, look at the *open*(2), *creat*(2), *read*(2), *write*(2), *dup*(2), *dup2*(2), *fcntl*(2), and *close*(2) entries in the Unix manual. (As the manual entries are aimed at the C programmer, their relationship to the shell concepts won't necessarily be obvious.)

File descriptors are integers starting at 0 that index an array of file information within a process. When a process starts, it has three file descriptors open. These correspond to the three *standards*: standard input (file descriptor 0), standard output (1), and standard error (2). If a process opens Unix files for input or output, they are assigned to the next available file descriptors, starting with 3.

By far the most common use of file descriptors with the Korn shell is in saving standard error in a file. For example, if you want to save the error messages from a long job in a file so that they don't scroll off the screen, append `2> file` to your command. If you also want to save standard output, append `> file1 2> file2`.

This leads to Task 7-3.

---

* Thanks to David Korn for providing me prerelease access to the version with this feature. ADR.

Task 7-3

You want to start a long job in the background (so that your terminal is freed up) and save both standard output and standard error in a single log file. Write a function that does this.

We'll call this function *start*. The code is very terse:

```
function start {
    "$@" > logfile 2>&1 &
}
```

This line executes whatever command and parameters follow *start*. (The command cannot contain pipes or output redirectors.) It first sends the command's standard output to *logfile*.

Then, the redirector 2>&1 says, "Send standard error (file descriptor 2) to the same place as standard output (file descriptor 1)." 2>&1 is actually a combination of two redirectors in Table 7-1: *n> file* and *>&n*. Since standard output is redirected to *logfile*, standard error will go there too. The final & puts the job in the background so that you get your shell prompt back.

As a small variation on this theme, we can send both standard output and standard error into a *pipe* instead of a file: *command* 2>&1 | ... does this. (Why this works is described shortly.) Here is a function that sends both standard output and standard error to the logfile (as above) and to the terminal:

```
function start {
    "$@" 2>&1 | tee logfile &
}
```

The command *tee*(1) takes its standard input and copies it to standard output *and* the file given as argument.

These functions have one shortcoming: you must remain logged in until the job completes. Although you can always type jobs (see Chapter 1) to check on progress, you can't leave your office for the day unless you want to risk a breach of security or waste electricity. We'll see how to solve this problem in Chapter 8.

The other file-descriptor-oriented redirectors (e.g., <&*n*) are usually used for reading input from (or writing output to) more than one file at the same time. We'll see an example later in this chapter. Otherwise, they're mainly meant for systems programmers, as are <&- (force standard input to close) and >&- (force standard output to close), <&*n*- (move file descriptor *n* to standard input) and >&*n*- (move file descriptor *n* to standard output).

Finally, we should just note that 0< is the same as <, and 1> is the same as >. (In fact, 0 is the default for any operator that begins with <, and 1 is the default for any operator that begins with >.)

Redirector ordering

The shell processes I/O redirections in a specific order. Once you understand how this works, you can take advantage of it, particularly for managing the disposition of standard output and standard error.

The first thing the shell does is set up the standard input and output for pipelines as indicated by the | character. After that, it processes the changing of individual file descriptors. As we just saw, the most common idiom that takes advantage of this is to send both standard output and standard error down the same pipeline to a pager program, such as *more* or *less.**

```
$ mycommand -h fred -w wilma 2>&1 | more
```

In this example, the shell first sets the standard output of *mycommand* to be the pipe to *more*. It then redirects standard error (file descriptor 2) to be the same as standard output (file descriptor 1), i.e., the pipe.

When working with just redirectors, they are processed left-to-right, as they occur on the command line. An example similar to the following has been in the shell man page since the original Version 7 Bourne shell:

program > file1 2>&1	*Standard output and standard error to file1*
program 2>&1 > file1	*Standard error to terminal and standard output to file1*

In the first case, standard output is sent to *file1*, and standard error is then sent to where standard output is, i.e., *file1*. In the second case, standard error is sent to where standard output is, which is still the terminal. The standard output is then redirected to *file1*, but only the standard output. If you understand this, you probably know all you need to know about file descriptors.

Special Filenames

Normally, when you provide a pathname after an I/O redirector such as < or >, the shell tries to open an actual file that has the given filename. However, there are two kinds of pathnames where the shell instead treats the pathnames specially.

---

* *less* is a nonstandard but commonly available paging program that has more features than *more*.

The first kind of pathname is /dev/fd/*N*, where *N* is the file descriptor number of an *already open* file. For example:

```
# assume file descriptor 6 is already open on a file
print 'something meaningful' > /dev/fd/6    # same as 1>&6
```

This works even on systems that don't have a */dev/fd* directory. This kind of pathname may also be used with the various file attribute test operators of the [[...]] command.

The second kind of pathname allows access to Internet services via either the TCP or UDP protocol. The pathnames are:

/dev/tcp/*host*/*port*

> Using TCP, connect to remote host *host* on remote port *port*. The *host* may be given as an IP address in dotted-decimal notation (1.2.3.4) or as a hostname (*www.oreilly.com*). Similarly, the *port* for the desired service may be a symbolic name (typically as found in */etc/services*) or a numeric port number.*

/dev/udp/*host*/*port*

> This is the same, but using UDP.

To use these files for two-way I/O, open a new file descriptor using the *exec* command (which is described in Chapter 9), using the "read and write" operator, <>. Then use *read −u* and *print −u* to read from and write to the new file descriptor. (The *read* command and the −*u* option to *read* and *print* are described later in this chapter.)

The following example, courtesy of David Korn, shows how to do this. It implements the *whois*(1) program, which provides information about the registration of Internet domain names:

```
host=rs.internic.net
port=43
exec 3<> /dev/tcp/$host/$port
print -u3 -f "%s\r\n" "$@"
cat <&3
```

Using the *exec* built-in command (see Chapter 9), this program uses the "read-and-write" operator, <>, to open a two-way connection to the host *rs.internic.net* on TCP port 43, which provides the *whois* service. (The script could have used

---

* The ability to use hostnames was added in *ksh93f*; use of service names was added in *ksh93m*.

port=whois as well.) It then uses the *print* command to send the argument strings to the *whois* server. Finally, it reads the returned result using *cat.* Here is a sample run:

```
$ whois.ksh kornshell.com

Whois Server Version 1.3

Domain names in the .com, .net, and .org domains can now be registered
with many different competing registrars. Go to http://www.internic.net
for detailed information.

    Domain Name: KORNSHELL.COM
    Registrar: NETWORK SOLUTIONS, INC.
    Whois Server: whois.networksolutions.com
    Referral URL: http://www.networksolutions.com
    Name Server: NS4.PAIR.COM
    Name Server: NS0.NS0.COM
    Updated Date: 02-dec-2001


    >>> Last update of whois database: Sun, 10 Feb 2002 05:19:14 EST <<<

The Registry database contains ONLY .COM, .NET, .ORG, .EDU domains and
Registrars.
```

Network programming is beyond the scope of this book. But for most things, you will probably want to use TCP connections instead of UDP connections if you do write any networking programs in *ksh.*

String I/O

Now we'll zoom back in to the string I/O level and examine the *print, printf,* and *read* statements, which give the shell I/O capabilities that are more analogous to those of conventional programming languages.

print

As we've seen countless times in this book, *print* simply prints its arguments to standard output. You should use it instead of the *echo* command, whose function-ality differs from system to system.* (The Korn shell's built-in version of *echo* emulates whatever the system's standard version of *echo* does.) Now we'll explore the *print* command in greater detail.

---

* Specifically, there is a difference between System V and BSD versions. The latter accepts options similar to those of *print,* while the former accepts C language-style escape sequences.

print escape sequences

print accepts a number of options, as well as several *escape sequences* that start with a backslash. (You must use a double backslash if you don't surround the string that contains them with quotes; otherwise, the shell itself "steals" a backslash before passing the arguments to *print*.) These are similar to the escape sequences recognized by *echo* and the C language; they are listed in Table 7-2.

These sequences exhibit fairly predictable behavior, except for \f. On some displays, it causes a screen clear, while on others it causes a line feed. It ejects the page on most printers. \v is somewhat obsolete; it usually causes a line feed.

Table 7-2. print escape sequences

Sequence	Character printed
\a	ALERT or CTRL-G
\b	BACKSPACE or CTRL-H
\c	Omit final newline and discontinue processing the string
\E	ESCAPE or CTRL-[
\f	FORMFEED or CTRL-L
\n	newline (not at end of command) or CTRL-J
\r	ENTER (RETURN) or CTRL-M
\t	TAB or CTRL-I
\v	VERTICAL TAB or CTRL-K
\0n	ASCII character with octal (base-8) value n, where n is 1 to 3 digits. Unlike C, C++, and many other languages, the initial 0 is required.
\\	Single backslash

The \0n sequence is even more device-dependent and can be used for complex I/O, such as cursor control and special graphics characters.

Options to print

print also accepts a few dash options; we've already seen *−n* for omitting the final newline. The options are listed in Table 7-3.

Table 7-3. print options

Option	Function
-e	Process escape sequences in the arguments (this is the default).
-f *format*	Print as if via *printf* with the given *format* (see the next section).
-n	Omit the final newline (same as the \c escape sequence).
-p	Print on pipe to coroutine; see Chapter 8.

Table 7-3. print options (continued)

Option	Function
-r	Raw; ignore the escape sequences listed above.
-R	Like *–r*, but furthermore ignore any other options except *–n*.
-s	Print to command history file (see Chapter 2).
-un	Print to file descriptor *n*.

Notice that some of these are redundant: print -n is the same as *print* with \c at the end of a line; print -un ... is equivalent to print ... >&*n* (though the former is slightly more efficient).

However, print -s is *not* the same as print ... >> $HISTFILE. The latter command renders the vi and emacs editing modes temporarily inoperable; you must use print -s if you want to print to your history file.

Printing to your history file is useful if you want to edit something that the shell expands when it processes a command line, for example, a complex environment variable such as PATH. If you enter the command print -s PATH=$PATH, hit ENTER, and then press CTRL-P in emacs-mode (or ESC k in vi-mode), you will see something like this:

```
$ PATH=/bin:/usr/bin:/etc:/usr/ucb:/usr/local/bin:/home/billr/bin
```

That is, the shell expands the variable (and anything else, like command substitutions, wildcards, etc.) before it writes the line to the history file. Your cursor will be at the end of the line (or at the beginning of the line in vi-mode), and you can edit your PATH without having to type in the whole thing again.

printf

If you need to produce formatted reports, the shell's *print* command can be combined with formatting attributes for variables to produce output data that lines up reasonably. But you can only do so much with these facilities.

The C language's *printf*(3) library routine provides powerful formatting facilities for total control of output. It is so useful that many other Unix-derived programming languages, such as *awk* and *perl*, support similar or identical facilities. Primarily because the behavior of *echo* on different Unix systems could not be reconciled, and recognizing *printf*'s utility, the POSIX shell standard mandates a *printf* shell-level command that provides the same functionality as the *printf*(3) library routine. This section describes how the *printf* command works and examines additional capabilities unique to the Korn shell's version of *printf*.

The *printf* command can output a simple string just like the *print* command.

```
printf "Hello, world\n"
```

The main difference that you will notice at the outset is that, unlike *print*, *printf* does not automatically supply a newline. You must specify it explicitly as \n.

The full syntax of the *printf* command has two parts:

```
printf format-string [arguments ...]
```

The first part is a string that describes the format specifications; this is best supplied as a string constant in quotes. The second part is an argument list, such as a list of strings or variable values, that correspond to the format specifications. (If there are more arguments than format specifications, *ksh* cycles through the format specifications in the format string, reusing them in order, until done.) A format specification is preceded by a percent sign (%), and the specifier is one of the characters described shortly. Two of the main format specifiers are %s for strings and %d for decimal integers.

The format string combines text to be output literally with specifications describing how to format subsequent arguments on the *printf* command line. For example:

```
$ printf "Hello, %s\n" World
Hello, World
```

Because the *printf* command is built-in, you are not limited to absolute numbers:

```
$ printf "The answer is %d.\n" 12+10+20
The answer is 42.
```

The allowed specifiers are shown in Table 7-4.

Table 7-4. Format specifiers used in printf

Specifier	Description
%c	ASCII character (prints first character of corresponding argument)
%d	Decimal integer
%i	Decimal integer
%e	Floating-point format ([-]*d.precision*e[+-]*dd*) (see following text for meaning of *precision*)
%E	Floating-point format ([-]*d.precision*E[+-]*dd*)
%f	Floating-point format ([-]*ddd.precision*)
%g	%e or %f conversion, whichever is shorter, with trailing zeros removed
%G	%E or %f conversion, whichever is shortest, with trailing zeros removed
%o	Unsigned octal value
%s	String

Table 7-4. Format specifiers used in printf (continued)

Specifier	Description
%u	Unsigned decimal value
%x	Unsigned hexadecimal number. Uses a–f for 10 to 15
%X	Unsigned hexadecimal number. Uses A–F for 10 to 15
%%	Literal %

The *printf* command can be used to specify the width and alignment of output fields. A format expression can take three optional modifiers following % and preceding the format specifier:

```
%flags width.precision format-specifier
```

The *width* of the output field is a numeric value. When you specify a field width, the contents of the field are right-justified by default. You must specify a flag of "-" to get left-justification. (The rest of the *flags* are discussed shortly.) Thus, "%-20s" outputs a left-justified string in a field 20 characters wide. If the string is less than 20 characters, the field is padded with whitespace to fill. In the following examples, a | is output to indicate the actual width of the field. The first example right-justifies the text:

```
printf "|%10s|\n" hello
```

It produces:

```
|     hello|
```

The next example left-justifies the text:

```
printf "|%-10s|\n" hello
```

It produces:

```
|hello     |
```

The *precision* modifier, used for decimal or floating-point values, controls the number of digits that appear in the result. For string values, it controls the maximum number of characters from the string that will be printed.

You can specify both the *width* and *precision* dynamically, via values in the *printf* argument list. You do this by specifying asterisks, instead of literal values.

```
$ myvar=42.123456
$ printf "|%*.*G|\n" 5 6 $myvar
|42.1235|
```

In this example, the width is 5, the precision is 6, and the value to print comes from the value of myvar.

The *precision* is optional. Its exact meaning varies by control letter, as shown in Table 7-5:

Table 7-5. Meaning of precision

Conversion	Precision means
%d, %i, %o, %u, %x, %X	The minimum number of digits to print. When the value has fewer digits, it is padded with leading zeros. The default precision is 1.
%e, %E	The minimum number of digits to print. When the value has fewer digits, it is padded with zeros after the decimal point. The default precision is 10. A precision of 0 inhibits printing of the decimal point.
%f	The number of digits to the right of the decimal point.
%g, %G	The maximum number of significant digits.
%s	The maximum number of characters to print.

Finally, one or more *flags* may precede the field width and the precision. We've already seen the "-" flag for left-justification. The rest of the flags are shown in Table 7-6.

Table 7-6. Flags for printf

Character	Description
-	Left-justify the formatted value within the field.
space	Prefix positive values with a space and negative values with a minus.
+	Always prefix numeric values with a sign, even if the value is positive.
#	Use an alternate form: %o has a preceding 0; %x and %X are prefixed with 0x and 0X, respectively; %e, %E and %f always have a decimal point in the result; and %g and %G do not have trailing zeros removed.
0	Pad output with zeros, not spaces. This only happens when the field width is wider than the converted result. In the C language, this flag applies to all output formats, even non-numeric ones. For *ksh*, it only applies to the numeric formats.

If *printf* cannot perform a format conversion, it returns a non-zero exit status.

Similar to *print*, the built-in *printf* command interprets escape sequences within the format string. However, *printf* accepts a larger range of escape sequences; they are the same as for the $'...' string. These sequences are listed later in Table 7-9.

Additional Korn shell printf specifiers

Besides the standard specifiers just described, the Korn shell accepts a number of additional specifiers. These provide useful features at the expense of nonportability to other versions of the *printf* command.

%b When used instead of **%s**, expands *print*-style escape sequences in the argument string. For example:

```
$ printf "%s\n" 'hello\nworld'
hello\nworld
$ printf "%b\n" 'hello\nworld'
hello
world
```

%H When used instead of **%s**, outputs HTML and XML special characters as their corresponding entity names. For example:

```
$ printf "%s\n" "Here are real < and > characters"
Here are real < and > characters
$ printf "%H\n" "Here are real < and > characters"
Here are real &lt; and &gt; characters
```

Interestingly enough, spaces are turned into , the unbreakable literal HTML and XML space character.

%n This is borrowed from ISO C. It places the number of characters written so far into the given variable. This is possible since *printf* is built-in to the shell.

```
$ printf "hello, world\n%n" msglen
hello, world
$ print $msglen
13
```

%P When used instead of **%s**, translates the *egrep*-style extended regular expression into an equivalent Korn shell pattern. For example:

```
$ printf "%P\n" '(.*\.o|.*\.obj|core)+'
*+(*\.o|*\.obj|core)*
```

%q When used instead of **%s**, prints the string argument in quotes in such a way that it could later be reused inside a shell script. For example:

```
$ printf "print %q\n" "a string with ' and \" in it"
print $'a string with \' and " in it'
```

(The $'...' notation is explained in the section "Extended quoting," later in this chapter.)

%R Goes the other way from %P, translating patterns into extended regular expressions. For example:

```
$ printf "%R\n" '+(*.o|*.c)'
^(.*\.o|.*\.c)+$
```

%(*date format*)T

The *date format* is a date command string similar to that of *date*(1). The argument is a string representing a date and time. *ksh* converts the given date string into the time it represents and then reformats it according to the *date*(1) format that you supply. *ksh* accepts a wide variety of date and time formats. For example:

```
$ date
Wed Jan 30 15:46:01 IST 2002
$ printf "%(It is now %m/%d/%Y %H:%M:%S)T\n" "$(date)"
It is now 01/30/2002 15:46:07
```

Unix systems keep time in "seconds since the Epoch." The Epoch is midnight, January 1, 1970, UTC. If you have a time value in this format, you can use it with the %T conversion specifier by preceding it with a # character, like so:

```
$ printf "%(It is now %m/%d/%Y %H:%M:%S)T\n" '#1012398411'
It is now 01/30/2002 15:46:51
```

%Z Print a byte whose value is zero.

Finally, for the %d format, after the precision you may supply an additional period and a number indicating the output base:

```
$ printf '42 is %.3.5d in base 5\n' 42
42 is 132 in base 5
```

read

The other side of the shell's string I/O facilities is the *read* command, which allows you to read values *into* shell variables. The basic syntax is:

```
read var1 var2 ...
```

There are a few options, which we cover in the section "Options to read," later in this chapter. This statement takes a line from the standard input and breaks it down into words delimited by any of the characters in the value of the variable IFS (see Chapter 4; these are usually a space, a TAB, and newline). The words are assigned to variables *var1*, *var2*, etc. For example:

```
$ read fred bob
dave pete
$ print "$fred"
dave
```

```
$ print "$bob"
pete
```

If there are more words than variables, excess words are assigned to the last variable. If you omit the variables altogether, the entire line of input is assigned to the variable REPLY.

You may have identified this as the missing ingredient in the shell programming capabilities we've seen so far. It resembles input statements in conventional languages, like its namesake in Pascal. So why did we wait this long to introduce it?

Actually, *read* is sort of an escape hatch from traditional shell programming philosophy, which dictates that the most important unit of data to process is a *text file*, and that Unix utilities such as *cut, grep, sort,* etc., should be used as building blocks for writing programs.

read, on the other hand, implies line-by-line processing. You could use it to write a shell script that does what a pipeline of utilities would normally do, but such a script would inevitably look like:

```
while (read a line) do
    process the line
        print the processed line
end
```

This type of script is usually much slower than a pipeline; furthermore, it has the same form as a program someone might write in C (or some similar language) that does the same thing much, *much* faster. In other words, if you are going to write it in this line-by-line way, there is no point in writing a shell script. (The authors have gone for years without writing a script with *read* in it.)

Reading lines from files

Nevertheless, shell scripts with *read* are useful for certain kinds of tasks. One is when you are reading data from a file small enough so that efficiency isn't a concern (say a few hundred lines or less), and it's really necessary to get bits of input into shell variables.

One task that we have already seen fits this description: Task 5-4, the script that a system administrator could use to set a user's TERM environment variable according to which terminal line he or she is using. The code in Chapter 5 used a case statement to select the correct value for TERM.

This code would presumably reside in */etc/profile*, the system-wide initialization file that the Korn shell runs before running a user's *.profile*. If the terminals on the system change over time—as surely they must—then the code would have to be changed. It would be better to store the information in a file and change just the file instead.

Assume we put the information in a file whose format is typical of such Unix "system configuration" files: each line contains a device name, a TAB, and a TERM value. If the file, which we'll call */etc/terms*, contained the same data as the case statement in Chapter 5, it would look like this:

```
console  s531
tty01    gl35a
tty03    gl35a
tty04    gl35a
tty07    t2000
tty08    s531
```

We can use *read* to get the data from this file, but first we need to know how to test for the end-of-file condition. Simple: *read*'s exit status is 1 (i.e., nonzero) when there is nothing to read. This leads to a clean while loop:

```
TERM=vt99          # assume this as a default
line=$(tty)
while read dev termtype; do
    if [[ $dev == $line ]]; then
        TERM=$termtype
        export TERM
        print "TERM set to $TERM."
        break
    fi
done
```

The while loop reads each line of the input into the variables dev and termtype. In each pass through the loop, the if looks for a match between $dev and the user's tty ($line, obtained by command substitution from the *tty* command). If a match is found, TERM is set and exported, a message is printed, and the loop exits; otherwise TERM remains at the default setting of vt99.

We're not quite done, though: this code reads from the standard input, not from */etc/terms!* We need to know how to redirect input to multiple commands. There are a few ways of doing this.

I/O redirection and multiple commands

One way to solve the problem is with a subshell, as we'll see in the next chapter. This involves creating a separate process to do the reading. However, it is usually more efficient to do it in the same process; the Korn shell gives us three ways of doing this.

The first, which we have seen already, is with a function:

```
function findterm {
    TERM=vt99          # assume this as a default
    line=$(tty)
    while read dev termtype; do
```

```
        if [[ $dev == $line ]]; then
            TERM=$termtype
            export TERM
            print "TERM set to $TERM."
            break
        fi
    done
}


findterm < /etc/terms
```

A function acts like a script in that it has its own set of standard I/O descriptors, which can be redirected in the line of code that calls the function. In other words, you can think of this code as if *findterm* were a script and you typed findterm < /etc/terms on the command line. The *read* statement takes input from */etc/terms* a line at a time, and the function runs correctly.

The second way is by putting the I/O redirector at the end of the loop, like this:

```
TERM=vt99          # assume this as a default
line=$(tty)
while read dev termtype; do
    if [[ $dev == $line ]]; then
        TERM=$termtype
        export TERM
        print "TERM set to $TERM."
        break
    fi
done < /etc/terms
```

You can use this technique with any flow-control construct, including if...fi, case...esac, for...done, select...done, and until...done. This makes sense because these are all *compound statements* that the shell treats as single commands for these purposes. This technique works fine—the *read* command reads a line at a time—as long as all of the input is done within the compound statement.

Putting the I/O redirector at the end is particularly important for making loops work correctly. Suppose you place the redirector after the *read* command, like so:

```
while read dev termtype < /etc/terms
do
    ...
done
```

In this case, the shell reopens */etc/terms* each time around the loop, reading the first line over and over again. This effectively creates an infinite loop, something you probably don't want.

Code blocks

Occasionally, you may want to redirect I/O to or from an arbitrary group of commands without creating a separate process. To do that, you need to use a construct that we haven't seen yet. If you surround some code with { and },* the code will behave like a function that has no name. This is another type of compound statement. In accordance with the equivalent concept in the C language, we'll call this a *block* of code.†

What good is a block? In this case, it means that the code within the curly braces ({ }) will take standard I/O descriptors just as we described for functions. This construct is also appropriate for the current example because the code needs to be called only once, and the entire script is not really large enough to merit breaking down into functions. Here is how we use a block in the example:

```
{
    TERM=vt99          # assume this as a default
    line=$(tty)
    while read dev termtype; do
        if [[ $dev == $line ]]; then
            TERM=$termtype
            export TERM
            print "TERM set to $TERM."
            break
        fi
    done
} < /etc/terms
```

To help you understand how this works, think of the curly braces and the code inside them as if they were one command, i.e.:

```
{ TERM=vt99; line=$(tty); while ... ; } < /etc/terms
```

Configuration files for system administration tasks like this one are actually fairly common; a prominent example is */etc/hosts*, which lists machines that are accessible in a TCP/IP network. We can make */etc/terms* more like these standard files by allowing comment lines in the file that start with #, just as in shell scripts. This way */etc/terms* can look like this:

```
#
# System Console is a Shande 531s
console s531
#
# Prof. Subramaniam's line has a Givalt GL35a
tty01   gl35a
...
```

---

* For obscure, historical syntactic reasons, the braces are shell *keywords*. In practice, this means that the closing } must be preceded by either a newline or a semicolon. Caveat emptor!

† LISP programmers may prefer to think of this as an *anonymous function* or *lambda-function*.

We can handle comment lines in two ways. First, we could modify the while loop so that it ignores lines beginning with #. We would take advantage of the fact that the equality and inequality operators (== and !=) under [[...]] do pattern matching, not just equality testing:

```
if [[ $dev != \#* && $dev == $line ]]; then
    ...
```

The pattern is #*, which matches any string beginning with #. We must precede # with a backslash so that the shell doesn't treat the rest of the line as a comment. Also, remember from Chapter 5 that the && combines the two conditions so that *both* must be true for the entire condition to be true.

This would certainly work, but the usual way to filter out comment lines is to use a pipeline with *grep*. We give *grep* the regular expression ^[^#], which matches anything except lines beginning with #. Then we change the call to the block so that it reads from the output of the pipeline instead of directly from the file.*

```
grep "^[^#]" /etc/terms | {
    TERM=vt99
    ...
}
```

We can also use *read* to improve our solution to Task 6-3, in which we emulate the multicolumn output of *ls*. In the solution in the previous chapter, we assumed for simplicity that filenames are limited to 14 characters, and we used 14 as a fixed column width. We'll improve the solution so that it allows *any* filename length (as in modern Unix versions) and uses the length of the longest filename (plus 2) as the column width.

In order to display the list of files in multicolumn format, we need to read through the output of *ls* twice. In the first pass, we find the longest filename and use that to set the number of columns as well as their width; the second pass does the actual output. Here is a block of code for the first pass:

```
ls "$@" | {
    let width=0
    while read fname; do
        if (( ${#fname} > $width )); then
            let width=${#fname}
        fi
    done
    let "width += 2"
    let numcols="int(${COLUMNS:-80} / $width)"
}
```

---

* Unfortunately, using *read* with input from a pipe is often very inefficient, because of issues in the design of the shell that aren't relevant here.

This code looks a bit like an exercise from a first-semester programming class. The while loop goes through the input looking for files with names that are longer than the longest found so far; if a longer one is found, its length is saved as the new longest length.

After the loop finishes, we add 2 to the width to allow for space between columns. Then we divide the width of the terminal by the column width to get the number of columns. As the shell does division in floating-point, the result is passed to the *int* function to produce an integer final result. Recall from Chapter 3 that the built-in variable COLUMNS often contains the display width; the construct ${COLUMNS:-80} gives a default of 80 if this variable is not set.

The results of the block are the variables width and numcols. These are global variables, so they are accessible by the rest of the code inside our (eventual) script. In particular, we need them in our second pass through the filenames. The code for this resembles the code to our original solution; all we need to do is replace the fixed column width and number of columns with the variables:

```
set -A filenames $(ls "$@")
typeset -L$width fname
let count=0

while (( $count < ${#filenames[*]} )); do
    fname=${filenames[$count]}
    print "$fname \c"
    let count++
    if [[ $((count % numcols)) == 0 ]]; then
        print           # output a newline
    fi
done

if (( count % numcols != 0 )); then
    print
fi
```

The entire script consists of both pieces of code. As yet another "exercise for the reader," consider how you might rearrange the code to only invoke the *ls* command once. (Hint: use at least one arithmetic for loop.)

Reading user input

The other type of task to which *read* is suited is prompting a user for input. Think about it: we have hardly seen any such scripts so far in this book. In fact, the only ones were the modified solutions to Task 5-4, which involved select.

As you've probably figured out, *read* can be used to get user input into shell variables. We can use *print* to prompt the user, like this:

```
print -n 'terminal? '
read TERM
print "TERM is $TERM"
```

Here is what this looks like when it runs:

```
terminal? vt99
TERM is vt99
```

However, in order that prompts don't get lost down a pipeline, shell convention dictates that prompts should go to standard error, not standard output. (Recall that select prompts to standard error.) We could just use file descriptor 2 with the output redirector we saw earlier in this chapter:

```
print -n 'terminal? ' >&2
read TERM
print TERM is $TERM
```

The shell provides a better way of doing the same thing: if you follow the first variable name in a *read* statement with a question mark (?) and a string, the shell uses that string as a prompt to standard error. In other words:

```
read TERM?'terminal? '
print "TERM is $TERM"
```

does the same as the above. The shell's way is better for the following reasons. First, this looks a bit nicer; second, the shell knows not to generate the prompt if the input is redirected to come from a file; and finally, this scheme allows you to use vi- or emacs-mode on your input line.

We'll flesh out this simple example by showing how Task 5-4 would be done if select didn't exist. Compare this with the code in Chapter 6:

```
set -A termnames gl35a t2000 s531 vt99
print 'Select your terminal type:'
while true;  do
    {
        print '1) gl35a'
        print '2) t2000'
        print '3) s531'
        print '4) vt99'
    } >&2
    read REPLY?'terminal? '

    if (( REPLY >= 1 && REPLY <= 4 )); then
        TERM=${termnames[REPLY-1]}
        print "TERM is $TERM"
        export TERM
        break
```

```
      fi
   done
```

The while loop is necessary so that the code repeats if the user makes an invalid choice.

This is roughly twice as many lines of code as the first solution in Chapter 5—but exactly as many as the later, more user-friendly version! This shows that select saves you code only if you don't mind using the same strings to display your menu choices as you use inside your script.

However, select has other advantages, including the ability to construct multicolumn menus if there are many choices, and better handling of empty user input.

Options to read

read takes a set of options that are similar to those for *print*. Table 7-7 lists them.

Table 7-7. read options

Option	Function
-A	Read words into indexed array, starting at index 0. Unsets all elements of the array first.
-d *delimiter*	Read up to character *delimiter*, instead of the default character, which is a newline.
-n *count*	Read at most *count* bytes.[a]
-p	Read from pipe to coroutine; see Chapter 8.
-r	Raw; do not use \ as line continuation character.
-s	Save input in command history file; see Chapter 1.
-t *nseconds*	Wait up to *nseconds* seconds for the input to come in. If *nseconds* elapses, return a failure exit status.
-u*n*	Read from file descriptor *n*.

[a] This option was added in *ksh93e*.

Having to type read word[0] word[1] word[2] ... to read words into an array is painful. It is also error-prone; if the user types more words than you've provided array variables, the remaining words are all assigned to the last array variable. The *–A* option gets around this, reading each word one at a time into the corresponding entries in the named array.

The *–d* option lets you read up to some other character than a newline. In practical terms, you will probably never need to do this, but the shell wants to make it possible for you to do it in case you ever need to.

Similarly, the *–n* option frees you from the default line-oriented way that *read* consumes input; it allows you to read a fixed number of bytes. This is very useful if you're processing legacy fixed-width data, although this is not very common on Unix systems.

read lets you input lines that are longer than the width of your display device by providing backslash (\) as a continuation character, just as in shell scripts. The *−r* option to *read* overrides this, in case your script reads from a file that may contain lines that happen to end in backslashes.

read −r also preserves any other escape sequences the input might contain. For example, if the file *fred* contains this line:

```
A line with a\n escape sequence
```

read −r fredline will include the backslash in the variable fredline, whereas without the *−r*, *read* will "eat" the backslash. As a result:

```
$ read -r fredline < fred
$ print "$fredline"
A line with a
 escape sequence
$
```

(Here, *print* interpreted the \n escape sequence and turned it into a newline.) However:

```
$ read fredline < fred
$ print "$fredline"
A line with an escape sequence
$
```

The *−s* option helps you if you are writing a highly interactive script and you want to provide the same command-history capability as the shell itself has. For example, say you are writing a new version of *mail* as a shell script. Your basic command loop might look like this:

```
while read -s cmd; do
     # process the command
done
```

Using read −s allows the user to retrieve previous commands to your program with the emacs-mode CTRL-P command or the vi-mode ESC k command. The *kshdb* debugger in Chapter 9 uses this feature.

The *−t* option is quite useful. It allows you to recover in case your user has "gone out to lunch," but your script has better things to do than just wait around for input. You tell it how many seconds you're willing to wait before deciding that the user just doesn't care anymore:

```
print -n "OK, Mr. $prisoner, enter your name, rank and serial number: "
# wait two hours, no more
if read -t $((60 * 60 * 2)) name rank serial
```

```
then
    # process information
    ...
else
    # prisoner is being silent
    print 'The silent treatment, eh? Just you wait.'
    call_evil_colonel -p $prisoner
    ...
fi
```

If the user enters data before the timeout expires, *read* returns 0 (success), and the then part of the if is processed. On the other hand, when the user enters nothing, the timeout expires and *read* returns 1 (failure), executing the else part of the statement.

Although not an option to the *read* command, the TMOUT variable can affect it. Just as for select, if TMOUT is set to a number representing some number of seconds, the *read* command times out if nothing is entered within that time, and returns a failure exit status. The *–t* option overrides the setting of TMOUT.

Finally, the *–un* option is useful in scripts that read from more than one file at the same time.

Task 7-4 is an example of this that also uses the *n<* I/O redirector that we saw earlier in this chapter.

Task 7-4

Write a script that prints the contents of two files side by side.

We'll format the output so the two output columns are fixed at 30 characters wide. Here is the code:

```
typeset -L30 f1 f2
while read -u3 f1 && read -u4 f2; do
    print "$f1$f2"
done 3<$1 4<$2
```

read –u3 reads from file descriptor 3, and 3<$1 directs the file given as first argument to be input on that file descriptor; the same is true for the second argument and file descriptor 4. Remember that file descriptors 0, 1, and 2 are already used for standard I/O. We use file descriptors 3 and 4 for our two input files; it's best to start from 3 and work upwards to the shell's limit, which is 9.

The *typeset* command and the quotes around the argument to *print* ensure that the output columns are 30 characters wide and that trailing whitespace in the lines from the file is preserved. The while loop reads one line from each file until at least one of them runs out of input.

Assume the file *dave* contains the following:

```
DAVE
Height: 177.8 cm.
Weight: 79.5 kg.
Hair: brown
Eyes: brown
```

And the file *shirley* contains this:

```
SHIRLEY
Height: 167.6 cm.
Weight: 65.5 kg.
Hair: blonde
Eyes: blue
```

If the script is called *twocols*, then `twocols dave shirley` produces this output:

```
DAVE                         SHIRLEY
Height: 177.8 cm.            Height: 167.6 cm.
Weight: 79.5 kg.             Weight: 65.5 kg.
Hair: brown                  Hair: blonde
Eyes: brown                  Eyes: blue
```

Command-Line Processing

We've seen how the shell processes input lines: it deals with single quotes (' '), double quotes (" "), and backslashes (\), and it separates parameter, command and arithmetic expansions into words, according to delimiters in the variable IFS. This is a subset of the things the shell does when processing *command lines*.

This section completes the discussion, in sometimes excruciating detail. We first examine two additional kinds of substitutions or expansions that the shell performs that may not be universally available. Then we present the full story of the order that the shell processes the command line. Covered next is the use of *quoting*, which prevents many or all of the substitution steps from occurring. Finally, we cover the *eval* command, which can be used for additional programmatic control of command line evaluations.

Brace Expansion and Process Substitution

Brace expansion is a feature borrowed from the Berkeley *csh* command interpreter and also available in the popular *bash* shell. Brace expansion is a way of saving typing when you have strings that are prefixes or suffixes of each other. For example, suppose you have the following files:

```
$ ls
cpp-args.c  cpp-lex.c  cpp-out.c  cpp-parse.c
```

You could type `vi cpp-{args,lex,parse}.c` if you wished to edit three out of the four C files, and the shell would expand this into `vi cpp-args.c cpp-lex.c cpp-parse.c`. Furthermore, brace substitutions may be nested. For example:

```
$ print cpp-{args,l{e,o}x,parse}.c
cpp-args.c cpp-lex.c cpp-lox.c cpp-parse.c
```

This is a handy feature. We haven't covered it up until now because it's possible that your version of *ksh* may not have it. It is an optional feature that is enabled when *ksh* is compiled. However, it is enabled by default when *ksh93* is compiled from source code.

Process substitution allows you to open multiple process streams and feed them into a single program for processing. For example:

```
awk '...' <(generate_data) <(generate_more_data)
```

(Note that the parentheses are part of the syntax; you type them literally.) Here, *generate_data* and *generate_more_data* represent arbitrary commands, including pipelines, that produce streams of data. The *awk* program processes each stream in turn, not realizing that the data is coming from multiple sources. This is shown graphically in Figure 7-1.a.

Process substitution may also be used for output, particularly when combined with the *tee*(1) program, which sends its input to multiple output files and to standard output. For example:

```
generate_data | tee >(sort | uniq > sorted_data) \
                     >(mail -s 'raw data' joe) > raw_data
```

This command uses *tee* to (1) send the data to a pipeline that sorts and saves the data, (2) send the data to the *mail* program to user joe, and (3) redirect the original data into a file. This is represented graphically in Figure 7-1.b. Process substitution, combined with *tee*, allows you to create nonlinear data graphs, freeing you from the straight "one input, one output" paradigm of traditional Unix pipes.

Process substitution is only available on Unix systems that support the */dev/fd/N* special files for named access to already open file descriptors. (This is different from the use of */dev/fd/N* described earlier in this chapter, where the shell itself interprets the pathname. Here, because external commands must be able to open files in */dev/fd*, the feature must be directly supported by the operating system.) Most modern Unix systems, including GNU/Linux, support this feature. Like brace substitution, it must be enabled at compile time, and may not be available in your version of *ksh*. As with brace expansion, it is enabled by default when *ksh93* is compiled from source code.

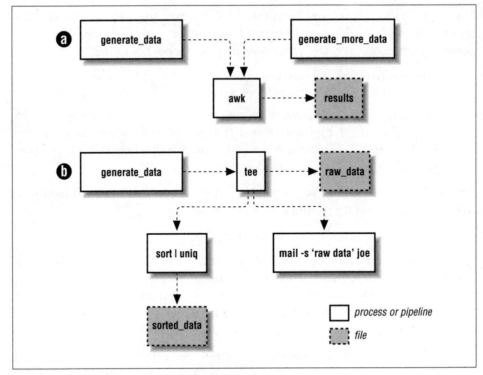

Figure 7-1. Process substitution for both input and output data streams

Substitution Order

We've touched upon command-line processing (see Figure 7-2) throughout this book; now is a good time to make the whole thing explicit.* Each line that the shell reads from the standard input or a script is called a *pipeline*; it contains one or more commands separated by zero or more pipe characters (|). For each pipeline it reads, the shell breaks it up into commands, sets up the I/O for the pipeline, and then does the following for each command:

1. Splits the command into tokens that are separated by the fixed set of metacharacters: space, TAB, newline, ;, (,), <, >, |, and &. Types of tokens include words, keywords, I/O redirectors, and semicolons.

2. Checks the first token of each command to see if it is a *keyword* with no quotes or backslashes. If it's an opening keyword (if and other control-structure openers, function, {, (, ((, or [[), the command is actually a *compound*

---

* Even this explanation is slightly simplified to elide the most petty details, e.g., "middles" and "ends" of compound commands, special characters within [[...]] and ((...)) constructs, etc. The last word on this subject is the reference book *The New KornShell Command and Programming Language* by Morris Bolsky and David Korn, published by Prentice-Hall.

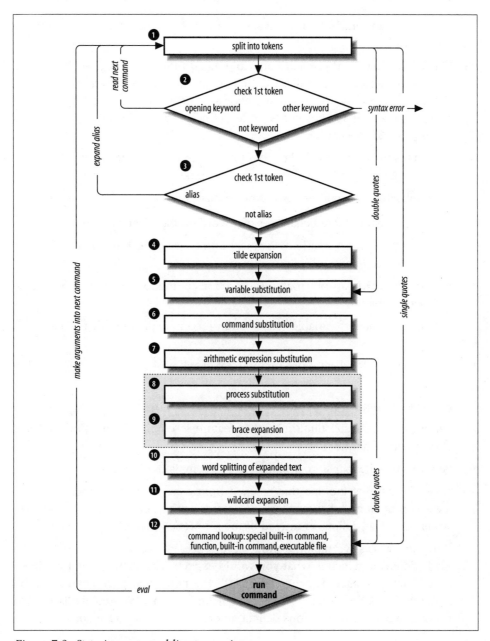

Figure 7-2. Steps in command-line processing

command. The shell sets things up internally for the compound command, reads the next command, and starts the process again. If the keyword isn't a compound command opener (e.g., is a control-structure "middle" like then, else, or do, an "end" like fi or done, or a logical operator), the shell signals a syntax error.

3. Checks the first word of each command against the list of *aliases*. If a match is found, it substitutes the alias's definition and goes back to Step 1; otherwise, it goes on to Step 4. This scheme allows recursive aliases; see Chapter 3. It also allows aliases for keywords to be defined, e.g., alias aslongas=while or alias procedure=function.

4. Substitutes the user's home directory ($HOME) for the tilde character (~) if it is at the beginning of a word. Substitutes *user*'s home directory for ~*user*.*

   Tilde substitution occurs at the following places:

   - As the first unquoted character of a word on the command line

   - After the = in a variable assignment and after any : in the value of a variable assignment

   - For the *word* part of variable substitutions of the form ${*variable op word*} (see Chapter 4)

5. Performs parameter (variable) substitution for any expression that starts with a dollar sign ($).

6. Does command substitution for any expression of the form $(*string*) or `*string*`.

7. Evaluates arithmetic expressions of the form $((*string*)).

8. Performs process substitution, if that feature is compiled into the shell and your system supports */dev/fd*.

9. Performs brace expansion, if that feature is compiled into the shell.

10. Takes the parts of the line that resulted from parameter, command, and arithmetic substitution and splits them into words again. This time it uses the characters in $IFS as delimiters instead of the set of metacharacters in Step 1.

    Normally, successive multiple input occurrences of characters in IFS act as a single delimiter, which is what you would expect. This is true only for whitespace characters, such as space and TAB. For non-whitespace characters, this is not true. For example, when reading the colon-separated fields of */etc/passwd*, two successive colons delimit an empty field. For example:

    ```
    IFS=:
    while read name passwd uid gid fullname homedir shell
    do
    ```

---

* Two obscure variations on this: the shell substitutes the current directory ($PWD) for ~+ and the previous directory ($OLDPWD) for ~-.

```
            . . .
        done < /etc/passwd
```

To get this behavior with whitespace-delimited fields (for example, where TAB characters delimit each field), put *two* successive instances of the delimiter character into IFS.

ksh ignores any inherited (environment) value of IFS. Upon startup, it sets the value of IFS to the default of space, TAB, and newline.

11. Performs filename generation, a.k.a. wildcard expansion, for any occurrences of *, ?, and [ ] pairs. It also processes the regular expression operators that we saw in Chapter 4.

12. Uses the first word as a command by looking up its location according to the rest of the list in Chapter 4, i.e., as a special built-in command, then as a function, then as a regular built-in command, and finally as a file in any of the directories in $PATH.

13. Runs the command after setting up I/O redirection and other such things.

That's a lot of steps—and it's not even the whole story! But before we go on, an example should make this process clearer. Assume that the following command has been run:

```
    alias ll="ls -l"
```

Further assume that a file exists called *.hist537* in user fred's home directory, which is */home/fred*, and that there is a double-dollar-sign variable $$ whose value is 2537 (we'll see what this special variable is in the next chapter).

Now let's see how the shell processes the following command:

```
    ll $(whence cc) ~fred/.*$(($$%1000))
```

Here is what happens to this line:

1. `ll $(whence cc) ~fred/.*$(($$%1000))`

   Splitting the input into words.

2. ll is not a keyword, so step 2 does nothing.

3. `ls -l $(whence cc) ~fred/.*$(($$%1000))`

   Substituting ls -l for its alias "ll". The shell then repeats steps 1 through 3; step 2 splits the ls -l into two words.

4. `ls -l $(whence cc) /home/fred/.*$(($$%1000))`

   Expanding ~fred into */home/fred*.

5. `ls -l $(whence cc) /home/fred/.*$((2537%1000))`

    Substituting 2537 for $$.

6. `ls -l /usr/bin/cc /home/fred/.*$((2537%1000))`

    Doing command substitution on "whence cc."

7. `ls -l /usr/bin/cc /home/fred/.*537`

    Evaluating the arithmetic expression 2537%1000.

8. `ls -l /usr/bin/cc /home/fred/.*537`

    This step does nothing. (No process substitution.)

9. `ls -l /usr/bin/cc /home/fred/.*537`

    This step does nothing. (No braces to expand.)

10. `ls -l /usr/bin/cc /home/fred/.*537`

    This step does nothing. (No expanded text to split.)

11. `ls -l /usr/bin/cc /home/fred/.hist537`

    Substituting the filename for the wildcard expression `.*537`.

12. The command *ls* is found in */usr/bin*.

13. */usr/bin/ls* is run with the option *–l* and the two arguments.

Although this list of steps is fairly straightforward, it is not the whole story. There are still two ways to subvert the process: by quoting, and by using the advanced command *eval*.

Quoting

You can think of quoting as a way of getting the shell to skip some of the 13 steps above. In particular:

*   **Single quotes** (`'...'`) bypass *everything* through Step 11, including aliasing. All characters inside a pair of single quotes are untouched. You can't have single quotes inside single quotes, even if you precede them with backslashes.[*]

*   **Double quotes** (`"..."`) bypass steps 1 through 4, plus steps 8 through 11. That is, they ignore pipe characters, aliases, tilde substitution, wildcard expansion, process substitution, brace expansion, and splitting into words via delimiters (e.g., spaces) inside the double quotes. Single quotes inside double quotes have no effect. But double quotes do allow parameter substitution, command substitution, and arithmetic expression evaluation. You can include a double

---

[*] However, as we saw in Chapter 1, `'\''` (i.e., single quote, backslash, single quote, single quote) acts pretty much like a single quote in the middle of a single-quoted string; e.g., `'abc'\''def'` evaluates to `abc'def`.

quote inside a double-quoted string by preceding it with a backslash (\). You must also backslash-escape $, ` (the archaic command substitution delimiter), and \ itself.

Table 7-8 contains some simple examples that show how these work; they assume the statement `dave=bob` was run and user `fred`'s home directory is */home/fred*.

If you are wondering whether to use single or double quotes in a particular shell programming situation, it is safest to use single quotes unless you specifically need parameter, command, or arithmetic substitution.

Table 7-8. Examples of quoting rules

Expression	Value
$dave	bob
"$dave"	bob
\$dave	$dave
'$dave'	$dave
\'$dave\'	'bob'
"'$dave'"	'bob'
~fred	/home/fred
"~fred"	~fred
'~fred'	~fred

Using double quotes on variable values is increasingly important when dealing with the results of wildcard expansion. Today, it is not unusual to have files and directories available on Unix systems that actually physically exist on Microsoft Windows and Apple Macintosh systems. On those systems, spaces and other unusual characters, such as apostrophes and back-quotes, are common in filenames. Thus, to pass the full pathname into your application, be sure you quote things properly.

Task 7-5 is a more advanced example of command-line processing that should give you deeper insight into the overall process.

Task 7-5

Customize your primary prompt string so that it contains the current directory with tilde (~) notation.

Recall from Chapter 4 that we found a simple way to set up the prompt string PS1 so that it always contains the current directory: `PS1=' ($PWD)-> '`.

One problem with this setup is that the resulting prompt strings can get very long. One way to shorten them is to substitute tilde notation for users' home directories. This cannot be done with a simple string expression analogous to the above. The solution is somewhat complicated and takes advantage of the command-line processing rules.

The basic idea is to create a "wrapper" around the *cd* command, as we did in Chapter 5, that installs the current directory with tilde notation as the prompt string. We will see how to make this wrapper function shortly. The code we need to insert tilde notation is complicated in its own right; we develop it first.

We start with a function that, given a pathname as argument, prints its equivalent in tilde notation if possible. In order to write this function, we assume that we already have an associative array named `tilde_ids`, in which the subscripts are home directories and the values are user names. Thus, `print ${tilde_ids[/home/arnold]}` would print the value `arnold`. Here's the function, named *tildize*:

```
function tildize {
    # subdir of our home directory
    if [[ $1 == $HOME* ]]; then
        print "\~${1#$HOME}"
        return 0
    fi

    # loop over homedirs trying to match current dir
    typeset homedir
    for homedir in ${!tilde_ids[*]}; do
        if [[ $1 == ${homedir}?(/*) ]]; then
            print "\~${tilde_ids[$homedir]}${1#$homedir}"
            return 0
        fi
    done
    print "$1"
    return 1
}
```

The first `if` clause checks if the given pathname is under the user's home directory. If so, it substitutes tilde (~) for the home directory in the pathname and returns.

If not, we loop over all the subscripts in `tilde_ids`, comparing each one to our current directory. The test matches home directories by themselves or with some other directory appended (the `?(/*)` part.) If a user's home directory is found, *~user* is substituted for the full home directory in the given pathname, the result is printed, and the function exits.

Finally, if the `for` loop exhausts all users without finding a home directory that is a prefix of the given pathname, *tildize* simply echoes back its input.

Now, how do we create the `tilde_ids` array? We use the function *init_tilde_db*. It should be called once, from the *.profile* file when we log in. The `tilde_ids` array must be explicitly declared as an associative array using `typeset -A`:

```
# tilde_ids[] is global associative array
# mapping directories to user names
typeset -A tilde_ids

function init_tilde_db {
    typeset user homedir    # local vars
    awk -F: '{ print $1, $6 }' /etc/passwd |
        while read user homedir; do
            if [[ $homedir != / ]]; then
                tilde_ids[$homedir]=$user
            fi
        done
}
```

We use the *awk* utility to extract the first and sixth fields of the file */etc/passwd*, which contain user IDs and home directories, respectively.* In this case, *awk* acts like *cut*. The `-F:` is analogous to `-d:`, which we saw in Chapter 4, except that *awk* prints the values on each line separated by spaces, not colons (`:`).

awk's output is fed into a `while` loop that checks the pathname given as argument to see if it contains some user's home directory. (The conditional expression eliminates "users" like `daemon` and `root`, whose home directories are root and therefore are contained in every full pathname.)

Now that we have the *tildize* function, you might think we could use it in a command substitution expression like this:

```
PS1='$(tildize $PWD)> '
```

In fact, you'd be right.† But there's a hidden cost here. The function is run *every* time that the shell prints the prompt. Even if all you do is hit ENTER, the shell runs the *tildize* function. If there are lots of users on your system, the shell loops through all of the home directories, each time. To avoid this, we write a *cd* function that only updates the prompt when we actually change directories. The following code should go into your *.profile* or environment file, along with the definition of `tilde_ids` and *tildize*:

```
init_tilde_db  # set up array once, upon login

function cd {
    command cd "$@"  # run real cd
```

---

* In large multi-machine environments, you may need to use something like `ypcat passwd | awk ...` or `niscat passwd.org_dir | awk ...` to get the same information. Check with your system administrator.

† This doesn't work in *ksh88*, though.

```
        typeset es=$?     # save exit status in a local var
        PS1="$(tildize $PWD)> "
        return $es
}

cd $PWD           # set prompt
```

As we saw in Chapter 5, writing a function with the same name as a built-in command looks pretty strange at first glance. But, following the POSIX standard, the Korn shell distinguishes between "special" built-in commands and regular built-in commands. When the shell looks for commands to execute, it finds functions before it finds regular built-in commands. *cd* is a regular built-in command, so this works. Within the function, we use the the cleverly named *command* command to actually get at the real *cd* command.* The statement `command cd "$@"` passes the function's arguments on to the real *cd* in order to change the directory. (As a side note, the shell defines an alias `command='command '`, which allows you to use *command* with aliases.)

When you log in, this code sets PS1 to the initial current directory (presumably your home directory). Then, whenever you enter a *cd* command, the function runs to change the directory and reset the prompt.

Of course, the function *tildize* can be any code that formats the directory string. See the exercises at the end of this chapter for a couple of suggestions.

Extended quoting

Single and double quoting have been in the Bourne shell and its derivatives from the beginning (although the original Bourne shell doesn't do arithmetic or $(...) substitution). The Korn shell offers variant versions of both single- and double-quoted strings, as follows.

$"..."

This version is the simplest. It is just like a regular double-quoted string. However, these strings are subject to *locale translation* at runtime. This is described further, below.

$'...'

This string is similar to a regular single-quoted string in that none of the shell's substitutions or expansions are performed on the contents. However, the contents are processed for escape sequences, similar to those used by the *print* command. *ksh* documentation refers to these as *ANSI C strings*.

---

* As mentioned earlier, *command* is *not* a special built-in. Woe be to the shell programmer who writes a function named *command*!

The Korn shell's internationalization features are beyond the scope of this book, but briefly, it works like this. When *ksh* is invoked on a script with the *−D* option, it prints a list of all $"..." strings to standard output. This list can then be saved and used to produce translations that are used at runtime when the script is actually executed. Thus, in a French locale, if a translation is available for this program:

```
print $"hello, world"    A well-known greeting among computer scientists
```

ksh would print bonjour, monde when the program runs.

The *print* command makes it possible to use C-style escape sequences for output. And most of the time, this is all you need. But occasionally, it's useful to use the same notation in arguments to other programs. This is the purpose of the $'...' string. The contents are not processed for variable, command, or arithmetic substitution. But they are processed for escape sequences, as shown in Table 7-9.

Table 7-9. String escape sequences

Sequence	Meaning	Sequence	Meaning
\a	Alert, ASCII bell	\t	TAB
\b	Backspace	\v	Vertical tab
\c*X*	CTRL-*X* [a] [b]	\x*HH*	Character with value of hexadecimal digits *HH*
\C[.*ce*.]	The collating element *ce*.[a] [b] (A collating element is two or more characters that are treated as one unit for sorting purposes.)	\x{*digs*}	Hexadecimal value of *digs*. Use the braces when following characters are hexadecimal digits that should not be interpreted.[a] [b]
\e	ASCII Escape character[a] [b]	\0	Rest of string ignored after this[b]
\E	ASCII Escape character[a]	*ddd*	Character with value of octal digits *ddd*
\f	Form feed	\'	Single quote
\n	Newline	\"	Double quote
\r	Carriage return	\\	Literal backslash

[a] Not in the C language.
[b] New, starting with *ksh93l*.

Of primary value is the fact that you can easily get single and double quotes inside the $'...' kind of string:

```
$ print $'A string with \'single quotes\' and \"double quotes\" in it'
A string with 'single quotes' and "double quotes" in it
```

Of interest is the fact that the double quote doesn't really need to be escaped, but that doing so doesn't hurt anything, either.

eval

We have seen that quoting lets you skip steps in command-line processing. Then there's the *eval* command, which lets you go through the process again. Performing command-line processing twice may seem strange, but it's actually very powerful: it lets you write scripts that create command strings on the fly and then pass them to the shell for execution. This means that you can give scripts "intelligence" to modify their own behavior as they are running.

The *eval* statement tells the shell to take *eval*'s arguments and run them through the command-line processing steps all over again. To help you understand the implications of *eval*, we'll start with a trivial example and work our way up to a situation in which we're constructing and running commands on the fly.

eval ls passes the string ls to the shell to execute; the shell prints a list of files in the current directory. Very simple; there is nothing about the string ls that needs to be sent through the command-processing steps twice. But consider this:

```
listpage="ls | more"
$listpage
```

Instead of producing a paginated file listing, the shell treats | and more as arguments to *ls*, and *ls* complains that no files of those names exist. Why? Because the pipe character "appears" in step 5 when the shell evaluates the variable, *after* it has actually looked for pipe characters (in step 2). The variable's expansion isn't even parsed until step 10. As a result, the shell treats | and more as arguments to *ls*, so that *ls* tries to find files called | and *more* in the current directory!

Now consider eval $listpage instead of just $listpage. When the shell gets to the last step, it runs the command *eval* with arguments ls, |, and more. This causes the shell to go back to Step 1 with a line that consists of these arguments. It finds | in Step 2 and splits the line into two commands, *ls* and *more*. Each command is processed in the normal (and in both cases trivial) way. The result is a paginated list of the files in your current directory.

Now you may start to see how powerful *eval* can be. It is an advanced feature that requires considerable programming cleverness to be used most effectively. It even has a bit of the flavor of artificial intelligence, in that it enables you to write programs that can "write" and execute other programs.* You probably won't use *eval* for everyday shell programming, but it's worth taking the time to understand what it can do.

---

* You could actually do this without *eval*, by *printing* commands to a temporary file and then "sourcing" that file with . filename. But that is *much* less efficient.

As a more interesting example, we'll revisit Task 4-1, the very first task in the book. In it, we constructed a simple pipeline that sorts a file and prints out the first *N* lines, where *N* defaults to 10. The resulting pipeline was:

```
sort -nr $1 | head -${2:-10}
```

The first argument specifies the file to sort; $2 is the number of lines to print.

Now suppose we change the task just a bit so that the default is to print the *entire file* instead of 10 lines. This means that we don't want to use *head* at all in the default case. We could do this in the following way:

```
if [[ -n $2 ]]; then
    sort -nr $1 | head -$2
else
    sort -nr $1
fi
```

In other words, we decide which pipeline to run according to whether or not $2 is null. But here is a more compact solution:

```
eval sort -nr \$1 ${2:+"| head -\$2"}
```

The last expression in this line evaluates to the string | head -\$2 if $2 exists (is not null); if $2 is null, then the expression is null too. We backslash-escape dollar signs (\$) before variable names to prevent unpredictable results if the variables' values contain special characters like > or |. The backslash effectively puts off the variables' evaluation until the *eval* command itself runs. So the entire line is either:

```
eval sort -nr \$1 | head -\$2
```

if $2 is given or:

```
eval sort -nr \$1
```

if $2 is null. Once again, we can't just run this command without *eval* because the pipe is "uncovered" after the shell tries to break the line up into commands. *eval* causes the shell to run the correct pipeline when $2 is given.

Next, we'll revisit Task 7-3 from earlier in this chapter, the *start* function that lets you start a command in the background and save its standard output and standard error in a logfile. Recall that the one-line solution to this task had the restriction that the command could not contain output redirectors or pipes. Although the former doesn't make sense when you think about it, you certainly would want the ability to start a pipeline in this way.

eval is the obvious way to solve this problem:

```
function start {
    eval "$@" > logfile 2>&1 &
}
```

The only restriction that this imposes on the user is that pipes and other such special characters must be quoted (surrounded by quotes or preceded by backslashes).

Task 7-6 is a way to apply *eval* in conjunction with various other interesting shell programming concepts.

Task 7-6

Implement the guts of the *make*(1) utility as a shell script.

make is known primarily as a programmer's tool, but it seems as though someone finds a new use for it every day. Without going into too much extraneous detail, *make* keeps track of multiple files in a particular project, some of which depend on others (e.g., a document depends on its word processor input file(s)). It makes sure that when you change a file, all of the other files that depend on it are processed.

For example, assume you're writing a book in DocBook XML. You have files for the book's chapters called *ch01.xml*, *ch02.xml*, and so on. The generated PostScript output for these files are *ch01.ps*, *ch02.ps*, etc. The tool to convert DocBook XML into PostScript is called (for some strange reason) *gmat*. You run commands like `gmat chN.xml` to do the processing. (*gmat* knows to create *ch01.ps* from *ch01.xml*; you don't need to use shell redirection.) While you're working on the book, you tend to make changes to several files at a time.

In this situation, you can use *make* to keep track of which files need to be reprocessed, so that all you need to do is type `make`, and it figures out what needs to be done. You don't need to remember to reprocess the files that have changed.

How does *make* do this? Simple: it compares the modification times of the input and output files (called *sources* and *targets* in *make* terminology), and if the input file is newer, *make* reprocesses it.

You tell *make* which files to check by building a file called *makefile* that has constructs like this:

```
target : source1 source2 ...
        commands to make target
```

This essentially says, "For *target* to be up to date, it must be newer than all of the *sources*. If it's not, run the *commands* to bring it up to date." The *commands* are on one or more lines that must start with TABs: e.g., to make *ch07.ps*:

```
ch07.ps : ch07.xml
        gmat ch07.xml
```

Now suppose that we write a shell function called *makecmd* that reads and executes a single construct of this form. Assume that the *makefile* is read from standard input. The function would look like the following code.

```
function makecmd {
    read target colon sources
    for src in $sources; do
        if [[ $src -nt $target ]]; then
            while read cmd && [[ $cmd == \t* ]]; do
                print "$cmd"
                eval $cmd
            done
            break
        fi
    done
}
```

This function reads the line with the target and sources; the variable colon is just a placeholder for the :. Then it checks each source to see if it's newer than the target, using the *–nt* file attribute test operator that we saw in Chapter 5. If the source is newer, it reads, prints, and executes the commands until it finds a line that doesn't start with a TAB or it reaches end-of-file. (The real *make* does more than this; see the exercises at the end of this chapter.) After running the commands, it breaks out of the for loop, so that it doesn't run the commands more than once. (It isn't necessary to strip the initial TAB from the command. The shell discards the leading whitespace automatically.)

The C compiler as pipeline

As a final example of *eval*, we'll revisit our old friend *occ*, the C compiler frontend from the previous three chapters. Recall that the compiler front-end does its work by calling separate programs to do the actual compile from C to object code (the ccom program), optimization of object code (*optimize*), assembly of assembler code files (*as*), and final linking of object code files into an executable program (*ld*). These separate programs use temporary files to store their outputs.

Now we'll assume that these components (except the linker) pass information in a pipeline to the final object code output. In other words, each component takes standard input and produces standard output instead of taking filename arguments. We'll also change an earlier assumption: instead of compiling a C source file directly to object code, *occ* compiles C to assembler code, which the assembler then assembles to object code.* This lets us suppose that *occ* works like this:

```
ccom < filename.c | as | optimize > filename.o
```

Or, if you prefer:

```
cat filename.c | ccom | as | optimize > filename.o
```

To get this in the proper framework for *eval*, let's assume that the variables src-name and objname contain the names of the source and object files, respectively. Then our pipeline becomes:

```
cat $srcname | ccom | as | optimize > $objname
```

As we've already seen, this is equivalent to:

```
eval cat \$srcname \| ccom \| as \| optimize \> \$objname
```

Knowing what we do about *eval*, we can transform this into:

```
eval cat \$srcname " | ccom" " | as" " | optimize" \> \$objname
```

and from that into:

```
compile=" | ccom"
assemble=" | as"
optimize=" | optimize"

eval cat \$srcname $compile $assemble $optimize \> \$objname
```

Now, consider what happens if you don't want to invoke the optimizer—which is the default case anyway. (Recall that the *−O* option invokes the optimizer.) We can do this:

```
optimize=""
if -O given then
    optimize=" | optimize"
fi
```

In the default case, $optimize evaluates to the empty string, causing the final pipeline to "collapse" into:

```
eval cat $srcname \| ccom \| as \> $objname
```

---

* For what it's worth, many Unix compilers generate assembly code, optimize the assembly code, and then generate object code.

Similarly, if you pass *occ* a file of assembler code (*filename.s*), you can collapse the compile step:*

```
assemble="| as"
if $srcname ends in .s then
    compile=""
fi
```

That results in this pipeline:

```
eval cat \$srcname \| as \> \$objname
```

Now we're ready to show the full "pipeline" version of *occ*. It's similar to the previous version, except that for each input file, it constructs and runs a pipeline as above. It processes the –g (debug) option and the link step in the same way as before. Here is the code:

```
# initialize option-related variables
do_link=true
debug=""
link_libs=""
clib="-lc"
exefile=""

# initialize pipeline components
compile=" | ccom"
assemble=" | as"
optimize=""

# process command-line options
while getopts "cgl:[lib]o:[outfile]O files ..." opt; do
    case $opt in
        c )     do_link=false ;;
        g )     debug="-g" ;;
        l )     link_libs+=" -l $OPTARG" ;;
        o )     exefile="-o $OPTARG" ;;
        O )     optimize=" | optimize" ;;
    esac
done
shift $(($OPTIND - 1))

# process the input files
for filename in "$@"; do
    case $filename in
        *.c )
            objname=${filename%.c}.o ;;
        *.s )
            objname=${filename%.s}.o
```

---

* Astute readers will notice that, according to this rationale, we would handle object-code input files (*filename.o*) with the pipeline `eval cat $srcname > $objname`, where the two names are the same. This will cause the shell to destroy *filename.o* by truncating it to zero length. We won't worry about this here.

```
                compile="" ;;
            *.o )
                objname=$filename  # just link it directly with the rest
                compile=""
                assemble="" ;;
            *  )
                print "error: $filename is not a source or object file."
                exit 1 ;;
        esac

        # run a pipeline for each input file
        eval cat \$filename $compile $assemble $optimize \> \$objname
        objfiles+=" $objname"
        compile=" | ccom"
        assemble=" | as"
    done

    if [[ $do_link == true ]]; then
        ld $exefile $objfiles $link_libs $clib
    fi
```

We could go on forever with increasingly complex examples of *eval*, but we'll set-
tle for concluding the chapter with a few exercises.

1. Here are a couple of ways to enhance *occ*, our C compiler:

    a. Real-world C compilers accept the option *−S*, which tells the compiler to
        suppress the assembly step and leave the output in files of assembler code
        whose names end in .s. Modify *occ* so that it recognizes this option.

    b. The language C++ is an evolutionary successor to C; it includes advanced
        features like operator overloading, mandatory function argument type
        checking, class definitions, templates, and many more. (Don't worry if you
        don't know what these are.) Some C++ compilers use C as an "assembly
        language", i.e., they compile C++ source files to C code and then pass
        them to a C compiler for further processing. Assume that C++ source files
        have names ending in *.cc*, and that */lib/cfront* is the C++ compiler "front-
        end" that produces C code on its standard output. Modify *occ* so that it
        accepts C++ as well as C, assembler, and object code files.

2. The possibilities for customizing your prompt string are practically endless.
    Here are two enhancements to the customization schemes that we've seen
    already:

    a. Enhance the current-directory-in-the-prompt scheme by limiting the
        prompt string's length to a number of characters that the user can define
        with an environment variable.

    b. Read the man page for *date*(1) and read about the SECONDS variable in the
        ksh(1) man page. Arrange things so that the shell prints the current time of
        day in the prompt. (Hint: remember that the shell does variable,

command, and arithmetic substitution on the value of PS1 before printing it out.)

3. The function *makecmd* in the solution to Task 7-6 represents an oversimplification of the real *make*'s functionality. *make* actually checks file dependencies *recursively*, meaning that a source on one line in a *makefile* can be a target on another line. For example, the book chapters in the example could themselves depend on figures in separate files that were made with a graphics package.

    a. Write a function called *readtargets* that goes through the *makefile* and stores all of the targets in a variable or temp file.

    b. Instead of reading the *makefile* from standard input, read it into an array variable called lines. Use the variable curline as the "current line" index. Modify *makecmd* so that it reads lines from the array starting with the current line.

    c. *makecmd* merely checks to see if any of the sources are newer than the given target. It should really be a recursive routine that looks like this:

        ```
        function makecmd {
            target=$1
            get sources for $target
            for each source src; do
                if $src is also a target in this makefile then
                    makecmd $src
                fi
                if [[ $src -nt $target ]]; then
                    run commands to make target
                    return
                fi
            done
        }
        ```

        Implement this. Remember to use *typeset* to create local variables, and think about how associative arrays might be helpful in tracking targets, sources, and commands to execute.

    d. Write the "driver" script that turns the *makecmd* function into a full *make* program. This should make the target given as argument, or if none is given, the first target listed in the makefile.

4. Finally, here are some problems that really test your knowledge of *eval* and the shell's command-line processing rules. Solve these and you're a true Korn shell wizard!

    a. Advanced shell programmers sometimes use a little trick that includes *eval*: using the value of a variable as the name of another variable. In other words, you can give a shell script control over the names of variables to which it assigns values. How would you do this? (Hint: if $fred equals "dave", and $dave is "bob", you might think that you could type print $$fred and get the response bob. This doesn't actually work, but it's on the right track. This exercise is actually easy to solve using namerefs. But it's worth doing it without them to test your understanding of *eval* and the shell's quoting rules.)

b. You could use the above technique together with other *eval* tricks to implement new control structures for the shell. For example, see if you can write a script (or function) that emulates the behavior of the C shell's *repeat* command:

```
repeat count command
```

This works in the obvious way: the *command* is executed *count* times.

8

Process Handling

The Unix operating system built its reputation on a small number of concepts, all of which are simple yet powerful. We've seen most of them by now: standard input/output, pipes, text-filtering utilities, the tree-structured filesystem, and so on. Unix also gained notoriety as the first small-computer* operating system to give each user control over more than one process. We call this capability *user-controlled multitasking.*

If Unix is the only operating system that you're familiar with, you might be surprised to learn that several other major operating systems have been sadly lacking in this area. For example, Microsoft's MS-DOS, for IBM PC compatibles, has no multitasking at all, let alone user-controlled multitasking. IBM's own VM/CMS system for large mainframes handles multiple users but gives them only one process each. Compaq's OpenVMS has user-controlled multitasking, but it is limited and difficult to use. The latest generation of small-computer operating systems, such as Apple's Macintosh OS X (which is BSD-based) and Microsoft's Windows (Windows 95 and later), finally include user-controlled multitasking at the operating system level.

But if you've gotten this far in this book, you probably don't think that multitasking is a big deal. You're probably used to the idea of running a process in the background by putting an ampersand (&) at the end of the command line. You have also seen the idea of a shell subprocess in Chapter 4, when we showed how shell scripts run.

In this chapter, we cover most of the Korn shell's features that relate to multitasking and process handling in general. We say "most" because some of these

---

* The PDP-11 systems on which Unix first became popular were considered small for the time.

features are, like the file descriptors we saw in Chapter 7, of interest only to low-level systems programmers.

We start out by looking at certain important primitives for identifying processes and for controlling them during login sessions and within shell scripts. Then we move out to a higher-level perspective, looking at ways to get processes to communicate with each other. The Korn shell's coroutine facility is the most sophisticated interprocess communication scheme that we'll examine; we also look in more detail at concepts we've already seen, like pipes and shell subprocesses.

Don't worry about getting bogged down in low-level technical details about Unix. We provide only the technical information that is necessary to explain higher-level features, plus a few other tidbits designed to pique your curiosity. If you are interested in finding out more about these areas, refer to your Unix Programmer's Manual or a book on Unix internals that pertains to your version of Unix.

We strongly recommend that you try out the examples in this chapter. The behavior of code that involves multiple processes is not as easy to understand on paper as most of the other examples in this book.

Process IDs and Job Numbers

Unix gives all processes numbers, called *process IDs*, when they are created. You will notice that, when you run a command in the background by appending & to it, the shell responds with a line that looks like this:

```
$ fred &
[1]     2349
```

In this example, 2349 is the process ID for the *fred* process. The [1] is a *job number* assigned by the shell (not the operating system). What's the difference? Job numbers refer to background processes that are currently running under your shell, while process IDs refer to all processes currently running on the entire system, for all users. The term *job* basically refers to a command line that was invoked from your login shell.

If you start up additional background jobs while the first one is still running, the shell numbers them 2, 3, etc. For example:

```
$ bob &
[2]     2367
$ dave | george &
[3]     2382
```

Clearly, 1, 2, and 3 are easier to remember than 2349, 2367, and 2382!

The shell includes job numbers in messages it prints when a background job completes, like this:

```
[1] +  Done            fred &
```

We'll explain what the plus sign means soon. If the job exits with nonzero status (see Chapter 5), the shell includes the exit status in parentheses:

```
[1] +  Done(1)         fred &
```

The shell prints other types of messages when certain abnormal things happen to background jobs; we'll see these later in this chapter.

Job Control

Why should you care about process IDs or job numbers? Actually, you could probably get along fine in your Unix life without ever referring to process IDs (unless you use a windowing workstation—as we'll see soon). Job numbers are more important, however: you can use them with the shell commands for *job control.*

You already know the most obvious way to control a job: you can create one in the background with &. Once a job is running in the background, you can let it run to completion, bring it into the *foreground*, or send it a message called a *signal*.

Foreground and Background

The built-in command *fg* brings a background job into the foreground. Normally this means that the job has control of your terminal or window and therefore is able to accept your input. In other words, the job begins to act as if you typed its command without the &.

If you have only one background job running, you can use *fg* without arguments, and the shell brings that job into the foreground. But if you have several jobs running in the background, the shell picks the one that you put into the background most recently. If you want a different job put into the foreground, you need to use the job's command name, preceded by a percent sign (%), or you can use its job number, also preceded by %, or its process ID without a percent sign. If you don't remember which jobs are running, you can use the *jobs* command to list them.

A few examples should make this clearer. Let's say you created three background jobs as above. If you type *jobs*, you see this:

```
[1]    Running         fred &
[2] -  Running         bob &
[3] +  Running         dave | george &
```

jobs has a few interesting options. Besides the job status, `jobs -l` also lists process group IDs:

```
[1]   2349      Running          fred &
[2] - 2367      Running          bob &
[3] + 2382      Running          dave | george &
```

How does all this work? Every time you run a job, the process(es) in the job are put into a new *process group*. Each process in a process group, besides its unique process ID number, also has a *process group ID*. The process group ID is the same as the process ID of the process group *leader*, which is one of the processes invoked as part of the job. (The last one in the pipeline, in fact.) The numbers that the shell prints are actually the process group IDs. (Note that for job 3, there are two processes, but only one number.)

Now, your terminal device, be it a real serial port or a pseudo-terminal such as you get in a windowing system or *telnet* session, also has a process group ID number. Processes whose process group ID matches that of the terminal "own" the terminal, in the sense that they are allowed to read input from it. In brief, job control works by setting the process group of the terminal to be the same as the process group of the current job. (There are lots more technical details, including the idea of a "session" introduced by POSIX, but those details aren't necessary for understanding the day-to-day use of job control.)

The *–p* option tells *jobs* to list *only* process group IDs:

```
$ jobs -p
2349
2367
2382
```

This could be useful with command substitution; see Task 8-1 later in this chapter. Finally, the *–n* option lists only those jobs whose status has changed since the shell last reported it—whether with a *jobs* command or otherwise.

If you type *fg* without an argument, the shell puts `dave | george` in the foreground, because it was put in the background most recently. But if you type `fg %bob` (or `fg %2`), *bob* will go in the foreground.

You can also refer to the job most recently put in the background by `%+`. Similarly, `%-` refers to the background job invoked *next*-most recently (*bob* in this case). That explains the plus and minus signs in the above: the plus sign shows the most recently invoked job; the minus sign shows the next most recently invoked job.*

---

* This is analogous to ~+ and ~– as references to the current and previous directory; see the footnote in Chapter 7. Also: `%%` is a synonym for `%+`.

If more than one background job has the same command, then %*command* will disambiguate by choosing the most recently invoked job (as you'd expect). If this isn't what you want, you need to use the job number instead of the command name. However, if the commands have different *arguments*, you can use %?*string* instead of %*command*. %?*string* refers to the job whose command contains the string. For example, assume you started these background jobs:

```
$ bob pete &
[1]     189
$ bob ralph &
[2]     190
$
```

Then you can use %?pete and %?ralph to refer to each of them, although actually %?pe and %?ra are sufficient to disambiguate.

Table 8-1 lists all of the ways to refer to background jobs. We have found that, given how infrequently people use job control commands, job numbers or command names are sufficient, and the other ways are superfluous.

Table 8-1. Ways to refer to background jobs

Reference	Background job
N	Process ID *N*
-*N*	Process group ID *N*
%*N*	Job number *N*
%*string*	Job whose command begins with *string*
%?*string*	Job whose command contains *string*
%+, %%	Most recently invoked background job
%-	Second most recently invoked background job

Suspending a Job

Just as you can put background jobs into the foreground with *fg*, you can also put a foreground job into the background. This involves suspending the job, so that the shell regains control of your terminal.

To suspend a job, type CTRL-Z* while it is running. This is analogous to typing CTRL-C (or whatever your interrupt key is), except that you can resume the job

---

* This assumes that the CTRL-Z key is set up as your suspend key; just as with CTRL-C and interrupts, this is conventional but by no means required.

after you have stopped it. When you type CTRL-Z, the shell responds with a message like this:

```
[1] + Stopped                    command
```

Then it gives you your prompt back. It also puts the suspended job at the top of the job list, as indicated by the + sign.

To resume a suspended job so that it continues to run in the foreground, just type *fg*. If, for some reason, you put other jobs in the background after you typed CTRL-Z, use *fg* with a job name or number. For example:

```
fred is running ...
CTRL-Z
[1] + Stopped                    fred
$ bob &
[2]       bob &
$ fg %fred
fred resumes in the foreground ...
```

The ability to suspend jobs and resume them in the foreground comes in very handy when you only have a single connection to your system,* and you are using a text editor like *vi* on a file that needs to be processed. For example, if you are editing an HTML file for your web server, you can do the following:

```
$ vi myfile.html
Edit the file ...  CTRL-Z
[1] + Stopped                    vi myfile.html
$ lynx myfile.html        Preview results with a text-only browser
You see that you made a mistake
$ fg
vi comes back up in the same place in your file
```

Programmers often use the same technique when debugging source code.

You will probably also find it useful to suspend a job and resume it in the background instead of the foreground. You may start a command in the foreground (i.e., normally) and find that it takes much longer than you expected—for example, a *grep*, *sort*, or database query. You need the command to finish, but you would also like control of your terminal back so that you can do other work. If you type CTRL-Z followed by *bg*, you move the job to the background.†

---

* Such as when you're dialed in from home to your office, or connected to a remote system over the Internet via *telnet* or *ssh*.

† Be warned, however, that not all commands are "well-behaved" when you do this. Be especially careful with commands that run over a network on a remote machine; you may end up "confusing" the remote program.

Disowning a Job

Normally, when you log out, the shell sends the HUP signal (see the next section) to any background jobs. If you've started a long-running job in the background and want it to complete no matter what, you should indicate this to the shell using the *disown* command with one or more job ID numbers as arguments. With no arguments, *all* background jobs are disowned.

Signals

We said earlier that typing CTRL-Z to suspend a job is similar to typing CTRL-C to stop a job, except that you can resume the job later. They are actually similar in a deeper way: both are particular cases of the act of sending a *signal* to a process.

A signal is a message that one process sends to another when some abnormal event takes place or when it wants the other process to do something. Most often, a process sends a signal to a subprocess it created. You're undoubtedly already comfortable with the idea that one process can communicate with another through an I/O pipeline; think of a signal as another way for processes to communicate with each other. (In fact, any textbook on operating systems will tell you that both are examples of the general concept of *interprocess communication*, or IPC.)*

Depending on the version of Unix, there are two or three dozen types of signals, including a few that can be used for whatever purpose a programmer wishes. Signals have numbers (from 1 to the number of signals the system supports) and names; we'll use the latter. You can get a list of all the signals on your system by typing `kill -l`. Bear in mind, when you write shell code involving signals, that signal names are more portable to other versions of Unix than signal numbers.

Control-Key Signals

When you type CTRL-C, you tell the shell to send the INT (for "interrupt") signal to the current job; CTRL-Z sends TSTP (for "terminal stop"). You can also send the current job a QUIT signal by typing CTRL-\ (control-backslash); this is sort of like a "stronger" version of CTRL-C.† You would normally use CTRL-\ when (and *only* when) CTRL-C doesn't work.

---

* Pipes and signals were the only IPC mechanisms in early versions of Unix. More modern versions have additional mechanisms, such as sockets, named pipes, and shared memory. Named pipes are accessible to shell programmers through the *mkfifo*(1) command, which is beyond the scope of this book.

† CTRL-\ can also cause the running program to leave a file called *core* in the program's current directory. This file contains an image of the process to which you sent the signal; a programmer could use it to help debug the program that was running. The file's name is a (very) old-fashioned term for a computer's memory. Other signals leave these "core dumps" as well; you should feel free to delete them unless a systems programmer tells you otherwise.

As we'll see soon, there is also a "panic" signal called KILL that you can send to a process when even CTRL-\ doesn't work. But it isn't attached to any control key, which means that you can't use it to stop the currently running process. INT, TSTP, and QUIT are the only signals you can use with control keys (although some systems have additional control-key signals).

You can customize the control keys used to send signals with options of the *stty*(1) command. These vary from system to system—consult your man page for the command—but the usual syntax is stty *signame char*. *signame* is a name for the signal that, unfortunately, is often not the same as the names we use here. Table 1-7 in Chapter 1 lists *stty* names for signals and tty-driver actions found on all modern versions of Unix. *char* is the control character, which you can give in the same notation we use. For example, to set your INT key to CTRL-X on most systems, use:

```
stty intr ^X
```

Now that we've told you how to do this, we should add that we don't recommend it. Changing your signal keys could lead to trouble if someone else has to stop a runaway process on your machine.

Most of the other signals are used by the operating system to advise processes of error conditions, like a bad machine code instruction, bad memory address, division by zero, or other events such as input being available on a file descriptor or a timer ("alarm" in Unix terminology) going off. The remaining signals are used for esoteric error conditions that are of interest only to low-level systems programmers; newer versions of Unix have more and more arcane signal types.

kill

You can use the built-in shell command *kill* to send a signal to any process you've created—not just the currently running job. *kill* takes as argument the process ID, job number, or command name of the process to which you want to send the signal. By default, *kill* sends the TERM ("terminate") signal, which usually has the same effect as the INT signal that you send with CTRL-C. But you can specify a different signal by using the *–s* option and the signal name, or the *–n* option and a signal number.

kill is so named because of the nature of the default TERM signal, but there is another reason, which has to do with the way Unix handles signals in general. The full details are too complex to go into here, but the following explanation should suffice.

Most signals cause a process that receives them to roll over and die; therefore, if you send any one of these signals, you "kill" the process that receives it. However, programs can be set up to "trap" specific signals and take some other action. For example, a text editor would do well to save the file being edited before terminating when it receives a signal such as INT, TERM, or QUIT. Determining what to do when various signals come in is part of the fun of Unix systems programming.

Here is an example of *kill*. Say you have a *fred* process in the background, with process ID 480 and job number 1, that needs to be stopped. You would start with this command:

```
kill %1
```

If you were successful, you would see a message like this:

```
[1] + Terminated           fred &
```

If you don't see this, then the TERM signal failed to terminate the job. The next step would be to try QUIT:

```
kill -s QUIT %1
```

If that worked, you would see this message:

```
[1] + Quit(coredump)       fred &
```

The shell indicates the signal that killed the program ("Quit") and the fact that it produced a *core* file. When a program exits normally, the exit status it returns to the shell is a value between 0 and 255. When a program dies from having been sent a signal, it exits, not with a status value of its own choosing, but rather with the status 256+N, where N is the number of the signal it received. (With *ksh88* and most other shells, normal exit statuses are between 0 and 127, and the "death by signal" exit status is 128+N. Caveat emptor.)

If even QUIT doesn't work, the last-ditch method would be to use KILL:

```
kill -s KILL %1
```

(Notice how this has the flavor of "yelling" at the runaway process.) This produces the message:

```
[1] + Killed               fred &
```

It is impossible for a process to trap a KILL signal—the operating system should terminate the process immediately and unconditionally. If it doesn't, then either your process is in one of the "funny states" that we'll see later in this chapter, or (far less likely) there's a bug in your version of Unix.

On job-control systems, there is an additional uncatchable signal: STOP. This is like TSTP, in that it suspends the targeted job. But unlike TSTP, it cannot be caught or ignored. It is a more drastic signal than TSTP, but less so than QUIT or TERM, since a stopped job may still be continued with *fg* or *bg*. The Korn shell provides the predefined alias `stop='kill -s STOP'` to make stopping jobs easier.

Task 8-1 is another example of how to use the *kill* command.

Task 8-1

Write a function called *killalljobs* that kills all background jobs.*

The solution to this task is simple, relying on `jobs -p`: \

```
function killalljobs {
    kill "$@" $(jobs -p)
}
```

You may be tempted to use the KILL signal immediately, instead of trying TERM (the default) and QUIT first. Don't do this. TERM and QUIT are designed to give a process the chance to clean up before exiting, whereas KILL will stop the process, wherever it may be in its computation. *Use KILL only as a last resort.*

You can use the *kill* command with any process you create, not just jobs in the background of your current shell. For example, if you use a windowing system, then you may have several terminal windows, each of which runs its own shell. If one shell is running a process that you want to stop, you can *kill* it from another window—but you can't refer to it with a job number because it's running under a different shell. You must instead use its process ID.

ps

This is probably the only situation in which a casual user would need to know the ID of a process. The command *ps*(1) gives you this information; however, it can give you lots of extra information that you must wade through as well.

ps is a complex command. It takes many options, some of which differ from one version of Unix to another. To add to the confusion, you may need different options on different Unix versions to get the same information! We will use options available on the two major types of Unix systems, those derived from System V (such as most of the versions for Intel x86 PCs, as well as Solaris, IBM's AIX and Hewlett-Packard's HP-UX) and BSD (Compaq's Ultrix, SunOS 4.x, and also GNU/Linux). If you aren't sure which kind of Unix version you have, try the System V options first.

---

* To test your understanding of how the shell works, answer this question: why can't this be done as a separate script?

You can invoke *ps* in its simplest form without any options. In this case, it prints a line of information about the current login shell and any processes running under it (i.e., background jobs). For example, if you invoked three background jobs, as we saw earlier in the chapter, *ps* on System V-derived versions of Unix would produce output that looks something like this:

```
PID TTY      TIME COMD
 146 pts/10  0:03 ksh
2349 pts/10  0:03 fred
2367 pts/10  0:17 bob
2387 pts/10  0:06 george
2389 pts/10  0:09 dave
2390 pts/10  0:00 ps
```

The output on BSD-derived systems looks like this:

```
PID TT STAT  TIME COMMAND
 146 10 S    0:03 /bin/ksh -i
2349 10 R    0:03 fred
2367 10 D    0:17 bob
2387 10 S    0:06 george
2389 10 R    0:09 dave
2390 10 R    0:00 ps
```

(You can ignore the STAT column.) This is a bit like the *jobs* command. PID is the process ID; TTY (or TT) is the terminal (or pseudo-terminal, if you are using a windowing system) the process was invoked from; TIME is the amount of processor time (not real or "wall clock" time) the process has used so far; COMD (or COMMAND) is the command. Notice that the BSD version includes the command's arguments, if any; also notice that the first line reports on the parent shell process, and in the last line, *ps* reports on itself.

ps without arguments lists all processes started from the current terminal or pseudo-terminal. But since *ps* is not a shell command, it doesn't correlate process IDs with the shell's job numbers. It also doesn't help you find the ID of the runaway process in another shell window.

To get this information, use *ps* *−a* (for "all"); this lists information on a different set of processes, depending on your Unix version.

System V

Instead of listing all of those that were started under a specific terminal, *ps* *−a* on System V-derived systems lists all processes associated with any terminal that aren't group leaders. For our purposes, a "group leader" is the parent shell of a terminal or window. Therefore, if you are using a windowing system, *ps* *−a* lists all jobs started in all windows (by all users), but not their parent shells.

Assume that, in the above example, you have only one terminal or window. Then *ps –a* prints the same output as plain *ps* except for the first line, since that's the parent shell. This doesn't seem to be very useful.

But consider what happens when you have multiple windows open. Let's say you have three windows, all running terminal emulators like *xterm* for the X Window System. You start background jobs *fred*, *dave*, and *bob* in windows with pseudo-terminal numbers 1, 2, and 3, respectively. This situation is shown in Figure 8-1.

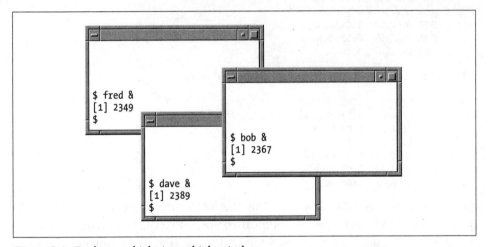

Figure 8-1. Background jobs in multiple windows

Assume you are in the uppermost window. If you type ps, you see something like this:

```
PID TTY      TIME COMD
146 pts/1    0:03 ksh
2349 pts/1   0:03 fred
2390 pts/1   0:00 ps
```

But if you type ps -a, you see this:

```
PID TTY      TIME COMD
2349 pts/1   0:03 fred
2367 pts/2   0:17 bob
2389 pts/3   0:09 dave
2390 pts/1   0:00 ps
```

Now you should see how *ps –a* can help you track down a runaway process. If it's *dave*, you can type kill 2389. If that doesn't work, try kill -s QUIT 2389, or in the worst case, kill -s KILL 2389.

BSD

On BSD-derived systems,* *ps* –*a* lists all jobs that were started on any terminal; in other words, it's a bit like concatenating the the results of plain *ps* for every user on the system. Given the above scenario, *ps* –*a* will show you all processes that the System V version shows, plus the group leaders (parent shells).

Unfortunately, *ps* –*a* (on any version of Unix) will not report processes that are in certain pathological conditions where they "forget" things like what shell invoked them and what terminal they belong to. Such processes have colorful names (zombies, orphans) that are actually used in Unix technical literature, not just informally by professional systems programmers. If you have a serious runaway process problem, it's possible that the process has entered one of these states.

Let's not worry about why or how a process gets this way. All you need to understand is that the process doesn't show up when you type ps -a. You need another option to *ps* to see it: on System V, it's *ps* –*e* ("everything"), whereas on BSD, it's *ps* –*ax*.

These options tell *ps* to list processes that either weren't started from terminals or "forgot" what terminal they were started from. The former category includes lots of processes that you probably didn't even know existed: these include basic processes that run the system and so-called *daemons* (pronounced "demons") that handle system services like mail, printing, network file systems, etc.

In fact, the output of *ps* –*e* or *ps* –*ax* is an excellent source of education about Unix system internals, if you're curious about them. Run the command on your system and, for each line of the listing that looks interesting, invoke *man* on the process name or look it up in the Unix Programmer's Manual for your system.

User shells and processes are listed at the very bottom of *ps* –*e* or *ps* –*ax* output; this is where you should look for runaway processes. Notice that many processes in the listing have ? instead of a terminal. Either these aren't supposed to have one (such as the basic daemons) or they're runaways. Therefore it's likely that if *ps* –*a* doesn't find a process you're trying to kill, *ps* –*e* (or *ps* –*ax*) will list it with ? in the TTY (or TT) column. You can determine which process you want by looking at the COMD (or COMMAND) column.

kill: The Full Story

The *kill* command is really misnamed. It should have been called *sendsignal* or something similar, since it sends signals to processes. (The name in fact derives

---

* *ps* on GNU/Linux systems acts like the BSD version.

from the *kill*(2) system call, which the *kill* command uses to send signals, and which is similarly misnamed.)

As we saw earlier, *kill –l* gives you the full list of available signal names on your system. The behavior of the built-in version of *kill* has been considerably rationalized in *ksh93*. The options and what they do are summarized in Table 8-2.

Table 8-2. Options for kill

Option	Meaning
`kill` *job* ...	Send the TERM signal to each named *job*. This is the normal usage.
`kill -l`	List the names of all supported signals.
`kill -l` *signal* ...	When *signal* is a number, print its name. If it's a name, print its number. If *signal* is a number greater than 256, it's treated as an exit status. The shell subtracts 256 and prints the corresponding signal.
`kill -s` *signal-name job* ...	Send the signal named by *signal-name* to each given *job*.
`kill -n` *signal-number job* ...	Send the numeric signal given by the *signal-number* to each given *job*.
`kill -`*signal job* ...	Send the signal specified by *signal* to each given *job*. *signal* may be either a number or a signal name. This form is considered to be obsolete; it is provided for compatibility with *ksh88* and the external *kill*(1) command.

One place to take advantage of *kill*'s ability to turn a number into a name is in issuing diagnostics. When a job dies due to a signal, the exit status is 256 plus the signal number. Thus, you might use code like this to produce a meaningful diagnostic from within a script:

```
es=$?          # save exit status
if ((es >= 256)); then
    print job received signal $(kill -l $((es - 256)) )
fi
```

trap

We've been discussing how signals affect the casual user; now let's talk a bit about how shell programmers can use them. We won't go into too much depth about this, because it's really the domain of systems programmers.

We mentioned earlier that programs in general can be set up to "trap" specific signals and process them in their own way. The *trap* built-in command lets you do this from within a shell script. *trap* is most important for "bullet-proofing" large shell programs so that they react appropriately to abnormal events—just as programs in any language should guard against invalid input. It's also important for certain systems programming tasks, as we'll see in the next chapter.

The syntax of *trap* is:

```
trap cmd sig1 sig2 ...
```

That is, when any of *sig1*, *sig2*, etc., are received, run *cmd*, then resume execution. After *cmd* finishes, the script resumes execution just after the command that was interrupted.*

Of course, *cmd* can be a script or function. The *sig*s can be specified by name or by number. You can also invoke *trap* without arguments, in which case the shell prints a list of any traps that have been set, using symbolic names for the signals. If you use trap -p, the shell prints the trap settings in a way that can be saved and reread later by a different invocation of the shell.

The shell scans the text of *cmd* twice. The first time is while it is preparing to run the *trap* command; all the substitutions as outlined in Chapter 7 are performed before executing the *trap* command. The second time is when the shell actually executes the trap. For this reason, it is best to use single quotes around the *cmd* in the text of the shell program. When the shell executes the trap's command, $? is always the exit status of the last command run before the trap started. This is important for diagnostics.

Here's a simple example that shows how *trap* works. Suppose we have a shell script called *loop* with this code:

```
while true; do
    sleep 60
done
```

This just pauses for 60 seconds (the *sleep*(1) command) and repeats indefinitely. *true* is a "do-nothing" command whose exit status is always 0. For efficiency, it is built-in to the shell. (The *false* command is a similar "do-nothing" command whose exit status is always 1. It is also built-in to the shell.) As it happens, *sleep* is also built-in to the shell. Try typing in this script. Invoke it, let it run for a little while, then type CTRL-C (assuming that is your interrupt key). It should stop, and you should get your shell prompt back.

---

* This is what *usually* happens. Sometimes the command currently running aborts (*sleep* acts like this, as we'll see soon); other times it finishes running. Further details are beyond the scope of this book.

Now insert the following line at the beginning of the script:

```
trap 'print "You hit control-C!"' INT
```

Invoke the script again. Now hit CTRL-C. The odds are overwhelming that you are interrupting the *sleep* command (as opposed to *true*). You should see the message "You hit control-C!", and the script will not stop running; instead, the *sleep* command will abort, and it will loop around and start another *sleep*. Hit CTRL-\ to get it to stop. Type `rm core` to get rid of the resulting core dump file.

Next, run the script in the background by typing `loop &`. Type `kill %loop` (i.e., send it the TERM signal); the script will terminate. Add TERM to the *trap* command, so that it looks like this:

```
trap 'print "You hit control-C!"' INT TERM
```

Now repeat the process: run it in the background and type `kill %loop`. As before, you will see the message and the process will keep running. Type `kill -KILL %loop` to stop it.

Notice that the message isn't really appropriate when you use *kill*. We'll change the script so it prints a better message in the *kill* case:

```
trap 'print "You hit control-C!"' INT
trap 'print "You tried to kill me!"' TERM

while true; do
    sleep 60
done
```

Now try it both ways: in the foreground with CTRL-C and in the background with *kill*. You'll see different messages.

Traps and Functions

The relationship between traps and shell functions is straightforward, but it has certain nuances that are worth discussing. The most important thing to understand is that Korn shell functions (those created using the `function` keyword; see Chapter 4) have their own local traps; these aren't known outside of the function. Old-style POSIX functions (those created using the *name*() syntax) *share* traps with the parent script.

Let's start with `function`-style functions, where traps are local. In particular, the surrounding script doesn't know about them. Consider this code:

```
function settrap {
    trap 'print "You hit control-C!"' INT
}
```

```
    settrap
    while true; do
        sleep 60
    done
```

If you invoke this script and hit your interrupt key, it just exits. The trap on INT in the function is known only inside that function. On the other hand:

```
function loop {
    trap 'print "How dare you!"' INT
    while true; do
        sleep 60
    done
}

trap 'print "You hit control-C!"' INT
loop
```

When you run this script and hit your interrupt key, it prints "How dare you!" But how about this:

```
function loop {
    while true; do
        sleep 60
    done
}

trap 'print "You hit control-C!"' INT
loop
print 'exiting ...'
```

This time the looping code is within a function, and the trap is set in the surrounding script. If you hit your interrupt key, it prints the message and then prints "exiting..." It does not repeat the loop as above.

Why? Remember that when the signal comes in, the shell aborts the current command, which in this case is a call to a function. The entire function aborts, and execution resumes at the next statement after the function call.

The advantage of traps that are local to functions is that they allow you to control a function's behavior separately from the surrounding code.

Yet you may want to define global traps inside functions. There is a rather kludgy way to do this; it depends on a feature that we introduce in Chapter 9, which we call a "fake signal." Here is a way to set *trapcode* as a global trap for signal *SIG* inside a function:

```
    trap "trap trapcode SIG" EXIT
```

This sets up the command trap *trapcode SIG* to run right after the function exits, at which time the surrounding shell script is in scope (i.e., is "in charge"). When that command runs, *trapcode* is set up to handle the *SIG* signal.

For example, you may want to reset the trap on the signal you just received, like this:

```
function trap_handler {
    trap "trap second_handler INT" EXIT
    print 'Interrupt: one more to abort.'
}

function second_handler {
    print 'Aborted.'
    exit
}

trap trap_handler INT
```

This code acts like the Unix *mail* utility: when you are typing in a message, you must press your interrupt key twice to abort the process.

There is a less kludgy way to this, taking advantage of the fact that POSIX-style functions *share* traps with the parent script:

```
# POSIX style function, trap is global
trap_handler () {
    trap second_handler INT
    print 'Interrupt: one more to abort.'
}

function second_handler {
    print 'Aborted.'
    exit
}

trap trap_handler INT

while true ; do
    sleep 60
done
```

If you type this in and run it, you get the same results as in the previous example, without the extra trickery of using the fake EXIT signal.

Speaking of *mail*, in Task 8-2 we'll show a more practical example of traps.

Task 8-2

As part of an electronic mail system, write the shell code that lets a user compose a message.

The basic idea is to use *cat* to create the message in a temporary file and then hand the file's name off to a program that actually sends the message to its destination. The code to create the file is very simple:

```
msgfile=/tmp/msg$$
cat > $msgfile
```

Since *cat* without an argument reads from the standard input, this just waits for the user to type a message and end it with the end-of-file character CTRL-D.

Process ID Variables and Temporary Files

The only thing new about this is $$ in the filename expression. This is a special shell variable whose value is the process ID of the current shell.

To see how $$ works, type ps and note the process ID of your shell process (*ksh*). Then type print "$$"; the shell responds with that same number. Now type ksh to start a shell subprocess, and when you get a prompt, repeat the process. You should see a different number, probably slightly higher than the last one.

You can examine the parent-child relationship in more detail by using the PPID (parent process ID) variable. *ksh* sets this to the process ID of the parent process. Each time you start a new instance of *ksh*, if you type print $PPID you should see a number that is the same as the $$ of the earlier shell.

A related built-in shell variable is ! (i.e., its value is $!), which contains the process ID of the most recently invoked background job. To see how this works, invoke any job in the background and note the process ID printed by the shell next to [1]. Then type print "$!"; you should see the same number.

To return to our mail example: since all processes on the system must have unique process IDs, $$ is excellent for constructing names of temporary files. We saw an example of this in Chapter 7, when discussing command-line evaluation steps, and there are also examples in Chapter 9.*

The directory */tmp* is conventionally used for temporary files. Files in this directory are usually erased whenever the computer is rebooted.

Nevertheless, a program should clean up such files before it exits, to avoid taking up unnecessary disk space. We could do this in our code very easily by adding the line rm $msgfile after the code that actually sends the message. But what if the program receives a signal during execution? For example, what if a user changes his or her mind about sending the message and hits CTRL-C to stop the process?

---

* In practice, temporary filenames based just on $$ can lead to insecure systems. If you have the *mktemp*(1) program on your system, you should use it in your applications to generate unique names for your temporary files.

We would need to clean up before exiting. We'll emulate the actual Unix *mail* system by saving the message being written in a file called *dead.letter* in the current directory. We can do this by using *trap* with a command string that includes an *exit* command:

```
trap 'mv $msgfile dead.letter; exit' INT TERM
msgfile=/tmp/msg$$
cat > $msgfile
# send the contents of $msgfile to the specified mail address ...
rm $msgfile
```

When the script receives an INT or TERM signal, it saves the temp file and then exits. Note that the command string isn't evaluated until it needs to be run, so $msgfile will contain the correct value; that's why we surround the string in single quotes.

But what if the script receives a signal before msgfile is created—unlikely though that may be? Then *mv* will try to rename a file that doesn't exist. To fix this, we need to test for the existence of the file $msgfile before trying to save it. The code for this is a bit unwieldy to put in a single command string, so we'll use a function instead:

```
function cleanup {
    if [[ -e $msgfile ]]; then
        mv $msgfile dead.letter
    fi
    exit
}

trap cleanup INT TERM

msgfile=/tmp/msg$$
cat > $msgfile
# send the contents of $msgfile to the specified mail address ...
rm $msgfile
```

Ignoring Signals

Sometimes a signal comes in that you don't want to do anything about. If you give the null string ("" or ' ') as the command argument to *trap*, the shell effectively ignores that signal. The classic example of a signal you may want to ignore is HUP (hangup), the signal all of your background processes receive when you log out. (If your line actually drops, Unix sends the HUP signal to the shell. The shell forwards the signal to all your background processes, or sends it on its own initiative if you logout normally.)

HUP has the usual default behavior: it kills the process that receives it. But there are bound to be times when you don't want a background job to terminate when you log out. For example, you may start a long compile or text formatting job; you want to log out and come back later when you expect the job to be finished. Under normal circumstances, your background job terminates when you log out. But if you run it in a shell environment where the HUP signal is ignored, the job finishes.

To do this, you could write a simple function that looks like this:

```
function ignorehup {
    trap "" HUP
    eval "$@"
}
```

We write this as a function instead of a script for reasons that will become clearer when we look in detail at subshells at the end of this chapter.

Actually, there is a Unix command called *nohup* that does precisely this. The *start* function from the last chapter could include *nohup*:

```
function start {
    eval nohup "$@" > logfile 2>&1 &
}
```

This prevents HUP from terminating your command and saves its standard and error output in a file. Actually, the following is just as good:

```
function start {
    nohup "$@" > logfile 2>&1 &
}
```

If you understand why *eval* is essentially redundant when you use *nohup* in this case, then you have a firm grasp on the material in Chapter 7.

Resetting Traps

Another "special case" of the *trap* command occurs when you give a dash (–) as the command argument. This resets the action taken when the signal is received to the default, which usually is termination of the process.

As an example of this, let's return to Task 8-2, our mail program. After the user has finished sending the message, the temporary file is erased. At that point, since there is no longer any need to "clean up," we can reset the signal trap to its default state. The code for this, apart from function definitions, is:

```
trap cleanup INT TERM

msgfile=/tmp/msg$$
cat > $msgfile
# send the contents of $msgfile to the specified mail address ...
rm $msgfile

trap - INT TERM
```

The last line of this code resets the handlers for the INT and TERM signals.

At this point you may be thinking that one could get seriously carried away with signal handling in a shell script. It is true that industrial strength programs devote considerable amounts of code to dealing with signals. But these programs are almost always large enough so that the signal-handling code is a tiny fraction of the whole thing. For example, you can bet that the real Unix *mail* system is pretty darn bullet-proof.

However, you will probably never write a shell script that is complex enough, and that needs to be robust enough, to merit lots of signal handling. You may write a prototype for a program as large as *mail* in shell code, but prototypes by definition do not need to be bullet-proofed.

Therefore, you shouldn't worry about putting signal-handling code in every 20-line shell script you write. Our advice is to determine if there are any situations in which a signal could cause your program to do something seriously bad and add code to deal with those contingencies. What is "seriously bad"? Well, with respect to the above examples, we'd say that the case where HUP causes your job to terminate on logout *is* seriously bad, while the temporary file situation in our mail program is not.

The Korn shell has several new options to *trap* (with respect to the same command in most Bourne shells) that make it useful as an aid for debugging shell scripts. We cover them in Chapter 9.

Coroutines

We've spent the last several pages on almost microscopic details of process behavior. Rather than continue our descent into the murky depths, we'll revert to a higher-level view of processes.

Earlier in this chapter, we covered ways of controlling multiple simultaneous jobs within an interactive login session; now we consider multiple process control within shell programs. When two (or more) processes are explicitly programmed to run simultaneously and possibly communicate with each other, we call them *coroutines*.

This is actually nothing new: a pipeline is an example of coroutines. The shell's pipeline construct encapsulates a fairly sophisticated set of rules about how processes interact with each other. If we take a closer look at these rules, we'll be better able to understand other ways of handling coroutines—most of which turn out to be simpler than pipelines.

When you invoke a simple pipeline, say ls | more, the shell invokes a series of Unix primitive operations, a.k.a. *system calls*. In effect, the shell tells Unix to do the following things; in case you're interested, we include in parentheses the actual system call used at each step:

1. Create the pipe that will handle I/O between the processes (the *pipe* system call).

2. Create two subprocesses, which we'll call P1 and P2 (*fork*).

3. Set up I/O between the processes so that P1's standard output feeds into P2's standard input (*dup*, *close*).

4. Start */bin/ls* in process P1 (*exec*).

5. Start */bin/more* in process P2 (*exec*).

6. Wait for both processes to finish (*wait*).

You can probably imagine how the above steps change when the pipeline involves more than two processes.

Now let's make things simpler. We'll see how to get multiple processes to run at the same time if the processes do not need to communicate. For example, we want the processes *dave* and *bob* to run as coroutines, without communication, in a shell script. Both should run to completion before the script exits. Our initial solution would be this:

```
dave &
bob
```

Assume for the moment that *bob* is the last command in the script. The above works—but only if *dave* finishes first. If *dave* is still running when the script finishes, it becomes an *orphan*, i.e., it enters one of the "funny states" we mentioned earlier in this chapter. Never mind the details of orphanhood; just believe that you don't want this to happen, and if it does, you may need to use the "runaway process" method of stopping it, discussed earlier in this chapter. (For example, consider the case where *dave* goes on a resource binge, slowing your system way down—it's much harder to stop it if the parent script has already exited.)

wait

There is a way of making sure the script doesn't finish before *dave* does: the built-in command *wait*. Without arguments, *wait* simply waits until all background jobs have finished. So to make sure the above code behaves properly, we would add *wait*, like this:

```
dave &
bob
wait
```

Here, if *bob* finishes first, the parent shell waits for *dave* to finish before finishing itself.

If your script has more than one background job and you need to wait for specific ones to finish, you can give *wait* the same type of job argument (with a percent sign) as you would use with *kill*, *fg*, or *bg*.

However, you will probably find that *wait* without arguments suffices for all coroutines you will ever program. Situations in which you would need to wait for specific background jobs are quite complex and beyond the scope of this book.

Advantages and Disadvantages of Coroutines

In fact, you may be wondering why you would ever need to program coroutines that don't communicate with each other. For example, why not just run *bob* after *dave* in the usual way? What advantage is there in running the two jobs simultaneously?

If you are running on a computer with one processor (CPU), there is a performance advantage—but only if you have the *bgnice* option turned off (see Chapter 3), and even then only in certain situations.

Roughly speaking, you can characterize a process in terms of how it uses system resources in three ways: whether it is *CPU intensive* (e.g., does lots of number crunching), *I/O intensive* (does a lot of reading or writing to the disk), or *interactive* (requires user intervention).

We already know from Chapter 1 that it makes no sense to run an interactive job in the background. But apart from that, the more two or more processes differ in these three criteria, the better it is to run them simultaneously. For example, a number-crunching statistical calculation would do well when running at the same time as a long, I/O-intensive database query.

On the other hand, if two processes use resources in similar ways, it may even be less efficient to run them at the same time as it would be to run them sequentially. Why? Basically, because under such circumstances, the operating system often has to "time-slice" the resource(s) in contention.

For example, if both processes are disk hogs, the operating system may enter a mode where it constantly switches control of the disk back and forth between the two competing processes; the system ends up spending at least as much time doing the switching as it does on the processes themselves. This phenomenon is known as *thrashing*; at its most severe, it can cause a system to come to a virtual standstill. Thrashing is a common problem; system administrators and operating system designers both spend lots of time trying to minimize it.

Parallelization

But if you have a computer with multiple CPUs* you should be less concerned about thrashing. Furthermore, coroutines can provide dramatic increases in speed on this type of machine, which is often called a *parallel* computer; analogously, breaking up a process into coroutines is sometimes called *parallelizing* the job.

Normally, when you start a background job on a multiple-CPU machine, the computer assigns it to the next available processor. This means that the two jobs are actually—not just metaphorically—running at the same time.

In this case, the running time of the coroutines is essentially equal to that of the longest-running job plus a bit of overhead, instead of the sum of the run times of all processes (although if the CPUs all share a common disk drive, the possibility of I/O-related thrashing still exists). In the best case—all jobs having the same run time and no I/O contention—you get a speedup factor equal to the number of CPUs.

Parallelizing a program is often not easy; there are several subtle issues involved and there's plenty of room for error. Nevertheless, it's worthwhile to know how to parallelize a shell script whether or not you have a parallel machine, especially since such machines are becoming more and more common, even on the desktop.

We'll show how to do this by means of Task 8-3, a simple task whose solution is amenable to parallelization.

Task 8-3

> Augment the C compiler front-end script to compile each source file in parallel.

If you have multiple CPUs, there is potential for considerable speedup by compiling multiple source files in parallel. Each file is independent of the next, and thus creating multiple object files simultaneously gets more work done, faster.

The changes are relatively straightforward: fire off the compilation pipeline into the background, and then add a *wait* statement before doing the final link step:

```
# initialize option-related variables
do_link=true
debug=""
link_libs=""
```

---

* Multiprocessor systems were once to be found only as large-scale servers kept in special climate-controlled machine rooms. Today, multiprocessor desktop systems are available and becoming increasingly common, although systems with more than around 4 CPUs still tend to be mostly in machine rooms.

```
clib="-lc"
exefile=""

# initialize pipeline components
compile=" | ccom"
assemble=" | as"
optimize=""

# process command-line options
while getopts "cgl:[lib]o:[outfile]O files ..." opt; do
    case $opt in
        c )     do_link=false ;;
        g )     debug="-g" ;;
        l )     link_libs+=" -l $OPTARG" ;;
        o )     exefile="-o $OPTARG" ;;
        O )     optimize=" | optimize" ;;
    esac
done
shift $(($OPTIND - 1))

# process the input files
for filename in "$@"; do
    case $filename in
        *.c )
            objname=${filename%.c}.o ;;
        *.s )
            objname=${filename%.s}.o
            compile="" ;;
        *.o )
            objname=$filename  # just link it directly with the rest
            compile=""
            assemble="" ;;
        *  )
            print "error: $filename is not a source or object file."
            exit 1 ;;
    esac

    # run a pipeline for each input file; parallelize by backgrounding
    eval cat \$filename $compile $assemble $optimize \> \$objname &
    objfiles+=" $objname"
    compile=" | ccom"
    assemble=" | as"
done

wait    # wait for all compiles to finish before linking
if [[ $do_link == true ]]; then
    ld $exefile $objfiles $link_libs $clib
fi
```

This is a straightforward example of parallelization, with the only "gotcha" being to make sure that all the compilations are done before doing the final link step. Indeed, many versions of *make* have a "run this many jobs in parallel" flag, precisely to obtain the speedup from simultaneous compilation of independent files.

But all of life is not so simple; sometimes just firing more jobs off into the background won't do the trick. For example, consider multiple changes to the same database: the database software (or something, somewhere) has to ensure that two different processes aren't trying to update the same record at the same time.

Things get even more involved when working at a lower level, with multiple threads of control within a single process (something not visible at the shell level, thankfully). Such problems, known as *concurrency control* issues, become much more difficult as the complexity of the application increases. Complex concurrent programs often have much more code for handling the special cases than for the actual job the program is supposed to do!

Therefore it shouldn't surprise you that much research has been and is being done on parallelization, the ultimate goal being to devise a tool that parallelizes code automatically. (Such tools do exist; they usually work in the confines of some narrow subset of the problem.) Even if you don't have access to a multiple-CPU machine, parallelizing a shell script is an interesting exercise that should acquaint you with some of the issues that surround coroutines.

Coroutines with Two-Way Pipes

Now that we have seen how to program coroutines that don't communicate with each other, we'll build on that foundation and discuss how to get them to communicate—in a more sophisticated way than with a pipeline. The Korn shell has a set of features that allow programmers to set up two-way communication between coroutines. These features aren't included in most Bourne shells.

If you start a background process by appending |& to a command instead of &, the Korn shell sets up a special two-way pipeline between the parent shell and the new background process. *read –p* in the parent shell reads a line of the background process' standard output; similarly, *print –p* in the parent shell feeds into the standard input of the background process. Figure 8-2 shows how this works.

This scheme has some intriguing possibilities. Notice the following things: first, the parent shell communicates with the background process independently of its own standard input and output. Second, the background process need not have any idea that a shell script is communicating with it in this manner. This means that the background process can be almost any preexisting program that uses its standard input and output in normal ways.*

---

* Note that *sort*(1) doesn't quite fit here. *sort* has to read *all* its input before it can generate any output. You can still use *sort* in a coprocess, but you'd have to close the file descriptor used to write to the coprocess first. The way to do this is to move the coprocess's input file descriptor to a numbered file descriptor and then close it. Both of these involve the *exec* command, which is covered in the next chapter.

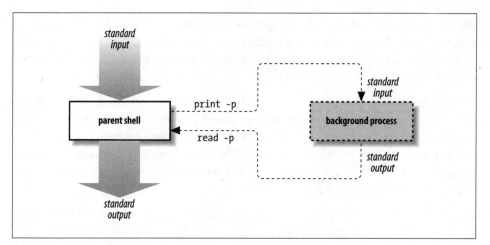

Figure 8-2. Coroutine I/O

Task 8-4 is a task that shows a simple example.

Task 8-4

You would like to have an online calculator, but the existing Unix utility *dc*(1) uses Reverse Polish Notation (RPN), a la Hewlett-Packard calculators. You'd rather have one that works like the $3.95 model you got with that magazine subscription. Write a calculator program that accepts standard algebraic notation.

The objective here is to write the program without reimplementing the calculation engine that *dc* already has—in other words, to write a program that translates algebraic notation to RPN and passes the translated line to *dc* to do the actual calculation. (The utility *bc*(1) actually provides similar functionality.)

We'll assume that the function *alg2rpn*, which does the translation, already exists: given a line of algebraic notation as argument, it prints the RPN equivalent on the standard output. If we have this, then the calculator program (which we'll call *adc*) is very simple:

```
dc |&

while read line'?adc> '; do
    print -p "$(alg2rpn $line)"
    read -p answer
    print "    = $answer"
done
```

The first line of this code starts *dc* as a coroutine with a two-way pipe. Then the while loop prompts the user for a line and reads it until the user types CTRL-D for end-of-input. The loop body converts the line to RPN, passes it to *dc* through the pipe, reads *dc*'s answer, and prints it after an equal sign. For example:

```
$ adc
adc> 2 + 3
    = 5
adc> (7 * 8) + 54
    = 110
adc> ^D
$
```

Actually—as you may have noticed—it's not entirely necessary to have a two-way pipe with *dc*. You could do it with a standard pipe and let *dc* do its own output, like this:

```
{ while read line'?adc> '; do
      print "$(alg2rpn $line)"
  done
} | dc
```

The only difference from the above is the lack of equal sign before each answer is printed.

But what if you wanted to make a fancy graphical user interface (GUI), like the *xcalc* program that comes with many X Window System installations? Then, clearly, *dc*'s own output would not be satisfactory, and you would need full control of your own standard output in the parent process. The user interface would have to capture *dc*'s output and display it in the window properly. The two-way pipe is an excellent solution to this problem: just imagine that, instead of `print " = $answer"`, there is a call to a routine that displays the answer in the "readout" section of the calculator window.

All of this suggests that the two-way pipe scheme is great for writing shell scripts that interpose a software layer between the user (or some other program) and an existing program that uses standard input and output. In particular, it's great for writing new interfaces to old, standard Unix programs that expect line-at-a-time, character-based user input and output. The new interfaces could be GUIs, or they could be network interface programs that talk to users over links to remote machines. In other words, the Korn shell's two-way pipe construct is designed to help develop very up-to-date software!

Two-Way Pipes Versus Standard Pipes

Before we leave the subject of coroutines, we'll complete the circle by showing how the two-way pipe construct compares to regular pipelines. As you may have been able to figure out by now, it is possible to program a standard pipeline by using |& with *print –p*.

This has the advantage of reserving the parent shell's standard output for other use. The disadvantage is that the child process' standard output is directed to the two-way pipe: if the parent process doesn't read it with *read –p*, it's effectively lost.

Shell Subprocesses and Subshells

Coroutines clearly represent the most complex relationship between processes that the Korn shell defines. To conclude this chapter, we will look at a much simpler type of interprocess relationship: that of a shell subprocess with its parent shell. We saw in Chapter 3 that whenever you run a shell script, you actually invoke another copy of the shell that is a subprocess of the main, or *parent*, shell process. Now let's look at them in more detail.

Shell Subprocess Inheritance

The most important things you need to know about shell subprocesses are what characteristics they get, or *inherit*, from their parents. These are as follows:

- The current directory

- Environment variables

- Standard input, output, and error plus any other open file descriptors

- Any characteristics defined in the environment file (see Chapter 3). Note that only interactive shells execute the environment file

- Signals that are ignored

The first three characteristics are inherited by all subprocesses, while the last two are unique to shell subprocesses. Just as important are the things that a shell subprocess does not inherit from its parent:

- Shell variables, except environment variables and those defined in the environment file

- Handling of signals that are not ignored

We covered some of this earlier (in Chapter 3), but these points are common sources of confusion, so they bear repeating.

Subshells

A special kind of shell subprocess is the *subshell*. The subshell is started within the same script (or function) as the parent. You do this in a manner very similar to the code blocks we saw in the last chapter. Just surround some shell code with parentheses (instead of curly braces), and that code runs in a subshell.

For example, here is the calculator program, from above, with a subshell instead of a code block:

```
( while read line'?adc> '; do
      print "$(alg2rpn $line)"
  done
) | dc
```

The code inside the parentheses runs as a separate process.* This is usually less efficient than a code block. The differences in functionality between subshells and code blocks are very few; they primarily pertain to issues of scope, i.e., the domains in which definitions of things like shell variables and signal traps are known. First, code inside a subshell obeys the above rules of shell subprocess inheritance, except that it knows about variables defined in the surrounding shell; in contrast, think of blocks as code units that inherit *everything* from the outer shell. Second, variables and traps defined inside a code block are known to the shell code after the block, whereas those defined in a subshell are not.

For example, consider this code:

```
{
    fred=bob
    trap 'print "You hit CTRL-C!"' INT
}
while true; do
    print "\$fred is $fred"
    sleep 60
done
```

If you run this code, you will see the message $fred is bob every 60 seconds, and if you type CTRL-C, you will see the message, You hit CTRL-C!. You will need to type CTRL-\ to stop it (don't forget to remove the *core* file). Now let's change it to a subshell:

```
(
    fred=bob
    trap 'print "You hit CTRL-C!"' INT
)
while true; do
    print "\$fred is $fred"
    sleep 60
done
```

If you run this, you will see the message $fred is; the outer shell doesn't know about the subshell's definition of fred and therefore thinks it's null. Furthermore,

---

* For performance reasons, the Korn shell tries very hard to avoid actually creating a separate process to run code in parentheses and inside $(...). But the results should always be the same *as if* the code ran in a separate process.

the outer shell doesn't know about the subshell's trap of the INT signal, so if you hit CTRL-C, the script terminates.

If a language supports code nesting, definitions inside a nested unit should have a scope limited to that nested unit. In other words, subshells give you better control than code blocks over the scope of variables and signal traps. Therefore we feel that you should use subshells instead of code blocks if they are to contain variable definitions or signal traps—unless efficiency is a concern.

This has been a long chapter, and it has covered a lot of territory. Here are some exercises that should help you make sure you have a firm grasp on the material. The last exercise is especially difficult for those without backgrounds in compilers, parsing theory, or formal language theory.

1. Write a function called *pinfo* that combines the *jobs* and *ps* commands by printing a list of jobs with their job numbers, corresponding process IDs, running times, and full commands. Extra credit: describe why this has to be a function and not a script.

2. Take the latest version of our C compiler shell script—or some other non-trivial shell script—and "bullet-proof" it with signal traps.

3. Redo the *findterms* program in the last chapter using a subshell instead of a code block.

4. The following doesn't have that much to do with the material in this chapter per se, but it is a classic programming exercise, and it will give you some good practice if you do it:

   a. Write the function *alg2rpn* used in *adc*. Here's how to do this: arithmetic expressions in algebraic notation have the form *expr op expr*, where each *expr* is either a number or another expression (perhaps in parentheses), and *op* is +, −, ×, /, or % (remainder). In RPN, expressions have the form *expr expr op*. For example: the algebraic expression 2+3 is 2 3 + in RPN; the RPN equivalent of (2+3) × (9−5) is 2 3 + 9 5 − ×. The main advantage of RPN is that it obviates the need for parentheses and operator precedence rules (e.g., the rule that × is evaluated before +). The *dc* program accepts standard RPN, but each expression should have "p" appended to it: this tells *dc* to print its result, e.g., the first example above should be given to *dc* as 2 3 + p.

   b. You need to write a routine that converts algebraic notation to RPN. This should be (or include) a function that calls itself (known as a *recursive* function) whenever it encounters a subexpression. It is especially important that this function keep track of where it is in the input string and how much of the string it eats up during its processing. (Hint: make use of the pattern matching operators discussed in Chapter 4 to ease the task of parsing input strings.)

To make your life easier, don't worry about operator precedence for now; just convert to RPN from left to right. e.g., treat 3+4×5 as (3+4)×5 and 3×4+5 as (3×4)+5. This makes it possible for you to convert the input string on the fly, i.e., without having to read in the whole thing before doing any processing.

c. Enhance your solution to the previous exercise so that it supports operator precedence in the usual order: ×, /, % (remainder) +, −. e.g., treat 3+4×5 as 3+(4×5) and 3×4+5 as (3×4)+5.

9

Debugging Shell Programs

We hope that we have convinced you that the Korn shell can be used as a serious Unix programming environment. It certainly has plenty of features, control structures, etc. But another essential part of a programming environment is a set of powerful, integrated *support tools*. For example, there is a wide assortment of screen editors, compilers, debuggers, profilers, cross-referencers, etc., for languages like C, C++ and Java. If you program in one of these languages, you probably take such tools for granted, and you would undoubtedly cringe at the thought of having to develop code with, say, the *ed* editor and the *adb* machine-language debugger.

But what about programming support tools for the Korn shell? Of course, you can use any editor you like, including *vi* and Emacs. And because the shell is an interpreted language, you don't need a compiler.* But there are no other tools available. The most serious problem is the lack of a debugger.

This chapter addresses that lack. The shell does have a few features that help in debugging shell scripts; we'll see these in the first part of the chapter. The Korn shell also has a couple of new features, not present in most Bourne shells, that make it possible to implement a full-blown debugging tool. We show these features; more importantly, we present *kshdb*, a Korn shell debugger that uses them. *kshdb* is basic yet quite usable, and its implementation serves as an extended example of various shell programming techniques from throughout this book.

---

* Actually, if you are really concerned about efficiency, there are shell code compilers on the market; some convert shell scripts to C code that often runs quite a bit faster; however, these tools are usually for Bourne shell scripts. Other "compilers" simply convert the script into a binary form so that customers can't read the program.

Basic Debugging Aids

What sort of functionality do you need to debug a program? At the most empirical level, you need a way of determining *what* is causing your program to behave badly and *where* the problem is in the code. You usually start with an obvious *what* (such as an error message, inappropriate output, infinite loop, etc.), try to work backwards until you find a *what* that is closer to the actual problem (e.g., a variable with a bad value, a bad option to a command), and eventually arrive at the exact *where* in your program. Then you can worry about *how* to fix it.

Notice that these steps represent a process of starting with obvious information and ending up with often obscure facts gleaned through deduction and intuition. Debugging aids make it easier to deduce and intuit by providing relevant information easily or even automatically, preferably without modifying your code.

The simplest debugging aid (for any language) is the output statement, *print* in the shell's case. Indeed, old-time programmers debugged their Fortran code by inserting WRITE cards into their decks. You can debug by putting lots of *print* statements in your code (and removing them later), but you will have to spend lots of time narrowing down not only *what* exact information you want but also *where* you need to see it. You will also probably have to wade through lots and lots of output to find the information that you really want.

Set Options

Luckily, the shell has a few basic features that give you debugging functionality beyond that of *print*. The most basic of these are options to the *set −o* command (as covered in Chapter 3). These options can also be used on the command line when running a script, as Table 9-1 shows.

The *verbose* option simply echoes (to standard error) whatever input the shell gets. It is useful for finding the exact point at which a script is bombing. For example, assume your script looks like this:

```
fred
bob
dave
pete
ed
ralph
```

Table 9-1. Debugging options

set -o option	Command-line option	Action
noexec	*−n*	Don't run commands; check for syntax errors only
verbose	*−v*	Echo commands before running them
xtrace	*−x*	Echo commands after command-line processing

None of these commands are standard Unix programs, and they all do their work silently. Say the script crashes with a cryptic message like "segmentation violation." This tells you nothing about which command caused the error. If you type `ksh -v` *scriptname*, you might see this:

```
fred
bob
dave
segmentation violation
pete
ed
ralph
```

Now you know that *dave* is the probable culprit—though it is also possible that *dave* bombed because of something it expected *fred* or *bob* to do (e.g., create an input file) that they did incorrectly.

The *xtrace* option is more powerful: it echoes each command and its arguments, after the command has been through parameter substitution, command substitution, and the other steps of command-line processing (as listed in Chapter 7). If necessary, the output is quoted in such as a way as to allow it to be reused later as input to the shell.

Here is an example:

```
$ set -o xtrace
$ fred=bob
+ fred=bob
$ print "$fred"
+ print bob
bob
$ ls -l $(whence emacs)
+ whence emacs
+ ls -l /usr/bin/emacs
-rwxr-xr-x   2 root     root       3471896 Mar 16 20:17 /usr/bin/emacs
$
```

As you can see, *xtrace* starts each line it prints with +. This is actually customizable: it's the value of the built-in shell variable PS4.* If you set PS4 to "xtrace-> " (e.g., in your *.profile* or environment file), you'll get *xtrace* listings that look like this:

```
$ ls -l $(whence emacs)
xtrace-> whence emacs
xtrace-> ls -l /usr/bin/emacs
-rwxr-xr-x    2 root     root       3471896 Mar 16 20:17 /usr/bin/emacs
$
```

An even better way of customizing PS4 is to use a built-in variable we haven't seen yet: LINENO, which holds the number of the currently running line in a shell script. Put this line in your *.profile* or environment file:

```
PS4='line $LINENO: '
```

We use the same technique as we did with PS1 in Chapter 3: using single quotes to postpone the evaluation of the string until each time the shell prints the prompt. This prints messages of the form line *N*: in your trace output. You could even include the name of the shell script you're debugging in this prompt by using the positional parameter $0:

```
PS4='$0 line $LINENO: '
```

As another example, say you are trying to track down a bug in a script called *fred* that contains this code:

```
dbfmq=$1.fmq
...
fndrs=$(cut -f3 -d' ' $dfbmq)
```

You type fred bob to run it in the normal way, and it hangs. Then you type ksh -x fred bob, and you see this:

```
+ dbfmq=bob.fmq
...
+ + cut -f3 -d
```

It hangs again at this point. You notice that *cut* doesn't have a filename argument, which means that there must be something wrong with the variable dbfmq. But it has executed the assignment statement dbfmq=bob.fmq properly... ah-*hah*! You made a typo in the variable name inside the command substitution construct.† You fix it, and the script works properly.

---

* As with PS1 and PS3, this variable also undergoes parameter, command, and arithmetic substitution before its value is printed.

† We should admit that if you turned on the *nounset* option at the top of this script, the shell would have flagged this error.

When set at the global level, the *xtrace* option applies to the main script and to any POSIX-style functions (those created with the `name ()` syntax). If the code you are trying to debug calls `function`-style functions that are defined elsewhere (e.g., in your *.profile* or environment file), you can trace through these in the same way with an option to the *typeset* command. Just enter the command `typeset -ft` *functname*, and the named function will be traced whenever it runs. Type `typeset +ft` *functname* to turn tracing off. You can also put `set -o xtrace` into the function body itself, which is good when the function is within the script being debugged.

The last option is *noexec*, which reads in the shell script and checks for syntax errors but doesn't execute anything. It's worth using if your script is syntactically complex (lots of loops, code blocks, string operators, etc.) and the bug has side effects (like creating a large file or hanging up the system).

You can turn on these options with `set -o` in your shell scripts, and, as explained in Chapter 3, turn them off with `set +o` *option*. For example, if you're debugging a script with a nasty side effect, and you have localized it to a certain chunk of code, you can precede that chunk with `set -o xtrace` (and, perhaps, close it with `set +o xtrace`) to watch it in more detail.

The *noexec* option is a "one-way" option. Once turned on, you can't turn it off again! That's because the shell only prints commands and doesn't execute them. This includes the `set +o noexec` command you'd want to use to turn the option off. Fortunately, this only applies to shell scripts; the shell ignores this option when it's interactive.

Fake Signals

A more sophisticated set of debugging aids is the shell's "fake debugging signals," which can be used in *trap* statements to get the shell to act under certain conditions. Recall from the previous chapter that *trap* allows you to install some code that runs when a particular signal is sent to your script.

Fake signals act like real ones, but they are generated by the shell (as opposed to real signals, which the underlying operating system generates). They represent runtime events that are likely to be interesting to debuggers—both human ones and software tools—and can be treated just like real signals within shell scripts. The four fake signals and their meanings are listed in Table 9-2.

Table 9-2. Fake signals

Fake signal	When sent
EXIT	The shell exits from a function or script
ERR	A command returns a non-zero exit status
DEBUG	Before every statement (*after* in *ksh88*)
KEYBD	When reading characters in the editing modes (not for debugging)

The KEYBD signal is not used for debugging. It is an advanced feature, for which we delay discussion until Chapter 10.

EXIT

The EXIT trap, when set, runs its code when the function or script within which it was set exits. Here's a simple example:

```
function func {
    trap 'print "exiting from the function"' EXIT
    print 'start of the function'
}

trap 'print "exiting from the script"' EXIT
print 'start of the script'
func
```

If you run this script, you see this output:

```
start of the script
start of the function
exiting from the function
exiting from the script
```

In other words, the script starts by setting the trap for its own exit. Then it prints a message and finally calls the function. The function does the same—sets a trap for its exit and prints a message. (Remember that function-style functions can have their own local traps that supersede any traps set by the surrounding script, while POSIX functions share traps with the main script.)

The function then exits, which causes the shell to send it the fake signal EXIT, which in turn runs the code print "exiting from the function". Then the script exits, and its own EXIT trap code is run. Note also that traps "stack;" the EXIT fake signal is sent to each running function in turn as each more recently called function exits.

An EXIT trap occurs no matter how the script or function exits, whether normally (by finishing the last statement), by an explicit *exit* or *return* statement, or by

receiving a "real" signal such as INT or TERM. Consider the following inane
number-guessing program:

```
trap 'print "Thank you for playing!"' EXIT

magicnum=$(($RANDOM%10+1))
print 'Guess a number between 1 and 10:'
while read guess'?number> '; do
    sleep 10
    if (( $guess == $magicnum )); then
        print 'Right!'
        exit
    fi
    print 'Wrong!'
done
```

This program picks a number between 1 and 10 by getting a random number (via
the built-in variable RANDOM, see Appendix B), extracting the last digit (the remainder when divided by 10), and adding 1. Then it prompts you for a guess, and after
10 seconds, it tells you if you guessed right.

If you did, the program exits with the message, "Thank you for playing!", i.e., it
runs the EXIT trap code. If you were wrong, it prompts you again and repeats the
process until you get it right. If you get bored with this little game and hit CTRL-C
while waiting for it to tell you whether you were right, you also see the message.

ERR

The fake signal ERR enables you to run code whenever a command in the surrounding script or function exits with non-zero status. Trap code for ERR can take
advantage of the built-in variable ?, which holds the exit status of the previous
command. It survives the trap and is accessible at the beginning of the trap-han-
dling code.

A simple but effective use of this is to put the following code into a script you
want to debug:

```
function errtrap {
    typeset es=$?
    print "ERROR: Command exited with status $es."
}

trap errtrap ERR
```

The first line saves the nonzero exit status in the local variable es.

For example, if the shell can't find a command, it returns status 1. If you put the
code in a script with a line of gibberish (like "lskdjfafd"), the shell responds with:

```
scriptname: line N: lskdjfafd:  not found
ERROR: command exited with status 1.
```

N is the number of the line in the script that contains the bad command. In this case, the shell prints the line number as part of its own error-reporting mechanism, since the error was a command that the shell could not find. But if the nonzero exit status comes from another program, the shell doesn't report the line number. For example:

```
function errtrap {
    typeset es=$?
    print "ERROR: Command exited with status $es."
}

trap errtrap ERR

function bad {
    return 17
}

bad
```

This only prints ERROR: Command exited with status 17.

It would obviously be an improvement to include the line number in this error message. The built-in variable LINENO exists, but if you use it inside a function, it evaluates to the line number in the function, not in the overall file. In other words, if you used $LINENO in the *print* statement in the *errtrap* routine, it would always evaluate to 2.

To get around this problem, we simply pass $LINENO as an argument to the trap handler, surrounding it in single quotes so that it doesn't get evaluated until the fake signal actually comes in:

```
function errtrap {
    typeset es=$?
    print "ERROR line $1: Command exited with status $es."
}
trap 'errtrap $LINENO' ERR
...
```

If you use this with the above example, the result is the message, ERROR line 12: Command exited with status 17. This is much more useful. We'll see a variation on this technique shortly.

This simple code is actually not a bad all-purpose debugging mechanism. It takes into account that a nonzero exit status does not necessarily indicate an undesirable condition or event: remember that every control construct with a conditional (if, while, etc.) uses a nonzero exit status to mean "false." Accordingly, the shell doesn't generate ERR traps when statements or expressions in the "condition" parts of control structures produce nonzero exit statuses.

But a disadvantage is that exit statuses are not as uniform (or even as meaningful) as they should be, as we explained in Chapter 5. A particular exit status need not say anything about the nature of the error or even that there was an error.

DEBUG

The final debugging-related fake signal, DEBUG, causes the trap code to be run before every statement in the surrounding function or script.* This has two possible uses. First is the use for humans, as a sort of a "brute force" method of tracking a certain element of a program's state that you notice is going awry.

For example, you notice that the value of a particular variable is running amok. The naive approach would be to put in lots of *print* statements to check the variable's value at several points. The DEBUG trap makes this easier:

```
function dbgtrap {
    print "badvar is $badvar"
}

trap dbgtrap DEBUG

... Section of code in which problem occurs ...

trap - DEBUG            # turn off DEBUG trap
```

This code prints the value of the wayward variable before every statement between the two *traps*.

The second and far more important use of the DEBUG trap is as a primitive for implementing Korn shell debuggers. In fact, it would be fair to say that the DEBUG trap reduces the task of implementing a useful shell debugger from a large-scale software development project to a manageable exercise. We will get to this shortly.

Signal delivery order

It is possible for multiple signals to arrive simultaneously (or close to it). In that case, the shell runs the trap commands in the following order:

1. DEBUG

2. ERR

---

* This is a notable change from *ksh88*, where the trap was run *after* each statement.

3. Real Unix signals, in order of signal number

4. EXIT

Discipline Functions

In Chapter 4, we introduced the Korn shell's compound variable notation, such as ${person.name}. Using this notation, *ksh93* provides special functions, called *discipline functions*, that give you control over variables when they are referenced, assigned to, and unset. Simple versions of such functions might look like this:

```
dave=dave                    Create the variable
function dave.set {          Called when dave is assigned to
    print "dave just got assigned '${.sh.value}'"
}

function dave.get {          Called when $dave retrieved
    print "dave's value referenced, it's '$dave'"    # this is safe

    .sh.value="dave was here"   Change what $dave returns, dave not changed
}

function dave.unset {        Called when dave is unset
    print "goodbye dave!"
    unset dave   # actually make dave go away
}
```

 The *unset* discipline function *must* actually use the *unset* command to unset the variable—this does not cause an infinite loop. Otherwise, the variable won't be unset, which in turn leads to very surprising behavior.

Here is what happens once all of these functions are in place:

```
$ print $dave
dave's value referenced, it's 'dave'              From dave.get
dave was here                                     From print
$ dave='who is this dave guy, anyway?'
dave just got assigned 'who is this dave guy, anyway?'  From dave.set
$ unset dave
goodbye dave!                                     From dave.unset
$ print $dave

$
```

Discipline functions may only be applied to global variables. They may not be used with local variables—those you create with *typeset* inside a function-style function.

Table 9-3 summarizes the built-in discipline functions.

Table 9-3. Predefined discipline functions

Name	Purpose
`variable.get`	Called when a variable's value is retrieved. Assigning to `.sh.value` changes the value returned but not the variable itself.
`variable.set`	Called when a variable is assigned to. `${.sh.value}` is the new value being assigned. Assigning to `.sh.value` changes the value being assigned.
`variable.unset`	Called when a variable is unset. This function must use *unset* on the variable to actually unset it.

As we've just seen, within the discipline functions, there are two special variables that the shell sets which give you information, as well as one variable that you can set to change how the shell behaves. Table 9-4 describes these variables and what they do.

Table 9-4. Special variables for use in discipline functions

Variable	Purpose
`.sh.name`	The name of the variable for which the discipline function is being run.
`.sh.subscript`	The current subscript for an array variable. (The discipline functions apply to the entire array, not each subscripted element.)
`.sh.value`	The new value being assigned in a *set* discipline function. If assigned to in a *get* discipline function, changes the value returned.

At first glance, it's not clear what the value of discipline functions is. But they're perfect for implementing a very useful debugger feature, called *watchpoints*. We're now ready to get down to writing our shell script debugger.

A Korn Shell Debugger

Commercially available debuggers give you much more functionality than the shell's *set* options and fake signals. The most advanced have fabulous graphical user interfaces, incremental compilers, symbolic evaluators, and other such amenities. But just about all modern debuggers—even the more modest ones—have features that enable you to "peek" into a program while it's running, to examine it in detail and in terms of its source language. Specifically, most debuggers let you do these things:

- Specify points at which the program stops execution and enters the debugger. These are called *breakpoints*.

- Execute only a bit of the program at a time, usually measured in source code statements. This ability is often called *stepping*.

- Examine and possibly change the state of the program (e.g., values of variables) in the middle of a run, i.e., when stopped at a breakpoint or after stepping.

- Specify variables whose values should be printed when they are changed or accessed. These are often called *watchpoints*.

- Do all of the above without having to change the source code.

Our debugger, called *kshdb*, has these features and a few more. Although it's a basic tool, without too many bells and whistles, it is not a toy. This book's web site, *http://www.oreilly.com/catalog/korn2/*, has a link for a downloadable copy of all the book's example programs, including *kshdb*. If you don't have access to the Internet, you can type or scan the code in. Either way, you can use *kshdb* to debug your own shell scripts, and you should feel free to enhance it. This is version 2.0 of the debugger. It includes some changes suggested to us by Steve Alston, and the watchpoints feature is brand new. We'll suggest some enhancements at the end of this chapter.

Structure of the Debugger

The code for *kshdb* has several features worth explaining in some detail. The most important is the basic principle on which it works: it turns a shell script into a debugger for itself, by prepending debugger functionality to it; then it runs the new script.

The driver script

Therefore the code has two parts: the part that implements the debugger's functionality, and the part that installs that functionality into the script being debugged. The second part, which we'll see first, is the script called *kshdb*. It's very simple:

```
# kshdb -- Korn Shell debugger
# Main driver: constructs full script (with preamble) and runs it

print "Korn Shell Debugger version 2.0 for ksh '${.sh.version}'" >&2
_guineapig=$1
if [[ ! -r $1 ]]; then       # file not found or readable
    print "Cannot read $_guineapig." >&2
    exit 1
fi
shift

_tmpdir=/tmp
_libdir=.                     # set to real directory upon installation
_dbgfile=$_tmpdir/kshdb$$     # temp file for script being debugged (copy)
```

```
cat $_libdir/kshdb.pre $_guineapig > $_dbgfile
exec ksh $_dbgfile $_guineapig $_tmpdir $_libdir "$@"
```

kshdb takes as argument the name of the script being debugged, which, for the sake of brevity, we'll call the guinea pig. Any additional arguments are passed to the guinea pig as its positional parameters. Notice that ${.sh.version} indicates the version of the Korn shell for the startup message.

If the argument is invalid (the file isn't readable), *kshdb* exits with an error status. Otherwise, after an introductory message, it constructs a temporary filename like we saw in Chapter 8. If you don't have (or don't have access to) */tmp* on your system, you can substitute a different directory for _tmpdir.* Also, make sure that _libdir is set to the directory where the *kshdb.pre* and *kshdb.fns* files (which we'll see soon) reside. */usr/share/lib* is a good choice if you have access to it.

The *cat* statement builds the temp file: it consists of a file that we'll see soon called *kshdb.pre*, which contains the actual debugger code, followed immediately by a copy of the guinea pig. Therefore the temp file contains a shell script that has been turned into a debugger for itself.

exec

The last line runs this script with *exec*, a statement that we haven't seen yet. We've chosen to wait until now to introduce it because—as we think you'll agree—it can be dangerous. *exec* takes its arguments as a command line and runs the command in place of the current program, in the same process. In other words, the shell running the above script will *terminate immediately* and be replaced by *exec*'s arguments. The situations in which you would want to use *exec* are few, far between, and quite arcane—though this is one of them.

In this case, *exec* just runs the newly constructed shell script, i.e., the guinea pig with its debugger, in another Korn shell. It passes the new script three arguments—the names of the original guinea pig ($_guineapig), the temp directory ($_tmpdir), and the directory where *kshdb.pre* and *kshdb.fns* are kept—followed by the user's positional parameters, if any.

exec can also be used with just an I/O redirector; this causes the redirector to take effect for the remainder of the script or login session. For example, the line exec 2>errlog at the top of a script directs the shell's own standard error to the file *errlog* for the entire script. This can also be used to move the input or output of a coprocess to a regular numbered file descriptor. For example, exec 5<&p moves

---

* All function names and variables (except those local to functions) in *kshdb* have names beginning with an underscore (_), to minimize the possibility of clashes with names in the guinea pig. A more *ksh93*-oriented solution would be to use a compound variable, e.g., _db.tmpdir, _db.libdir, and so on.

the coprocess's output (which is input to the shell) to file descriptor 5. Similarly, `exec 6>&p` moves the coprocess's input (which is output from the shell) to file descriptor 6. The predefined alias `redirect='command exec'` is more mnemonic.

The Preamble

Now we'll see the code that gets prepended to the script being debugged; we call this the *preamble*. It's kept in the following file, *kshdb.pre*, which is also fairly simple:

```
# kshdb preamble for kshdb version 2.0
# prepended to shell script being debugged
# arguments:
# $1 = name of original guinea-pig script
# $2 = directory where temp files are stored
# $3 = directory where kshdb.pre and kshdb.fns are stored

_dbgfile=$0
_guineapig=$1
_tmpdir=$2
_libdir=$3
shift 3                         # move user's args into place

. $_libdir/kshdb.fns            # read in the debugging functions
_linebp=
_stringbp=
let _trace=0                    # initialize execution trace to off

typeset -A _lines
let _i=1                        # read guinea-pig file into lines array
while read -r _lines[$_i]; do
    let _i=$_i+1
done < $_guineapig

trap _cleanup EXIT              # erase files before exiting
let _steps=1                    # no. of stmts to run after trap is set
LINENO=0
trap '_steptrap $LINENO' DEBUG
```

The first few lines save the three fixed arguments in variables and shift them out of the way, so that the positional parameters (if any) are those that the user supplied on the command line as arguments to the guinea pig. Then the preamble reads in another file, *kshdb.fns*, that contains the meat of the debugger as function definitions. We put this code in a separate file to minimize the size of the temp file. We'll examine *kshdb.fns* shortly.

Next, *kshdb.pre* initializes the two breakpoint lists to empty and execution tracing to off (see below), then reads the guinea pig into an array of lines. We do the latter so that the debugger can access lines in the script when performing certain checks, and so that the execution trace feature can print lines of code as they execute. We use an associative array to hold the shell script source, to avoid the built-in (if large) limit of 4096 elements for indexed arrays. (Admittedly our use is a bit unusual; we use line numbers as indices, but as far as the shell is concerned, these are just strings that happen to contain nothing but digits.)

The real fun begins in the last group of code lines, where we set up the debugger to start working. We use two *trap* commands with fake signals. The first sets up a cleanup routine (which just erases the temporary file) to be called on EXIT, i.e., when the script terminates for any reason. The second, and more important, sets up the function *_steptrap* to be called before every statement.

_steptrap gets an argument that evaluates to the number of the line in the guinea pig that was just executed. We use the same technique with the built-in variable LINENO that we saw earlier in the chapter, but with an added twist: if you assign a value to LINENO, it uses that as the *next* line number and increments from there. The statement LINENO=0 re-starts line numbering so that the first line in the guinea pig is line 1.

After the DEBUG trap is set, the preamble ends. The DEBUG trap executes *before* the next statement, which is the first statement of the guinea pig. The shell thus enters *_steptrap* for the first time. The variable *_steps* is set up so that *_steptrap* executes its last elif clause, as you'll see shortly, and enters the debugger. As a result, execution halts just before the first statement of the guinea pig is run, and the user sees a kshdb> prompt; the debugger is now in full operation.

Debugger Functions

The function *_steptrap* is the entry point into the debugger; it is defined in the file *kshdb.fns*, listed in its entirety at the end of this chapter. Here is *_steptrap*:

```
# Here before each statement in script being debugged.
# Handle single-step and breakpoints.
function _steptrap {
    _curline=$1                           # arg is no. of line that just ran
    (( $_trace )) && _msg "$PS4 line $_curline: ${_lines[$_curline]}"
    if (( $_steps >= 0 )); then           # if in step mode
        let _steps="$_steps - 1"          # decrement counter
    fi

    # first check: if line num breakpoint reached
    if _at_linenumbp; then
        _msg "Reached line breakpoint at line $_curline"
        _cmdloop                          # breakpoint, enter debugger

    # second check: if string breakpoint reached
    elif _at_stringbp; then
        _msg "Reached string breakpoint at line $_curline"
        _cmdloop                          # breakpoint, enter debugger
```

```
    # if neither, check whether break condition exists and is true
    elif [[ -n $_brcond ]] && eval $_brcond; then
        _msg "Break condition '$_brcond' true at line $_curline"
        _cmdloop                        # break condition, enter debugger

    # finally, check if step mode and number of steps is up
    elif (( _steps == 0 )); then        # if step mode and time to stop
        _msg "Stopped at line $_curline"
        _cmdloop                        # enter debugger
    fi
}
```

_steptrap starts by setting _curline to the number of the guinea pig line that just ran. If execution tracing is turned on, it prints the PS4 execution trace prompt (a la *xtrace* mode), the line number, and the line of code itself.

Then it does one of two things: enter the debugger, the heart of which is the function *_cmdloop*, or just return so that the shell can execute the next statement. It chooses the former if a *breakpoint* or *break condition* (see below) has been reached, or if the user stepped into this statement.

Commands

We'll explain shortly how *_steptrap* determines these things; now we'll look at *_cmdloop*. It's a typical command loop, resembling a combination of the case statements we saw in Chapter 5 and the calculator loop we saw in Chapter 8.

```
    # Debugger command loop.
    # Here at start of debugger session, when breakpoint reached,
    # after single-step.  Optionally here inside watchpoint.
    function _cmdloop {
        typeset cmd args

        while read -s cmd"?kshdb> " args; do
            case $cmd in
                \#bp ) _setbp $args ;;      # set breakpoint at line num or string.
                \#bc ) _setbc $args ;;      # set break condition.
                \#cb ) _clearbp ;;          # clear all breakpoints.
                \#g  ) return ;;            # start/resume execution
                \#s  ) let _steps=${args:-1} # single-step N times (default 1)
                       return ;;
                \#wp ) _setwp $args ;;      # set a watchpoint
                \#cw ) _clearwp $args ;;    # clear one or more watchpoints

                \#x  ) _xtrace ;;           # toggle execution trace
                \#\? | \#h ) _menu ;;       # print command menu
                \#q  ) exit ;;              # quit
                \#*  ) _msg "Invalid command: $cmd" ;;
                *    ) eval $cmd $args ;;   # otherwise, run shell command
            esac
        done
```

At each iteration, *_cmdloop* prints a prompt, reads a command, and processes it. We use *read –s* so that the user can take advantage of command-line editing within *kshdb*. All *kshdb* commands start with # to prevent confusion with shell commands. Anything that isn't a *kshdb* command (and doesn't start with #) is passed off to the shell for execution. Using # as the command character prevents a mistyped command from having any ill effect when the last case catches it and runs it through *eval*. Table 9-5 summarizes the debugger commands.

Table 9-5. kshdb commands

Command	Action
#bp *N*	Set breakpoint at line *N*.
#bp *str*	Set breakpoint at next line containing *str*.
#bp	List breakpoints and break condition.
#bc *str*	Set break condition to *str*.
#bc	Clear break condition.
#cb	Clear all breakpoints.
#g	Start or resume execution (go).
#s [*N*]	Step through *N* statements (default 1).
#wp [–c] *var* get	Set a watchpoint on variable *var* when the value is retrieved. With –c, enter the command loop from within the watchpoint.
#wp [–c] *var* set	Set a watchpoint on variable *var* when the value is assigned. With –c, enter the command loop from within the watchpoint.
#wp [–c] *var* unset	Set a watchpoint on variable *var* when the variable is unset. With –c, enter the command loop from within the watchpoint.
#cw *var discipline*	Clear the given watchpoint.
#cw	Clear all watchpoints.
#x	Toggle execution tracing.
#h, #?	Print a help menu.
#q	Quit.

Before we look at the individual commands, it is important that you understand how control passes through *_steptrap*, the command loop, and the guinea pig.

_steptrap runs before every statement in the guinea pig as a result of the trap ... DEBUG statement in the preamble. If a breakpoint has been reached or the user previously typed in a step command (#s), *_steptrap* calls the command loop. In doing so, it effectively interrupts the shell that is running the guinea pig to hand control over to the user.*

The user can invoke debugger commands as well as shell commands that run in the same shell as the guinea pig. This means that you can use shell commands to check values of variables, signal traps, and any other information local to the script being debugged.

The command loop runs, and the user stays in control, until the user types #g, #s, or #q. Let's look in detail at what happens in each of these cases.

#g has the effect of running the guinea pig uninterrupted until it finishes or hits a breakpoint. But actually, it simply exits the command loop and returns to _steptrap_, which exits as well. The shell takes control back; it runs the next statement in the guinea pig script and calls _steptrap_ again. Assuming that there is no breakpoint, this time _steptrap_ just exits again, and the process repeats until there is a breakpoint or the guinea pig is done.

Stepping

When the user types #s, the command loop code sets the variable _steps to the number of steps the user wants to execute, i.e., to the argument given. Assume at first that the user omits the argument, meaning that _steps is set to 1. Then the command loop exits and returns control to _steptrap_, which (as above) exits and hands control back to the shell. The shell runs the next statement and returns to _steptrap_, which sees that _steps is 1 and decrements it to 0. Then the third elif conditional sees that _steps is 0, so it prints a "stopped" message and calls the command loop.

Now assume that the user supplies an argument to #s, say 3. _steps is set to 3. Then the following happens:

1. After the next statement runs, _steptrap_ is called again. It enters the first if clause, since _steps is greater than 0. _steptrap_ decrements _steps to 2 and exits, returning control to the shell.

2. This process repeats, another step in the guinea pig is run, and _steps becomes 1.

3. A third statement is run and we're back in _steptrap_. _steps is decremented to 0, the third elif clause is run, and _steptrap_ breaks out to the command loop again.

---

* In fact, low-level systems programmers can think of the entire *trap* mechanism as quite similar to an interrupt-handling scheme.

The overall effect is that three steps run and then the debugger takes over again.

Finally, the #q command exits. The EXIT trap then calls the function _cleanup, which just erases the temp file and exits the entire program.

All other debugger commands (#bp, #bc, #cb, #wp, #cw, #x, and shell commands) cause the shell to stay in the command loop, meaning that the user prolongs the interruption of the shell.

Breakpoints

Now we'll examine the breakpoint-related commands and the breakpoint mechanism in general. The #bp command calls the function _setbp, which can set two kinds of breakpoints, depending on the type of argument given. If it is a number, it's treated as a line number; otherwise, it's interpreted as a string that the breakpoint line should contain.

For example, the command #bp 15 sets a breakpoint at line 15, and #bp grep sets a breakpoint at the next line that contains the string *grep*—whatever number that turns out to be. Although you can always look at a numbered listing of a file,* string arguments to #bp can make that unnecessary.

Here is the code for _setbp:

```
# Set breakpoint(s) at given line numbers or strings
# by appending patterns to breakpoint variables
function _setbp {
    if [[ -z $1 ]]; then
        _listbp
    elif [[ $1 == +([0-9]) ]]; then  # number, set bp at that line
        _linebp="${_linebp}$1|"
        _msg "Breakpoint at line " $1
    else                             # string, set bp at next line w/string
        _stringbp="${_stringbp}$@|"
        _msg "Breakpoint at next line containing '$@'."
    fi
}
```

_setbp sets the breakpoints by storing them in the variables _linebp (line number breakpoints) and _stringbp (string breakpoints). Both have breakpoints separated by pipe character delimiters, for reasons that will become clear shortly. This implies that breakpoints are cumulative; setting new breakpoints does not erase the old ones.

---

* pr -n *filename* prints a numbered listing to standard output on System V-derived versions of Unix. Some very old BSD-derived systems don't support it. If this doesn't work on your system, try cat -n *filename*, or if that doesn't work, create a shell script with the single line awk '{ printf("%d\t%s\n", NR, $0 }' $1

The only way to remove breakpoints is with the command #cb, which (in function *_clearbp*) clears all of them at once by simply resetting the two variables to null. If you don't remember what breakpoints you have set, the command #bp without arguments lists them.

The functions *_at_linenumbp* and *_at_stringbp* are called by *_steptrap* after every statement; they check whether the shell has arrived at a line number or string breakpoint, respectively.

Here is *_at_linenumbp*:

```
# See if next line no. is a breakpoint.
function _at_linenumbp {
    [[ $_curline == @(${_linebp%\|}) ]]
}
```

_at_linenumbp takes advantage of the pipe character as the separator between line numbers: it constructs a regular expression of the form @(*N1*|*N2*|...) by taking the list of line numbers *_linebp*, removing the trailing |, and surrounding it with @(and). For example, if $_linebp is 3|15|19|, the resulting expression is @(3|15|19).

If the current line is any of these numbers, the conditional becomes true, and *_at_linenumbp* also returns a "true" (0) exit status.

The check for a string breakpoint works on the same principle, but it's slightly more complicated; here is *_at_stringbp*:

```
# Search string breakpoints to see if next line in script matches.
function _at_stringbp {
    [[ -n $_stringbp && ${_lines[$_curline]} == *@(${_stringbp%\|})* ]]
}
```

The conditional first checks if $_stringbp is non-null (meaning that string breakpoints have been defined). If not, the conditional evaluates to false, but if so, its value depends on the pattern match after the &&—which tests the current line to see if it contains any of the breakpoint strings.

The expression on the right side of the double equal sign is similar to the one in *_at_linenumbp* above, except that it has * before and after it. This gives expressions of the form *@(*S1*|*S2*|...)*, where the *S*s are the string breakpoints. This expression matches any line that contains any one of the possibilities in the parentheses.

The left side of the double equal sign is the text of the current line in the guinea pig. So, if this text matches the regular expression, we've reached a string breakpoint; accordingly, the conditional expression and *_at_stringbp* return exit status 0.

_steptrap tests each condition separately, so that it can tell you which kind of breakpoint stopped execution. In both cases, it calls the main command loop.

Break conditions

kshdb has another feature related to breakpoints: the *break condition*. This is a string that the user can specify that is evaluated as a command; if it is true (i.e., returns exit status 0), the debugger enters the command loop. Since the break condition can be any line of shell code, there's lots of flexibility in what can be tested. For example, you can break when a variable reaches a certain value (e.g., (($x < 0))) or when a particular piece of text has been written to a file (grep *string file*). You will probably think of all kinds of uses for this feature.* To set a break condition, type #bc *string*. To remove it, type #bc without arguments—this installs the null string, which is ignored. *_steptrap* evaluates the break condition $_brcond only if it's non-null. If the break condition evaluates to 0, the if clause is true and, once again, *_steptrap* calls the command loop.

Execution tracing

The next feature is execution tracing, available through the #x command. This feature is meant to overcome the fact that a *kshdb* user can't use set -o xtrace while debugging (by entering it as a shell command), because its scope is limited to the *_cmdloop* function.†

The function *_xtrace* toggles execution tracing by simply assigning to the variable _trace the logical "not" of its current value, so that it alternates between 0 (off) and 1 (on). The preamble initializes it to 0.

Watchpoints

kshdb takes advantage of the shell's discipline functions to provide watchpoints. You can set a watchpoint on any variable when the variable's value is retrieved or changed, or when the variable is unset. Optionally, the watchpoint can be set up to drop into the command loop as well. You do this with the #wp command, which in turn calls *_setwp*:

```
# Set a watchpoint on a variable
# usage: _setwp [-c] var discipline
# $1 = variable
# $2 = get|set|unset
typeset -A _watchpoints
function _setwp {
    typeset funcdef do_cmdloop=0
    if [[ $1 == -c ]]; then
```

---

* Bear in mind that if your break condition produces any standard output (or standard error), you will see it before every statement. Also, make sure your break condition doesn't take a long time to run; otherwise your script will run very, very slowly.

† Actually, by entering typeset -ft *funcname*, the user can enable tracing on a per-function basis, but it's probably better to have it all under the debugger's control.

```
                do_cmdloop=1
                shift
        fi

        funcdef="function $1.$2 { "

        case $2 in
        get)     funcdef+="_msg $1 \(\$$1\) retrieved, line \$_curline"
                 ;;
        set)     funcdef+="_msg $1 set to "'${.sh.value}'", line \$_curline"
                 ;;
        unset)   funcdef+="_msg $1 cleared at line \$_curline"
                 funcdef+=$'\nunset '"$1"
                 ;;
        *)       _msg invalid watchpoint function $2
                 return 1
                 ;;
        esac

        if ((do_cmdloop)); then
                funcdef+=$'\n_cmdloop'
        fi
        funcdef+=$'\n}'

        eval "$funcdef"

        _watchpoints[$1.$2]=1
    }
```

This function illustrates several interesting techniques. The first thing it does is declare some local variables and check if it was invoked with the *−c* option. This indicates that the watchpoint should enter the command loop.

The general idea is to build up the text of the appropriate discipline function in the variable funcdef. The initial value is the function keyword, the discipline function name, and the opening left curly brace. The space following the brace is important, so that the shell will correctly recognize it as a keyword.

Then, for each kind of discipline function, the case construct appends the appropriate function body to the funcdef string. The code uses judiciously placed backslashes to get the correct mixture of immediate and delayed shell variable evaluation. Consider the get case: for the \(, the backslash stays intact for use as a quoting character inside the body of the discipline function. For \$$1, the quoting happens as follows: the \$ becomes a $ inside the function, while the $1 is evaluated immediately inside the double quoted string.

In the case that the *−c* option was supplied, it uses the $'...' notation to append a newline and a call to *_cmdloop* to the function body, and then at the end appends another newline and closing right brace. Finally, by using *eval*, it installs the newly created function.

For example, if –c was used, the text of the generated *get* function for the variable count ends up looking like this:

```
function count.get { _msg count \($count\) retrieved, line $_curline
_cmdloop
}
```

At the end of *_setwp*, _watchpoints[$1.$2] is set to 1. This creates an entry in the associative array _watchpoints indexed by discipline function name. This conveniently stores the names of all watchpoints for when we want to clear them.

Watchpoints are cleared with the #cw command, which in turn runs the *_clearwp* function. Here it is:

```
# Clear watchpoints:
# no args: clear all
# two args: same as for setting: var get|set|unset
function _clearwp {
    if [ $# = 0 ]; then
        typeset _i
        for _i in ${!_watchpoints[*]}; do
            unset -f $_i
            unset _watchpoints[$_i]
        done
    elif [ $# = 2 ]; then
        case $2 in
        get | set | unset)
            unset -f $1.$2
            unset _watchpoints[$1.$2]
            ;;
        *)  _msg $2: invalid watchpoint
            ;;
        esac
    fi
}
```

When invoked with no arguments, *_clearwp* clears all the watchpoints, by looping over all the subscripts in the _watchpoints associative array. Otherwise, if invoked with two arguments, the variable name and discipline function, it unsets the function using unset -f. In either case, the entry in _watchpoints is also unset.

Limitations

kshdb was not designed to push the state of the debugger art forward or to have an overabundance of features. It has the most useful basic features; its implementation is compact and (we hope) comprehensible. But it does have some important limitations. The ones we know of are described in the list that follows:

• String breakpoints cannot begin with digits or contain pipe characters (|) unless they are properly escaped.

- You can only set breakpoints—whether line number or string—on lines in the guinea pig that contain what the shell's documentation calls *simple commands*, i.e., actual Unix commands, shell built-ins, function calls, or aliases. If you set a breakpoint on a line that contains only whitespace or a comment, the shell always skips over that breakpoint. More importantly, control keywords like while, if, for, do, done, and even conditionals ([[...]] and ((...))) won't work either, unless a simple command is on the same line.

- *kshdb* does not "step down" into shell scripts that are called from the guinea pig. To do this, you have to edit your guinea pig and change a call to *scriptname* to kshdb *scriptname*.

- Similarly, subshells are treated as one gigantic statement; you cannot step down into them at all.

- The guinea pig should not trap on the fake signals DEBUG or EXIT; otherwise the debugger won't work.

- Variables that are *typeset* (see Chapter 4) are not accessible in break conditions. However, you can use the shell command *print* to check their values.

- Command error handling is weak. For example, a non-numeric argument to #s will cause it to bomb.

- Watchpoints that invoke the command loop are fragile. For *ksh93m* under GNU/Linux, trying to unset a watchpoint when in the command loop invoked from the watchpoint causes the shell to core dump. But this does not happen on all platforms, and this will eventually be fixed.

Many of these are not insurmountable; see the exercises.

A Sample kshdb Session

Now we'll show a transcript of an actual session with *kshdb*, in which the guinea pig is (a slightly modified version of) the solution to Task 6-3. For convenience, here is a numbered listing of the script, which we'll call *lscol*.

```
1     set -A filenames $(ls $1)
2     typeset -L14 fname
3     let numfiles=${#filenames[*]}
4     let numcols=5
5
6     for ((count = 0; $count < $numfiles ; )); do
7         fname=${filenames[count]}
8         print -n "$fname   "
9         let count++
10        if (( count % numcols == 0 )); then
11            print              # newline
12        fi
13    done
```

```
14
15    if (( count % numcols != 0 )); then
16        print
17    fi
```

Here is the *kshdb* session transcript:

```
$ kshdb lscol book
Korn Shell Debugger version 2.0 for ksh Version M 1993-12-28 m
Stopped at line 1
kshdb> #bp 4
Breakpoint at line  4
kshdb> #g
Reached line breakpoint at line 4
kshdb> #s
Stopped at line 6
kshdb> print $numcols
5
kshdb> #bc (( count == 10 ))
Break when true: (( count == 10 ))
kshdb> #g
appa.xml        appb.xml        appc.xml        appd.xml        appf.xml
book.xml        ch00.xml        ch01.xml        ch02.xml        ch03.xml
Break condition '(( count == 10 ))' true at line 10
kshdb> #bc
Break condition cleared.
kshdb> #bp newline
Breakpoint at next line containing 'newline'.
kshdb> #g
Reached string breakpoint at line 11
kshdb> print $count
10
kshdb> let count=9
kshdb> #g

ch03.xml        Reached string breakpoint at line 11
kshdb> #bp
Breakpoints at lines:
4
Breakpoints at strings:
newline
Break on condition:

kshdb> #g

ch04.xml        ch05.xml        ch06.xml        ch07.xml        ch08.xml
Reached string breakpoint at line 11
kshdb> #g

ch09.xml        ch10.xml        colo1.xml       copy.xml
$
```

First, notice that we gave the guinea pig script the argument book, meaning that
we want to list the files in that directory. We begin by setting a simple breakpoint

at line 4 and starting the script. It stops before executing line 4 (let numcols=5). We issue the #s command to single step through the command (i.e., to actually execute it). Then we issue a shell *print* command to show that the variable numcols is indeed set correctly.

Next, we set a break condition, telling the debugger to kick in when count is 10, and we resume execution. Sure enough, the guinea pig prints 10 filenames and stops at line 10, right after count is incremented. We clear the break condition by typing #bc without an argument, since otherwise the shell would stop after every statement until the condition becomes false.

The next command shows how the string breakpoint mechanism works. We tell the debugger to break when it hits a line that contains the string newline. This string is in a comment on line 11. Notice that it doesn't matter that the string is in a comment—just that the line it's on contains an actual command. We resume execution, and the debugger hits the breakpoint at line 11.

After that, we show how we can use the debugger to change the guinea pig's state while running. We see that $count is still greater than 10; we change it to 9. In the next iteration of the while loop, the script accesses the same filename that it just did (*ch03.xml*), increments count back to 10, and hits the string breakpoint again. Finally, we list breakpoints and step through to the end, at which point it exits.

Exercises

We conclude this chapter with a few exercises, which are suggested enhancements to *kshdb*.

1. Improve command error handling in these ways:

   a. For numeric arguments to #bp, check that they are valid line numbers for the particular guinea pig.

   b. Check that arguments to #s are valid numbers.

   c. Any other error handling you can think of.

2. Enhance the #cb command so that the user can delete specific breakpoints (by string or line number).

3. Remove the major limitation in the breakpoint mechanism:

   a. Improve it so that if the line number selected does not contain an actual Unix command, the next closest line above it is used as the breakpoint instead.

   b. Do the same thing for string breakpoints. (Hint: first translate each string breakpoint command into one or more line-number breakpoint commands.)

4. Implement an option that causes a break into the debugger whenever a command exits with nonzero status:

   a. Implement it as the command-line option −*e*.

   b. Implement it as the debugger commands #be (to turn the option on) and #ne (to turn it off). (Hint: you won't be able to use the ERR trap, but bear in mind that when you enter _*steptrap*, $? is still the exit status of the last command that ran.)

5. Add the ability to "step down" into scripts that the guinea pig calls (i.e., shell subprocesses) as the command-line option −*s*. One way to implement this is to change the *kshdb* script so it plants recursive calls to *kshdb* in the guinea pig. You can do this by filtering the guinea pig through a loop that reads each line and determines, with the whence −v and *file*(1) (see the man page) commands, if the line is a call to another shell script.* If so, prepend kshdb −s to the line and write it to the new file; if not, just pass it through as is.

6. Add support for multiple break conditions, so that *kshdb* stops execution when any one of them becomes true and prints a message that says which one is true. Do this by storing the break conditions in a colon-separated list or an array. Try to make this as efficient as possible, since the checking has to take place before every statement.

7. Add any other features you can think of.

Finally, here is the complete source code for the debugger function file *kshdb.fns*:

```
# Here before each statement in script being debugged.
# Handle single-step and breakpoints.
function _steptrap {
    _curline=$1                         # arg is no. of line that just ran
    (( $_trace )) && _msg "$PS4 line $_curline: ${_lines[$_curline]}"
    if (( $_steps >= 0 )); then         # if in step mode
        let _steps="$_steps - 1"        # decrement counter
    fi

    # first check: if line num breakpoint reached
    if _at_linenumbp; then
        _msg "Reached line breakpoint at line $_curline"
        _cmdloop                        # breakpoint, enter debugger

    # second check: if string breakpoint reached
    elif _at_stringbp; then
        _msg "Reached string breakpoint at line $_curline"
        _cmdloop                        # breakpoint, enter debugger
```

---

* Notice that this method should catch most separate shell scripts, but not all of them. For example, it won't catch shell scripts that follow semicolons (e.g., cmd1; cmd2).

```
        # if neither, check whether break condition exists and is true
        elif [[ -n $_brcond ]] && eval $_brcond; then
            _msg "Break condition '$_brcond' true at line $_curline"
            _cmdloop                    # break condition, enter debugger

        # finally, check if step mode and number of steps is up
        elif (( _steps == 0 )); then      # if step mode and time to stop
            _msg "Stopped at line $_curline"
            _cmdloop                      # enter debugger
        fi
}


# Debugger command loop.
# Here at start of debugger session, when breakpoint reached,
# after single-step.  Optionally here inside watchpoint.
function _cmdloop {
    typeset cmd args

    while read -s cmd"?kshdb> " args; do
        case $cmd in
            \#bp ) _setbp $args ;;        # set breakpoint at line num or string.
            \#bc ) _setbc $args ;;        # set break condition.
            \#cb ) _clearbp ;;            # clear all breakpoints.
            \#g  ) return ;;              # start/resume execution
            \#s  ) let _steps=${args:-1}  # single-step N times (default 1)
                   return ;;
            \#wp ) _setwp $args ;;        # set a watchpoint
            \#cw ) _clearwp $args ;;      # clear one or more watchpoints

            \#x  ) _xtrace ;;             # toggle execution trace
            \#\? | \#h ) _menu ;;         # print command menu
            \#q  ) exit ;;                # quit
            \#*  ) _msg "Invalid command: $cmd" ;;
            *  ) eval $cmd $args ;;       # otherwise, run shell command
        esac
    done
}


# See if next line no. is a breakpoint.
function _at_linenumbp {
    [[ $_curline == @(${_linebp%\|}) ]]
}


# Search string breakpoints to see if next line in script matches.
function _at_stringbp {
    [[ -n $_stringbp && ${_lines[$_curline]} == *@(${_stringbp%\|})* ]]
}


# Print the given message to standard error.
function _msg {
    print -r -- "$@" >&2
}
```

```
# Set breakpoint(s) at given line numbers or strings
# by appending patterns to breakpoint variables
function _setbp {
    if [[ -z $1 ]]; then
        _listbp
    elif [[ $1 == +([0-9]) ]]; then  # number, set bp at that line
        _linebp="${_linebp}$1|"
        _msg "Breakpoint at line " $1
    else                             # string, set bp at next line w/string
        _stringbp="${_stringbp}$@|"
        _msg "Breakpoint at next line containing '$@'."
    fi
}


# List breakpoints and break condition.
function _listbp {
    _msg "Breakpoints at lines:"
    _msg "$(print $_linebp | tr '|' ' ')"
    _msg "Breakpoints at strings:"
    _msg "$(print $_stringbp | tr '|' ' ')"
    _msg "Break on condition:"
    _msg "$_brcond"
}


# Set or clear break condition
function _setbc {
    if [[ $# = 0 ]]; then
        _brcond=
        _msg "Break condition cleared."
    else
        _brcond="$*"
        _msg "Break when true: $_brcond"
    fi
}


# Clear all breakpoints.
function _clearbp {
    _linebp=
    _stringbp=
    _msg "All breakpoints cleared."
}


# Toggle execution trace feature on/off
function _xtrace {
    let _trace="! $_trace"
    if (( $_trace )); then
        _msg "Execution trace on."
    else
        _msg "Execution trace off."
    fi
}
```

```
# Print command menu
function _menu {
    _msg 'kshdb commands:
    #bp N                      set breakpoint at line N
    #bp str                    set breakpoint at next line containing str
    #bp                        list breakpoints and break condition
    #bc str                    set break condition to str
    #bc                        clear break condition
    #cb                        clear all breakpoints
    #wp [-c] var discipline    set a watchpoint on a variable
    #cw                        clear all watchpoints
    #g                         start/resume execution
    #s [N]                     execute N statements (default 1)
    #x                         toggle execution trace on/off
    #h, #?                     print this menu
    #q                         quit'
}


# Erase temp files before exiting.
function _cleanup {
    rm $_dbgfile 2>/dev/null
}


# Set a watchpoint on a variable
# usage: _setwp [-c] var discipline
# $1 = variable
# $2 = get|set|unset
typeset -A _watchpoints
function _setwp {
    typeset funcdef do_cmdloop=0
    if [[ $1 == -c ]]; then
        do_cmdloop=1
        shift
    fi

    funcdef="function $1.$2 { "

    case $2 in
    get)    funcdef+="_msg $1 \(\$$1\) retrieved, line \$_curline"
            ;;
    set)    funcdef+="_msg $1 set to "'${.sh.value}'", line \$_curline"
            ;;
    unset)  funcdef+="_msg $1 cleared at line \$_curline"
            funcdef+=$'\nunset '"$1"
            ;;
    *)      _msg invalid watchpoint function $2
            return 1
            ;;
    esac

    if ((do_cmdloop)); then
        funcdef+=$'\n_cmdloop'
    fi
    funcdef+=$'\n}'
```

```
        eval "$funcdef"

        _watchpoints[$1.$2]=1
}


# Clear watchpoints:
# no args: clear all
# two args: same as for setting: var get|set|unset
function _clearwp {
    if [ $# = 0 ]; then
        typeset _i
        for _i in ${!_watchpoints[*]}; do
            unset -f $_i
            unset _watchpoints[$_i]
        done
    elif [ $# = 2 ]; then
        case $2 in
        get | set | unset)
            unset -f $1.$2
            unset _watchpoints[$1.$2]
            ;;
        *) _msg $2: invalid watchpoint
            ;;
        esac
    fi
}
```

10

Korn Shell Administration

System administrators use the shell as part of their job of setting up a system-wide environment for all users. In this chapter, we discuss the Korn shell's features that relate to this task from two perspectives: customization that is available to all users and system security. We assume that you already know the basics of Unix system administration.*

Installing the Korn Shell as the Standard Shell

As a prelude to system-wide customization, we want to emphasize something about the Korn shell that doesn't apply to most other shells: you can install it as if it were the standard Bourne shell, i.e., as */bin/sh*. Just save the real Bourne shell as another filename, such as */bin/bsh*, in case anyone actually needs it for anything (which is doubtful), then rename (or link) your Korn shell as */bin/sh*.

Many installations have done this with absolutely no ill effects. Not only does this make the Korn shell your system's standard login shell, but it also makes most existing Bourne shell scripts run faster, and it has security advantages that we'll see later in this chapter.

As we will see in Appendix A, the Korn shell is backward-compatible with the Bourne shell except that it doesn't support ^ as a synonym for the pipe character |. Unless you have an ancient Unix system, or you have some very, very old shell scripts, you needn't worry about this.

---

* A good source of information on system administration is *Essential System Administration* by Æleen Frisch. It is published by O'Reilly & Associates.

But if you want to be absolutely sure, simply search through all shell scripts in all directories in your PATH. An easy way to do this is to use the *file*(1) command, which we saw in Chapter 5 and Chapter 9. *file* prints "executable shell script" when given the name of one. (The exact message varies from system to system; make sure that yours prints this message when given the name of a shell script. If not, just substitute the message your *file* command prints for "shell script" in the following example.) Here is a script that looks for ^ in shell scripts in every directory in your PATH:*

```
dirs=$(print -- $PATH |
        sed -e 's/^:/.:/' -e 's/::/:.:/' -e s'/:$/:./' -e 's/:/ /g')
for d in $dirs
do
        print "checking $d:"
        cd "$d"
        scripts=$(file * | grep 'shell script' | cut -d: -f1)
        grep -l '\^' $scripts /dev/null
done
```

The first statement of this script pulls $PATH apart into separate directories, including handling the several cases of empty separators which signify the current directory. The *sed*(1) program is a stream editor that performs editing operations on its input, and prints the changed contents on its output. The result is assigned to dirs, which is then used as the item list in the for loop. For each directory, it *cd*s there and finds all shell scripts by piping the *file* command into *grep* and then, to extract the filename only, into *cut*. Then it searches each script for the ^ character. The *–l* option to *grep* simply lists all filenames that match the pattern, without printing the matching lines. The *grep* command has */dev/null* on the end of the list of files in case $scripts happens to be empty. If you're adventurous, you could do all the work on one line:

```
grep -l '\^' $(file * | grep 'shell script' | cut -d: -f1) /dev/null
```

If you run this script, you will probably find several occurrences of ^, but these should be used within regular expressions in *grep*, *sed*, or *awk* commands, not as pipe characters. Assuming this is the case, it is safe for you to install the Korn shell as */bin/sh*.

---

* This script will fail if your PATH has directories whose names contain spaces. Consider fixing this problem as an advanced exercise for the reader.

Environment Customization

Like the Bourne shell, the Korn shell uses the file */etc/profile* for system-wide customization. When a user logs in, the shell reads and runs */etc/profile* before running the user's *.profile*.

We don't cover all the possible commands you might want to put in */etc/profile*. But the Korn shell has a few unique features that are particularly relevant to system-wide customization; we discuss them here.

We'll start with two built-in commands that you can use in */etc/profile* to tailor your users' environments and constrain their use of system resources. Users can also use these commands in their *.profile*, or at any other time, to override the default settings.

umask

umask, like the same command in most other shells, lets you specify the default permissions that files have when users create them. With *ksh*, it takes the same types of arguments that the *chmod* command does, i.e., absolute (octal numbers) or symbolic permission values.

The *umask* contains the permissions that are turned off by default whenever a process creates a file, regardless of what permission the process specifies.[*] Another way to think of this is as a bitwise borrow-free subtraction: *actual permissions = requested permissions − the umask*.

We'll use octal notation to show how this works. As you should know, the digits in a permission number stand (left to right) for the permissions of the owner, the owner's group, and all other users, respectively. Each digit, in turn, consists of three bits, which specify read, write, and execute permissions from left to right. (If a file is a directory, the "execute" permission becomes "search" permission, i.e., permission to *cd* to it, and to traverse it as part of a pathname.)

For example, the octal number 640 equals the binary number 110 100 000. If a file has this permission, then its owner can read and write it; users in the owner's group can only read it; everyone else has no permission on it. A file with permission 755 (111 101 101 in binary) gives its owner the right to read, write, and execute it and everyone else the right to read and execute (but not write).

022 is a common *umask* value. This implies that when a file is created, the most permission it could possibly have is 755—which is the usual permission of an executable that a compiler might create. A text editor, on the other hand, might create

---

[*] If you know C, C++, or Java, and are comfortable with bitwise operations, the umask operation works like this: `actual_permission = requested_permission & (~ umask)`.

a file with 666 permission (read and write for everyone), but the *umask* forces it to be 644 instead.

The *–S* option to *umask* causes it to work with symbolic values instead of with octal numbers. When used without an argument, *umask –S* prints the umask in symbolic form. With an argument, the mask is changed. In both cases, a symbolic mask represents the permissions to *keep* for a file. (This ends up being the bitwise complement of the traditional octal umask, which represents permissions to remove.) If you're confused, some examples should clear things up:

```
$ umask                          Print the current umask, in octal
0022
$ umask -S                       Print the current umask, in symbolic form
u=rwx,g=rx,o=rx
$ umask -S u=rwx,g=r,o=          Change the umask using the symbolic form
$ umask -S                       Print it back out symbolically
u=rwx,g=r,o=
$ umask                          Print it in octal
0037
```

ulimit

Early Unix systems didn't impose any limits on what resources a process could use. If a program wanted to run forever, it could. If a program wanted to create large files and fill up a disk, it could. And so on.

As Unix developed and matured, it became possible to explicitly control, or *limit*, a variety of different system resources, such as CPU time and disk space. The *ulimit* command is the Korn shell's interface for viewing and changing the limits on system resources. Table 10-1 lists the options it accepts and the corresponding resources. Not all options are available on all Unix systems. Many won't be available on non-Unix systems.

Table 10-1. ulimit resource options

Option	Resource limited	Option	Resource limited
-a	All (for printing values only)	-n	File descriptors
-c	Core file size (½ kb blocks)	-p	Pipe buffer size (½ kb blocks)[a]
-d	Process data segment (kb)	-s	Process stack segment (kb)
-f	File size (½ kb blocks)	-t	Process CPU time (seconds)
-m	Physical memory (kb)	-v	Virtual memory (kb)

[a] Most Unix systems don't have this feature.

Each takes a numerical argument that specifies the limit in units shown in the table. (You may use an arithmetic expression for the limit; *ksh* automatically evaluates the expression.) You can also give the argument "unlimited" (which may actually mean some physical limit), or you can omit the argument, in which case it prints the current limit. `ulimit -a` prints the limits (or "unlimited") for all types. You can only specify one type of resource at a time. If you don't specify any option, *–f* is assumed.

Some of these options depend on operating system capabilities that don't exist in older Unix versions. In particular, some older versions have a fixed limit of 20 file descriptors per process (making *–n* irrelevant), and some don't support virtual memory (making *–v* irrelevant).

The *–d* and *–s* options have to do with *dynamic memory allocation,* i.e., memory for which a process asks the operating system at runtime. It's not necessary for casual users to limit these, though software developers may want to do so to prevent buggy programs from trying to allocate endless amounts of memory due to infinite loops.

The *–v* option is similar; it puts a limit on all uses of memory. You don't need this unless your system has severe memory constraints or you want to limit process size to avoid thrashing.

You may want to specify limits on file size (*–f* and *–c*) if you have constraints on disk space. Sometimes users actually mean to create huge files, but more often than not, a huge file is the result of a buggy program that goes into an infinite loop. Software developers who use debuggers like *gdb* and *dbx* should not limit core file size, because core dumps are often helpful for debugging.

The *–t* option is another possible guard against infinite loops. On single-user systems, a program that is in an infinite loop but isn't allocating memory, writing files, or using the network is not particularly dangerous; it's better to leave this unlimited and just let the user kill the offending program. However, on shared server systems, such programs definitely degrade the overall environment. The problem in that case is that it's difficult to know what limit to set: there are important and legitimate uses for long-running programs.

In addition to the types of resources you can limit, *ulimit* lets you specify hard or soft limits. Hard limits can be lowered by any user but only raised by the superuser (`root`); users can lower soft limits and raise them—but only as high as the hard limit for that resource.

If you give *–H* along with one (or more) of the options above, *ulimit* sets hard limits; *–S* sets soft limits. Without either of these, *ulimit* sets both. For example, the following commands set the soft limit on file descriptors to 64 and the hard limit to unlimited:

```
ulimit -Sn 64
ulimit -Hn unlimited
```

When *ulimit* prints current limits, it prints the soft limits unless you specify *–H*.

Types of Global Customization

The best possible approach to globally available customization would be a system-wide environment file that is separate from each user's environment file—just like */etc/profile* is separate from each user's *.profile*.

Unfortunately, the Korn shell doesn't have this feature. If you assign a filename to the ENV environment variable, it could be overridden in a user's *.profile*. This allows you to make a default environment file available for users who don't have their own, but it doesn't let you have a system-wide environment file that runs in addition to the users'. Furthermore, the environment file is only run for interactive shells, not all shells.

Nevertheless, the shell gives you a few ways to set up customizations that are available to all users at all times. Environment variables are the most obvious; your */etc/profile* file will undoubtedly contain definitions for several of them, including PATH and TERM.

The variable TMOUT is useful when your system supports dialup lines. We have already seen that it affects the *read* command and the select menu loop. When set to a number *N*, if a user doesn't enter a command within *N* seconds after the shell last issued a prompt, the shell prints the warning message shell will time-out in 60 seconds due to inactivity. If, after a further 60 seconds, the user does not enter anything, the shell terminates. This feature is helpful in preventing people from "hogging" the dialup lines. Just make sure you set it to a reasonable value!

You may want to include some more complex customizations involving environment variables, such as the prompt string PS1 containing the current directory, user name, or hostname (as seen in Chapter 4).

You can also turn on options, such as emacs or vi editing modes, *noclobber* to protect against inadvertent file overwriting, and perhaps *ignoreeof* to keep people from logging off by accident when they type too many CTRL-D characters. Any shell scripts you have written for general use also contribute to customization.

Unfortunately, it's not possible to create a global alias. You can define aliases in */etc/profile*, but there is no way to make them part of the environment so that their definitions will propagate to shell subprocesses.

However, you can set up global functions. These are an excellent way to customize your system's environment, because functions are part of the shell, not separate processes. For example, you might wish to make *pushd* and *popd* (see Chapter 4 through Chapter 6) globally available.

The best way to create global functions is to use the built-in variable FPATH for autoloading of functions that we introduced in Chapter 4. Just define FPATH as a function library directory, perhaps */usr/local/functions*, and make it an environment variable by *export*ing it. Then make sure that the directory listed in FPATH is also included in PATH. In other words, put this or similar code in */etc/profile*:

```
FPATH=/usr/local/functions
PATH=$PATH:$FPATH
export FPATH PATH
```

Then put each global function's definition in a file in that directory with the same name as the function.

In any case, we suggest using global functions for global customization instead of shell scripts. Given how cheap memory is nowadays, there is no reason why you shouldn't make generally useful functions part of your users' environment.

Customizing the Editing Modes

As we saw in Chapter 2, you have your choice of either emacs or vi editing modes when editing your command line. Besides the commands available in each mode, you can customize the behavior of the editing modes to suit your needs or environment.

Appendix A discusses a number of third party shells based on the Bourne and Korn shell design. Those shells generally provide command-line editing, as well as the ability to customize the editor via a special built-in command, a special start-up file, or both.

The Korn shell's approach is different. It is based on a paradigm where you program the behavior you want from the shell. This is accomplished via a fake trap, named KEYBD. If it exists, the trap set for KEYBD is evaluated when *ksh* processes normal command-line input characters.* Within the code executed for the trap, two special variables contain the text of the command line and the text being entered that caused the trap. Additional special variables allow you to distinguish between emacs- and vi-modes and indicate the current position on the input line. These variables are listed in Table 10-2.

---

* Characters for search strings and numeric arguments to vi- and emacs-mode commands do not trigger the KEYBD trap.

Table 10-2. Special editing variables

Variable	Meaning
.sh.edchar	The character or escape sequence entered by the user that caused the KEYBD trap. The value of .sh.edchar at the end of the trap is then used to direct the actions of the built-in editor.
.sh.edcol	The position of the cursor on the current input line.
.sh.edmode	Equal to ESC in vi-mode, empty otherwise. (Use [[-n ${.sh.edmode}]] to test it.)
.sh.edtext	The text of the current input line.

Upon entering the KEYBD trap, the contents of .sh.edchar will be either a single character, ESC followed by a single character, or ESC, [, and a single character. You can assign a new value to .sh.edchar to change the input that the current editing mode receives. Thus, the KEYBD trap allows you to interpose a "filter" between what the user enters and what the shell editing modes actually process. The following example is from page 98 of *The New KornShell Command and Programming Language.** It presents a *keybind* function that allows you to bind new actions to input key sequences, similar to the built-in *bind* command of many other shells.

```
    # Quoted from Page 98 of
    # The New KornShell Command and Programming Language

1   typeset -A Keytable
2   trap 'eval "${Keytable[${.sh.edchar}]}"' KEYBD
3   function keybind # key [action]
4   {
5       typeset key=$(print -f "%q" "$2")
6       case $# in
7       2)      Keytable[$1]=' .sh.edchar=${.sh.edmode}'"$key"
8               ;;
9       1)      unset Keytable[$1]
10              ;;
11      *)      print -u2 "Usage: $0 key [action]"
12              return 2 # usage errors return 2 by default
13              ;;
14      esac
15  }
```

This is an interesting function. Let's go through it line by line. Line 1 creates an associative array to act as a table of key/action pairs. Line 2 sets the KEYBD trap. It gets the action out of the associative array and then executes it using *eval.* Line 3 starts the *keybind* function, which takes one or two arguments. With two arguments, the second argument is first quoted appropriately (line 5—the key variable

---

* This is the book on *ksh93* written by David Korn and Morris Bolsky and published by Prentice Hall.

would have been better-named `action`). Line 7 then creates the entry in the array, using `$1` (the user key sequence) as the index, and quoted action as the value to assign to `.sh.edchar`. Note how `${.sh.mode}` is also included. This has the effect of forcing a switch to command mode for the vi editing mode. It is this generated assignment statement that is *eval*ed every time the trap executes.

The rest of the function is mostly bookkeeping: with one argument (line 9), the given entry in the `Keytable` array is removed. If more than two arguments (line 11), *keybind* prints a message and then returns the (false) value 2.

While somewhat unusual, the KEYBD trap mechanism for dealing with user input is both general and extensible; you can do whatever you want, as just a Simple Matter of Programming. With other shells, you're limited to whatever built-in facilities they provide.

System Security Features

Unix security is a problem of legendary notoriety. Just about every aspect of a Unix system has some security issue associated with it, and it's usually the system administrator's job to worry about this issue.

This is not a textbook on Unix system security. Be aware that this section merely touches the tip of the iceberg and that there are myriad other aspects to Unix system security besides how the shell is set up. See the end of the chapter for one book that we recommend.

We first present a list of "tips" for writing shell scripts that have a better chance of avoiding security problems. Next we cover the *restricted shell*, which attempts to put a straitjacket around the user's environment. Then we present the idea of a "trojan horse," and why such things should be avoided. Finally we discuss the Korn shell's *privileged mode*, which is used with shell scripts that run as if the user were root.

Tips for Secure Shell Scripts

Here are some tips for writing more secure shell scripts, courtesy of Professor Eugene (Gene) Spafford, the director of Purdue University's Center for Education and Research in Information Assurance and Security:*

---

* See *http://www.cerias.purdue.edu.*

Don't put dot in PATH

> This issue was described in Chapter 3. This opens the door wide for "trojan horses," described in the next section.

Protect bin directories

> Make sure that every directory in $PATH is writable only by its owner and by no one else. The same applies to all the programs *in* the *bin* directories.

Design before you code

> Spend some time thinking about what you want to do and how to do it; don't just type stuff in with a text editor and keep hacking until it seems to work. Include code to handle errors and failures gracefully.

Check all input arguments for validity

> If you expect a number, verify that you got a number. Check that the number is in the correct range. Do the same thing for other kinds of data; the shell's regular expression facilities are particularly useful for this.

Check error codes from all commands that can return errors

> Things you may not expect to fail might be mischievously forced to fail to cause the script to misbehave. For instance, it is possible to cause some commands to fail even as root if the argument is a NFS-mounted disk or a character-oriented device file.

Don't trust passed-in environment variables

> Check and reset them to known values if they are used by subsequent commands (e.g., TZ, FPATH, PATH, IFS, etc.). The Korn shell automatically resets IFS to its default upon startup, ignoring whatever was in the environment, but many other shells don't. In all cases it's an excellent idea to explicitly set PATH to contain just the system *bin* directories.

Start in a known place

> Explicitly *cd* to a known directory when the script starts so that any subsequent relative pathnames are to a known location. Be sure the that *cd* succeeds:

```
cd app-dir || exit 1
```

Use full pathnames for commands

> Do this so you know which version you are getting, regardless of $PATH.

Use syslog(8) to keep an audit trail

> Log the date and time of invocation, username, etc.; see *logger*(1). If you don't have *syslog*, create a function to keep a log file:

```
function logsys {
    print -r -- "$@"  >>  /var/adm/logsysfile
}
logsys "Run by user " $(/bin/whoami)  "($USER) at "  $(/bin/date)
```

(*whoami*(1) prints the login name of the effective user ID, a concept described later in this chapter.)

Always quote user input when using that input

E.g., `"$1"` and `"$*"`. This prevents malicious user input from being further evaluated and executed.

Don't use eval on user input

Beside quoting user input, *don't* hand it to the shell to reprocess with *eval*. If the user reads your script and sees that it uses *eval*, it's easy to subvert the script into doing almost anything.

Quote the results of wildcard expansion

There are several nasty things you can do to a system administrator by creating files with spaces, semicolons, back-quotes, and so on in the filenames. If administrative scripts don't quote the filename arguments, the scripts can trash—or give away—the system.

Check user input for metacharacters

Look for metacharacters such as `$` or ` (old-style command substitution) if using the input in an *eval* or `$(...)`.

Test your code and read it critically

Look for assumptions and mistakes that can be exploited. Put yourself into a nasty mood, and read your code with the intent of trying to figure out how to subvert it. Then fix whatever problems you find.

Be aware of race conditions

If an attacker can execute arbitrary commands between any two commands in your script, will it compromise security? If so, find another way to do it.

Suspect symbolic links

When *chmod*ing or editing a file, check it to be sure it is a file and not a symbolic link to a critical system file. (Use `[[ -L file ]]` or `[[ -h file ]]` to test if *file* is a symbolic link.)

Have someone else review your code for mistakes

Often a fresh pair of eyes can spot things that the original author of a program misses.

Use setgid instead of setuid, if possible

These terms are discussed later in this chapter. In brief, by using *setgid*, you restrict the amount of damage that can be done to the group that is compromised.

Use a new user instead of root

If you must use *setuid* to access a group of files, consider making a new, non-root user for that purpose, and *setuid* to it.

Limit setuid code as much as possible

Make the amount of *setuid* code as small as you can. Move it into a separate program, and invoke that from within a larger script when necessary. However, be sure to code defensively as if the script can be invoked by anyone from anywhere else!

Chet Ramey, the maintainer of *bash*, offers the following prologue for use in shell scripts that need to be more secure:

```
# reset IFS, even though ksh doesn't import IFS from the environment,
# $ENV could set it
IFS=$' \t\n'

# make sure unalias is not a function, since it's a regular builtin
# unset is a special builtin, so it will be found before functions
unset -f unalias

# unset all aliases
# quote unalias so it's not alias-expanded
\unalias -a

# make sure command is not a function, since it's a regular builtin
# unset is a special builtin, so it will be found before functions
unset -f command

# get a reliable path prefix, handling case where getconf is not
# available (not too necessary, since getconf is a ksh93 built-in)
SYSPATH="$(command -p getconf PATH 2>/dev/null)"
if [[ -z "$SYSPATH" ]]; then
        SYSPATH="/usr/bin:/bin"          # pick your poison
fi
PATH="$SYSPATH:$PATH"
```

Restricted Shell

The restricted shell is designed to put the user into an environment where his or her ability to move around and write files is severely limited. It's usually used for guest accounts. When invoked as *rksh* (or with the *−r* option), *ksh* acts as a restricted shell. You can make a user's login shell restricted by putting the full pathname to *rksh* in the user's */etc/passwd* entry. The *ksh* executable file must have a link to it named *rksh* for this to work.

The specific constraints imposed by the restricted shell disallow the user from doing the following:

- Changing working directories: *cd* is inoperative. If you try to use it, you will get the error message ksh: cd: restricted.

- Redirecting output to a file: the redirectors >, >|, <>, and >> are not allowed. This includes using *exec*.

- Assigning a new value to the environment variables ENV, FPATH, PATH, or SHELL, or trying to change their attributes with *typeset*.

- Specifying any pathnames of commands with slashes (/) in them. The shell only runs commands found along $PATH.

- Adding new built-in commands with the *builtin* command. (This very advanced feature is outside the scope of this book.)

These restrictions go into effect after the user's *.profile* and environment files are run. This means that the restricted shell user's entire environment is set up in *.profile*. This lets the system administrator configure the environment as she sees fit.

To keep the user from overwriting ~/*.profile*, it is not enough to make the file read-only by the user. Either the home directory should not be writable by the user, or the commands in ~/*.profile* should *cd* to a different directory.

Two common ways of setting up such environments are to set up a directory of "safe" commands and have that directory be the only one in PATH, and to set up a command menu from which the user can't escape without exiting the shell. In any case, make sure that there is no other shell in any directory listed in $PATH; otherwise the user can just run that shell and avoid the restrictions listed earlier.

Although the ability to restrict the shell has been available (if not necessarily compiled in or documented) since the original Version 7 Bourne shell, it is rarely used. Setting up a usable yet correctly restricted environment is difficult in practice. So, caveat emptor.

Trojan Horses

The concept of a *trojan horse* was introduced briefly in Chapter 3. A trojan horse is something that looks harmless, or even useful, but which contains a hidden danger.

Consider the following scenario. User John Q. Programmer (login name jprog) is an excellent programmer and has quite a collection of personal programs in ~*jprog/bin*. This directory occurs first in the PATH variable in ~*jprog/.profile*. Since he is such a good programmer, management recently promoted him to system administrator.

This is a whole new field of endeavor, and John—not knowing any better—has unfortunately left his *bin* directory writable. Along comes W. M. Badguy, who creates the following shell script, named *grep*, in John's *bin* directory:

```
/bin/grep "$@"
case $(whoami) in                        Check effective user ID name
root)     nasty stuff here               Danger Will Robinson, danger!
          rm ~/jprog/bin/grep            Hide the evidence
          ;;
esac
```

In and of itself, this script can do no damage when jprog is working *as himself.*
The problem comes when jprog uses the *su*(1) command. This command allows a
regular user to "switch user" to a different user. By default, it allows a regular user
to become root (as long as that user knows the password, of course). The problem is that normally, *su* uses whatever PATH it inherits.* In this case, $PATH includes
˜jprog/bin. Now, when jprog, working as root, runs *grep,* he actually executes the
trojan horse version in his *bin.* This version runs the real *grep,* so jprog gets the
results he expects. But it also silently executes the *nasty stuff here* part, as root.
This means that Unix will let the script do anything it wants to. *Anything.* And to
make things worse, by removing the trojan horse when it's done, there's no longer
any evidence.

Writable *bin* directories open one door for trojan horses, as does having dot in
PATH. Having writable shell scripts in any *bin* directory is another door. Just as you
close and lock the doors of your house at night, you should make sure that you
close any doors on your system!

Setuid and Privileged Mode

Many problems with Unix security hinge on a Unix file attribute called the *setuid*
(set user ID) bit. This is like a permission bit (see the earlier discussion of *umask*):
when an executable file has it turned on, the file runs with an effective user ID
equal to the owner of the file. The effective user ID is distinct from the real user
ID of the process, and Unix applies its permission tests to the process's effective
user ID.

For example, suppose you've written a really nifty game program that keeps a private score file showing the top 15 players on your system. You don't want to
make the score file world-writable, because anyone could just come along and
edit the file to make themselves the high scorer. By making your game setuid to
your user ID, the game program can update the file, which you own, but no one
else can update it. (The game program can determine who ran it by looking at its
real user ID and using that to determine the login name.)

The setuid facility is a nice feature for games and score files, but it becomes much
more dangerous when used for root. Making programs setuid root lets

---

* Get in the habit of using su - *user* to switch to *user* as if the user were doing a real login. This prevents the importing of the existing PATH.

administrators write programs that do certain things that require root privilege (e.g., configure printers) in a controlled way. To set a file's *setuid* bit, the superuser can type chmod 4755 *filename*; the 4 is the *setuid* bit.

A similar facility exists at the group level, known (not surprisingly) as *setgid* (set group ID). Use chmod 2755 *filename* to turn on setgid permissions. When you do an *ls –l* on a setuid or setgid file, the x in the permission mode is replaced with an s; for example, –rws–s–x for a file that is readable and writable by the owner, executable by everyone, and has both the setuid and setgid bits set (octal mode 6711).

Modern system administration wisdom says that creating setuid and setgid shell scripts is a very, very bad idea. This has been especially true under the C shell, because its *.cshrc* environment file introduces numerous opportunities for break-ins. In particular, there are multiple ways of tricking a setuid shell script into becoming an *interactive* shell with an effective user ID of root. This is about the best thing a cracker could hope for: the ability to run any command as root.

There is an important difference between a setuid shell script and a *setuid shell*. The latter is a copy of the shell executable, which has been made to belong to root and had the setuid bit applied. In the previous section on trojan horses, suppose that the *nasty stuff here* was this code:

```
cp /bin/ksh ~badguy/bin/myls
chown root ~badguy/bin/myls
chmod 4755 ~badguy/bin/myls
```

Remember, this code executes as root, so it will work. When badguy executes *myls*, it's a machine-code executable file, and the setuid bit *is* honored. Hello shell that runs as root. Goodbye security!

Privileged mode was designed to protect against setuid shell scripts. This is a *set –o* option (set -o privileged or set -p), but the shell enters it automatically whenever it executes a script whose *setuid* bit is set, i.e., when the effective user ID is different from the real user ID.

In privileged mode, when a *setuid* Korn shell script is invoked, the shell runs the file */etc/suid_profile*. This file should be written so as to restrict *setuid* shell scripts in much the same way as the restricted shell does. At a minimum, it should make PATH read-only (typeset -r PATH or readonly PATH) and set it to one or more "safe" directories. Once again, this prevents any decoys from being invoked.

Since privileged mode is an option, it is possible to turn it off with the command set +o privileged (or set +p). But this doesn't help the potential system cracker: the shell automatically changes its effective user ID to be the same as the real user ID—i.e., if you turn off privileged mode, you also turn off *setuid*.

In addition to privileged mode, *ksh* provides a special "agent" program, */etc/suid_exec*, that runs setuid shell scripts (or shell scripts that are executable but not readable).

For this to work, the script should *not* start with #! /bin/ksh. When the program is invoked, *ksh* attempts to run the program as a regular binary executable. When the operating system fails to run the script (because it isn't binary, and because it doesn't have the name of an interpreter specified with #!), *ksh* realizes that it's a script and invokes */etc/suid_exec* with the name of the script and its arguments. It also arranges to pass an authentication "token" to */etc/suid_exec* indicating the real and effective user and group IDs of the script. */etc/suid_exec* verifies that it is safe to run the script and then arranges to invoke *ksh* with the proper real and effective user and group IDs on the script.

Although the combination of privileged mode and */etc/suid_exec* allows you to avoid many of the attacks on setuid scripts, actually writing scripts that can safely be run setuid is a difficult art, requiring a fair amount of knowledge and experience. It should be done very carefully.

In fact, the dangers of setuid and setgid shell scripts (at least for shells besides *ksh*) are so great that modern Unix systems, meaning both commercial Unix systems and freeware clones (4.4–BSD-derived and GNU/Linux), disable the setuid and setgid bits on shell scripts. Even if you apply the bits to the file, the operating system does not honor them.*

Although setuid shell scripts don't work on modern systems, there are occasions where privileged mode is still useful. In particular, there is a widely used third party program named *sudo*, which, to quote the web page, "allows a system administrator to give certain users (or groups of users) the ability to run some (or all) commands as root or another user while logging the commands and arguments." The home page for *sudo* is *http://www.courtesan.com/sudo/*. A system administrator could easily execute sudo /bin/ksh -p in order to get a known environment for performing administrative tasks.

Finally, if you would like to learn more about Unix security, we recommend *Practical UNIX & Internet Security* by Simson Garfinkel and Gene Spafford. It is published by O'Reilly & Associates.

---

* MacOS X seems to be a notable exception. Be extra careful if you run one or more such systems!

Related Shells

The fragmentation of the Unix marketplace has had its advantages and disadvantages. The advantages came mostly in the early days: lack of standardization and proliferation among technically savvy academics and professionals contributed to a healthy "free market" for Unix software, in which several programs of the same type (e.g., shells, text editors, system administration tools) would often compete for popularity. The best programs would usually become the most widespread, while inferior software tended to fade away.

But often there was no single "best" program in a given category, so several would prevail. This led to the current situation, where multiplicity of similar software has led to confusion, lack of compatibility, and—most unfortunate of all—Unix's inability to capture as big a share of the market as other operating platforms. In particular, Unix has been relegated to its current position as a very popular operating system for servers, but it's a rarity on desktop machines.

The "shell" category has probably suffered in this way more than any other type of software. As we said in the Preface and Chapter 1, it is one of the strengths of Unix that the shell is replaceable, and thus a number of shells are currently available; the differences between them are often not all that great. We believe that the Korn shell is one of the best of the most widely used shells, but other shells certainly have their staunch adherents, so they aren't likely to fade into obscurity. In fact, it seems that shells, Bourne-compatible or not, continue to proliferate.

Therefore we felt it necessary to include information on shells similar to the Korn shell. This Appendix summarizes the differences between the Korn shell and the following shells:

- The System V Release 4 Bourne shell, as a kind of baseline

- The 1988 version of the Korn shell

- The IEEE POSIX 1003.2 Shell Standard, to which the Korn shell and other shells adhere

- The Desk Top Korn shell (*dtksh*), a Korn shell with enhancements for X Window System programming, as part of the Common Desktop Environment (CDE)

- The *tksh* shell, an interesting blend of *ksh93* with Tcl/Tk

- *pdksh*, a widely used public domain version of the Korn shell

- The *bash* shell, another enhanced Bourne shell with some C shell and Korn shell features

- The Z shell, *zsh*, yet another enhanced Bourne shell with some C shell and Korn shell features and many, many more of its own

- Korn shell workalikes on desktop PC platforms

The Bourne Shell

The Korn shell is almost completely backward-compatible with the Bourne shell. The only significant feature of the latter that the Korn shell doesn't support is ^ (caret) as a synonym for the pipe (|) character.* This is an archaic feature that the Bourne shell includes for its own backward compatibility with earlier shells. No modern Unix version has any shell code that uses ^ as a pipe.

To describe the differences between the Bourne shell and the Korn shell, we'll go through each chapter of this book and enumerate the features discussed in the chapter that the Bourne shell does *not* support.

Chapter 1, Korn Shell Basics

The cd *old new* and cd – forms of the *cd* command.

Tilde (~) expansion.

The Bourne shell always follows the physical file layout, which affects what happens when you cd .. out of somewhere that was a symbolic link.

---

* There are also a few differences in how the two shells react to certain extremely pathological input. Usually, the Korn shell processes correctly what causes the Bourne shell to "choke."

The built-in commands don't have online help.

Some older versions of the Bourne shell don't support the *jobs* command and job control, or they may require being invoked as *jsh* in order to enable job control features.

Chapter 2, Command-Line Editing

All (i.e., the Bourne shell doesn't support any of the history and editing features discussed in Chapter 2).

Chapter 3, Customizing Your Environment

Aliases are not supported.

set −o options don't work. The Bourne shell supports the abbreviations listed in the "Options" table in Appendix B, except *−A*, *−b*, *−C*, *−m*, *−p*, and *−s*.

Environment files aren't supported; neither is the *print* command (use *echo* instead). The following built-in variables aren't supported:

.sh.edchar	.sh.version	HISTEDIT	LINENO	PS4
.sh.edcol	COLUMNS	HISTFILE	LINES	PWD
.sh.edmode	EDITOR	HISTSIZE	OLDPWD	RANDOM
.sh.edtext	ENV	LANG	OPTARG	REPLY
.sh.match	FCEDIT	LC_ALL	OPTIND	SECONDS
.sh.name	FIGNORE	LC_COLLATE	PPID	TMOUT
.sh.subscript	FPATH	LC_CTYPE	PS3	VISUAL
.sh.value	HISTCMD	LC_NUMERIC		

Some of these variables (e.g., EDITOR and VISUAL) are still used by other programs, like *mail* and news readers.

Chapter 4, Basic Shell Programming

Extended variable names (those with a dot in them), as well as compound variable assignment are not available, nor is string concatenation with the += operator.

Indirect variables (namerefs) are not available.

The *whence* command is not available; use *type* instead.

The pattern-matching variable operators (%, %%, #, ##, etc.) and advanced (regular expression) wildcards are not available; use the external command *expr* instead.

Autoloaded functions are not available, and only POSIX-style functions (those defined using the *name*() syntax) may be used.

Command substitution syntax is different: use the older `command` instead of
$(command). (Some vendors have enhanced their Bourne shells to support the
$(command) notation, since it's defined by the POSIX standard.)

Chapter 5, Flow Control

return may only be used from within a function.

Conditional tests use older syntax: [*condition*] or test *condition* instead of
[[*condition*]]. These are actually two forms of the same command (see the
test(1) manual page).

The logical operators && and || are -a and -o instead. Supported test opera-
tors differ from system to system.*

The ! keyword to reverse the exit status of a command was not in the SVR4
Bourne shell, although it may be available on your system, since it is required
by POSIX.

The select construct isn't supported. Neither is the arithmetic for loop, and
there is no way to fall through from one case to another inside a case statement.

There is no equivalent for TMOUT.

Chapter 6, Command-Line Options and Typed Variables

The SVR4 Bourne shell *getopts* command is similar, but not identical to, that in
ksh. It does not allow options that begin with a plus sign, nor any of the
advanced features described in Appendix B.

Arithmetic isn't supported: use the external command *expr* instead of the
$((...)) syntax. For numeric conditionals, use the old condition test syntax
and relational operators *–lt*, *–eq*, etc., instead of ((...)). *let* isn't supported.

Array variables and the *typeset* command are not supported.

Chapter 7, Input/Output and Command-Line Processing

The following I/O redirectors are not supported:†

>| <>   <<<   <&p   >&p   <&*n*-   >&*n*- |&

print isn't supported (use *echo* instead). *printf* is generally available as an
external command.

---

* In the original Version 7 Bourne Shell (and in Berkeley Unix systems through 4.3BSD), *test* and
  [*condition*] were actually external commands. (They were hard links to each other in */bin*.) However, they've been built into the Bourne shell in all systems since System III (circa 1981).

† The <> operator was in the original Version 7 Bourne shell, but not documented, since it didn't
  always work correctly across all Unix systems. Its availability should not be relied upon for Bourne
  shell programming.

None of the options to *read* are supported, nor is the ability to supply a prompt with the first variable's name.

The Bourne shell does not do special interpretations of pathnames, such as */dev/fd/2* or */dev/tcp/ftp.oreilly.com/ftp.*

The $"..." and $'...' quoting mechanisms are not available.

Chapter 8, Process Handling

Job control is supported, but only if the shell is invoked with the –*j* option or as *jsh.*

The - option to *trap* (reset trap to the default for that signal) is not available. Instead, a missing trap indicates that the supplied traps should be reset. *trap* accepts only signal numbers, not logical names.

Coroutines aren't supported.

The *wait* command only accepts process IDs.

Chapter 9, Debugging Shell Programs

The ERR and DEBUG fake signals are not available. The EXIT fake signal *is* supported, as signal 0.

set –*n* takes effect even in interactive shells.

The output from tracing with *set* –*x* is not customizable (no PS4 variable).

Discipline functions are not available.

Chapter 10, Korn Shell Administration

Privileged mode isn't supported. (Some Bourne shells do have it.)

The *ulimit* and *umask* commands are not as capable.

The KEYBD trap is not available.

The 1988 Korn Shell

Perhaps the most obvious shell with which to compare *ksh93* is *ksh88*, the 1988 version of the Korn shell. This section briefly describes those features of *ksh93* that are either different or nonexistent in *ksh88*. As with the presentation for the Bourne shell, the topics are covered in the same order as they're presented in the rest of the book.

Chapter 1, Korn Shell Basics

The built-in help facilities (such as –*?*, ––*man*, and so on) are not available.

Tilde substitution does not occur during variable expansion (${var op word}).

Chapter 2, Command-Line Editing

CTRL-T works differently in emacs editing mode. In *ksh88*, it transposes the two characters to the right of point and moves point forward by one character.

In emacs-mode, ESC ESC, ESC *, and ESC = don't work on the first word of a command line, i.e., there is no command completion facility. The ESC # command always prepends a # character. It never removes them.

Similarly, in vi-mode, the *, \ and = commands don't work on the first word of a command line, and the # command always prepends a # character. It never removes them.

Finally, there is no variable completion, the *hist* command is called *fc*, FCEDIT is used in place of HISTEDIT, and the HISTCMD variable is not available.

Chapter 3, Customizing Your Environment

The ENV file is sourced for all shells, and *ksh88* only does variable substitution on the value of $ENV.

Alias tracking can be turned off in *ksh88*.

The *–p* option to *alias* is not present in *ksh88*, nor is the *–a* option to *unalias*.

The following built-in variables aren't supported:

.sh.edchar	.sh.match	.sh.version	LANG
.sh.edcol	.sh.name	FIGNORE	LC_ALL
.sh.edmode	.sh.subscript	HISTCMD	LC_COLLATE
.sh.edtext	.sh.value	HISTEDIT	LC_CTYPE

Chapter 4, Basic Shell Programming

In *ksh88*, both syntaxes for defining functions produce functions with Korn shell semantics. You cannot apply the dot command to a function name.

The command search order in *ksh88* is keywords, aliases, all built-in commands, functions, and then external commands and scripts. The order was changed in *ksh93* for POSIX compliance.

In *ksh88*, undefined (autoloaded) functions are searched for exclusively along the list in the FPATH variable, and PATH is not involved.

The *.paths* file feature is not available.

Many of the variable substitution features described in the main text are new to *ksh93*. Only the following are available in *ksh88*: ${name:-string}, ${name:=string}, ${name:?string}, ${name:+string}, ${name#pattern}, ${name##pattern}, ${name%pattern}, ${name%%pattern}, ${#name}, ${#name[*]}, and ${#name[@]}.

Compound variables, namerefs and the += operator for appending to a variable are not in *ksh88*.

The \n notation in patterns is not available, nor are non-greedy matching, the use of backslash escapes in patterns, options in subpatterns, nor any of the [:...:] character classes.

The .sh.match array is not available.

Chapter 5, Flow Control

Exit values in *ksh88* only go up to 128. Programs that die due to a signal have exit status 128 plus signal number.

There is no *command* built-in command. To replace a built-in, you have to use an awkward combination of aliasing, functions, and quoting.

The *set –o pipefail* option and the the ! keyword for reversing the sense of a test are not available. Instead of the == operator for [[...]], *ksh88* uses =.

The arithmetic for loop is not in *ksh88*. The use of ;& for falling through cases existed in *ksh88* but was undocumented. The TMOUT variable existed in *ksh88*, but it only applied to the shell itself, not to the *select* loop or the *read* command.

Chapter 6, Command-Line Options and Typed Variables

The *ksh88* getopts did not have the ability to specify numeric arguments to options, nor a way to specify optional arguments to options.

The built-in arithmetic only supports integers, and the ++, --, ?: and comma operators aren't available. Numeric constants of the form *base#number* can only go up to base 36. There are no built-in arithmetic functions.

Only indexed arrays exist, and the maximum index is 1023.

Chapter 7, Input/Output and Command-Line Processing

The following I/O redirectors are not supported:

```
<&n-    >&n-    <<<
```

TCP/IP networking is available starting with *ksh88e*, but you must use IP addresses.

ksh88 does not have the *printf* command, nor the *–A, –d, –n,* and *–t* options to *read*. TMOUT does not affect *read*.

Brace expansion and process substitution are compile-time options that are generally not available in *ksh88*.

Locale translation with $"..." and ANSI C strings with $'...' are not available.

Chapter 8, Process Handling

The *disown* command is not available, and neither are the *–n* and *–s* options to *kill*. *kill –l* can only be used by itself to list the available signals.

true and *false* are predefined aliases instead of built-in commands.

Functions and aliases are exported to shell subprocesses; this is not true of *ksh93*.

Chapter 9, Debugging Shell Programs

Traps for the DEBUG fake signal are executed *after* each command is executed, not before.

Discipline functions are not available.

Chapter 10, Korn Shell Administration

The *umask* command only works with octal masks.

You cannot customize the built-in editors; the KEYBD fake signal does not exist.

The IEEE 1003.2 POSIX Shell Standard

There have been many attempts to standardize Unix. Hardware companies' monolithic attempts at market domination, fragile industry coalitions, marketing failures, and other such efforts are the stuff of history—and the stuff of frustration.

Only one standardization effort has not been tied to commercial interests: the Portable Operating System Interface, known as POSIX. This effort started in 1981 with the */usr/group* (now UniForum) Standards Committee, which produced the */usr/group Standard* three years later. The list of contributors grew. Eventually, the effort to create a formal standard moved under the umbrella of the Institute of Electrical and Electronic Engineers (IEEE) and the International Organization for Standardization (ISO).

The first POSIX standard was published in 1988 and revised in 1996. This one, called IEEE Standard 1003.1, covered low-level issues at the system call level. IEEE Standard 1003.2, covering the shell, utility programs, and user interface issues, was ratified in September 1992 after a six-year effort. In September 2001, a joint revision of both standards was approved. The new standard, covering all the material in the two earlier separate documents, is known as IEEE Standard 1003.1-2001.

The POSIX standards were never meant to be rigid and absolute. The committee members certainly weren't about to put guns to the heads of operating system implementers and force them to adhere. Instead, the standards are designed to be flexible enough to allow for both coexistence of similar available software, so that existing code isn't in danger of obsolescence, and the addition of new features, so that vendors have the incentive to innovate. In other words, they are supposed to be the kind of third-party standards that vendors might actually be interested in following.

As a result, most Unix vendors currently comply with both standards. The Korn shell is no exception; it is intended to be 100% POSIX-compliant. It pays to be familiar with what's in the standard if you want to write code that is portable to different systems.

The shell part of the standard describes utilities that must be present on all systems, and others that are optional, depending upon the nature of the system. One such option is the User Portability Utilities option, which defines standards for interactive shell use and interactive utilities like the *vi* editor. The standard—on the order of 2000 pages—is available through the IEEE; for information, contact the IEEE:

> IEEE Customer Service
> 445 Hoes Lane, PO Box 1331
> Piscataway, NJ 08855-1331
> (800) 678-IEEE (United States and Canada)
> (732) 981-0060 (international/local)
> (732) 981-9667 (fax)
> *customer.service@ieee.org*
> *http://www.standards.ieee.org/catalog/ordering.html*

The committee members had two motivating factors to weigh when they designed the shell standard. On the one hand, the design had to accomodate, as much as possible, existing shell code written under various Bourne-derived shells (the Version 7, System V, BSD, and Korn shells). These shells are different in several extremely subtle ways, most of which have to do with the ways certain syntactic elements interact with each other.

It must have been quite difficult and tedious to spell out these differences, let alone to reach compromises among them. Throw in biases of some committee members towards particular shells, and you might understand why it took six years to ratify the first 1003.2 standard and another five years to merge the two standards.

On the other hand, the shell design had to serve as a standard on which to base future shell implementations. This implied goals of simplicity, clarity, and precision—objectives that seem especially elusive in the context of the above problems.

The designers found one way of ameliorating this dilemma: they decided that the standard should include not only the features included in the shell, but also those explicitly omitted and those included but with unspecified functionality. The latter category allows some of the existing shells' innovations to "sneak through" without becoming part of the standard, while listing omitted features helps programmers determine which features in existing shell scripts won't be portable to future shells.

The POSIX standard is primarily based on the System V Bourne shell. Therefore you should assume that Korn shell features that aren't present in the Bourne shell also aren't included in the POSIX standard.

However, the Korn shell did contribute a few of its features to the POSIX standard, including:

- $((...)) syntax for arithmetic expressions.

- $(...) syntax for command substitution, except that the $(< *filename*) shorthand for $(cat *filename*) isn't supported.

- Tilde expansion (originally derived from the C shell).

The following Korn shell features are left "unspecified" in the standard, meaning that their syntax is acceptable but their functionality is not standardized:

- The ((...)) syntax for arithmetic conditionals. The arithmetic test operators introduced in Chapter 5 (e.g., *–eq*, *–lt*), however, are included.

- The [[...]] syntax for conditional tests. The external *test* or [...] utility should be used instead. The Korn shell's version of *test* is POSIX-compliant when used with no more than three arguments. (It also complies with four arguments, if the first argument is !.)

- The syntax for defining functions that this book uses. The other syntax shown in Chapter 4 (*fname*() instead of function *fname*) is supported, with what we described as "POSIX semantics;" see below.

- The select control structure.

- Signal numbers are only allowed if the numbers for certain key signals (INT, TERM, and a few others) are the same as on the most important historical versions of Unix. In general, shell scripts should use symbolic names for signals.

The POSIX standard supports functions, but the semantics are weaker than the Korn shell's function-style functions: functions do not have local traps or options, and it is not possible to define local variables. (For this reason, *ksh93* has two different syntaxes for defining functions, with different semantics.)

Code blocks ({...; }) are supported. For maximum portability, when you want literal curly braces, you should quote them (for reasons too complicated to go into here).

The POSIX standard introduced the following features, which are different from traditional Bourne shell behavior. *ksh93* supports them all:

- The command lookup order has been changed to allow certain built-in commands to be overridden by functions—since aliases aren't included in the standard. Built-in commands are divided into two sets by their positions in the command lookup order: some are processed before functions, some after. Specifically, the built-in commands *break*, *:* (do nothing), *continue*, *.* (dot), *eval*, *exec*, *exit*, *export*, *readonly*, *return*, *set*, *shift*, *trap*, and *unset* take priority over functions.

- A new built-in command, *command*, allows you to use built-in commands other than the above even if there are functions of the same name.*

- A new keyword, !, takes the logical "not" of a command's exit status: if *command* returns exit status 0, ! `command` returns 1; if *command* returns a non-zero value, ! `command` returns 0. ! can be used with &&, ||, and parentheses (for nested subshells) to create logical combinations of exit statuses in conditionals.

- The command `unset -v` is used instead of `unset` (without an option) to remove the definition of a variable. This provides a better syntactic match with `unset -f`, for unsetting functions.

Finally, because the POSIX standard is meant to promote shell script portability, it explicitly avoids mention of features that only apply to interactive shell use—including aliases, editing modes, control keys, and so on. The User Portability Utilities option covers these. It also avoids mentioning certain key implementation issues: in particular, there is no requirement that multitasking be used for background jobs, subshells, etc. This was done to allow portability to non-multitasking systems like MS-DOS, so that, for example, the MKS Toolkit (see later in this appendix) can be POSIX compliant.

dtksh

The Desk Top Korn Shell (*dtksh*) is a standard part of the Common Desktop Environment (CDE), available on commercial Unix systems such as Solaris, HP-UX, and AIX. It is based on a somewhat older version of *ksh93*. It evolved from the earlier program *wksh*, the Windowing Korn shell, released by Unix System Laboratories in late 1992. It's a full Korn shell, compatible with the version that this book describes,† that has extensions for graphical user interface (GUI) programming in the X Window System environment. It is typically found in */usr/dt/bin/dtksh*.

dtksh supports the OSF/Motif graphical Toolkit by making its routines available as built-in commands. This allows programmers to combine the Korn shell's strength as a Unix systems programming environment with the power and abstraction of the Toolkit. The result is a unified environment for quick and easy development of graphics-based software.

---

* But note that it's *not* a special built-in! Design by committee shows through here.

† Features listed throughout the book as being introduced for "recent" versions won't be in *dtksh*.

There are various GUI development tools that allow you to construct user interfaces with a graphics-based editor rather than with programming language code. But such tools are typically huge, expensive, and complex. *dtksh*, on the other hand, is inexpensive and unbeatable for the smoothness of its integration with Unix—it's the only such tool that you can use as your login shell! (Well, almost; see the next section.) It is a definite option for systems programmers who use X-based workstations and need a rapid prototyping tool.

To give you the flavor of *dtksh* code, here is a script that implements the canonical "Hello World" program by displaying a small box with an "OK" button. It is from the article *Graphical Desktop Korn Shell*, in the July, 1998 issue of *Linux Journal*, by George Kraft IV. (See *http://www.linuxjournal.com/article.php?sid=2643*.) This code should hold no surprises for X and Motif programmers:

```
#!/usr/dt/bin/dtksh

XtInitialize TOPLEVEL dtHello DtHello "$@"

XmCreateMessageDialog HELLO $TOPLEVEL hello \
        dialogTitle:"DtHello" \
        messageString:"$(print "Hello\nWorld")"
XmMessageBoxGetChild HELP $HELLO \
        DIALOG_HELP_BUTTON
XtUnmanageChild $HELP
XmMessageBoxGetChild CANCEL $HELLO \
        DIALOG_CANCEL_BUTTON
XtUnmanageChild $CANCEL
XtAddCallback $HELLO okCallback exit
XtManageChild $HELLO
XtMainLoop
```

http://www.cactus.org/~gk4/kraft/george/papers/dtksh/ is Mr. Kraft's web presentation on *dtksh*.

The following book is devoted to *dtksh*: *Desktop KornShell Graphical Programming* by J. Stephen Pendergast, Jr., published by Addison-Wesley, 1995 (ISBN: 0-201-63375-2). Examples from the book are online at *ftp://ftp.aw.com/aw.prof.comp.series/pendergrast.examples.tar.Z*. Also available is *ftp://ftp.aw.com/aw.prof.comp.series/pend.dtksh1*, a text file that provides an overview of the book. Unfortunately, as of this writing, this book is out of print.

tksh

Back in 1996, while a computer science graduate student at Princeton University, Dr. Jeffrey L. Korn* wrote *tksh*. This is an integration of *ksh93* with Tcl/Tk. The following quote (from Dr. Korn's research web page) summarizes it well:

> Tksh is a graphical language (similar to Visual Basic or Tcl/Tk) that uses KornShell (*ksh93*) for scripting and Tk for graphical user interface. Tksh is implemented as a *ksh93* extension, and allows Tcl libraries such as Tk to run on top of *ksh93* unchanged. *ksh93* is well suited for graphical scripting because it is backward compatible with *sh*, making it both easy to learn and easy to extend existing scripts to provide user interface. Tksh also allows Tcl scripts to run without modification, making it possible to mix and match components written in either Tcl or *ksh93*.

The *tksh* home page is still at Princeton: *http://www.cs.princeton.edu/~jlk/tksh/*. It has links to papers and documentation that can be downloaded and printed. However, the link to *tksh* executables is out-of-date. The *tksh* source is available from AT&T Research as part of the *ast-open* package, which also contains *ksh93* and reimplementations of many other Unix tools. See Appendix C for more information.

The following example script, from the USENIX paper on *tksh*, is called *watchdir*:

```
# Tksh Demo
# Jeff Korn
#
# This script keeps track of visited directories and shows the files
# in the current directory.   You can double-click on files and
# directories.  The script should be used interactively, so to run:
#    $ tksh
#    $ . scripts/watchdir

function winsetup
{
    pack $(frame .f)
    frame .f.dirname -relief raised -bd 1
    pack .f.dirname -side top -fill x
    pack $(frame .f.ls) $(frame .f.dirs) -side left
    label .f.dirname.label -text "Current directory: "
    label .f.dirname.pwd -textvariable PWD
    pack .f.dirname.label .f.dirname.pwd -side left

    scrollbar .f.ls.scroll -command ".f.ls.list yview"
    listbox .f.ls.list -yscroll ".f.ls.scroll set" -width 20 -setgrid 1
    pack $(label .f.ls.label -text "Directory Contents") -side top
    pack .f.ls.list .f.ls.scroll -side left -fill y -expand 1
```

---

* Yes, David Korn's son. He now works in the same research center as his father at AT&T Laboratories, although in a different area.

```
        scrollbar .f.dirs.scroll -command ".f.dirs.list yview"
        listbox .f.dirs.list -yscroll ".f.dirs.scroll set" -width 20 -setgrid 1
        pack $(label .f.dirs.label -text "Visited Directories") -side top
        pack .f.dirs.list .f.dirs.scroll -side left -fill y -expand 1
        bind .f.dirs.list "<Double-1>" 'cd $(selection get)'
        bind .f.ls.list "<Double-1>" 'tkfileselect $(selection get)'
}

function tkfileselect
{
        [[ -d "$1" ]] && tkcd "$1"
        [[ -f "$1" ]] && ${EDITOR-${VISUAL-emacs}} "$1"
}

function tkcd
{
        cd $1 > /dev/null || return
        .f.ls.list delete 0 end
        set -o markdirs
        .f.ls.list insert end .. *
        [[ ${VisitedDir["$PWD"]} == "" ]] && .f.dirs.list insert end "$PWD"
        VisitedDir["$PWD"]=1
}

typeset -A VisitedDir
winsetup > /dev/null
alias cd=tkcd
tkcd .
```

What's nice about *tksh*, besides the interesting blend of complementary technologies, is that it brings Tk programming out to the shell level. Graphics programming with Tk is much higher level than with the Motif toolkit; thus the learning curve is easier to climb, and the scripts are easier to read and write.

pdksh

Many of the Open Source Unix-like systems, such as GNU/Linux, come with the Public Domain Korn Shell, *pdksh*. *pdksh* is available as source code; start at its home page: *http://www.cs.mun.ca/~michael/pdksh/*. It comes with instructions for building and installing on various Unix platforms.

pdksh was originally written by Eric Gisin, who based it on Charles Forsyth's public-domain clone of the Version 7 Bourne shell. It is mostly compatible with the 1988 Korn shell and POSIX, with some extensions of its own.

Its emacs editing mode is actually more powerful than that of the 1988 Korn shell. Like the full Emacs editor, you can customize the keystrokes that invoke editing commands (known as *key bindings* in Emacs terminology). Editing commands have full names that you can associate with keystrokes by using the *bind* command.

For example, if you want to set up CTRL-U to do the same thing as CTRL-P (i.e., go back to the previous command in the history file), you could put this command in your *.profile*:

```
bind '^U'=up-history
```

You can even set up two-character escape sequences, which (for example) allow you to use ANSI arrow keys as well as control characters, and you can define *macros*, i.e., abbreviations for sequences of editing commands.

The public domain Korn shell's additional features include *alternation* wildcards (borrowed from the C shell) and user-definable tilde notation, in which you can set up ~ as an abbreviation for anything, not just user names. There are also a few subtle differences in integer expression evaluation and aliasing.

pdksh lacks the following features of the official version:

- The built-in variable LINES.

- The DEBUG fake signal. The fake signals ERR and EXIT within functions.

- Functions inherit the trap settings of the main script.

- The POSIX file expansion character classes ([[:alpha:]], etc.) are not available.

- The *read* command and select loop do not use the command-line editing modes.

- The last command of a pipeline is not run in the parent shell. Thus, echo hi | read x; print $x doesn't work the same as in *ksh*. (Most Bourne-style shells work this same way.)

- The *set −o option* form of *ksh* is *set −X option* in *pdksh*.

Although it lacks most *ksh93* extensions, *pdksh* is a worthwhile alternative to the C and Bourne shells.

bash

bash is probably the most popular "third-party" shell that is available for Unix and other systems. In particular, it is the default shell on GNU/Linux systems. (It also comes on the "freeware" CD with Solaris 8.) You can get it from the Internet, via anonymous FTP to *ftp.gnu.org* in the directory */pub/gnu/bash*. You can also order it from its maker at the address listed here.

The Free Software Foundation
59 Temple Place – Suite 330
Boston, MA 02111-1307
(617) 542-2652
(617) 542-5942 (fax)
gnu@gnu.org
http://www.gnu.org

Bash was written by Brian Fox and Chet Ramey. Chet Ramey currently maintains
it. Its name is in line with the FSF's penchant for bad puns: it stands for Bourne-
Again Shell. Although *bash* is easily available and you don't have to pay for it
(other than the cost of media, phone calls, etc.), it's not really public domain software. While public domain software doesn't have licensing restrictions, the FSF's
software does. But those restrictions are diametrically opposed to those in a commercial license:* instead of agreeing not to distribute the software further, you
agree not to prevent it from being distributed further! In other words, you enjoy
unrestricted use of the software as long as you agree not to inhibit others from
doing the same. Richard Stallman, the founder of the FSF, invented this intriguing
and admirable concept.

These days, the ideals of the Free Software and Open Source movements, the
GNU project, and the quality of GNU software are all well known. The most popular GNU system is GNU/Linux, which uses the Linux kernel and GNU utilities to
make a complete, fully functional, Unix- and POSIX-compatible computing environment.

bash is fully compatible with the 1992 POSIX standard. It has several of the most
important Korn shell features and the C shell features that the Korn shell has
appropriated, including aliases, functions, tilde notation, emacs and vi editing
modes, arithmetic expressions, job control, etc.

The overlap of features between *bash* and the Korn shell has increased in recent
years. It includes many *ksh93* features. But it is not an exact *ksh* clone. The *bash*
FAQ, published monthly by Chet Ramey, lists the following differences between
bash and *ksh93*. Items enclosed in square brackets ([...]) are listed in this book, but
not in the FAQ.

The following new things in *ksh93* are not available in *bash* 2.05:

- Associative arrays

- Floating-point arithmetic and variables

---

* Accordingly, the document that spells out these restrictions is called a *copyleft*.

- Math library functions
- `${!name[sub]}` name of subscript for associative array
- "." is allowed in variable names to create a hierarchical namespace
- More extensive compound assignment syntax
- Discipline functions
- *sleep* and *getconf* built-ins (*bash* has loadable versions)
- *typeset −n* and nameref variables
- The KEYBD trap
- The variables: `.sh.edchar`, `.sh.edmode`, `.sh.edcol`, `.sh.edtext`, `.sh.version`, `.sh.name`, `.sh.subscript`, `.sh.value`, `HISTEDIT` [The `.sh.match` variable also]
- Backreferences in pattern matching (*N*)
- The `&` operator in pattern lists for matching
- *print −f* (*bash* uses *printf*)
- *fc* has been renamed to *hist*
- The dot command (.) can execute shell functions
- Exit statuses between 0 and 255
- The `set -o pipefail` option
- The `+=` variable assignment operator
- `TMOUT` is default timeout for *read* and `select`
- `<&n-` and `>&n-` redirections (combination *dup* and *close*) [Here-strings with `<<<`]
- `FPATH` and `PATH` mixing
- *getopts −a*
- The *−R* invocation option
- DEBUG trap now executed before each simple command, instead of after
- The *printf* `%H`, `%P`, `%T` modifiers, and an output base for `%d` [Also `%Z`.]

The following new things in *ksh93* are present in *bash* 2.05:

- The `for ((...;...;...))` ; `do list; done` arithmetic for command
- The `?:`, `++`, `--`, and comma (,) arithmetic operators
- The shell variable expansions: `${!param}`, `${param:offset[:len]}`, `${param/pat[/str]}`, `${!param*}`
- Compound array assignment

- The ! reserved word
- Loadable built-ins—but *ksh* uses *builtin* while *bash* uses *enable*
- The *command, builtin,* and *disown* built-ins
- New $'...' and $"..." quoting
- FIGNORE (but *bash* uses GLOBIGNORE), HISTCMD
- set -o notify, set -C
- Changes to *kill* built-in
- *read –A* (*bash* uses *read –a*)
- *read –t/ read –d*
- *trap –p*
- *exec –a/ exec –c*
- The dot command (.) restores the positional parameters when it completes
- The *test* command conforms to POSIX.
- *umask –S*
- *unalias –a*
- Command and arithmetic substitution performed on PS1, PS4, and ENV
- Command name completion
- ENV processed only for interactive shells

bash has many features of its own that make it a very powerful and flexible environment. Here are some of the highlights:

- You can put backslash-escapes in the primary prompt string (PS1) for which *bash* substitutes things like the date, time, current working directory, machine name, user name, shell, etc.

- The commands *builtin, command,* and *enable* give you more control over the steps *bash* goes through to look for commands—i.e., *bash*'s analogue to the list of command search steps in Chapter 7.

- The emacs editing mode is customizable, even more so than its equivalent in *pdksh.* You can use the *bind* command to set up your own keystroke preferences, and there are several more commands available—including the ability to undo your last command.

- You can also rebind keystrokes in vi editing mode.

- *pushd* and *popd* are built-in, as they are in the C shell.

- Indexed arrays may be of unlimited size.

- Many new options and variables let you customize your environment with unprecedented flexibility. This includes `set -o posix` for strict POSIX conformance.

We're compelled to say that many users prefer *bash* to the Korn shell. With the increasing popularity of GNU/Linux and various BSD-derived systems, it's not clear which shell has the larger user base. In any case, *bash* is definitely an excellent choice. We recommend the book *Learning the bash Shell* by Cameron Newham and Bill Rosenblatt, published by O'Reilly & Associates. (It is based on the first edition of this book.)

zsh

zsh is a powerful interactive shell and scripting language with many features found in *ksh*, *bash*, and *tcsh*, as well as several unique features. *zsh* has most of the features of *ksh88* but few of *ksh93*. It is freely available and should compile and run on just about any modern version of Unix. Ports for other operating systems are also available. The *zsh* home page is *http://www.zsh.org*. The current version is 4.0.2.

In this section we cover:

- Extended globbing
- Completion
- Command-line editing
- Prompts and prompt themes
- Differences between *zsh* and *ksh*

Extended Globbing

A very useful feature is the recursive glob* operator, `**`. For example, a recursive *grep* is simple to construct:

```
grep foo **/*.c
```

Or to recursively find all files or directories named *core*, try:

```
print **/core
```

---

* *Globbing* is technical slang for wildcard expansion.

Another useful feature is *glob qualifiers*. There are many of these, for example, to print out only regular files in the current directory:

```
print *(.)
```

or just the directories:

```
print *(/)
```

Combining these with the recursive glob operator can be handy. We can improve the above example of finding *core* files by limiting the search to regular files only:

```
print **/core(.)
```

Another qualifier is U for file system objects you own. The following prints all files you own in */tmp* and below:

```
print /tmp/**/*(U)
```

The glob qualifiers can also be combined. For example, using the socket file keyword = in combination with U, it's easy to find socket files in */tmp* and below that you own:

```
print /tmp/**/*(U=)
```

File size qualifiers are also available. For example, to find all files in your home directory that are greater than 10 megabytes in size:

```
print ~/**/*(Lm+10)
```

And file permission qualifiers are also available. For example, the W qualifier selects world-writable file system objects. You can use it to find all directories in your home directory and below that are owned by you and that are world-writeable:

```
print ~/**/*(UW/)
```

See *zshexpn*(1) for more information.

Completion

The *zsh* completion system is extremely sophisticated. The main idea is that any time you are about to type something on the command line, if you hit TAB, *zsh* will try to complete it. *zsh* comes with many defaults for completion and is also fully customizable.

To get a full set of default completion features, run the following commands (normally in your ˜/.zshrc startup file):

```
autoload -U compinit
compinit
```

Now let's look at some examples. We represent the TAB key in examples as [TAB].

First, *zsh* is smart about doing completions. For example, cd[TAB] only expands directories, thus eliminating completion noise.

Have you ever been frustrated because you can't think of exactly the name of the command you want to find more information on, and *man –k*[*] hasn't been configured on your system? Well, *zsh* will complete available man pages for you:

```
g@sifl:pts/7% man zsh[TAB]
zsh           zshcompctl    zshcontrib    zshmodules    zshzftpsys
zshall        zshcompsys    zshexpn       zshoptions    zshzle
zshbuiltins   zshcompwid    zshmisc       zshparam
```

Or maybe you want to find out a process name or PID you want to kill:

```
g@sifl:pts/2% kill [TAB]
 9652 pts/2    00:00:00 zsh
 9653 pts/2    00:00:00 ps
```

For *finger*, it expands users:

```
g@sifl:pts/7% finger o[TAB]
odin      omg      oof         operator      orb
```

and hosts:

```
g@sifl:pts/7% finger oof@[TAB]
brak      localhost      sifl      zorak
```

Using the distributed *compdef* function, you can define your own completions, using either your own custom functions or the completion functions that come with *zsh*. For example, the distribution defines the *kill* command to use the *_pids* distribution function to provide process identifiers. You can also use it to define completion for other commands, such as the Solaris *pstack* command:

```
compdef _pids pstack
```

Once this is done, you can apply completion to the *pstack* command like so:

```
g@sifl:pts/7% pstack [TAB]
13606 pts/7    00:00:00 zsh
13607 pts/7    00:00:00 ps
```

Another very useful distribution completion function is *_gnu_generic*. This can be applied to any command that uses the GNU --long-option command-line option

---

* This does a keyword search of an online database extracted from the man pages.

conventions. The *zsh* distribution specifies many GNU commands to complete
with this function (such as *tar*):

```
g@sifl:pts/7% tar --v[TAB]
--verbose      --verify       --version      --volno-file
```

And this is just the tip of the proverbial iceberg. There is much more to the *zsh*
completion system; see *zshcompsys*(1) for the (gory) details.

Command-Line Editor

The *zsh* command-line editor is extremely powerful. It has several unique features,
including multiline editing and an input buffer stack. The multiline command editor makes composing small scripts on the command line much easier then just
having one line to edit with.

The input buffer stack comes in very handy. While you are typing a command,
you can type ESC q, and the current line is pushed onto the buffer stack. The
input line is then cleared, and you can type another command. When that has
been executed, the previous line is popped off the stack and you can continue
with that command. See *zshzle*(1) for more details.

Prompts and Prompt Themes

While most modern shells have customizable prompts, *zsh* raises it to an art form.
One of the unique features is a right side prompt, RPROMPT, which is very useful for
holding the current directory. This in turn removes clutter from the left hand
prompt:

```
g@sifl:pts/2% RPROMPT='%~'
g@sifl:pts/2%                                              ~/src/xemacs-21.1.14
```

Also, you can define colors and bold fonts, and the prompt can be more than one
line.

And as the notion of *themes** has become popular in GUIs such as GNOME, *zsh*
prompt themes can be defined; the distribution ships with several to choose from.
To enable prompt themes, add these lines to your *~/.zshrc*:

```
autoload -U promptinit
promptinit
```

---

* Some popular GUIs, such as GNOME, support themes. Rather than having one immutable look and
  feel, they can be changed to different styles, or themes. The distributions of these GUIs often contain
  several to choose from. Some of these tend to emulate other GUI's, while others are new and are
  mostly fun window dressing.

To see what themes are available, run:

```
g@sifl:pts/2% prompt -l                                        ~
Currently available prompt themes:
adam1 adam2 bart bigfade clint elite2 elite fade fire off oliver
redhat suse zefram
```

To enable a theme, use the *–s* option. For example:

```
g@sifl:pts/7% prompt -s bart                                   ~
sifl [prompt -s bart] ~                         01-10-04 11:58PM
g@sifl:pts/7%                                                  ~
```

You can see that *bart* is a two-line prompt with several components such as the host name, the previous command, the current directory, and the date and time. See *zshcontrib*(1) for more details on prompt themes.

Differences Between zsh and ksh

This section is derived from information in the *zsh* FAQ.

Most features of *ksh88* (and hence also of the Bourne shell, *sh*) are implemented in *zsh*; problems can arise because the implementation is slightly different. Note also that not all *ksh*'s are the same either. This is based on the 11/16/88f version of *ksh*; differences from *ksh93* are more substantial.

As a summary of the status:

1. Because of all the options, it is not safe to assume a general *zsh* run by a user will behave as if *sh* or *ksh* compatible.

2. Invoking *zsh* as *sh* or *ksh* (or if either is a symbolic link to *zsh*) sets appropriate options and improves compatibility (from within *zsh* itself, calling ARGV0=sh zsh will also work).

3. From Version 3.0 onward, the degree of compatibility with *sh* under these circumstances is very high: *zsh* can now be used with GNU *configure* or *perl*'s *Configure*, for example.

4. The degree of compatibility with *ksh* is also high, but a few things are missing: for example, the more sophisticated pattern-matching expressions are different for versions before 3.1.3—see the detailed list below.

5. Also from 3.0, the command *emulate* is available: emulate ksh and emulate sh set various options as well as changing the effect of single-letter option flags, as if the shell had been invoked with the appropriate name. Including the command emulate sh; setopt localoptions in a shell function turns on *sh* emulation for that function only. In 4.0 (and in 3.0.6 through 8), this can be abbreviated as emulate -L sh.

The classic difference is word splitting: *zsh* keeps the result of plain $variable as one word, even if the variable contains white space. This trips up many beginning *zsh* users. The answer is to set SH_WORD_SPLIT for backward compatibility. The next most classic difference is that unmatched glob patterns cause the command to abort; set NO_NOMATCH for those.

zsh has a large set of options which increase *ksh* compatibility, though maybe decreasing *zsh*'s abilities: see the manual entries for the details. If invoked as *ksh*, the shell sets suitable options.

Here are some differences from *ksh* which might prove significant for *ksh* programmers, some of which may be interpreted as bugs. Note that this list is deliberately rather full and that most of the items are fairly minor. Those marked with † perform in a *ksh*-like manner if the shell is invoked with the name *ksh* or if emulate ksh is in effect. Capitalized words with underscores in their names refer to shell options.

Syntax

- † Shell word splitting: see above.

- † Arrays are (by default) more *csh*-like than *ksh*-like: subscripts start at 1, not 0; array[0] refers to array[1]; $array refers to the whole array, not $array[0]; braces are unnecessary: $a[1] is the same as ${a[1]}, etc. Set the KSH_ARRAYS option for compatibility.

- Coprocesses are established by *coproc*; |& behaves like *csh*.* Handling of coprocess file descriptors is also different.

- For cmd1 && cmd2 &, only *cmd2*, instead of the whole expression, is run in the background in *zsh*. The manual implies that this is a bug. Use { cmd1 && cmd2 } & as a workaround.

Command-line substitutions, globbing, etc.

- † Failure to match a globbing pattern causes an error (use NO_NOMATCH).

- † The results of parameter substitutions are treated as plain text: foo="*"; print $foo prints all files in *ksh* but prints * in *zsh* (use GLOB_SUBST).

- † The prompt variables (e.g., PS1) do not undergo parameter substitution by default (use PROMPT_SUBST).

- † Standard globbing does not allow *ksh*-style pattern-lists. Table A-1 shows equivalent patterns.

---

* In *csh*, |& sends both standard output and standard error down the same pipeline; it is equivalent to ... 2>&1 | ....

The ^, ~ and # (but not |) forms require setting EXTENDED_GLOB. From version 3.1.3, the *ksh* forms are fully supported when the option KSH_GLOB is in effect; for previous versions you must use the equivalents given in Table A-1.

- Unquoted assignments do file expansion after colons (intended for PATH-style variables).

- *integer* does not allow *–i*.

- *typeset* and *integer* have special behavior for assignments in *ksh*, but not in *zsh*. For example, this doesn't work in *zsh*:

    ```
    integer k=$(wc -l ~/.zshrc)
    ```

because the return value from *wc* includes leading whitespace, which causes wordsplitting. *ksh* handles the assignment specially, as a single word.

Table A-1. ksh/zsh pattern equivalents

ksh	zsh	Meaning
!(foo)	^foo	Anything but foo.
	foo1~foo2	Anything matching foo1 but not foo2.[a]
@(foo1|foo2|...)	(foo1|foo2|...)	One of foo1 or foo2 or ...
?(foo)	(foo|)	Zero or one occurrences of foo.
*(foo)	(foo)#	Zero or more occurrences of foo.
+(foo)	(foo)##	One or more occurrences of foo.

[a] Note that ~ is the only globbing operator to have a lower precedence than /. For example, **/foo~*bar* matches any file in a subdirectory called *foo*, except where *bar* occurred somewhere in the path (e.g. *users/barstaff/foo* will be excluded by the ~ operator). As the ** operator cannot be grouped (inside parentheses it is treated as *), this is the way to exclude some subdirectories from matching a **.

Command execution

- † There is no ENV variable (use */etc/zshrc*, *~/.zshrc*; note also $ZDOTDIR).

- $PATH is not searched for commands specified at invocation without *–c*.

Aliases and functions

- The order in which aliases and functions are defined is significant: function definitions with () expand aliases.

- Aliases and functions cannot be exported.

- There are no tracked aliases: command hashing replaces these.

- The use of aliases for key bindings is replaced by *bindkey*.

- † Options are not local to functions (use LOCAL_OPTIONS; note this may always be unset locally to propagate options settings from a function to the calling level).

- Functions defined with function *funcname* { *body* ;} behave the same way as those defined with *funcname* () { *body* ;}. In *ksh93*, only the former behave as true functions, and the latter behave as if the body were read from a file with the dot command.

Traps and signals

- † Traps are not local to functions. The option LOCAL_TRAPS is available from 3.1.6.

- TRAPERR has become TRAPZERR (this was forced by UNICOS which has SIGERR).

Editing

- The options *emacs, gmacs,* and *viraw* are not supported. Use *bindkey* to change the editing behavior: set -o emacs becomes bindkey -e and set -o vi becomes bindkey -v; for *gmacs*, go to emacs-mode and use bindkey \^t gosmacs-transpose-characters.

- The *keyword* option does not exist and *set –k* is instead *interactivecomments*.

- † Management of histories in multiple shells is different: the history list is not saved and restored after each command. The option SHARE_HISTORY appeared in 3.1.6 and is set in *ksh* compatibility mode to remedy this.

- \ does not escape editing chars (use CTRL-V).

- Not all *ksh* bindings are set (e.g. ESC #; try ESC q).

- † # in an interactive shell is not treated as a comment by default.

Built-in commands

- Some built-ins (*r, autoload, history, integer, ...*) are aliases in *ksh*.

- There is no built-in command *newgrp*: use alias newgrp="exec newgrp".

- *jobs* has no *–n* flag.

- *read* has no *–s* flag.

Other idiosyncrasies

- select always redisplays the list of selections on each loop.

Workalikes on PC Platforms

The proliferation of the Korn shell has not stopped at the boundaries of Unix-dom. Many programmers who got their initial experience on Unix systems and subsequently crossed over into the PC world wished for a nice Unix-like environment (especially when faced with the horrors of the MS-DOS command line!), so it's not surprising that several Unix shell-style interfaces to small-computer operating systems have appeared, Korn shell emulations among them.

In the past several years, not just shell clones have appeared, but entire Unix "environments." Two of them use shells that we've already discussed. Two others provide their own shell reimplementations. Providing lists of major and minor differences is counterproductive. Instead, this section describes each environment in turn (in alphabetical order), along with contact and Internet download information.

Cygwin

Cygnus Consulting (now Red Hat), created the *cygwin* environment. First creating *cgywin.dll*, a shared library that provides Unix system call emulation, they ported a large number of GNU utilities to various versions of Microsoft Windows. The emulation includes TCP/IP networking with the Berkeley socket API. The greatest functionality comes under Windows/NT, Windows 2000, and Windows XP, although the environment can and does work under Windows 95/98/ME, as well.

The *cygwin* environment uses *bash* for its shell, GCC for its C compiler, and the rest of the GNU utilities for its Unix toolset. A sophisticated *mount* command provides a mapping of the Windows C:\path notation to Unix filenames.

The starting point for the *cygwin* project is *http://www.cygwin.com*. The first thing to download is an installer program. Upon running it, you choose what additional packages you wish to install. Installation is entirely Internet-based; there are no official *cygwin* CD's, at least not from the project maintainers.

DJGPP

The DJGPP suite provides 32-bit GNU tools for the MS-DOS environment. To quote the web page:

> DJGPP is a complete 32-bit C/C++ development system for Intel 80386 (and higher) PCs running MS-DOS. It includes ports of many GNU development utilities. The development tools require a 80386 or newer computer to run, as do the programs they produce. In most cases, the programs it produces can be sold commercially without license or royalties.

The name comes from the initials of D.J. Delorie, who ported the GNU C++ compiler, *g++* to MS-DOS, and the text initials of *g++*, GPP. It grew into essentially a full Unix environment on top of MS-DOS, with all the GNU tools and *bash* as its shell. Unlike *cygwin* or UWIN (see later in this chapter), you don't need a version of Windows, just a full 32-bit processor and MS-DOS. (Although, of course, you can use DJGPP from within a Windows MS-DOS window.) The web site is *http://www.delorie.com/djgpp/*.

MKS Toolkit

Perhaps the most established Unix environment for the PC world is the MKS Toolkit from Mortice Kern Systems:

> MKS Canada – Corporate Headquarters
> 410 Albert Street
> Waterloo, ON N2L 3V3
> Canada
> (519) 884-2251
> (519) 884-8861 (fax)
> (800) 265-2797 (sales)
> *http://www.mks.com*

The MKS Toolkit comes in various versions depending upon the development environment and the number of developers who will be using it. It includes a shell that is POSIX compliant, along with just about all the features of the 1988 Korn shell, as well as over 300 utilities, such as *awk, perl, vi, make*, and so on. Their library supports over 1500 Unix APIs, making it extremely complete and easing porting to the Windows environment. More information is available at *http://www.mkssoftware.com/products/tk/ds_tkpdev.asp*.

Thompson Automation Software Toolkit

Thompson Automation Software provides the Thompson Toolkit, which includes a shell and over 100 utilities. The toolkit is available MS-DOS 2.1 and higher, OS/2 1.2 or WARP, and for Microsoft Windows 95 and higher. The contact information is:

> Thompson Automation Software
> 5616 SW Jefferson
> Portland, OR 97221
> 1-800-944-0139 (U.S. and Canada)
> 1-503-224-1639 (international/local)
> 1-503-224-3230 (FAX)
> *sales@tasoft.com*
> *http://www.teleport.com/~thompson/*

Thompson software is best known for their implementation of *awk*, which is both fast and reliable, with many powerful extensions to the *awk* language. The toolkit shell is compatible with POSIX and the 1988 version of the Korn shell.

AT&T UWIN

The UWIN package is a project by David Korn and his colleagues to make a Unix environment available under Microsoft Windows. It is similar in structure to *cygwin*, discussed earlier. A shared library, *posix.dll*, provides emulation of the Unix system call APIs. The system call emulation is quite complete. An interesting twist is that the Windows registry can be accessed as a filesystem under */reg*. On top of the Unix API emulation, *ksh93* and over 200 Unix utilities (or rather, reimplementations) have been compiled and run. The UWIN environment relies on the native Microsoft Visual C/C++ compiler, although the GNU development tools are available for download and use with UWIN.

http://www.research.att.com/sw/tools/uwin/ is the web page for the project. It describes what is available, with links for downloading binaries, as well as information on commercial licensing of the UWIN package. Also included are links to various papers on UWIN, additional useful software, and links to other, similar packages.

The most notable advantage to the UWIN package is that its shell *is* the authentic *ksh93*. Thus, compatibility with the Unix version of *ksh93* isn't an issue.

B

Reference Information

This appendix contains reference lists for invocation options, built-in commands and keywords, predefined aliases, built-in shell variables, *test* operators, shell options, *typeset* options, arithmetic, emacs-mode commands, and vi-mode control commands. Furthermore, it describes how to use the full facilities of the built-in *getopts* command.

Invocation Options

Here is a list of the options you can use when invoking the Korn shell. In addition to these, any *set* option can be used on the command line; see the table on options later in this appendix. Login shells are usually invoked with the options *−i* (interactive), *−s* (read from standard input), and *−m* (enable job control).

Option	Meaning
-c *string*	Execute *string*, then exit.
-D	Print all $"..." strings in the script. This is for use in creating a database of locale-specific translations of strings in a script.
-i	Interactive shell. Ignore signals TERM, INTR, and QUIT.
-r	Restricted shell. See Chapter 10.
-R *filename*	Create a cross-reference database for variable and command definitions in *filename*. May not be compiled in.
-s	Read commands from the standard input. If an argument is given, this flag takes precedence (i.e., the argument won't be treated as a script name and standard input will be read).

Built-in Commands and Keywords

Here is a summary of all built-in commands and keywords.

Name	Command / keyword	Chapter	Summary
!	Keyword	5	Invert the true/false result of the following pipeline.
:	Command	7	Do nothing (just do expansions of arguments).
.	Command	4	Read file and execute its contents in current shell.
alias	Command	3	Set up shorthand for command or command line.
bg	Command	8	Put job in background.
builtin	Command		Add or remove built-in commands; print information about them.
break	Command	5	Exit from surrounding for, select, while, or until loop.
case	Keyword	5	Multiway conditional construct.
cd	Command	1	Change working directory.
command	Command	5	Locate built-in and external commands; find a built-in command instead of an identically named function.
continue	Command	4	Skip to next iteration of for, select, while, or until loop.
disown	Command	8	Disassociate a background job from the current shell. The effect is that the job is not sent the HUP signal when the shell exits.
echo	Command	4	Expand and print arguments (obsolete).
exec	Command	9	Replace shell with given program.
exit	Command	5	Exit from shell.
export	Command	3	Create environment variables.
eval	Command	7	Process arguments as a command line.
false	Command	8	Do nothing and exit unsuccessfully. Useful for making infinite loops.
fg	Command	8	Put background job in foreground.
for	Keyword	5	Looping construct.
function	Keyword	4	Define function.
getconf	Command		Get system-specific information. The parameters are defined by POSIX.
getopts	Command	6	Process command-line options.
hist	Command	2	Work with command history.
if	Keyword	5	Conditional construct.
jobs	Command	1	List background jobs.
kill	Command	8	Send signal to process.
let	Command	6	Arithmetic variable assignment.
newgrp	Command		Start new shell with new group ID (obsolete).
print	Command	1	Expand and print arguments on standard output.

Name	Command / keyword	Chapter	Summary
printf	Command	7	Expand and print arguments on standard output, using ANSI C *printf*(3) format specifiers.
pwd	Command	1	Print working directory.
read	Command	7	Read a line from standard input.
readonly	Command	6	Make variables read-only (unassignable).
return	Command	5	Return from surrounding function or script.
select	Keyword	5	Menu generation construct.
set	Command	3	Set options.
shift	Command	6	Shift command-line arguments.
sleep	Command	8	Suspend execution for the given number of seconds.
test	Command	5	Old version of conditional test program. Use [[...]] instead.
time	Keyword		Run command and print execution times. By itself, prints cumulative times for the shell and all children.
trap	Command	8	Set up signal-catching routine.
true	Command	8	Do nothing and exit successfully. Useful for making infinite loops.
typeset	Command	6	Set special characteristics of variables and functions.
ulimit	Command	10	Set/show process resource limits.
umask	Command	10	Set/show file permission mask.
unalias	Command	3	Remove alias definitions.
unset	Command	3	Remove definitions of variables or functions.
until	Keyword	5	Looping construct.
wait	Command	8	Wait for background job(s) to finish.
whence	Command	3	Identify source of command.
while	Keyword	5	Looping construct.

Assignments for the *alias, export, readonly*, and *typeset* commands are processed like variable assignments, in that tilde expansion is done after the = character, and field splitting is not done on any variable substitutions in the value being assigned.

Predefined Aliases

A number of aliases are predefined, i.e. automatically built-in to *ksh* at compile time. They are listed in the table below. Note that some of them are defined with a trailing space character. This enables alias expansion on the word following the alias on the command line.

Name	Chapter	Full value
autoload	4, 6	`alias autoload='typeset -fu'`
command	7	`alias command='command '`
fc	2	`alias fc=hist`

Name	Chapter	Full value
float	6	alias float='typeset -E'
functions	6	alias functions='typeset -f'
hash	3	alias hash='alias -t --'
history	2	alias history='hist -l'
integer	6	alias integer='typeset -i'
nameref	4	alias nameref='typeset -n'
nohup	3, 8	alias nohup='nohup '
r	2	alias r='hist -s'
redirect	9	alias redirect='command exec'
stop	8	alias stop='kill -s STOP'
times		alias times='{ {time;} 2>&1;}'
type	4	alias type='whence -v'

Built-in Shell Variables

Here is a summary of all built-in shell variables:

Variable	Chapter	Meaning
#	4	Number of arguments given to current process.
@	4	Command-line arguments to current process. Inside double quotes, expands to individual arguments.
*	4	Command-line arguments to current process. Inside double quotes, expands to a single argument.
- (hyphen)		Options given to shell on invocation.
?	5	Exit status of previous command.
$	8	Process ID of shell process.
_ (underscore)	3	Inside $MAILPATH: the filename that triggered a "you have mail" message. On the command line: last argument to previous command. Inside a script: the full pathname used to find and run the script.
!	8	Process ID of last background command.
.sh.edchar	10	Characters entered when processing a KEYBD trap.
.sh.edcol	10	Position of the cursor in the most recent KEYBD trap.
.sh.edmode	10	Equal to ESC in vi-mode, empty otherwise.
.sh.edtext	10	Characters in the input buffer during a KEYBD trap.
.sh.match	4	Array variable with text that matched pattern in variable substitution. (Starting with *ksh93l*.)
.sh.name	9	Name of a variable executing a discipline function.
.sh.subscript	9	Subscript of an array variable executing a discipline function.
.sh.value	9	Value of the variable executing a discipline function.
.sh.version	4, 9	Version of *ksh*.
CDPATH	3	List of directories for *cd* command to search.
COLUMNS	3	Width of display in columns (for editing modes and select).

Variable	Chapter	Meaning
EDITOR	2	Used to set editing mode; also used by *mail* and other programs. Overriden by VISUAL, if that is set.
ENV	3	Name of file to run as environment file when shell is invoked.
FCEDIT	2	Obsolete default editor for *hist* command.
FIGNORE	1	Pattern for files to ignore during pattern expansion.
FPATH	4	Search path for autoloaded functions.
HISTCMD	2	Number of current command in command history.
HISTEDIT	2	Default editor for *hist* command.
HISTFILE	2	Name of command history file.
HISTSIZE	2	Number of lines kept in history file.
HOME	3	Home (login) directory.
IFS	7	Internal field separator: list of characters that act as word separators. Normally set to space, TAB, and newline.
LANG		Default name of current locale; overridden by the other LC_* variables.
LC_ALL		Name of current locale; overrides LANG and the other LC_* variables.
LC_COLLATE		Name of current locale for character collation (sorting) purposes.
LC_CTYPE		Name of current locale for character class determination during pattern matching; see Chapter 4.
LC_NUMERIC		Name of current locale for number formatting (decimal point, thousands separator).
LINENO	9	Number of line in script or function that just ran.
LINES	3	Height of display in lines (for select command).
MAIL	3	Name of file to check for new mail.
MAILCHECK	3	How often (in seconds) to check for new mail.
MAILPATH	3	List of file names to check for new mail, if MAIL is not set.
OLDPWD	3	Previous working directory.
OPTARG	6	Argument to option being processed by *getopts*.
OPTIND	6	Number of first argument after options.
PATH	3	Search path for commands.
PPID	8	Process ID of parent process.
PS1	3	Primary command prompt string.
PS2	3	Prompt string for line continuations.
PS3	5	Prompt string for select command.
PS4	9	Prompt string for *xtrace* option.
PWD	3	Current working directory.
RANDOM	9	Random number between 0 and 32767 ($2^{15}-1$).
REPLY	5, 7	User's response to select command; result of *read* command if no variable names given.
SECONDS	3	Number of seconds since shell was invoked.
SHELL	3	Full pathname of shell programs should use to run commands.

Variable	Chapter	Meaning
TMOUT	5, 7, 10	If set to a positive integer, number of seconds between commands after which shell automatically terminates. Also applies to reading responses to select and *read*.
VISUAL	2	Used to set editing mode.

Test Operators

These are the operators that are used with the [[...]] construct. They can be logically combined with && ("and") and || ("or") and grouped with parenthesis. When used with filenames of the form /dev/fd/*N*, they test the corresponding attribute of open file descriptor *N*.

Operator	True if...
-a *file*	*file* exists. (Obsolete. -e is preferred.)
-b *file*	*file* is a block device file.
-c *file*	*file* is a character device file.
-C *file*	*file* is a contiguous file. (Not for most Unix versions.)
-d *file*	*file* is a directory.
-e *file*	*file* exists.
-f *file*	*file* is a regular file.
-g *file*	*file* has its setgid bit set.
-G *file*	*file*'s group ID is the same as the effective group ID of the shell.
-h *file*	*file* is a symbolic link.
-k *file*	*file* has its sticky bit set.
-l *file*	*file* is a symbolic link. (Only works on systems where */bin/test −l* tests for symbolic links.)
-L *file*	*file* is a symbolic link.
-n *string*	*string* is non-null.
-o *option*	*option* is set.
-O *file*	*file* is owned by the shell's effective user ID.
-p *file*	*file* is a pipe or named pipe (FIFO file).
-r *file*	*file* is readable.
-s *file*	*file* is not empty.
-S *file*	*file* is a socket.
-t *N*	File descriptor *N* points to a terminal.
-u *file*	*file* has its setuid bit set.
-w *file*	*file* is writable.
-x *file*	*file* is executable, or *file* is a directory that can be searched.
-z *string*	*string* is null.
fileA -nt *fileB*	*fileA* is newer than *fileB*, or *fileB* does not exist.
fileA -ot *fileB*	*fileA* is older than *fileB*, or *fileB* does not exist.
fileA -ef *fileB*	*fileA* and *fileB* point to the same file.

Operator	True if...
string = pattern	*string* matches *pattern* (which can contain wildcards). Obsolete; == is preferred.
string == pattern	*string* matches *pattern* (which can contain wildcards).
string != pattern	*string* does not match *pattern*.
stringA < stringB	*stringA* comes before *stringB* in dictionary order.
stringA > stringB	*stringA* comes after *stringB* in dictionary order.
exprA -eq exprB	Arithmetic expressions *exprA* and *exprB* are equal.
exprA -ne exprB	Arithmetic expressions *exprA* and *exprB* are not equal.
exprA -lt exprB	*exprA* is less than *exprB*.
exprA -gt exprB	*exprA* is greater than *exprB*.
exprA -le exprB	*exprA* is less than or equal to *exprB*.
exprA -ge exprB	*exprA* is greater than or equal to *exprB*.

The operators *−eq*, *−ne*, *−lt*, *−le*, *−gt*, and *−ge* are considered obsolete in *ksh93*; the *let* command or ((...)) should be used instead.

For =, ==, and !=, quote *pattern* to do literal string comparisons.

Options

These are options that can be turned on with the *set −o* command. All are initially off except where noted. Abbreviations, where listed, are options to *set* that can be used instead of the full *set −o* command (e.g., set -a is an abbreviation for set -o allexport). For the most part, the abbreviations are actually backward-compatible Bourne shell options. To disable an option, use *set +o long-name* or *set +X*, where *long-name* and *X* are the long form or the single character form of the option, respectively.

Option	Abbrev	Meaning
allexport	-a	Export all subsequently defined variables.
bgnice		Run all background jobs at decreased priority (on by default).
emacs		Use Emacs-style command-line editing.
errexit	-e	Exit the shell when a command exits with nonzero status.
gmacs		Use Emacs-style command-line editing, but with a slightly different meaning for CTRL-T (See Chapter 2).
ignoreeof		Disallow CTRL-D to exit the shell.
keyword	-k	Execute assignments in the middle of command lines. (Very obsolete.)
markdirs		Add / to all directory names generated from wildcard expansion.
monitor	-m	Enable job control (on by default).
noclobber	-C	Don't allow > redirection to existing files.
noexec	-n	Read commands and check for syntax errors, but don't execute them.

Option	Abbrev	Meaning
noglob	-f	Disable wildcard expansion.
nolog		Disable command history for function definitions.
notify	-b	Print job completion messages right away, instead of waiting for next prompt.
nounset	-u	Treat undefined variables as errors, not as null.
pipefail		Wait for all jobs in a pipeline to complete. Exit status is that of last command that failed, or zero otherwise. (*ksh93g* and later.)
privileged	-p	Script is running in *suid* mode.
trackall	-h	Create an alias for each full pathname found in a command search. (*ksh93* ignores this option; the behavior is always on, even if this option is turned off.)
verbose	-v	Print commands (verbatim) before running them.
vi		Use *vi*-style command-line editing.
viraw		Use vi-mode and have each keystroke take effect immediately. (This is required on some very old systems for vi-mode to work at all, and is necessary on all systems in order to use TAB for completion. Starting with *ksh93n*, it is automatically enabled when vi-mode is being used.)
xtrace	-x	Print commands (after expansions) before running them.

The *set* command has a few additional options that don't have corresponding *set* −*o* versions, as follows:

Option	Meaning
set -A ...	Indexed array assignment.
set -s	Sort the positional parameters.
set -t	Read and execute one command, and then exit. (Obsolete.)

Typeset Options

These are the options to the *typeset* command. Use +*option* to turn an option off, e.g., typeset +x foo to stop exporting the variable foo.

Option	Meaning
	With no option, create local variable within function.
-A	Declare variable as an associative array.
-E[*n*]	Declare variable as a floating-point number. Optional *n* is number of significant figures.
-F[*n*]	Declare variable as a floating-point number. Optional *n* is number of significant digits.
-f	With no arguments, prints all function definitions.
-f *fname*	Print the definition of function *fname*.
+f	Print all function names.

Option	Meaning
-ft	Turn on trace mode for named function(s).
+ft	Turn off trace mode for named function(s).
-fu	Define given name(s) as autoloaded function(s).
-fx	Obsolete; does nothing in *ksh93*.
-H	Unix to host filename mapping for non-Unix system.
-i[*n*]	Declare variable as an integer. Optional *n* is output base.
-l	Convert all letters to lowercase.
-L	Left-justify and remove leading spaces.
-n	Declare variable as a nameref.
-p	Print *typeset* commands to re-create variables with the same attributes.
-r	Make variable read-only.
-R	Right-justify and remove trailing spaces.
-t	Tag the variable. (Obsolete.)
-u	Convert all letters to uppercase.
-ui[*n*]	Declare variable as an unsigned integer. Optional *n* is output base. (*ksh93m* and newer.)
-x	Export variable, i.e., put in environment so that it is passed to subprocesses.
-z[*n*]	Right-justify and fill with leading zeros. *n* is width, or width is set from value used in first assignment.

Arithmetic

Starting with *ksh93m*, the built-in arithmetic facility understands a large percentage of the C language's expressions. This makes the shell more attractive as a full-blown programming language. The following features are available:

Trailing type suffixes

Integer constants can have a trailing U or L suffix to indicate that they are unsigned or long, respectively. While the lowercase versions may also be used, this is not recommended, since it is easy to confuse an l (letter ell) with a 1 (digit one).

C character constants

C single-quoted character constants are recognized. As in C, they act like integer constants. For example:

```
$ typeset -i c
$ for ((c = 'a'; c <= 'z'; c++))
> do print $c
> done
97
98
99
100
...
```

Octal and hexadecimal constants

You can use the C format for octal (base 8) and hexadecimal (base 16) constants. Octal constants start with a leading 0, and hexadecimal constants start with a leading 0x or 0X. For example:

```
$ print $((010 + 1))        Octal 10 is decimal 8
9
$ print $((0x10 + 1))       Hexadecimal 10 is decimal 16
17
```

Unsigned integer arithmetic

By using *typeset −ui*, you can create unsigned integers. Regular integers represent both positive and negative numbers. Unsigned integers start at 0, go up to some implementation-dependent value, and then "wrap" around again to 0. Similarly, subtracting 1 from 0 wraps around the other way, yielding the largest unsigned number:

```
$ typeset -ui u=0
$ let u--
$ print $u
4294967295
```

C operators and precedence

ksh supports the full set of C operators, with the same precedence and associativity. The operators were presented in detail in Chapter 6 and are summarized again below.

Operator	Meaning	Associativity
++ −−	Increment and decrement, prefix and postfix	Left to right
+ − ! ~	Unary plus and minus; logical and bitwise negation	Right to left
**	Exponentiation[a]	Right to left
* / %	Multiplication, division, and remainder	Left to right
+ −	Addition and subtraction	Left to right
<< >>	Bit-shift left and right	Left to right
< <= > >=	Comparisons	Left to right
== !=	Equal and not equal	Left to right
&	Bitwise and	Left to right
^	Bitwise exclusive-or	Left to right
|	Bitwise or	Left to right
&&	Logical and (short circuit)	Left to right
||	Logical or (short circuit)	Left to right
?:	Conditional expression	Right to left
= += −= *= /= %= &= ^= <<= >>=	Assignment operators	Right to left
,	Sequential evaluation	Left to right

[a] *ksh93m* and newer. The ** operator is not in the C language.

Emacs Mode Commands

Here is a complete list of all emacs editing mode commands. Some of these, such as "ESC [A," represent ANSI standard terminal arrow key sequences; they were added for *ksh93h*.

Command	Meaning
CTRL-A	Move to beginning of line
CTRL-B	Move backward one character without deleting
CTRL-C	Capitalize character after point
CTRL-D	Delete one character forward
CTRL-E	Move to end of line
CTRL-F	Move forward one character
CTRL-I (TAB)	Do filename completion on current word (starting with *ksh93h*)
CTRL-J	Same as ENTER.
CTRL-K	Delete ("kill") forward to end of line
CTRL-L	Redisplay the line
CTRL-M	Same as ENTER
CTRL-N	Next line
CTRL-O	Same as ENTER, then display next line in history file
CTRL-P	Previous line
CTRL-R	Search backward
CTRL-T	Transpose the two characters on either side of point
CTRL-U	Repeat the following command four times
CTRL-V	Print the version of the Korn shell
CTRL-W	Delete ("wipe") all characters between point and mark
CTRL-X CTRL-E	Invoke the *emacs* program on the current command
CTRL-X CTRL-X	Exchange point and mark
CTRL-Y	Retrieve ("yank") last item deleted
CTRL-] *x*	Search forward for *x*, where *x* is any character
CTRL-@	Set mark at point
DEL	Delete one character backward
CTRL-[	Same as ESC (most keyboards)
ESC b	Move one word backward
ESC c	Change word after point to all capital letters
ESC d	Delete one word forward
ESC f	Move one word forward
ESC h	Delete one word backward
ESC l	Change word after point to all lowercase letters
ESC p	Save characters between point and mark as if deleted
ESC CTRL-H	Delete one word backward
ESC CTRL-] *x*	Search backward for *x*, where *x* is any character
ESC SPACE	Set mark at point
ESC #	Insert line in history file for future editing

Command	Meaning
ESC DEL	Delete one word backward
ESC <	Move to first line of history file
ESC >	Move to last line of history file
ESC .	Insert last word in previous command line after point
ESC _	Same as above
ESC ESC	Do filename/command/variable completion on current word
ESC *	Do filename/command/variable expansion on current word
ESC =	Do filename/command/variable listing on current word
ESC [A	Previous line (*ksh93h* and newer)
ESC [B	Next line (*ksh93h* and newer)
ESC [C	Move forward one character (*ksh93h* and newer)
ESC [D	Move backward one character (without deleting) (*ksh93h* and newer)
ESC [H	Move to beginning of line (*ksh93h* and newer)
ESC [Y	Move to end of line (*ksh93h* and newer)
Kill	The *stty*(1) kill character, often CTRL-U or @ or CTRL-X. This erases everything on the line. Typing it twice toggles "line feed" mode, which issues a line-feed character to start over on a new line. This is appropriate for paper-only terminals

vi Control Mode Commands

Here is a complete list of all vi-mode control commands. As for the emacs mode commands, the sequences such as "[A" are for ANSI standard terminal arrow keys and were added for *ksh93h*.

Command	Meaning
h	Move left one character
[D	Move left one character (*ksh93h* and newer)
l	Move right one character
space	Move right one character
[C	Move right one character (*ksh93h* and newer)
w	Move right one word
b	Move left one word
W	Move to beginning of next nonblank word
B	Move to beginning of preceding nonblank word
e	Move to end of current word
E	Move to end of current nonblank word
0	Move to beginning of line
[H	Move to beginning of line (*ksh93h* and newer)
^	Move to first nonblank character in line
$	Move to end of line
[Y	Move to end of line (*ksh93h* and newer)

Command	Meaning
i	Insert text before current character
a	Insert text after current character
I	Insert text at beginning of line
A	Insert text at end of line
r	Replace one character (doesn't enter input mode)
R	Overwrite existing text
dh	Delete one character backwards
dl	Delete one character forwards
db	Delete one word backwards
dw	Delete one word forwards
dB	Delete one nonblank word backwards
dW	Delete one nonblank word forwards
d$	Delete to end of line
d0	Delete to beginning of line
D	Equivalent to d$ (delete to end of line)
dd	Equivalent to 0d$ (delete entire line)
C	Equivalent to c$ (delete to end of line, enter input mode)
cc	Equivalent to 0c$ (delete entire line, enter input mode)
s	Equivalent to xi (delete current character, enter input mode)
S	Equivalent to cc (delete entire line, enter input mode)
x	Equivalent to dl (delete character backwards)
X	Equivalent to dh (delete character forwards)
k or -	Move backward one line
[A	Move backward one line (*ksh93h* and newer)
j or +	Move forward one line
[B	Move forward one line (*ksh93h* and newer)
G	Move to line given by repeat count
/string	Search forward for *string*
?string	Search backward for *string*
n	Repeat search forward
N	Repeat search backward
f *x*	Move right to next occurrence of *x*
F *x*	Move left to previous occurrence of *x*
t *x*	Move right to next occurrence of *x*, then back one space
T *x*	Move left to previous occurrence of *x*, then forward one space
yh	Yank one character backwards
yl	Yank one character forwards
yb	Yank one word backwards
yw	Yank one word forwards
yB	Yank one nonblank word backwards
yW	Yank one nonblank word forwards
y$	Yank to end of line
y0	Yank to beginning of line

Command	Meaning
Y	Equivalent to y$ (yank to end of line)
yy	Equivalent to 0y$ (yank entire line)
u	Undo last editing change
U	Undo all editing changes made to the line
. (dot)	Repeat last editing command
|	Move to absolute column position
;	Redo last character finding command
,	Redo last character finding command, but in opposite direction
%	Move to matching (,), {, }, [, or]
\	Do filename/command/variable completion
CTRL-I (TAB)	Do filename/command/variable completion (only for *set –o viraw*) (starting with *ksh93h*)
*	Do filename/command/variable expansion (onto command line)
=	Do filename/command/variable expansion (as printed list)
~	Invert ("twiddle") case of current character(s)
_	Append last word of previous command, enter input mode
v	Run the *hist* command on the current line (actually, run the command hist -e ${VISUAL:-${EDITOR:-vi}}); usually this means run the full *vi* on the current line
CTRL-J	Same as ENTER
CTRL-L	Start a new line and redraw the current line on it
CTRL-M	Same as ENTER
CTRL-V	Print the version of the Korn shell
#	Prepend # (comment character) to the line and send it. If the line starts with #, remove the leading # and all leading # characters after any embedded newlines
@ *x*	Insert expansion of alias _*x* as command mode input

Using getopts

The *getopts* command is extremely capable. With it, you can make your shell scripts accept long options, specify that arguments are optional or numeric, and provide descriptions of the arguments and values such that the –?, ––*man*, ––*html* and ––*nroff* options work the same for your program as they do for the *ksh93* built-in commands.

The price for this power is the complexity of the option description "language." Based on a description provided by Dr. Glenn Fowler of AT&T Research, we describe how the facilities evolved, how they work, and summarize how to use them in your own programs. We use the the extended *getopts* command in the solution to Task B-1.

Task B-1

Design the program *phaser4*, that combines the features of the *phaser3* and *tricorder* programs. Make sure it is self-documenting.*

The first step is to describe the options. This is done with a comment at the top of the script:

```
# usage: phaser4 [ options ] files
#    -k, --kill              use kill setting (default)
#    -l n, --level n         set phaser level (default = 2)
#    -s, --stun              use stun-only setting
#    -t [lf], --tricorder [lf]   tricorder mode, opt. scan for life form lf
```

Now the fun begins. This outline of capabilities follows the order in which features were added to *getopts*.

1. Start with the *getopts* command as described in Chapter 6. This yields a simple option string that only allows one-letter options:

    ```
    USAGE="kl#st:"
    while getopts "$USAGE" optchar ...
    ```

2. Add a textual description for the option argument. This is done by enclosing arbitrary text in between [and]:

    ```
    USAGE="kl#[level]st:[life_form]"
    while getopts "$USAGE" optchar ...
    ```

3. Allow a default value for an option's argument. This is done by specifying := *value* within the description in between the brackets:

    ```
    USAGE="kl#[level:=2]st:[life_form]"
    while getopts "$USAGE" optchar ...
    ```

4. Add ? after the : to indicate an optional argument:

    ```
    USAGE="kl#[level:=2]st:?[life_form]"
    while getopts "$USAGE" optchar ...
    ```

5. Allow long options that start with --. This is done by using [*let*:*long*] *instead of* the single option letter:

    ```
    USAGE="[k:kill]"
    USAGE+="[l:level]#[level:=2]"
    USAGE+="[s:stun]"
    USAGE+="[t:tricorder]:?[life_form]"
    while getopts "$USAGE" optchar ...
    ```

---

* No, the walls of my room are not covered with Star Trek posters. I outgrew that a long time ago, and besides, my wife wouldn't let me anyway. ADR.

Here, we've split each option out into its own line, to make things easier to follow, and concatenated them together using the += assignment operator. Note that there are no newlines in the string.

6. Within the square brackets for an option letter, allow descriptive text to follow a question mark. This text is ignored, as are any whitespace characters, including newlines:

```
USAGE="[k:kill?Use kill setting (default).]"
USAGE+="[l:level]#[level:=2?Set the phaser level.]"
USAGE+="[s:stun?Stun-only.]"
USAGE+="[t:tricorder?Tricorder mode.]:?[life_form]"
while getopts "$USAGE" optchar ...
```

7. Now it gets interesting. Unix man page style section headings come *before* the option description. They are distinguished from option descriptions by starting with a + inside square brackets:

```
USAGE="[+NAME?phaser4 --- combined phaser and tricorder]"
USAGE+="[+DESCRIPTION?The phaser4 program combines the operation "
USAGE+="of the phaser3 and tricorder programs in one handy tool.]"
USAGE+="[k:kill?Use kill setting (default).]"
USAGE+="[l:level]#[level:=2?Set the phaser level.]"
USAGE+="[s:stun?Stun-only.]"
USAGE+="[t:tricorder?Tricorder mode.]:?[life_form]"
while getopts "$USAGE" optchar ...
```

Note that *getopts* automatically understands that the actual options description comes after the man page headings; there is no explicit [+OPTIONS?...] in the text of the string.

8. Additional descriptive text for the short usage summary can be given after the options description, separated by two newlines:

```
USAGE="[+NAME?phaser4 --- combined phaser and tricorder]"
USAGE+="[+DESCRIPTION?The phaser4 program combines the operation "
USAGE+="of the phaser3 and tricorder programs in one handy tool.]"
USAGE+="[k:kill?Use kill setting (default).]"
USAGE+="[l:level]#[level:=2?Set the phaser level.]"
USAGE+="[s:stun?Stun-only.]"
USAGE+="[t:tricorder?Tricorder mode.]:?[life_form]"
USAGE+=$'\n\nfile ...\n\n'          Use ANSI C string for \n character
USAGE+="[+SEE ALSO?phaser3(1), tricorder(1)]"
while getopts "$USAGE" optchar ...
```

9. To indicate text to be italicized, enclose it in between pairs of \a characters. To indicate text to be emboldened, enclose it between pairs of \b:

```
USAGE="[+NAME?phaser4 --- combined phaser and tricorder]"
USAGE+="[+DESCRIPTION?The \aphaser4\a program combines the operation "
USAGE+="of the \aphaser3\a and \atricorder\a programs in one handy tool.]"
USAGE+="[k:kill?Use kill setting (default).]"
USAGE+="[l:level]#[level:=2?Set the phaser level.]"
```

```
USAGE+="[s:stun?Stun-only.]"
USAGE+="[t:tricorder?Tricorder mode.]:?[life_form]"
USAGE+=$'\n\nfile ...\n\n'
USAGE+=$'[+SEE ALSO?\aphaser3\a(1), \atricorder\a(1)]'
while getopts "$USAGE" optchar ...
```

10. Dynamic control of descriptive output is possible. To do this, write a function that prints whatever you want, and then enclose the function name in a pair of \f characters: \f*name*\f (this isn't needed for *phaser4*).

11. If an option (or anything else) needs a verbose description, enclosing the text between { and } creates an indented list. This is particularly useful for describing different option values:

```
USAGE="[+NAME?phaser4 --- combined phaser and tricorder]"
USAGE+="[+DESCRIPTION?The \aphaser4\a program combines the operation "
USAGE+="of the \aphaser3\a and \atricorder\a programs in one handy tool.]"
USAGE+="[k:kill?Use kill setting (default).]"
USAGE+="[l:lev*el]#[level:=2?Set the phaser level.]{    Add value descriptions
               [level=0-2?non-lethal settings]
               [level=3-10?lethal, use with caution]
       }"
USAGE+="[s:stun?Stun-only.]"
USAGE+="[t:tricorder?Tricorder mode.]:?[life_form]"
USAGE+=$'\n\nfile ...\n\n'
USAGE+=$'[+SEE ALSO?\aphaser3\a(1), \atricorder\a(1)]'
while getopts "$USAGE" optchar ...
```

12. Almost done. Text in between square brackets that begins with a minus sign provides version and identification information. Such text comes at the very beginning. The empty item indicates a version and may contain both SCCS and RCS ID strings as shown here:

```
USAGE=$'[-?\n@(#)$Id: phaser4 (Starfleet Research and Development)'
USAGE+=$' Stardate 57234.22 $\n]'
USAGE+="[-author?J. Programmer <J.Prog@r-d.starfleet.mil.fed>]"
USAGE+="[-copyright?Copyright (c) Stardate 57000 Starfleet.]"
USAGE+="[-license?http://www.starfleet.mil.fed/weapons-license.xml23]"
USAGE+="[+NAME?phaser4 --- combined phaser and tricorder]"
USAGE+="[+DESCRIPTION?The \aphaser4\a program combines the operation "
USAGE+="of the \aphaser3\a and \atricorder\a programs in one handy tool.]"
USAGE+="[k:kill?Use kill setting (default).]"
USAGE+="[l:lev*el]#[level:=2?Set the phaser level.]{
               [level=0-2?non-lethal settings]
               [level=3-10?lethal, use with caution]
       }"
USAGE+="[s:stun?Stun-only.]"
USAGE+="[t:tricorder?Tricorder mode.]:?[life_form]"
USAGE+=$'\n\nfile ...\n\n'
USAGE+=$'[+SEE ALSO?\aphaser3\a(1), \atricorder\a(1)]'
while getopts "$USAGE" optchar ...
```

13. Finally, allow escapes within the strings.]] represents a literal] when *getopts* might otherwise take it to mean a closing bracket. Similarly, ?? stands for a literal ? that might otherwise start a description.

Whew! That's a lot of stuff. However, seeing it in the order it was added helps it to make sense. Here is a summary of the items that go in the usage string, in the order that *getopts* requires:

1. Identification strings for the version, author, license, and so on are the very first part. They are enclosed in square brackets and begin with a minus sign. The item name, such as author, follows the minus sign and ends at a question mark. Following the question mark is the associated information.

   The empty item indicates version information, and should be of the form as shown earlier; *getopts* strips out the special SCCS and RCS identification characters.

2. Unix man page–style section headings and text come next. These are enclosed in square brackets and begin with a + sign. The section heading name ends at the ? character, and the descriptive text follows.

   Text separated by two successive newlines from the options description is appended to the short usage message.

3. Option descriptions form the third section. The original short form as described in Chapter 6 is still allowed:

   - Use : for options that require arguments.

   - Use # for options that require numeric arguments.

   - Use :? and #? for options that allow arguments but don't require them.

4. Follow options by descriptive text in between [and]. Use := within the descriptive text to specify a default value for an option argument.

5. Long options are matched with a short option letter by enclosing them in square brackets, separated by a colon. This replaces the single letter form.

6. Enclose items to be italicized between two \a characters. Enclose items to be emboldened between two \b characters. Enclose the name of a customizing function to call between two \f characters.

7. Use { and } to enclose nested, indented option descriptions.

8. Follow the options section with two newlines and additional text for the short options summary.

9. Use]] to represent a literal] and ?? to represent a literal ?.

Here is the skeletal version of *phaser4*:

```ksh
#! /bin/ksh

# usage: phaser4 [ options ] files
#   -k, --kill              use kill setting (default)
#   -l n, --level n         set phaser level (default = 2)
#   -s, --stun              use stun-only setting
#   -t [lf], --tricorder [lf]   tricorder mode, opt. scan for life form lf

USAGE=$'[-?\n@(#)$Id: phaser4 (Starfleet Research and Development)'
USAGE+=$' Stardate 57234.22 $\n]'
USAGE+="[-author?J. Programmer <J.Prog@r-d.starfleet.mil.fed>]"
USAGE+="[-copyright?Copyright (c) Stardate 57000 Starfleet.]"
USAGE+="[-license?http://www.starfleet.mil.fed/weapons-license.xml23]"
USAGE+="[+NAME?phaser4 --- combined phaser and tricorder]"
USAGE+="[+DESCRIPTION?The \aphaser4\a program combines the operation "
USAGE+="of the \aphaser3\a and \atricorder\a programs in one handy tool.]"
USAGE+="[k:kill?Use kill setting (default).]"
USAGE+="[l:lev*el]#[level:=2?Set the phaser level.]{
                [0-2?non-lethal settings]
                [3-10?lethal, use with caution]
}"
USAGE+="[s:stun?Stun-only.]"
USAGE+="[t:tricorder?Tricorder mode.]:?[life_form]"
USAGE+=$'\n\nfile ...\n\n'
USAGE+=$'[+SEE ALSO?\aphaser3\a(1), \atricorder\a(1)]'

kill=1 stun=0 level=2    # defaults
tricorder=0 phaser=1
life_form=
while getopts "$USAGE" optchar ; do
    case $optchar in
    k)  kill=1 stun=0 ;;
    s)  kill=0 stun=1 ;;
    l)  level=$OPTARG
        if ((level < 0)) ; then level=0 ; fi
        if ((level > 10)) ; then level=10 ; fi
        ;;
    t)  phaser=0 tricorder=1
        life_form=${OPTARG:-"general_unknown"}
        ;;
    esac
done

print kill=$kill
print stun=$stun
print level=$level
print phaser=$phaser
print tricorder=$tricorder
print life_form=$life_form
```

Here is the output from phaser4 --man:

NAME

    phaser4 --- combined phaser and tricorder

SYNOPSIS

    phaser4 [**options**] file ...

DESCRIPTION

    The **phaser4** program combines the operation of the **phaser3** and **tricorder**
    programs in one handy tool.

OPTIONS

    -**k**, --**kill**   Use kill setting (default).

    -**l**, --**level=level**

               Set the phaser level.

                 level=0-2

                      non-lethal settings

                 level=3-10

                      lethal, use with caution

               The default value is 2.

    -**s**, --**stun**   Stun-only.

    -**t**, --**tricorder**[=**life form**]

               Tricorder mode. The option value may be omitted.

SEE ALSO

    phaser3(1), **tricorder**(1)

IMPLEMENTATION

    version   phaser4 (Starfleet Research and Development) Stardate
               57234.22

    author   J. Programmer <J.Prog@r-d.starfleet.mil.fed>

    copyright   Copyright (c) Stardate 57000 Starfleet.

    license   http://www.starfleet.mil.fed/weapons-license.xml23

C

Building ksh from Source Code

This appendix describes how to download binaries for *ksh93*, as well as how to download the source code for *ksh93* and build a working version. You should do this if your system does not have *ksh93* at all or if you need any of the features that are only available in the most recent releases.

Korn Shell Web Sites

The starting place for all things related to the Korn shell is *http://www.korn-shell.com*, maintained by David Korn, with links grouped by the following topics:

Information
> Clicking this link leads to a one-page overview on the Korn shell.

Software
> Clicking this link leads to pointers to the AT&T download site (see the next section), some sample code, an online article for *dtksh*, and a link for *tksh*. These last two are described in Appendix A.

Documentation
> This link leads to a page with pointers to online info, including general information, man pages for both *ksh88* and *ksh93*, books and references on the Korn shell, and papers about the Korn shell from various conferences.

Resources
> A list of links to other WWW resources for *ksh* and many of the other shells described in Appendix A, such as *bash* and *dtksh*.

Fun
> David G. Korn, the programmer, meets KoRN, the rock group. 'Nuff said.

What You Can Download

http://www.research.att.com/sw/download is the starting point for actually downloading the *ksh* software. The software is covered by an Open Source–style license. The current version of the license is at *http://www.research.att.com/sw/license/ast-open.html*. This license is reproduced in Appendix D. You should read and understand it first; if its terms aren't acceptable to you, you should not download the software source code or binaries from the AT&T web site.

The software on the AT&T web site is available in different "packages," most of which have names prefixed with "ast," which stands for "Advanced Software Tools." The source packages come as *gzip*ed *tar* files, using the *.tgz* file name suffix. Choose one or more of the following packages to download:

ratz

> A standalone executable program for reading *gzip*ed *tar* files. Use this if you don't have *gzip* on your system and don't want to go to the trouble to first download and build *gzip*. You may download source code for this package or a binary executable for any of the architectures listed in Table C-1.

ksh

> This is the fastest way to get a *ksh93* executable. Versions are available for the architectures listed in Table C-1.

INIT

> This package must be downloaded when building any of the following source packages. It contains the files and directory structures that the AST tools and build system rely upon.

ast-ksh

> This package builds just the support infrastructure (libraries, environment test programs, etc.) for *ksh* and the *ksh* executable. It is the simplest thing to build.

ast-base

> This package builds everything in the *ast-ksh* package and a few additional basic AST tools. In particular, it includes *pax*, an archiving tool that combines features from *tar*(1) and *cpio*(1), and *nmake*, a significantly enhanced version of the standard Unix *make*(1) program. It also includes the *sfio* (Safe Fast I/O) and *ast* libraries, which you can use for your own programs.

ast-open

> This package builds everything in the *ast-base* package and many additional tools. Note particularly that *tksh* (see Appendix A) is included in this package.

Each of the packages (except *INIT*) is also available as prebuilt binaries. Table C-1 lists the available architectures for these packages. Locale translations for some locales for some of the programs are also available.

Table C-1. Supported architectures for AST programs

Name	OS/Architecture
darwin.ppc	Apple's MacOS X (a.k.a. Darwin) for the Motorola Power PC
hp.pa	Hewlett-Packard HP-UX for HP Precision Architecture
ibm.risc	IBM's AIX for RS/6000
linux.i386	GNU/Linux on Intel 80386 and higher
linux.s390	GNU/Linux on the IBM S/390 mainframe
mvs.390	IBM's MVS on the IBM S/390 mainframe
netbsd.i386	NetBSD on Intel 80386 and higher (see *http://www.netbsd.org*)
openbsd.i386	OpenBSD on Intel 80386 and higher (see *http://www.openbsd.org*)
osf.alpha	OSF/1 on the Compaq (nee Digital) Alpha processor
sgi.mips3	Silicon Graphics (SGI) Irix on the MIPS processor
sol.sun4	Solaris 5.4 on the Sun SPARC architecture
sol6.sun4	Solaris 5.6 on the Sun SPARC architecture
sol7.i386	Solaris 7 on Intel 80386 and higher
sol7.sun4	Solaris 7 on the Sun SPARC architecture
sol8.sun4	Solaris 8 on the Sun SPARC architecture
sun4	SunOS 4.x on the Sun SPARC architecture
unixware.i386	UnixWare (the latest official version of System V) on Intel 80386 and higher

Building ksh

Building any of the packages from source code is pretty straightforward. The full details, with a FAQ and notes, are given on the AT&T web site. Here is a walk-through of the steps. We show the steps for the *ast-open* package, but they're identical for the other source code packages.

1. Make sure you have a C compiler for your system. An ANSI/ISO C compiler is preferred, but a K&R compiler will work too. Getting a C compiler if you don't have one is beyond the scope of this book; contact your local system administrator.

2. Download the package(s) you wish to build into an otherwise empty directory. Here, we build the *ast-open* package from October 31, 2001:

    ```
    $ ls
    INIT.2001-10-31.tgz  ast-open.2001-10-31.tgz
    ```

3. Make the directory *lib/package/tgz* and move the files there:

    ```
    $ mkdir lib lib/package lib/package/tgz
    $ mv *.tgz lib/package/tgz
    ```

4. Extract the *INIT* package manually:

    ```
    $ gzip -d < lib/package/tgz/INIT.2001-10-31.tgz | tar -xvpf -
    \r\v\vNOTICE -- LICENSED SOFTWARE -- SEE README FOR DETAILS\r\v\v
    README
    src/Makefile
    src/cmd/Makefile
    src/lib/Makefile
    ...
    ```

    If you don't have *gzip*, use the *ratz* program, as described earlier.

5. Initialize the list of available packages:

    ```
    $ bin/package read
    \r\v\vNOTICE -- LICENSED SOFTWARE -- SEE README FOR DETAILS\r\v\v
    README
    src/Makefile
    src/cmd/Makefile
    src/lib/Makefile
    src/Mamfile
    ...
    ```

6. Start the compilation. This step is quite verbose and will take a while. Exactly how long depends upon the speed of your system and compiler, and upon which package you are building:

    ```
    $ bin/package make
    package: initialize the /home/arnold/ast-open/arch/linux.i386 view
    package: update /home/arnold/ast-open/arch/linux.i386/bin/proto
    package: update /home/arnold/ast-open/arch/linux.i386/bin/mamake
    package: update /home/arnold/ast-open/arch/linux.i386/bin/ratz
    package: update /home/arnold/ast-open/arch/linux.i386/bin/release
    ...
    ```

7. Install the created files. This can be done with the command bin/package install *directory* where *directory* is the location to place things in.

    Alternatively, if all you're interested in is the *ksh* binary, you can just copy it. The compiled binary will be in a directory named *arch/ARCH/bin*, where *ARCH* represents your architecture, such as *linux.i386*:

    ```
    cp arch/linux.i386/bin/ksh $HOME/bin/ksh93
    ```

8. Enjoy!

D

AT&T ast Source Code License Agreement

SOURCE CODE AGREEMENT
Version 1.2D

PLEASE READ THIS AGREEMENT CAREFULLY. By accessing and using the **Source Code**, you accept this Agreement in its entirety and agree to only use the **Source Code** in accordance with the following terms and conditions. If you do not wish to be bound by these terms and conditions, do not access or use the **Source Code**.

1. *YOUR REPRESENTATIONS*

    1. You represent and warrant that:

        a. If you are an entity, or an individual other than the person accepting this Agreement, the person accepting this Agreement on your behalf is your legally authorized representative, duly authorized to accept agreements of this type on your behalf and obligate you to comply with its provisions;

        b. You have read and fully understand this Agreement in its entirety;

        c. Your **Build Materials** are either original or do not include any **Software** obtained under a license that conflicts with the obligations contained in this Agreement;

        d. To the best of your knowledge, your **Build Materials** do not infringe or misappropriate the rights of any person or entity; and,

        e. You will regularly monitor the **Website** for any notices.

2. *DEFINITIONS AND INTERPRETATION*

1. For purposes of this Agreement, certain terms have been defined below and elsewhere in this Agreement to encompass meanings that may differ from, or be in addition to, the normal connotation of the defined word.

    a. **"Additional Code"** means **Software** in source code form which does *not* contain any

        i. of the **Source Code**, or

        ii. derivative work (such term having the same meaning in this Agreement as under U.S. Copyright Law) of the **Source Code**.

    b. **"AT&T Patent Claims"** means those claims of patents (i) owned by AT&T and (ii) licensable without restriction or obligation, which, absent a license, are necessarily and unavoidably infringed by the use of the functionality of the **Source Code**.

    c. **"Build Materials"** means, with reference to a **Derived Product**, the **Patch** and **Additional Code**, if any, used in the preparation of such **Derived Product**, together with written instructions that describe, in reasonable detail, such preparation.

    d. **"Capsule"** means a computer file containing the exact same contents as a computer file downloaded from the **Website**.

    e. **"Derived Product"** means a **Software Product** which is a derivative work of the **Source Code**.

    f. **"IPR"** means all rights protectable under intellectual property law anywhere throughout the world, including rights protectable under patent, copyright and trade secret laws, but not trademark rights.

    g. **"Patch"** means **Software** for **changing** all or any portion of the **Source Code**.

    h. **"Proprietary Notice"** means the following statement:

        "This product contains certain software code or other information ("AT&T Software") proprietary to AT&T Corp. ("AT&T"). The AT&T Software is provided to you "AS IS". YOU ASSUME TOTAL RESPONSIBILITY AND RISK FOR USE OF THE AT&T SOFTWARE. AT&T DOES NOT MAKE, AND EXPRESSLY DISCLAIMS, ANY EXPRESS OR IMPLIED WARRANTIES OF ANY KIND WHATSOEVER, INCLUDING, WITHOUT LIMITATION, THE IMPLIED WARRANTIES OF MERCHANTABILITY OR FITNESS FOR A PARTICULAR PURPOSE, WARRANTIES OF TITLE OR NON-INFRINGEMENT OF ANY INTELLECTUAL PROPERTY RIGHTS, ANY WARRANTIES ARISING BY USAGE OF TRADE, COURSE OF DEALING OR COURSE OF PERFORMANCE,

OR ANY WARRANTY THAT THE AT&T SOFTWARE IS "ERROR FREE" OR WILL MEET YOUR REQUIREMENTS.

Unless you accept a license to use the AT&T Software, you shall not reverse compile, disassemble or otherwise reverse engineer this product to ascertain the source code for any AT&T Software.

© AT&T Corp. All rights reserved. AT&T is a registered trademark of AT&T Corp."

i. "**Software**" means, as the context may require, source or object code instructions for controlling the operation of a central processing unit or computer, and computer files containing data or text.

j. "**Software Product**" means a collection of computer files containing **Software** in object code form only, which, taken together, reasonably comprise a product, regardless of whether such product is intended for internal use or commercial exploitation. A single computer file can comprise a **Software Product**.

k. "**Source Code**" means the **Software** contained in compressed form in the **Capsule**.

l. "**Website**" means the Internet website having the URL *http://www.research.att.com/sw/download/*. AT&T may **change** the content or URL of the **Website**, or remove it from the Internet altogether.

2. By way of clarification only, the terms **Capsule**, **Proprietary Notice** and **Source Code** when used in this Agreement shall mean the materials and information defined by such terms without any change, enhancement, amendment, alteration or modification (collectively, "**change**").

3. *GRANT OF RIGHTS*

    1. Subject to third party intellectual property claims, if any, and the terms and conditions of this Agreement, AT&T grants to you under:

        a. the **AT&T Patent Claims** and AT&T's copyright rights in the **Source Code**, a non-exclusive, fully paid-up license to:

            i.   Reproduce and distribute the **Capsule**;

            ii. Display, perform, use, and compile the **Source Code** and execute the resultant binary **Software** on a computer;

            iii. Prepare a **Derived Product** solely by compiling **Additional Code**, if any, together with the code resulting from operating a **Patch** on the **Source Code**; and,

iv. Execute on a computer and distribute to others **Derived Products**,

except that, with respect to the **AT&T Patent Claims**, the license rights granted in clauses (iii) and (iv) above shall only .extend, and be limited, to that portion of a **Derived Product** which is **Software** compiled from some portion of the **Source Code**; and,

b. AT&T's copyright rights in the **Source Code**, a non-exclusive, fully paid-up license to prepare and distribute **Patches** for the **Source Code**.

2. Subject to the terms and conditions of this Agreement, you may create a hyperlink between an Internet website owned and controlled by you and the **Website**, which hyperlink describes in a fair and good faith manner where the **Capsule** and **Source Code** may be obtained, provided that, you do not frame the **Website** or otherwise give the false impression that AT&T is somehow associated with, or otherwise endorses or sponsors your website. Any goodwill associated with such hyperlink shall inure to the sole benefit of AT&T. Other than the creation of such hyperlink, nothing in this Agreement shall be construed as conferring upon you any right to use any reference to AT&T, its trade names, trademarks, service marks or any other indicia of origin owned by AT&T, or to indicate that your products or services are in any way sponsored, approved or endorsed by, or affiliated with, AT&T.

3. Except as expressly set forth in Section 3.1 above, no other rights or licenses under any of AT&T's **IPR** are granted or, by implication, estoppel or otherwise, conferred. By way of example only, no rights or licenses under any of AT&T's patents are granted or, by implication, estoppel or otherwise, conferred with respect to any portion of a **Derived Product** which is *not* **Software** compiled from some portion, without **change**, of the **Source Code**.

4. *YOUR OBLIGATIONS*

1. If you distribute **Build Materials** (including if you are required to do so pursuant to this Agreement), you shall ensure that the recipient enters into and duly accepts an agreement with you which includes the minimum terms set forth in Appendix A (*http://www.research.att.com/sw/license/ast-terms.html*) (completed to indicate you as the LICENSOR) and no other provisions which, in AT&T's opinion, conflict with your obligations under, or the intent of, this Agreement. The agreement required under this Section 4.1 may be in electronic form and may be distributed with the **Build Materials** in a form such that the recipient accepts the agreement by using or installing the **Build Materials**. If any **Additional Code** contained in your **Build Materials** includes **Software** you obtained under license, the agreement shall also include complete details concerning the license and any

restrictions or obligations associated with such **Software**.

2. If you prepare a **Patch** which you distribute to anyone else you shall:

   a. Contact AT&T, as may be provided on the **Website** or in a text file included with the **Source Code**, and describe for AT&T such **Patch** and provide AT&T with a copy of such **Patch** as directed by AT&T; or,

   b. Where you make your **Patch** generally available on your Internet website, you shall provide AT&T with the URL of your website and hereby grant to AT&T a non-exclusive, fully-paid up right to create a hyperlink between your website and a page associated with the **Website**.

3. If you prepare a **Derived Product**, such product shall conspicuously display to users, and any corresponding documentation and license agreement shall include as a provision, the **Proprietary Notice**.

5. *YOUR GRANT OF RIGHTS TO AT&T*

   1. You grant to AT&T under any **IPR** owned or licensable by you which in any way relates to your **Patches**, a non-exclusive, perpetual, worldwide, fully paid-up, unrestricted, irrevocable license, along with the right to sublicense others, to (a) make, have made, use, offer to sell, sell and import any products, services or any combination of products or services, and (b) reproduce, distribute, prepare derivative works based on, perform, display and transmit your Patches in any media whether now known or in the future developed.

6. *AS IS CLAUSE / LIMITATION OF LIABILITY*

   1. The **Source Code** and **Capsule** are provided to you "AS IS". YOU ASSUME TOTAL RESPONSIBILITY AND RISK FOR YOUR USE OF THEM INCLUDING THE RISK OF ANY DEFECTS OR INACCURACIES THEREIN. AT&T DOES NOT MAKE, AND EXPRESSLY DISCLAIMS, ANY EXPRESS OR IMPLIED WARRANTIES OF ANY KIND WHATSOEVER, INCLUDING, WITHOUT LIMITATION, THE IMPLIED WARRANTIES OF MERCHANTABILITY OR FITNESS FOR A PARTICULAR PURPOSE, WARRANTIES OF TITLE OR NON-INFRINGEMENT OF ANY **IPR** OR TRADEMARK RIGHTS, ANY WARRANTIES ARISING BY USAGE OF TRADE, COURSE OF DEALING OR COURSE OF PERFORMANCE, OR ANY WARRANTY THAT THE **SOURCE CODE** OR **CAPSULE** ARE "ERROR FREE" OR WILL MEET YOUR REQUIREMENTS.

   2. IN NO EVENT SHALL AT&T BE LIABLE FOR (a) ANY INCIDENTAL, CONSEQUENTIAL, OR INDIRECT DAMAGES (INCLUDING, WITHOUT LIMITATION, DAMAGES FOR LOSS OF PROFITS, BUSINESS INTERRUPTION, LOSS OF PROGRAMS OR INFORMATION, AND THE LIKE) ARISING OUT OF THE USE OF OR INABILITY TO USE THE SOURCE CODE OR

CAPSULE, EVEN IF AT&T OR ANY OF ITS AUTHORIZED REPRESENTA-TIVES HAS BEEN ADVISED OF THE POSSIBILITY OF SUCH DAMAGES, (b) ANY CLAIM ATTRIBUTABLE TO ERRORS, OMISSIONS, OR OTHER INACCURACIES IN THE **SOURCE CODE** OR **CAPSULE**, OR (c) ANY CLAIM BY ANY THIRD PARTY.

3. BECAUSE SOME STATES DO NOT ALLOW THE EXCLUSION OR LIMITA-TION OF LIABILITY FOR CONSEQUENTIAL OR INCIDENTAL DAMAGES, THE ABOVE LIMITATIONS MAY NOT APPLY TO YOU. IN THE EVENT THAT APPLICABLE LAW DOES NOT ALLOW THE COMPLETE EXCLU-SION OR LIMITATION OF LIABILITY OF CLAIMS AND DAMAGES AS SET FORTH IN THIS AGREEMENT, AT&T'S LIABILITY IS LIMITED TO THE GREATEST EXTENT PERMITTED BY LAW.

7. *INDEMNIFICATION*

1. You shall indemnify and hold harmless AT&T, its affiliates and authorized representatives against any claims, suits or proceedings asserted or com-menced by any third party and arising out of, or relating to, your use of the **Source Code**. This obligation shall include indemnifying against all damages, losses, costs and expenses (including attorneys' fees) incurred by AT&T, its affiliates and authorized representatives as a result of any such claims, suits or proceedings, including any costs or expenses incurred in defending against any such claims, suits, or proceedings.

8. *GENERAL*

1. You shall not assert against AT&T, its affiliates or authorized representa-tives any claim for infringement or misappropriation of any **IPR** or trade-mark rights in any way relating to the **Source Code**, including any such claims relating to any **Patches**.

2. In the event that any provision of this Agreement is deemed illegal or unenforceable, AT&T may, but is not obligated to, post on the **Website** a new version of this Agreement which, in AT&T's opinion, reasonably pre-serves the intent of this Agreement.

3. Your rights and license (but not any of your obligations) under this Agree-ment shall terminate automatically in the event that (a) notice of a non-frivolous claim by a third party relating to the **Source Code** or **Capsule** is posted on the **Website**, (b) you have knowledge of any such claim, (c) any of your representations or warranties in Article 1.0 or Section 8.4 are false or inaccurate, (d) you exceed the rights and license granted to you or (e) you fail to fully comply with any provision of this Agreement. Noth-ing in this provision shall be construed to restrict you, at your option and subject to applicable law, from replacing the portion of the Source Code

that is the subject of a claim by a third party with non-infringing code or from independently negotiating for necessary rights from the third party.

4. You acknowledge that the **Source Code** and **Capsule** may be subject to U.S. export laws and regulations, and, accordingly, you hereby assure AT&T that you will not, directly or indirectly, violate any applicable U.S. laws and regulations.

5. Without limiting any of AT&T's rights under this Agreement or at law or in equity, or otherwise expanding the scope of the license and rights granted hereunder, if you fail to perform any of your obligations under this Agreement with respect to any of your **Patches** or **Derived Products**, or if you do any act which exceeds the scope of the license and rights granted herein, then such **Patches**, **Derived Products** and acts are not licensed or otherwise authorized under this Agreement and such failure shall also be deemed a breach of this Agreement. In addition to all other relief available to it for any breach of your obligations under this Agreement, AT&T shall be entitled to an injunction requiring you to perform such obligations.

6. This Agreement shall be governed by and construed in accordance with the laws of the State of New York, USA, without regard to its conflicts of law rules. This Agreement shall be fairly interpreted in accordance with its terms and without any strict construction in favor of or against either AT&T or you. Any suit or proceeding you bring relating to this Agreement shall be brought and prosecuted only in New York, New York, USA.

Index

Symbols

& ampersand, 22
&& for condition tests, 230
&& in exit status syntax, 141–143
&& logical operator, 150
as bitwise operator, 183
(see also background jobs)
< > angle brackets, 209
<< >> bitwise operators, 183
in I/O redirection, 20
* asterisk, 15
for accessing entire array, 195
as built-in variable, 100
as command (vi-mode), 58
as default in case statement, 161
as regular expression operator, 114–118
as wildcard, 17
@ at sign
for accessing entire array, 195
as built-in variable, 100
as default list in for statement, 154
as default list in select statement, 165
for preserving whitespace, 196
as regular expression operator, 114, 117
\ backslash, 27
as command, 57
{ } curly braces, 105
[ ] square brackets, 118
[[. . .]] for comparison tests, 144–154

[. . .] for condition tests (old syntax), 144
set construct wildcards and, 16
^ caret character, 41
as bitwise operator, 183
as command, 48
matching beginning of line in regular
expressions, 322
: colon, 21, 109–112
, comma, as command, 56
$ dollar sign
$@/$* variables, 100–104
$((. . .)), 183
as built-in variable, 36, 275
as command, 48
as pattern-substitution operator, 124
as variable name operator, 126
. dot
.. indicating parent of working
directory, 11
indicating hidden files, 14
as redo command, 52
to run scripts, 91
indicating working directory, 11
= equal sign, 230
== string comparison operator, 144
as command, 58
as string comparison operator, 144
as variable assignment operator, 73

We'd like to hear your suggestions for improving our indexes. Send email to *index@oreilly.com*.

About the Authors

Bill Rosenblatt is president of GiantSteps/Media Technology Strategies, a consulting firm in New York City. Before founding GiantSteps, Bill was CTO of Fathom, an online content and education company associated with Columbia University and other scholarly institutions. He has been a technology executive at McGraw-Hill and Times Mirror, and head of strategic marketing for media and publishing at Sun Microsystems. Bill was also one of the architects of the Digital Object Identifier (DOI), a standard for online content identification and DRM.

Arnold Robbins, an Atlanta native, is a professional programmer and technical author. He is also a happy husband, the father of four very cute children, and an amateur Talmudist (Babylonian and Jerusalem). Since late 1997, he and his family have been living in Israel. Arnold has been working with Unix systems since 1980, when he was introduced to a PDP-11 running a version of Sixth Edition Unix. He has been working with the Korn shell since 1984 and is the author of SSC's pocket reference on the Korn shell. (A few minor features are in the Korn shell at his suggestion.) Arnold has also been a heavy *awk* user since 1987, when he became involved with *gawk*, the GNU project's version of *awk*. As a member of the POSIX 1003.2 balloting group, he helped shape the POSIX standard for *awk*. He is currently the maintainer of *gawk* and its documentation. In previous incarnations he has been a systems administrator and a teacher of Unix and networking continuing education classes. He has also had more than one poor experience with start-up software companies, which he prefers not to think about anymore. One day he hopes to put up his own web site at *http://www.skeeve.com*. O'Reilly has been keeping him busy: he is author and/or coauthor of the bestselling titles *Learning the vi Editor*, *Effective awk Programming*, *sed & awk*, *Unix in a Nutshell*, and several pocket references.

Colophon

Our look is the result of reader comments, our own experimentation, and feedback from distribution channels. Distinctive covers complement our distinctive approach to technical topics, breathing personality and life into potentially dry subjects.

The animal on the cover of *Learning the Korn Shell* is a hawksbill turtle. The name "hawksbill" refers to its prominent hooked beak. This marine reptile is one of the smaller sea turtles, having a carapace (upper shell) length of about two feet and weighing about one hundred pounds. Among pelagic turtles, the hawksbill alone has the tendency to feed and breed in the same area, preferring the tropical shoals and reefs of the world's oceans.

Primarily carnivorous, the hawksbill feeds on crabs, fish, sponges, and jellyfish. The turtle's flesh can be poisonous; in some places, fisherman test for poison by throwing the turtle's liver to the crows. If the birds reject the liver, the hawksbill is toxic.

The hawksbill turtle is the sole source of authentic "tortoiseshell," which comes from the scutes, or outer layer of the carapace. Tortoiseshell has been harvested through the years—from ancient Egypt to the present—and is highly valued for its beauty and plasticity. As a result, the hawksbill is endangered. Illegal trade continues to threaten this species' existence.

Leanne Soylemez was the production editor and proofreader for *Learning the Korn Shell*, Second Edition. Kate Briggs was the copyeditor. Mary Brady and Jane Ellin provided quality control. Brenda Miller wrote the index.

Edie Freedman designed the cover of this book. The cover image is a 19th-century engraving from the Dover Pictorial Archive. Emma Colby produced the cover layout with QuarkXPress 4.1 using Adobe's ITC Garamond font.

Melanie Wang and David Futato designed the interior layout based on a series design by Nancy Priest. The print version of this book was created by translating the DocBook XML markup of its source files into a set of *gtroff* macros using a filter developed at O'Reilly & Associates by Norman Walsh. Steve Talbott designed and wrote the underlying macro set on the basis of the GNU *troff –mgs* macros; Lenny Muellner adapted them to XML and implemented the book design. The GNU *groff* text formatter version 1.11.1 was used to generate PostScript output. The text and heading fonts are ITC Garamond Light and Garamond Book; the code font is Constant Willison. The illustrations that appear in the book were produced by Robert Romano, Jessamyn Read, and Chris Reilley, using Macromedia FreeHand 9 and Adobe Photoshop 6. This colophon was written by Michael Kalantarian.